LITERARY CRITICISM

An Introduction
to Theory and Practice

FOURTH EDITION

Charles E. Bressler
Houghton College

PEARSON
Prentice
Hall

Upper Saddle River, New Jersey 07458

Library of Congress Cataloging-in-Publication Data

Bressler, Charles E.

Literary criticism : an introduction to theory and practice / Charles E. Bressler.—4th ed.

p. cm.

Includes bibliographical references and index.

ISBN-13: 978-0-13-153448-3 (pbk.)

ISBN-10: 0-13-153448-3 (pbk.)

1. Criticism. I. Title.

PN81.B666 2007

801'.95—dc22

2006014748

Once again, for Darlene, my best friend and loving wife,
and Heidi, my much loved daughter

Editor-in-Chief: Leah Jewell
Acquisitions Editor: Vivian Garcia
Editorial Assistant: Christina Volpe
Production Liaison: Joanne Hakim
Executive Marketing Manager:
  Brandy Dawson
Marketing Manager: Vivian Garcia
Marketing Assistant: Vicki DeVita
Manufacturing Buyer: Christina Amato
Permissions Specialist: Lisa Black

Cover Art Director: Jayne Conte
Cover Design: Kiwi Design
Cover Illustration/Photo: Kristen
  Ankiewicz
**Manager, Cover Visual Research
  & Permissions:** Karen Sanatar
**Composition/Full-Service Project
  Management:** Babitha Balan/GGS
  Book Services
Printer/Binder: The Courier Companies

Credits and acknowledgments borrowed from other sources and reproduced, with permission, in this textbook appear on appropriate page within text.

Pearson Education LTD., London
Pearson Education Singapore, Pte. Ltd
Pearson Education, Canada, Ltd
Pearson Education–Japan
Pearson Education Australia
  PTY, Limited

Pearson Education North Asia Ltd
Pearson Educación de Mexico,
  S.A. de C.V.
Pearson Education Malaysia, Pte. Ltd
Pearson Education, Upper Saddle River,
  New Jersey

10 9 8 7 6 5 4 3
ISBN 0-13-153448-3

CONTENTS

FOREWORD

Some years ago now, as an undergraduate, I remember sitting down to study in the law library of a large university. To find the solitude in which to begin my work, I settled into a small carrel in the far corner of the library, surrounded by books, an inexhaustible variety of them—shelves upon shelves, rows upon rows of law books. Distracted from my immediate task, I looked into a few of the volumes close at hand. Case law, law history, legal precedent—these subjects did not mean much to me then, but I recall being struck by the impression that such subjects, and the specific texts I perused, amounted to a long, complex, and demanding conversation, which was entailed in the practice of law. As I read selected portions of these texts, just from the few volumes that I had slipped off the shelves, I could not yet imagine how a person found access to such a conversation, much less to the meanings of these texts. I wondered how they all comprised, in any consistent way, the "discipline" of law, even and especially when they sometimes seemed to contradict each other.

For the student coming to literary theory, perhaps for the first time, he or she confronts an equally bewildering array of texts in a variety of interdisciplinary forms—texts upon texts, theories upon theories. One might think that this proliferation of theory warns of yet more duplicating mirrors or winding staircases in what the Argentinean writer Jorge Luis Borges calls the "library of Babel," a multiform library of infinite proportion, in which "official searchers, *inquisitors*"—readers and interpreters—try to clarify humanity's "basic mysteries," unlock certain codes, only to return home disenchanted from the exhausting, even confounding, search for knowledge.

Since 1994, with the publication of *Literary Criticism: An Introduction to Theory and Practice*, which is now in its 4th edition, Charles Bressler has been helping students to navigate the daunting, and potentially dizzying, subject of literary theory and practice. Bressler's primary commitment, true to the first three editions of *Literary Criticism*, is to equip students to ask important questions about literature. What is a literary text, and does it have multiple meanings? What is the relationship between a text and the context in which it is situated? How does history inform the activity of reading? What role does the reader play in shaping meaning? Does the reader's gender matter at all? Who is the author? Is there an author? How does language "mean"? Are there moral questions at stake in reading? Asking penetrating questions, as *Literary Criticism* makes clear, is an indispensable part of the practice of critical reading and writing.

Yet teachers and students, wearied and embattled by theoretical wrangling and academic politics, might wonder, now more than ever, whether discussions about literary theory are really rather beside the point, especially for undergraduates, who simply want to "read" good books. Some critics argue that literary theory seems more often to close rather than open dialogue. Mary Lefkowitz has written that "as the university has become more politicized, the notion of dialogue has disappeared, and been replaced by speechifying and the kind of pronouncements that are intended to end discussion rather than to stimulate it" ("Literary Politics," ALSC *Newsletter* 7.1 [2001]). Another critic, Mark Edmundson, contends that setting theory "between readers and literature—if you make theory a prerequisite to discussing a piece of writing—you effectively deny students a chance to encounter the first level of literary density, the level they're ready to negotiate" (*Why Read?* New York: Bloomsbury, 41). Yet to dismiss literary theory entirely, in a fit of trying to protect readers from its influence, or to deny its heuristic possibilities, with the silent hope that whole fields of theoretical inquiry will vanish in the night, seems to be a defensive posture at best, a dodge, another way of closing dialogue.

Although it is not the goal of *Literary Criticism* to substitute for or detract from a student's direct encounter with literature, the book does drive home the point that the most introductory statements about literary texts rest on certain philosophical assumptions; deploy different, often contradictory interpretative approaches; and advance arguments. For students to become more active readers, then, it is important for them to wrestle with such varying approaches to literature while keeping in mind Terry Eagleton's memorable claim that "Hostility to theory usually means an opposition to other people's theories and an oblivion of one's own" (*Literary Theory*, viii). Yet what exactly is literary theory, and what are its uses?

Charles Bressler's *Literary Criticism* faces up to this question. As in its three previous editions, the book explores the major literary theories, in detail, examining both the philosophical assumptions driving them and the methodologies by which they are applied in the activity of reading and interpreting. This approach is intended to help students formulate their ideas about literature as they prepare for classroom discussions or prepare to write essays about the texts they have been assigned to read. Replete with student essays, in-depth discussions, focused questions for analyses, and other important tools for critical reading, this book is designed to support the literature classroom as a vital forum for literary study.

Literary Criticism, 4th edition, begins, appropriately, with a section entitled, "Listening to a Conversation," to prompt readers to think about the significance of human messages. Charles Bressler describes how even a routine human conversation, between a mother and her son, opens up an array of interpretive possibilities. Here is an excerpt from Bressler's discussion:

> By listening to the conversation, you have become, in a real sense, a part of
> it. For a moment, the concerns of the two participants, Tim and his mother,
> became part of your world. You looked at them, evaluated their social position,

thought about their feelings, and conjectured about the social structure of their family. And even your personal feelings were temporarily affected as you noted that Tim walked cockily away and that his mother had a saddened look as he did so. When the conversation was over, you returned to reading the newspaper.

This example prepares the reader for a more detailed discussion about the literature classroom as a place of "conversation," where readers exchange ideas and ask penetrating questions as active participants, not as passive observers.

Literary Criticism has developed over the years, matured, through three successful editions, within the ambience of a liberal arts setting, "the great conversation," in which students consider important ideas in relation to a broad range of profoundly human concerns. One of the chief merits of the book is that its author is a scholar–teacher who believes, firmly, that theory needs and finds nourishment in practical applications. Plenty of books on literary theory are published each year. Few of them, however, distill such complex theoretical concepts in terms helpful both to the student and the teacher as well as to the professional literary critic.

Daniel H. Strait
Asbury College
Wilmore, KY

To the Reader

Like the first three editions, this new edition of *Literary Criticism* is designed as a supplemental text for introductory courses in literature, literary criticism, and other courses in the humanities. In all four editions, the purpose of this text has remained the same: to enable students to approach literature from a variety of practical and theoretical perspectives and to equip them with a theoretical and a practical understanding of how critics develop their interpretations. The text's overall aim is to take the mystery out of working with and interpreting texts. My hope is that this text will allow students to join in the conversations taking place at the various literary tables around the world.

Like the three previous editions, this fourth edition holds to several key premises. First, I assume that there is no such thing as an "innocent" reading of a text. Whether our responses to texts are emotional and spontaneous or well reasoned and highly structured, all of our interpretations are rooted in underlying factors that cause us to respond in a particular way to a particular text. What elicits these responses and how a reader makes sense of a text is what really matters. Knowing literary theory allows us to analyze both our initial and all further responses to any text and to question our beliefs, our values, our feelings, and eventually our overall interpretation of a text at hand. To understand why we respond to texts in certain ways, we must first understand literary theory and its practical application, literary criticism.

Second, because our responses to texts have theoretical bases, I believe that all readers have a literary theory. Consciously or unconsciously, we, as readers, have developed a mindset that provides us with certain expectations when reading various kinds of texts. Somehow, we usually make sense of any text we are reading. The methods we use to frame both our private (personal) and our public interpretations involve us directly in literary theory and criticism, automatically making us practicing literary critics, whether we know it or not.

My third premise rests on the observation that each reader's literary theory and accompanying methodology (i.e., literary criticism) is either conscious or unconscious, most nearly complete or incomplete, informed or ill formed, eclectic or unified. Because an unconscious, incomplete, ill-informed, and eclectic literary theory more frequently than not leads to illogical, unsound, and haphazard interpretations, I believe that a well-defined, logical, and clearly articulated literary theory will enable readers to develop their own methods of interpreting texts—their personal hermeneutics—and help them as readers to order, clarify, and justify their appraisals of any text in a consistent manner.

Unfortunately, many readers cannot articulate their own literary theory and have little or no knowledge of the history and development of the ever-evolving principles of literary criticism. The goal of this text is to introduce such students and readers to literary theory and criticism, its historical development, and the various theoretical positions or schools of criticism that will enable them as readers to make conscious, informed, and well-thought-out choices about their own methods of interpretation.

But why a new edition? Like many other academic studies, literary criticism is an ever-developing discipline. Since the third edition of this text, much creative scholarship in literary theory and criticism has been written, published, and now debated. This new edition highlights many of these new concerns developed by literary theorists and allows you, the reader, to participate in the cutting-edge discussions taking place in such areas as cultural poetics, cultural studies, postcolonialism, and queer theory. In addition, this fourth edition includes 95 new critical terms that will help readers understand more fully the various concepts being discussed by the advocates of the different schools of literary criticism.

Like the previous three editions, this new edition introduces students to the basic concerns of literary theory in Chapter 1, which now includes a more detailed discussion of the nature and concerns of theory and criticism and provides updated reading resources and web sites. Chapter 2 places literary theory and criticism in historical perspective, beginning with the writings of Plato and ending with one of the giants of literary criticism of the twentieth century, Mikhail Bakhtin. Readers will notice the addition of such critical theorists as Plotinus, Giovanni Boccaccio, John Dryden, Joseph Addison, and Percy Bysshe Shelley to help round out the historical perspectives that such writers provide for discussing contemporary literary theory. Chapters 3 to 10 have all been greatly revised, adding new terminology where appropriate. In some chapters, such as Chapters 3 and 10, new schools or branches of previous schools of criticism have been added such as Russian Formalism and queer theory. All these chapters present the major schools of criticism that have been developed and continue to develop in the twenty-first century: Russian Formalism, New Criticism, Reader-oriented Criticism, Structuralism, Deconstruction, Psychoanalytic Criticism, Feminism, Marxism, New Historicism or Cultural Poetics, Cultural Studies, Postcolonialism, African American Criticism, and Queer Theory.

To maintain consistency and for ease of study, each of the chapters is identically organized. We begin with a brief introductory section that is followed by the historical development of each school of criticism. The assumptions section, which sets forth the philosophical principles on which each school of criticism is based, is next. The methodology section follows and serves as a "how-to" manual for explaining the techniques used by the various schools of criticism to formulate their interpretations of texts based on their philosophical assumptions.

After the methodology section, a newly revised questions for analysis section appears in Chapters 3 to 10. This feature provides students with key questions to ask of a text in order to view that text from the perspective of the school of criticism under discussion. Some of the questions also ask students to apply their newfound knowledge to a particular text. Then a new section appears, critiques and responses. This section briefly explains the key concepts of each school of criticism followed by concerns raised by other schools of criticism that do not necessarily agree with the assumptions of the school of criticism under discussion. By adding this section to each chapter, you, the reader, will be better able to join in the discussions and debates concerning which theories and practices you will ultimately use in your interpretive methodology. Following the critiques and responses section are the updated further reading section and web sites for exploration. The newly revised further reading section complements the the updated web sites and provides additional avenues of exploration for each of the schools of criticism. Often the web addresses include links to other sites, providing additional opportunities to venture into the ever-expanding world of literary theory. Following the web site section are newly written student essays. These essays provide examples for analysis in which an undergraduate student applies the principles and methods of interpretation of the school of criticism under discussion. All student authors were free to choose their own texts for interpretation. Most of the texts they chose for analysis appear in the literary selections section at the end of this edition.

All chapters in this new edition have undergone careful revision and editing. In every chapter, key terms appear in boldface type and are included in the updated glossary that appears at the back of this edition. This glossary continues 95 more terms than the third edition. Readers of previous editions may also note that one chapter appears to be eliminated; this edition contains only 10, not 11 chapters. Chapters 5 (Structuralism) and 6 (Deconstruction) from the third edition have been combined. Because structuralism provides the foundation for deconstruction theory, these two chapters were combined to provide consistency, avoid unnecessary repetition, and add clarity to the discussion and development of deconstruction theory and practice.

Because *Literary Criticism* is an introductory text, the explanations of the various schools of criticism should not be viewed as exhaustive but as a first step toward developing an understanding of some rather difficult and at times provocative concepts, principles, and methodologies for textual analysis. Similarly, the undergraduate student essays should not be viewed as literary masterpieces but as attempts to use differing literary theories and to practice various critical methodologies. Instructors and students alike should freely critique these essays, exploring both their strengths and weaknesses. After reading this new edition, I hope that readers will continue their own investigations of literary theory and criticism by exploring not only advanced theoretical texts but also the primary documents of theoretical and practical critics. By contacting their local Prentice Hall representative, instructors can obtain a complete reference section for all chapters and a test bank for examinations.

ACKNOWLEDGMENTS

Because I believe in the intertextuality of texts, I readily acknowledge that the creation of this text and its previous editions involves an intricate web of relationships with many people. First, to those students who enrolled in my literary criticism classes, I say a huge thank you. Your thoughtful questions, class presentations and discussions, and seemingly countless essays have all helped me clarify my thinking about many complex theoretical issues. Without you, this book could not have been written. In particular, I wish to thank those students who contributed new essays for this edition: Hilary S. Brautigam, Danielle Bowers, Ian J. Galloway, Brandon W. Hawk, Matt Hepler, Lori Huth, Matthew S. Lasher, Anna L. Kruse, and Benjamin K. Walker.

I am also deeply grateful to Houghton College. By awarding me released time from teaching, you have made this book possible. Special thanks must go to my academic dean, Dr. Ron Oakerson, and to Dr. Linda Mills Woolsey, my department chair, for their strong support and encouragement throughout this extended project. In addition, my fellow faculty members of the Department of English, Communication, and Writing have also encouraged me in my research and writing. Thank you one and all, with special thanks to Andy Gallman, Wes Oden, Todd Leach, and Willis Beardsley for their ever-faithful friendship and support.

Words of great praise have been earned by my faithful and bold editor at Prentice Hall, Vivian Garcia, and to her assistant, Christina Volpe. Their necessary prodding to keep on schedule, their kind words, and their shepherding of this new edition through all its various stages of production are extremely appreciated. Also, the following reviewers are acknowledged for reviewing the manuscript: Yuan Yuan, California State University—San Marcos; Harold Hellwig, Idaho State University; Thomas Cassidy, South Carolina State University; Albert Rouzie, Ohio University; Alan Richardson, Boston College; Diane R. Pingatore, Lake Superior State University; Willie Tolliver, Agnes Scott College; Kathryn N. Benzel, University of Nebraska- Kearney.

Most of all, I want to express my undying gratitude, appreciation, and love to my best friend, Darlene, who is also my wife: You are my joy, my life's companion, and my most beloved critic. Thank you for your patience and support through all stages of this project. And to the apple of my eye, my daughter, Heidi Elizabeth, I say thank you and I love you. How proud I am of you, and what great joy you bring me because you are you. Your many encouragements to keep on keeping on throughout this project enabled me to keep researching, writing, revising, and editing. Without the help and encouragement of my thoughtful and gifted students, colleagues, friends, and family, this book could not have been written. Any errors in this edition, however, are solely mine.

Charles E. Bressler
Houghton College
Houghton, New York

1

DEFINING CRITICISM,
THEORY, AND LITERATURE

Literary theory has permeated our thinking to the point that it has defined for our times how discourse about literature, as well as about culture in general, shall proceed. Literary theory has arrived, and no student of literature can afford not to come to terms with it.

Thomas McLaughlin, *Critical Terms for Literary Study*

LISTENING TO A CONVERSATION

Imagine for a moment that you are sitting at the food court of a local shopping mall. Your seat is front and center, the chair located closest to the mall's walkway where all the shoppers have to pass you by as they continue seeking out those bargains while chatting with their friends. Sipping on your energy-boosted fruit drink, you begin reading your copy of the local newspaper. As you read, you cannot help but hear a conversation between a middle-aged woman and her apparent teenage son as they stop in front of you:

"Mom, can I have five dollars to go to the arcade while you shop for shoes for your dinner party next week?"

"No! I want you to come with me to the store to help me pick out my new shoes. I want to buy something a little daring, and I need your support."

"But, mom, what do I know about shoes for you? I promised to meet some of my friends at the arcade around noon, and it is already 12:49!"

"Tim, I really want you to come, but if you want to go to the arcade, just go. Here's the money."

As you look up, the smiling teen grabs the bills from his mother's hand and saunters cockily to the arcade. As his mom is walking away with a somewhat sad look on her face, you wonder how she is feeling. Is she disappointed? Angry? Hurt? Did she really expect her son to join her as she tried on pair after pair of shoes? Should she even have asked Tim to go with her in the first place? And what about Tim: Is he a spoiled brat? Does he hold a part-time job after school? What about his siblings? Is he an only child? One of many? These and similar questions keep popping into your head as you watch the mother and son separate and travel in opposite directions.

By listening to the conversation, you have become, in a real sense, a part of it. For a moment, the concerns of the two participants, Tim and his mother, became part of your world. You looked at them, evaluated their social position, thought about their feelings, and conjectured about the social structure of their family. And even your personal feelings were temporarily affected as you noted that Tim walked cockily away and that his mother had a sad look as he did so. When the conversation was over, you returned to reading the newspaper. Briefly, however, you became an observer of this mother and son's story. As if they were in a story, you "read" not only what was said but also what was left unsaid because you imagined their feelings, their desires, and the results of their interaction. You filled in the gaps about their characters while simultaneously developing them not as they really were but as you personally imagined them to be. Being an outsider, you quickly became a participant in the actions of their tale, asking questions about the nature of the characters, the events of their story, and their and your emotional responses to the story line. Although you were not actually reading a story, you asked the same kinds of questions that a literary critic asks when reading a work of fiction. Like a literary critic, you became an evaluator, an interpreter, and, for a moment, a participant in the story itself.

As you "overheard" the voices of the two characters—Tim and his mother—in their story, similarly, literary critics eavesdrop on the multiple conversations in literary works. To help them articulate and analyze their eavesdropping, these critics assign names to the various elements of the multiple conversations of which they become a part: author, reader, narrator, naratee, text, nature of reality, and so forth. One such critic, the Russian writer, essayist, and literary theorist Mikhail Bakhtin, coined the term **dialogic heteroglossia** ("many voices in multiple conversations") to explain the multiple conversations occurring in one such literary genre, the novel. All genres, however, have developed such technical vocabulary to explain not only their constituent elements but also avenues to discovering their meanings.

Let us now eavesdrop on another conversation taking place about a short story.

EAVESDROPPING ON A LITERATURE CLASSROOM

Having assigned her literature class Flannery O'Connor's short story "A Good Man Is Hard to Find" and knowing O'Connor's canon and her long list of curious protagonists, Professor Linda Blackwell could not anticipate whether her students would greet her with silence, bewilderment, or frustration when asked to discuss this work. Her curiosity would soon be satisfied. As she stands before the class, she asks a seemingly simple, direct question: "What do you believe O'Connor is trying to tell us in this story? In other words, how do you, as readers, interpret this text?"

Although some students stare out the window and others suddenly find the covers of their books fascinating, a few shoot up their hands. Given a nod from Professor Blackwell, Alice is the first to respond: "I believe O'Connor is trying to tell us the state of the family in rural Georgia during the 1950s. Just look at how the children, June Star and John Wesley, behave. They don't respect their grandmother. In fact, they mock her."

"But she deserves to be mocked," interrupts Peter. "Her life is one big act. She wants to act like a lady—to wear white cotton gloves and carry a purse— but she really cares only for herself. She is selfish, self-centered, and arrogant."

"That may be," responds Karen, "but I think the real message of O'Connor's story is not about family or one particular character, but about a philosophy of life. O'Connor uses the Misfit to articulate her personal view of life. When the Misfit says Jesus has thrown 'everything off balance,' O'Connor is really asking each of her readers to choose his or her own way of life or to follow the teachings of Jesus. In effect, O'Connor is saying we all have a choice: to live for ourselves or to live for and through others."

"I don't think we should bring Christianity or any other philosophy or religion into the story," says George. "Through analyzing O'Connor's individual words—words like *tall*, *dark*, and *deep*—and noting how often she repeats them and in what context, we can deduce that O'Connor's text, not O'Connor herself or her view of life, is melancholy and a bit dark. But to equate O'Connor's personal philosophy about life with the meaning of this particular story is somewhat silly."

"But we can't forget that O'Connor is a woman," says Betty, "and an educated one at that! Her story has little to do with an academic or pie-in-the-sky, meaningless philosophical discussion but a lot to do with being a woman. Being raised in the South, O'Connor would know and would have experienced prejudice because she is female. And as we all know, the Southern male's opinion of women is that they are to be kept 'barefoot, pregnant, and in the kitchen,' to be as nondescript as Bailey's wife is in this story. Unlike all the other characters, we don't even know this woman's name. How much more nondescriptive could O'Connor be? O'Connor's message, then, is simple: Women are oppressed and suppressed. If they open their mouths, if they have an opinion, and if they voice that opinion, they will end up like the grandmother, with a bullet in their head."

"I don't think that's her point at all," says Barb. "I do agree that she is writing from personal experience about the South, but her main point is about prejudice itself—prejudice against African Americans. Through the voice of the grandmother we see the Southern lady's opinion of African Americans: They are inferior to whites, uneducated, poor, and basically ignorant. O'Connor's main point is that we are all equal."

"Yes, I agree," says Mike. "But if we look at this story in the context of all the other stories we have read this semester, I see a theme we have discussed countless times before: appearance versus reality. This is O'Connor's main point. The grandmother acts like a lady—someone who cares greatly about others—but inwardly, she cares only for herself. She's a hypocrite."

"I disagree. In fact, I disagree with everybody," shouts Daniel. "I like the grandmother. She reminds me of my grandmother. O'Connor's grandmother is a bit self-centered, but whose old grandmother isn't? Like my grandma, O'Connor's grandmother likes to be around her grandchildren, to read and to play with them. She's funny, and she has spunk. And she even likes cats."

"But, Professor Blackwell, can we ever know what Flannery O'Connor really thinks about this story?" asks Jessica. "After all, she's dead, and she didn't write an essay titled "What 'A Good Man Is Hard to Find' Really Means." And since she never tells us its meaning, can't the story have more than one meaning?"

Professor Blackwell instantly realizes that Jessica's query—can a story have multiple meanings?—is a pivotal question not only for English professors and their students but also for anyone who reads any text.

CAN A TEXT HAVE MORE THAN ONE INTERPRETATION?

A quick glance at the discussion of O'Connor's "A Good Man Is Hard to Find" in Professor Blackwell's classroom reveals that not all readers interpret texts in the same way. In fact, all of the eight students who voiced their understandings of the story gave fundamentally different interpretations. Was only one of these eight interpretations correct and the remaining seven wrong? If so, how does one arrive at the correct interpretation? Put another way, if there is only one correct interpretation of a text, what are the **hermeneutical principles** (the rules of interpretation) readers must use to discover this interpretation? Should each of the eight students attempt to reconstruct the intentions O'Connor held while writing her story or the meaning her story had for her readers in the 1950s (**hermeneutics of recovery**)? Or should each student attempt to examine O'Connor's unspoken but implied assumptions concerning politics, sexuality, religion, linguistics, and a host of other topics (**hermeneutics of suspicion**)? In so doing, Connor's work may then have have multiple interpretations. Are all such interpretations valid? Can and should each interpretation be considered a satisfactory and legitimate analysis of the text? In other words, can a text mean anything a reader declares it to mean, or are there guiding principles for interpreting a text that must be followed if a reader is to arrive at a valid interpretation? And who, anyway, can declare that one's interpretation is valid or legitimate? English professors? Professional critics? Published scholars? Or any reader?

Need a reader, however, be thinking of any of these particulars when reading a text? Can't one simply enjoy a novel, for example, without considering its interpretation? Need one be able to state the work's theme, discuss its structure, or analyze its tone in order to enjoy the actual act of reading the novel itself?

These and similar questions are the domain of **literary criticism**, which is the act of studying, analyzing, interpreting, evaluating, and enjoying a work of art. At first glance, the study of literary criticism appears daunting and formidable. Jargon such as **hermeneutics**, **Aristotelian poetics**, **metaphysics of presence**, **deconstruction**, and a host of other intimidating terms confront the would-be **literary critic**. Nevertheless, the actual process or act of literary criticism is not as ominous as it may first appear.

HOW TO BECOME A LITERARY CRITIC

When the students in Professor Blackwell's class were discussing O'Connor's short story "A Good Man Is Hard to Find," each of them was directly responding to the instructor's initial question: What do you believe O'Connor is trying to tell us in and through this story? Although not all responses were radically different, each student viewed the story from a unique perspective. For example, some students expressed a liking for the grandmother, but others thought her a selfish, arrogant woman. Still others believed O'Connor was voicing a variety of philosophical, social, and cultural concerns, such as the place of women and African Americans in Southern society or adherence to tenets of Christianity as the basis for one's view of life, or the structure of the family in rural Georgia in the 1950s. All had an opinion about and therefore an interpretation of O'Connor's story.

When Professor Blackwell's students stated their personal interpretations of O'Connor's story, they had become practicing literary critics. All of them had already interacted with the story, thinking about their likes and dislikes of the various characters; their impressions of the setting, plot, and structure; and their overall assessment of the story itself, whether that assessment was a full-fledged interpretation that seeks to explain every facet of the text or simply bewilderment as to the story's overall meaning.

None of the students, however, had had formal training in literary criticism. None knew the somewhat complicated jargon (**discourse**) of literary theory. And none were acquainted with any of the formal and informal schools of literary criticism.

What each student did was read the story. The reading process itself produced within the students an array of responses, taking the form of questions, statements, opinions, and feelings evoked by the text. These responses coupled with the text itself are the concerns of literary criticism and theory.

Although these students may need to master the terminology, the many philosophical approaches, and the diverse methodologies of formal literary criticism to become trained literary critics, they automatically became literary critics as they read and thought about O'Connor's text. They needed no formal training in literary criticism or working understanding of literary theory. By mastering the concepts of formal literary criticism and theory, however, these students, like all readers, can become critical readers who are better able to understand and articulate their own reactions and analyze those of others to any text.

WHAT IS LITERARY CRITICISM?

Matthew Arnold, a nineteenth-century literary critic, describes literary criticism as "A disinterested endeavor to learn and propagate the best that is known and thought in the world." Implicit in this definition is that literary criticism is a disciplined activity that attempts to describe, study, analyze, justify, interpret, and evaluate works of art. By necessity, Arnold would argue, this discipline attempts to formulate aesthetic and methodological principles on which the critic can evaluate a text. Anyone who attempts to evaluate texts in this fashion is a **literary critic**, a term derived from two Greek words, *krínō*, meaning "to judge," and *krités*, meaning "a judge or jury person." A literary critic, or *kritikós*, is therefore a "judge of literature." The first recorded such judge is the fourth century B.C.E. teacher Philitas, who arrived in Alexandria in 305 B.C.E. to tutor a child who would become King Ptolemy II. When judging literature, Philitas was actively engaged in the disciplined activities of literary criticism.

When we consider its function and its relationship to texts, literary criticism is not usually considered a discipline in and of itself because it must be related to something else—that is, a work of art. Without the work of art, the activity of criticism cannot exist. And it is through this discerning activity that we can knowingly explore the questions that help define our humanity, critique our culture, evaluate our actions, or simply increase our appreciation and enjoyment of both a literary work and our fellow human beings.

When analyzing a text, literary critics ask basic questions such as these about the philosophical, psychological, functional, and descriptive nature of the text itself:

*   Does a text have only one correct meaning?
*   Is a text always didactic—that is, must a reader learn something from every text?
*   Can a text be read only for enjoyment?
*   Does a text affect every reader in the same way?

- How is a text influenced by the culture of its author and the culture in which it is written?
- Can a text become a catalyst for change in a given culture?

Since the time of the Greek philosophers Plato and Aristotle and continuing to the present day, critics and readers have been hotly debating the answers to these and similar questions. By asking questions of O'Connor's or any other text and by contemplating answers, we, too, can participate in this debate. We can question, for example, the grandmother's motives in O'Connor's "A Good Man Is Hard to Find" for wanting to take her cat on the family's vacation. Or we can ask if the presence of the Misfit and his companions is the primary reason the grandmother experiences her **epiphany**. No matter what question we may ask concerning O'Connor's text, we are participating in an ongoing discussion of the value and enjoyment of O'Connor's short story while simultaneously engaging in literary criticism and functioning as practical literary critics.

Traditionally, literary critics involve themselves in either theoretical or practical criticism. **Theoretical criticism** formulates the theories, principles, and tenets of the nature and value of art. By citing general aesthetic and moral principles of art, theoretical criticism provides the necessary framework for practical criticism. **Practical criticism** (also known as **applied criticism**) applies the theories and tenets of theoretical criticism to a particular work. Using the theories and principles of theoretical criticism, the **practical critic** defines the standards of taste and explains, evaluates, or justifies a particular piece of literature. A further distinction is made between a practical critic who posits that there is only one theory or set of principles a critic may use when evaluating a literary work—an **absolutist critic**—and a **relativistic critic**, one who uses various and even contradictory theories in critiquing a text. The basis for either kind of critic or any form of criticism is literary theory. Without theory, practical criticism could not exist.

WHAT IS LITERARY THEORY?

When reading O'Connor's "A Good Man Is Hard to Find," we necessarily interact with the text, asking many specific, text-related questions and often rather personal ones as well. For example, such questions as these may concern us, the readers:

- What kind of person is the grandmother? Is she like my grandmother or any grandmother I know?
- What is the function or role of June Star? John Wesley? Bailey? The mother?
- Why was the grandmother taking Pitty Sing, the cat, on the family vacation?

- What is the significance of the restaurant scene at The Tower?
- Right before she is shot, what does the grandmother recognize about the Misfit? What is the significance of this recognition?

Such questions immediately involve us in practical criticism. What we tend to forget during the reading of O'Connor's short story or any other text, however, is that we have read other literary works (**intertextuality**). Our response to any text—or the principles of practical criticism we apply to it—is largely a conditioned or socially constructed one—that is, how we arrive at meaning in fiction is partly determined by our past experiences. Consciously or unconsciously, we have developed a mindset or framework that accommodates our expectations when reading a novel, short story, poem, or any other type of literature. In addition, what we choose to value or uphold as good or bad, moral or immoral, or beautiful or ugly within a given text also depends on this ever-evolving framework. When we can clearly articulate our mental framework when reading a text and explain how this mindset directly influences our values and aesthetic judgments about the text, we are well on our way to developing a coherent, unified **literary theory**—the assumptions (conscious or unconscious) that undergird one's understanding and interpretation of language, the construction of meaning, art, culture, aesthetics, and ideological positions. Whereas literary criticism involves our analysis of a text, literary theory is concerned with our understanding of the ideas, concepts, and intellectual assumptions upon which our actual literary critique rests.

Because anyone who responds to a text is already a practicing literary critic and because practical criticism is rooted in the reader's preconditioned expectations (i.e., his or her mindset) when reading a text, every reader espouses some kind of literary theory. Each reader's theory may be conscious or unconscious, whole or partial, informed or ill informed, eclectic or unified. An incomplete, unconscious, and, therefore, unclear literary theory leads to illogical, unsound, and haphazard interpretations. On the other hand, a well-defined, logical, and clearly articulated theory enables readers to develop a method by which to establish principles that enable them to justify, order, and clarify their own appraisals of a text in a consistent manner.

A better understanding of literary theory can be gained by investigating the etymology of the word *theory* itself. Derived from the Greek word *theoria*, the word *theory* means a "view or perspective of the Greek stage." Literary theory, then, offers to us a view of life, an understanding of why we interpret texts the way we do. Consider the various places in the theatre we, the audience, may sit. Depending on our seats—whether we are close to the stage, far back, to the far left, to the far right, or in the middle row—our view and, therefore, our interpretation of the events taking place on the stage will alter. Literary theory figuratively and literally asks where we are "sitting" when we are reading a text. What exactly is influencing us during the reading process? Our culture? Our understanding of the nature of literature itself? Our political or social views? These and similar questions (and their answers) directly and indirectly and consciously and unconsciously affect our interpretation and our enjoyment of a text. To be able to articulate such underlying assumptions about how we read texts enables us, the readers, to establish for ourselves a lucid and logical practical criticism.

A well-articulated literary theory also assumes that an innocent reading of a text or a sheerly emotional or spontaneous reaction to a work cannot exist because theory questions the assumptions, beliefs, and feelings of readers, asking why they respond to a text in a certain way. In one very real sense, literary theory questions our "common sense" interpretation of a text, asking us to probe beneath our initial responses. A consistent and informed literary theory assumes that a simple emotional or intuitive response to a text does not explain the underlying factors that cause such a reaction. What matters is what elicits that response or how the reader constructs meaning through or with the text.

MAKING MEANING FROM TEXT

How we as readers construct meaning through or with a text depends on the mental framework each of us has developed and continues to develop concerning the nature of reality. This framework or **worldview** consists of the assumptions or presuppositions that we all hold (either consciously or unconsciously) about the basic makeup of our world. For example, most people struggle to find answers to such questions as:

- What is the basis of morality or ethics?
- What is the meaning of human history?
- Is there an overarching purpose for humanity's existence?
- What is beauty? Truth? Goodness?
- Is there an ultimate reality?

Interestingly, our answers to these and other questions do not remain static because as we interact with other people, our environment, our culture, and our own inner selves, we are continually shaping and developing our personal philosophies, rejecting former ideas, and replacing old ideas with newly discovered ones. It is our dynamic answers—including our doubts and fears about these answers—that largely determine our responses to a literary text.

Upon such a conceptual framework rests literary theory. Whether that framework is well reasoned or simply a matter of habit and past teachings, readers respond to works of art via their worldview. From this philosophical core of beliefs spring their evaluations of the goodness, worthiness, and value of art itself. Using their worldviews either consciously or unconsciously as a yardstick by which to measure and value their experiences, readers respond to individual works of literature, ordering and valuing each separate or collective experience in each text based on the system of beliefs housed in their worldviews.

THE READING PROCESS AND LITERARY THEORY

The relationship between literary theory and a reader's personal worldview is best illustrated in the act of reading itself. When reading, we are constantly interacting with the text. According to Louise M. Rosenblatt's text *The Reader, the Text, the Poem* (1978), during the act or event of reading:

> A reader brings to the text his or her past experience and present personality. Under the magnetism of the ordered symbols of the text, the reader marshals his or her resources and crystallizes out from the stuff of memory, thought, and feeling a new order, a new experience, which he/she sees as the poem. This becomes part of the ongoing stream of the reader's life experience, to be reflected on from any angle important to him or her as a human being. (p.12)

Accordingly, Rosenblatt declares that the relationship between the reader and the text is not linear, but **transactional**—that is, it is a process or event that takes place at a particular time and place in which the text and the reader condition each other. The reader and the text transact, creating meaning, because meaning does not exist solely within the reader's mind or within the text, Rosenblatt maintains, but in the transaction between them. To arrive at an interpretation of a text (what Rosenblatt calls the **poem**), readers bring their own "temperament and fund of past transactions to the text [what some critics call **forestructure**] and live through a process of handling new situations, new attitudes, new personalities, [and] new conflicts in value. They can reject, revise, or assimilate into the resource with which they engage their world." Through this transactional experience, readers consciously and unconsciously amend their worldviews.

Because no literary theory can account for all the various factors included in everyone's conceptual framework, and because we as readers all have different literary experiences, there can exist no **metatheory**—no one overarching literary theory that encompasses all possible interpretations of a text suggested by its readers. Additionally, there can be no one correct literary theory because, in and of itself, each literary theory asks valid questions of and about a text, and no one theory is capable of exhausting all legitimate questions to be asked about any text.

The valid and legitimate questions asked about a text by the various literary theories differ, often widely. Espousing separate critical orientations, each theory focuses primarily on one element of the interpretative process, although in practice different theories may address several areas of concern in interpreting a text. For example, one theory may stress the work itself, believing that the text alone contains all the necessary information to arrive at an interpretation. This theory isolates the text from its historical or socio-logical setting and concentrates on the literary forms found in the text, such as figures of speech, word choice (**diction**), and style. Another theory may attempt to place a text in its historical, political, sociological, religious, and economic settings. By placing the text in historical perspective, this theory asserts that its adherents can arrive at an interpretation that both the text's author and its original audience would support. Still another theory may direct its chief concern toward the text's audience. It asks how the readers' emotions and personal backgrounds affect each reader's interpretation of a particular text. Whether the primary focus of concern is psychological, linguistic, mythical, historical, or from any other critical orientation, each literary theory establishes its own theoretical basis and then proceeds to develop its own methodology whereby readers can apply the particular the-ory to an actual text. In effect, each literary theory or perspective is similar to taking a different seat in the theatre and thereby obtaining a different view of the stage. Different literary theories and theorists may all study the same text, but being in different seats, the various literary theorists all respond dif-ferently to the text—or the performance on the stage—because of their unique perspectives.

Although each reader's theory and methodology for arriving at a text's interpretation differs, sooner or later groups of readers and critics declare allegiance to a similar core of beliefs and band together, founding **schools of criticism**. For example, whereas critics who believe that social and historical concerns must be highlighted in a text are known as Marxist critics, reader-oriented critics (sometimes referred to as reader-response critics) concentrate on readers' personal reactions to the text. Because new points of view concern-ing literary works are continually evolving, new schools of criticism—and, therefore, new literary theories—will continue to develop. One of the more recent schools to emerge in the 1980s and 1990s, New Historicism or Cultural Poetics, declares that a text must be analyzed through historical research that assumes that history and fiction are inseparable. The members of this school, known as New Historicists, hope to blur the boundaries between history and literature and thereby produce criticism that accurately reflects what they believe to be the proper relationship between texts and their historical contexts. Still other newly evolving schools of criticism, such as postcolonial-ism, African American studies, and gender studies, continue to emerge and challenge previous ways of thinking about and critiquing texts.

Because the various schools of criticism (and the theories on which they are based) ask different questions about the same work of literature, these theoretical schools provide an abundance of options from which readers can choose to broaden their understanding not only of texts but also of their society, their culture, and their own humanity. By embracing literary theory, we learn about literature, but importantly, we are also taught tolerance for other people's beliefs. By rejecting or ignoring theory, we are in danger of canonizing ourselves as literary saints who possess divine knowledge and who can, therefore, supply the one and only correct interpretation for a given text. When we oppose, disregard, or ignore literary theory, we are in danger of blindly accepting our often unquestioned prejudices and assumptions. By embracing literary theory and literary criticism (its practical application), we can participate in that seemingly endless historical conversation about the nature of humanity and of humanity's concerns as expressed in literature. In the process, we can begin to question our concepts of ourselves, our society, and our culture and how texts themselves help define and continually redefine these concepts.

WHAT IS LITERATURE?

Because literary criticism presupposes that there exists a work of literature to be interpreted, we could assume that formulating a definition of literature would be simple. This is, however, not the case. For centuries, writers, literary historians, and others have debated but have failed to agree on a definition for this term. Some assume that literature is simply anything that is written, thereby declaring a city telephone directory, a cookbook, and a road atlas to be literary works along with *David Copperfield* and the *Adventures of Huckleberry Finn*. Derived from the Latin *littera*, meaning "letter," the root meaning of the word *literature* refers primarily to the written word and seems to support this broad definition. Yet such a definition eliminates the important oral traditions upon which much of our literature is based, including Homer's *Iliad* and *Odyssey*, the English epic *Beowulf*, and many Native American legends, among many other examples.

To solve this difficulty, others choose to define *literature* as an art, thereby leaving open the question of its being written or oral. This definition further narrows its meaning, equating literature to works of the imagination or creative writing. To emphasize the imaginative qualities of literature, some critics choose to use the German word for literature, **Wortkunst** instead of its English equivalent because *Wortkunst* automatically implies that the imaginative and creative aspects of literature are essential components of the word *literature* itself. By this definition, written works such as a telephone directory or a cookbook can no longer be considered literature; these kinds of works are superseded by poetry, drama, fiction, and other imaginative writings. Some scholars believe that the imaginative qualities of a work of literature were first articulated for Western literature in a work written by the French

Baroness Madame de Stael, a German Romantic theorist, who authored *On Literature Considered in its Relations with Social Institutions* in 1800.

Although the narrowing of the definition of literature accomplished by equating it to the defining terms of art seemingly simplifies what can and cannot be considered a literary work, such is not the case. That the J. Crew and Victoria's Secret clothes catalogues are imaginative (and colorful) writing is unquestioned, but should they then be considered works of literature? Who declares whether a written document is a work of art? Many readers assume that if an imaginative work of fiction is published— be it signally or in an anthology—such a work is worthy of being read. It has, after all, been judged acceptable as a literary work and has been published and presumably approved by an editorial board. This belief that published works are deemed worthy to be dubbed literature is called the **hyper-protected cooperative principle**—that is, published works have been evaluated and declared literary texts by a group of well-informed people who are protecting the overall **canon** of literature. But even this principle does not stop many from arguing that some published works are unworthy of being called works of art or literature. Specifying and narrowing the definition of literature to a "work of art" does not, then, immediately provide consensus or a consistent rule about how to declare a text a "work of literature."

Whether one accepts the broad or narrow definition, many argue that a text must have certain peculiar qualities before it can be dubbed "literature." Those who hold this view believe that an artist's creation or secondary world often mirrors the author's primary world, the world where the writer lives, moves, and breathes. Because reality or the primary world is highly structured, the secondary world must also be this structured. To achieve this structure, the artist must create plot, character, tone, symbols, conflict, and a host of other elements or parts of the artistic story, with all of these elements working in a dynamic relationship to produce a literary work. Some argue that it is the creation of these elements—how they are used and in what context—that determines whether a piece of writing is literature.

Still other critics add the "test of time" criterion to their essential components of literature. If a work such as Dante's *Divine Comedy* withstands the passage of time and is still being read centuries after its creation, it is deemed valuable and worthy of being called literature. This criterion also denotes literature's functional or cultural value: If people value a written work, for whatever reason, they often declare it to be literature whether or not it contains the prescribed elements of a text.

What this work may contain is a peculiar aesthetic quality—that is, some element of beauty—that distinguishes it as literature from other forms of writing. **Aesthetics**, the branch of philosophy that deals with the concept of the beautiful, strives to determine the criteria for beauty in a work of art.

Theorists such as Plato and Aristotle declare that the source of beauty is inherent within the art object itself. Other critics, such as David Hume, say that beauty is in the eye of the beholder. And some contemporary theorists argue that one's perception of beauty in a text rests in the dynamic relationship between the object (i.e., the text) and the perceiver (i.e., the reader) at a given moment in time. Wherever the criteria for judging the beauty of a work of art finally resides, most critics agree that a work of literature has an appealing aesthetic quality.

Although distinguishing literature from other forms of writings, this appealing aesthetic quality directly contributes to literature's chief purpose: telling a story. Although it may simultaneously communicate facts, literature's primary aim is to tell a story. The subject of this story is particularly human, describing and detailing a variety of human experiences, not stating facts or bits and pieces of information. For example, literature does not define the word *courage*; rather, it shows us a courageous character acting courageously. By so doing, literature concretizes an array of human values, emotions, actions, and ideas in story form. It is this concretization that allows us to experience vicariously the stories of a host of characters. Through these characters, we observe people in action, making decisions, struggling to maintain their humanity in often inhumane circumstances, and embodying for us a variety of values and human characteristics that we may embrace, discard, enjoy, or detest.

LITERARY THEORY AND THE DEFINITION OF LITERATURE

Is literature simply a story that contains certain aesthetic and literary qualities that all somehow pleasingly culminate in a work of art? If so, can texts be considered **artifacts** that can be analyzed, dissected, and studied to discover their essential nature or meaning? Or does a literary work have **ontological** status—that is, does it exist in and of itself, perhaps in a special **neo-Platonic** realm? Or must it have an audience, a reader, before it becomes literature? And can we define the word *text*? Is it simply print on a page? If pictures are included, do they automatically become part of the text? Who determines when print becomes a work of art? The reader? The author? Both?

The answers to these and similar questions have been long debated, and the various responses make up the corpus of literary theory. Providing the academic arena in which those interested in literary theory (literary theorists) can posit philosophical assumptions as to the nature of the reading process, the **epistemological** nature of learning, the nature of reality itself, and a host of related concerns, literary theory offers a variety of methodologies that enable readers to interpret a text from different and often conflicting points of view. Such theorizing empowers readers to examine their personal world-views, to articulate their individual assumptions about the nature of reality, and to understand how these assumptions directly affect their interpretation not only of a work of art but also of the definition of literature itself.

Although any definition of literature is debatable, most would agree that an examination of a text's total artistic situation would help us decide what constitutes literature. This total picture of the work involves such elements as the work itself (e.g., an examination of the fictionality or secondary world created within the story), the artist, the universe or world the work suppos-edly represents, and the audience or readers. Although readers and critics may emphasize one, two, or even three of these elements while deemphasiz-ing the others, such a consideration of a text's artistic situation immediately broadens the definition of literature from the concept that it is simply a writ-ten work that contains certain qualities to a definition that must include the dynamic interrelationship of the actual text and the readers. Perhaps, then, the literary competence of the readers themselves helps determine whether a work should be considered literature. If this is so, then a literary work may be more functional than ontological, its existence and, therefore, its value being determined by its readers and not by the work itself.

Overall, the definition of literature depends on the particular kind of literary theory or school of criticism that the reader or critic espouses. For formalists, for example, the text and text alone contains certain qualities that make a particular piece of writing literature. On the other hand, for reader-oriented critics, the interaction and psychological relationships between the text and the reader help determine whether a document should be deemed literary. A working knowledge of literary theory can thus help all readers formulate their ever-developing definitions of literature and what they believe constitutes a literary work.

THE FUNCTION OF LITERATURE AND LITERARY THEORY

Critics continually debate literature's chief function. Tracing their arguments to Plato, many contend that literature's primary function is moral, its chief value being its usefulness for cultural or societal purposes. But others, such as Aristotle, hold that a work of art can be analyzed and broken down into its various parts, with each part contributing to the overall enjoyment of the work itself. For these critics, the value of a text is found within the text itself or is inseparably linked to the work itself. In its most simple terms, the debate centers around two concerns: Is literature's chief function to teach (extrinsic) or to entertain (intrinsic)? In other words, can we read a text for the sheer fun of it, or must we always be studying and learning from what we read?

Such questions and their various answers lead us directly to literary theory because literary theory concerns itself not only with ontological questions (e.g., whether a text really exists) but also with epistemological issues (e.g., how we know or ways of knowing). When we ask, then, if literature's chief function is to entertain or to teach, we are really asking epistemological questions. Whether we read a text to learn from it or to be entertained, we can say that after we have read a text, we "know" that text.

We can know a text, however, in two distinct ways. The first way involves the typical literature classroom analysis. When we have studied, analyzed, and critiqued a text and arrived at an interpretation, we can then confidently assert that we know the text. On the other hand, when we stay up all night turning the pages of P.D. James's latest mystery novel *The Lighthouse* to discover who the murderer is, we can also say that we know the text because we have spent time devouring its pages, lost in its secondary world, consumed by its characters, and by the novel's end, eagerly seeking the resolution of its tensions. Both methods—one with its chief goal to learn, the other to entertain—involve similar yet distinct epistemological endpoints: to know a text, but in two different ways.

The French verbs *savoir* and *connaître* can both be translated "to know" and can highlight for us the difference between these two epistemological goals or ways of knowing a text. *Savoir* means "to analyze" (from the Greek *analuein*, to undo) and "to study." The word is used to refer to knowing something that is the object of study and assumes that the object, such as a text, can be examined, analyzed, and critiqued. Knowledge or learning *about* is the ultimate goal.

Connaître, on the other hand, implies that we intimately know or have experienced the text. Interestingly, *connaître* is used for knowing people and also refers to knowing an author's canon. Both knowing persons and knowing all a writer's works imply intimacy, learning the particular qualities of one person or author, the ins and outs of each. Indeed, it is this intimacy that one often experiences while reading a mystery novel all night long. It is knowing or knowledge *of* that the word means.

To know how to analyze a text, discuss its literary elements, and apply the various methodologies of literary criticism mean that we know that text (*savoir*). To have experienced the text, to have cried with or about its characters, to have lost time and sleep immersed in the secondary world of the text, and to have felt our emotions stirred also means that we know that text (*connaître*). From one way of knowing, we learn facts or information; from the other, we encounter and participate in an intimate experience.

At times, however, we have actually known the text from both these perspectives, *savoir* and *connaître*. While analyzing and critiquing a text (*savoir*), we have at times (and perhaps more often than not) simultaneously experienced it, becoming emotionally involved with its characters' choices and destinies (*connaître*) and imagining ourselves to be these characters—or at least recognizing some of our own characteristics dramatized by the characters.

To say that we know a text is no simple statement. Underlying our private and public reactions and our scholarly critiques and analyses is our literary theory, the fountainhead of our most intimate and our most public declarations. The formal study of literary theory therefore enables us to explain our responses to any text and allows us to articulate the function of literature in an academic and a personal way.

BEGINNING THE FORMAL STUDY OF LITERARY THEORY

This chapter has stressed the importance of literary theory and criticism and its relationship to literature and the interpretative processes. It has also articulated the underlying premises of why a study of literary theory is essential:

- Literary theory assumes that there is no such thing as an innocent reading of a text. Whether our responses are emotional and spontaneous or well reasoned and highly structured, all such interactions with and about a text are based on some underlying factors that cause us to respond to that text in a particular fashion. What elicits these responses and how a reader makes sense of a text is at the heart of literary theory.

- Because our reactions to any text have theoretical bases, all readers must have a literary theory. The methods we use to frame our personal interpretations of any text directly involve us in the process of literary criticism and theory, automatically making us practicing literary critics.

- Many readers have a literary theory that is more often than not unconscious, incomplete, ill informed, and eclectic; therefore, readers' interpretations can easily be illogical, unsound, and haphazard. A well-defined, logical, and clearly articulated literary theory enables readers to consciously develop their own methods of interpretation, permitting them to order, clarify, and justify their appraisals of a text in a consistent and logical manner.

- Today, many critics use the terms *literary criticism* and *literary theory* interchangeably. Still others use the terms *literary theory* and *Continental philosophy* synonymously. Although the semantic boundaries between literary criticism and literary theory (and sometimes Continental philosophy) are a bit blurred, literary criticism implies that literary theory exists and that literary criticism rests upon literary theory's concepts, ideas, and ever-developing principles.

It is the goal of this text to enable readers to make such conscious, informed, and intelligent choices, and in doing so, refine their own methods of literary interpretation and more precisely understand their personal and public reactions to texts. To accomplish this goal, the text introduces readers to literary theory and criticism, its historical development, and the various theoretical positions or schools of criticism, enabling readers to become knowledgeable critics of their own and others' interpretations. By becoming acquainted with diverse and often contradictory approaches to texts, readers will broaden their perspectives not only about themselves but also about others and the world in which they live.

FURTHER READING

Culler, Jonathan. *Literary Theory: A Very Short Introduction*. New York: Oxford University Press, 2000.

During, Simon, ed. *The Cultural Studies Reader*, 2nd ed. London: Routledge, 1999.

Eagleton, Terry. *Literary Theory: An Introduction*, 2nd ed. Minneapolis, MN: University of Minnesota Press, 1996.

Groden, Michael, Martin Kreiswirth, and Imre Szeman, eds. *The Johns Hopkins Guide to Literary Theory and Criticism*, 2nd ed. Baltimore, MD: Johns Hopkins University Press, 2005.

Harmon, William, and Hugh Holman. *A Handbook to Literature*, 10th ed. Upper Saddle River, NJ: Prentice Hall, 2005.

Kaplan, Charles, and William Anderson. *Criticism: Major Statements*, 4th ed. New York: Bedford, 1999.

Leitch, Vincent B., ed. *The Norton Anthology of Theory and Criticism*. New York: Norton, 2001.

Lentricchia, Frank. *After the New Criticism*. Chicago, IL: University of Chicago Press, 1981.

Lodge, David, ed. *Modern Criticism and Theory: A Reader*, 2nd ed. New York: Longman, 1999.

Makaryk, Irena R., ed. *Encyclopedia of Contemporary Literary Theory: Approaches, Scholars, Terms (Theory/Culture)*. Toronto: University of Toronto Press, 1993.

Reiss, Timothy J. *The Meaning of Literature*. Ithaca, NY: Cornell University Press, 1992.

Rice, Philip, and Patricia Waugh, eds. *Modern Literary Theory: A Reader*, 4th ed. London: Hodder Arnold, 2001.

Richter, David H. *Falling into Theory: Conflicting Views of Reading Literature*, 2nd ed. Boston, MA: Bedford, 1999.

Rosenblatt, Louise M. *The Reader, the Text, the Poem: The Transactional Theory of the Literary Work*. Carbondale, IL: Southern Illinois University Press, 1978.

Ryan, Michael. *Literary Theory: A Practical Introduction*. Malden, MA: Blackwell, 1999.

Tyson, Lois. *Critical Theory Today: A User-Friendly Guide*. New York: Garland, 1998.

Wolfreys, Julian, et al. *Continuum Encyclopedia of Modern Criticism and Theory*. New York: Continuum, 2004.

WEB SITES FOR EXPLORATION

http://www.library.utoronto.ca/utel/glossary/headerindex.html
> A solid glossary of terms used in discussing literary theory and includes an index of primary entries

http://www.kristisiegel.com/theory.htm
> A good overview of modern literary theory

http://andromeda.rutgers.edu/~jlynch/Lit/theory.html
> A valuable resource for finding literary theory and cultural studies web sites

http://litguide.press.jhu.edu
> An indispensable tool for studying literary theory and criticism

http://vos.ucsb.edu/browse.asp?id=2718
> An excellent listing of general literary theory resources from classical to modern theories

2

A HISTORICAL SURVEY
OF LITERARY CRITICISM

No poet, no artist, has his [or her] complete meaning alone.

T.S. Eliot, "Tradition and the Individual Talent"

Questions about the value, the structure, and even the definition of litera-ture undoubtedly arose in all cultures as people heard or read works of art. Such practical criticism probably began with the initial hearing or reading of the first literary works. The Greeks of the fifth century B.C.E., however, first articulated and developed the philosophy of art and life that serves as the foundation for most theoretical and practical criticism. Assuredly, hearers and performers of the Homeric poems commented on and interpreted these works before the fifth century B.C.E., but the fifth-century Athenians questioned the very act of reading and writing itself while pondering the purpose of litera-ture. Some scholars date the origin of literary criticism by citing the perfor-mance of Aristophanes's play *The Frogs* in 405 B.C.E. The play was performed as a part of a contest among dramatists, with Aristophanes receiving first prize. To win the contest, a literary judge or judges had to declare *The Frogs* the "best" play, thus initiating literary criticism. By so doing, these early critics began a debate about the nature and function of literature that continues to the present day, and they inaugurated the formal study of literary criticism.

From the fifth century B.C.E. to the present, numerous critics, such as Plato, Dante Alighieri, William Wordsworth, Mikhail Bakhtin, Jacques Derrida, Louise Rosenblatt, Stephen Greenblatt, Judith Butler, and a host of others, have developed principles of criticism that have had a major influ-ence on the continuing discussion of literary criticism. By examining these critics' ideas, we can gain an understanding of and participate in this critical debate while acquiring an appreciation for and a working knowledge of both practical and theoretical criticism.

PLATO (c. 427–347 B.C.E.)

Alfred North Whitehead, a modern British philosopher, once quipped that "all of Western philosophy is but a footnote to Plato." Although others have, indeed, contributed to Western thought, Plato's ideas, expressed in his *Ion, Crito, The Republic*, and other works, laid the foundation for many, if not most, of the pivotal issues of philosophy and literature, including the concepts of truth, beauty, and goodness; the nature of reality; the structure of society; the nature and relations of being (ontology); questions about how we know what we know (epistemology); and ethics and morality. Since Plato's days, such ideas have been debated, changed, debunked, or simply accepted. None, however, have been ignored.

Before Plato, only fragmentary comments about the nature and value of literature can be found. In the plays and writings of the comic dramatist Aristophanes, a contemporary of Plato, a few tidbits of practical criticism arise, but no clearly articulated literary theory can be found. Plato, on the other hand, systematically begins for us the study of literary theory and criticism. Plato's theories and criticism, however, would be more clearly articulated and developed several hundred years later by the philosopher Plotinus (204–270 C.E.) who reintroduced Plato's ideas to the Western world. Nevertheless, Plato's writings form the foundation upon which literary theory rests.

The core of Platonic thought resides in Plato's doctrine of essences, ideas, or forms. Ultimate reality, he states, is spiritual. This spiritual realm, which Plato calls **The One**, is composed of "ideal" forms or absolutes that exist whether or not any mind posits their existence or reflects their attributes. These ideal forms give shape to our physical world because our material world is nothing more than a shadow, a replica, of the absolute forms found in the spiritual realm. In the material world we can therefore recognize a chair as a chair because the ideal chair exists in this spiritual realm and preceded the existence of the material chair. Without the existence of the ideal chair, the physical chair, which is nothing more than a shadow or replica (representation, imitation, reflection) of the ideal chair, could not exist.

Such an emphasis on philosophical ideals earmarks the beginning of the first articulated literary theory and becomes the foundation for literary criticism. Before Plato and his Academy, Greek culture ordered its world through poetry and the poetic imagination—that is, by hearing such epics as the *Iliad* and *Odyssey* or by attending the play cycles, the Greeks saw good characters in action performing good deeds. From such stories, they formulated their theories of goodness and other similar standards, thereby using the presentational mode for discovering truth: observing good characters acting justly, honorably, and courageously and inculcating these characteristics within themselves. With the advent of Plato and his Academy, philosophical inquiry and abstract thinking usurped the narrative as a method for discovering truth. Not by accident, then, Plato places above his school door the words, "Let no one enter here who is not a geometer" (a master of geometry; one skilled in formal logic and reasoning). All his students had to value the art of reason and abstraction as opposed to the presentational mode for discovering truth.

This art of abstract reasoning and formal logic not only usurps literature's role as an evaluating mode for discerning truth but also condemns it. If ultimate reality rests in the spiritual realm, and the material world is only a shadow or replica of the world of ideals, then according to Plato and his followers, poets (those who compose imaginative literature) are merely imitating an imitation when they write about any object in the material world. Accordingly, Plato declares that a poet's craft is "an inferior who marries an inferior and has inferior offspring" because the poet, declares Plato, is one who is now two steps removed from ultimate reality. These imitators of mere shadows, contends Plato, cannot be trusted.

While condemning poets for producing art that is nothing more than a copy of a copy, Plato also argues that poets produce their art irrationally, relying on untrustworthy intuition rather than reason for their inspiration. He writes, "For the poet is a light and winged and holy thing, and there is no invention in him until he has been inspired and is out of his senses, and then the mind is no longer in him." Because such inspiration opposes reason and asserts that truth can be attained intuitively, Plato condemns all poets.

Because poets are untrustworthy and damned, their works can no longer be the basis of the Greeks' morality or ethics. Lies abound in the works of poets, argues Plato—critical lies about the nature of ultimate reality and dangerous lies about human reality. In the *Iliad*, for example, the gods lie and cheat and are one of the main causes of suffering among humans. Even the mortals in these works steal, complain, and hate each other. Such writings, contends Plato, set a bad example for Greek citizens and may lead normally law-abiding people down paths of wickedness and immorality. In *The Republic*, Plato ultimately concludes that the poets must be banished.

In a later work, Plato recants the total banishment of poets from society. Seemingly, he recognizes society's need for poets and their craft to "celebrate the victors" of the state. Plato then asserts that only those poets "who are themselves good and also honourable in the state" can be tolerated. In making this statement, Plato decrees poetry's function and value in and for his society: to sing the praises of loyal Greeks. Accordingly, poets must be supporters of the state or risk exile from their homeland. Being mere imitators of reality—in effect, good liars—these artisans and their craft must be religiously censured.

By directly linking politics and literature in a moral and reasoned worldview, Plato and his Academy founded a complex theory of literary criticism that initiated the debate, still ongoing, on the value, nature, and worth of artists and literature itself.

ARISTOTLE (384–322 B.C.E.)

Whereas literary criticism's concern with morality began with Plato, its emphasis on the elements of which a work is composed began with Plato's famous pupil, Aristotle. Rejecting some of Plato's beliefs about the nature of reality, Aristotle opts for a detailed investigation of the material world.

The son of a medical doctor from Thrace, Aristotle reveled in the physical world. After studying at Plato's Academy and mastering the philosophy and techniques of inquiry taught there, Aristotle founded the Lyceum, a school of scientific and philosophical thought and investigation. Applying his scientific methods of investigation to the study of literature, Aristotle answers Plato's accusations against poetry in a series of lectures known as the *Poetics*. Unlike **exoteric treatises** meant for general publication, the *Poetics* is an **esoteric work**, one meant for private circulation to those who attended the Lyceum. This work therefore lacks the unity and coherence of Aristotle's other works, but it remains one of the most important critical influences on literary theory and criticism.

Aristotle's *Poetics* has become the cornerstone of Western literary criticism. By applying his analytic abilities to a definition of tragedy, Aristotle began a discussion of the components of a literary work that continues to the present day. Unfortunately, many critics and scholars mistakenly assume that the *Poetics* is a how-to-manual, defining and setting the standards for literature (particularly tragedy) for all time. Aristotle's purpose, however, was not to formulate a series of absolute rules for evaluating a tragedy but to state the general principles of tragedy, as he viewed them in his time, while at the same time responding to many of Plato's doctrines and arguments. Even his title, the *Poetics*, reveals Aristotle's purpose because in Greek, the word *poetikes* means "things that are made or crafted." Similar to a biologist, Aristotle dissects tragedy to discover its component or crafted parts.

At the beginning of the *Poetics*, Aristotle notes that "epic poetry, tragedy, comedy, dithyrambic poetry, and most forms of flute and lyre playing all happen to be, in general, imitations." All seemingly differ in how and what they imitate, but Aristotle agrees with Plato that all the arts are imitations. In particular, the art of poetry exists because people are imitative creatures who enjoy such imitation. Whereas Plato contends that this is a pleasure that can undermine the structure of society and all its values, Aristotle strongly disagrees. His disagreement is basically a metaphysical argument concerning the nature of imitation itself. Whereas Plato decrees that imitation is two steps removed from the truth or realm of the ideal (the poet imitating an object that is itself an imitation of an ideal form), Aristotle contends that poetry is more universal, more general than things as they are because "it is not the function of the poet to relate what has happened, but what may happen—what is possible according to the law of probability or necessity."

The historian, not the poet, writes of what has already happened. The poet's task, declares Aristotle, is to write of what *could* happen. "Poetry, therefore, is a more philosophical and a higher thing than history: for poetry tends to express the universal, history the particular." In arguing that poets present things not as they are but as they should be, Aristotle rebuffs Plato's concept that poets merely imitate an imitation because Aristotle's poet, with his emphasis on the universal, actually attains something nearer to the ideal than does Plato's.

In Aristotle's view, not all imitations by poets are the same because "writers of greater dignity imitated the noble actions of noble heroes; the less dignified sort of writers imitated the actions of inferior men." "Comedy," writes Aristotle, "is an imitation of base men . . . characterized not by every kind of vice but specifically by 'the ridiculous,' some error or ugliness that is painless and has no harmful effects." It is to tragedy, written by poets imitating noble actions and heroes, that Aristotle turns his major attention.

Aristotle's complex definition of **tragedy** as found in the Poetics has perplexed and frustrated many readers:

> Tragedy is, then, an imitation of a noble and complete action, having the proper magnitude; it employs language that has been artistically enhanced by each of the kinds of linguistic adornment, applied separately in the various parts of the play; it is presented in dramatic, not narrative form, and achieves, through the representation of pitiable and fearful incidents, the catharsis of such pitiable and fearful incidents.

When put in context with other ideas in the *Poetics*, this complex definition highlights Aristotle's chief contributions to literary criticism:

1. Tragedy, or a work of art, is an imitation of nature that reflects a high form of art in exhibiting noble characters and noble deeds, the act of imitation itself giving us pleasure.
2. Art possesses form—that is, tragedy, unlike life, has a defined beginning, a middle, and an end, with each of the parts being related to every other part. A tragedy is therefore an organic whole, with its various parts all formally interrelated.
3. In tragedy, concern for form must be given to the characters as well as to the structure of the play, because the tragic hero must be "a man who is not eminently good and just, yet whose misfortune is brought about not by vice or depravity, but by some error or frailty. He must be one who is highly renowned and prosperous." In addition, all tragic heroes have a tragic flaw, or **hamartia**, that leads to their downfall in such a way as not to offend the audience's sense of justice.
4. The tragedy must have an emotional effect on its audience and "through pity and fear" effect a **catharsis**; that is, by the play's end, the audience's emotions should be purged, purified, or clarified. (What Aristotle really meant by *catharsis* is debatable; see the Glossary under *catharsis* for further details.)

5. The universal, not the particular, should be stressed, because unlike history, which deals with what happens, poetry or tragedy deals with what *could* happen and is, therefore, closer to perfection or truth.

6. The poet must give close attention to diction or language itself, whether it is in verse, prose, or song; but ultimately, the thoughts expressed through language are of utmost concern.

Interestingly, nowhere in the *Poetics* does Aristotle address the didactic value of poetry or literature. Unlike Plato, whose chief concern is the subject matter of poetry and its effects on the reader, Aristotle emphasizes literary form or structure, examining the component parts of a tragedy and how these parts must work together to produce a unified whole.

From the writings of these philosopher–artists, Plato and Aristotle, arise the concerns, questions, and debates that have spearheaded the development of most literary criticism. By addressing different aspects of these fifth-century critics' ideas and concepts, other literary critics from the Middle Ages to the present have formulated theories of literary criticism that force us to ask different—but also legitimate—questions of a text. Nevertheless, the shadows of Plato and Aristotle and their concerns loom over much of what these later theorists espouse.

HORACE (65–8 B.C.E.)

With the passing of the glory that was Greece and its philosopher–artists came the grandeur of Rome and its chief stylist, Quintus Horatius Flaccus or, simply, Horace. Friend of Emperor Augustus and many other members of the Roman aristocracy, Horace enjoyed the wealth and influence of these associates. In a letter to the sons of one of his friends and patrons, Maecenas, Horace articulated what became the official canon of literary taste during the Middle Ages, the Renaissance, and much of the Neoclassic period. By reading this letter and his *Ars Poetica* (*The Art of Poetry*), any Roman aristocrat, any medieval knight, and even Alexander Pope himself could learn the standards of good or proper literature.

Although Horace was probably acquainted with Aristotle's works, his concerns are quite different. Whereas both Plato and Aristotle decree that poets must, and do, imitate nature, Horace declares that poets must imitate other poets, particularly those of the past and especially the Greeks. Less concerned with **metaphysics** than his predecessors, Horace establishes the practical do's and don'ts for a writer. To be considered a good writer, he maintains, one should write about traditional subjects in unique ways. In addition, the poet should avoid all extremes in subject matter, diction (word choice), vocabulary, and style. Gaining mastery in these areas could be achieved by reading and following the examples of the classical Greek and

Roman authors. For example, because authors of antiquity began their epics in the middle of things, all epics must begin **in medias res**. Above all, writers should avoid appearing ridiculous and must therefore aim their sights low, not attempting to be a new Virgil or Homer.

Literature's ultimate aim, declares Horace, is *"dulce et utile,"* to be "sweet and useful." The best writings, he argues, both teach and delight. To achieve this goal, poets must understand their audience: Whereas learned readers may want to be instructed, others may simply read to be amused. The poet's task is to combine usefulness and delight in the same literary work.

Often oversimplified and misunderstood, Horace opts for giving would-be writers practical guidelines for the author's craft, while leaving unattended and unchallenged many of Plato and Aristotle's philosophical concerns. For Horace, a poet's greatest reward is the adulation of the public.

LONGINUS (FIRST CENTURY c.e.)

Although his date of birth and national origin remain controversial, Longinus garners an important place in literary history for his treatise *On the Sublime*. Probably Greek, Longinus often peppers his Greek and Latin writings with Hebrew quotations, making him the first literary critic to borrow from a different literary tradition than his own and earning him the title of the first comparative critic in literary history.

Unlike Plato, Aristotle, and Horace, who focus, respectively, on a work's essence, the constituent parts of a work, and literary taste, Longinus concentrates on single elements of a text. In addition, he is the first critic to define a literary classic.

One cannot accurately judge a literary work, he argues, unless one is exceedingly well read. A well-read critic can evaluate and recognize what is great, or what Longinus calls sublime: "For that is really great which bears a repeated examination, and which it is difficult or rather impossible to withstand, and the memory of which is strong and hard to efface." Longinus also contends that all readers are innately capable of recognizing the sublime, for "Nature has appointed us to be no base or ignoble animals . . . for she implants in our souls the unconquerable love of whatever is elevated and more divine than we." When our intellects, emotions, and wills harmoniously respond to a given work of art, we know we have been touched by the sublime.

Until the late seventeenth century, few people considered Longinus's *On the Sublime* important or had even read it. By the eighteenth century, its significance was recognized, and the treatise was quoted and debated by most public authors. Emphasizing the author (one who must possess a great mind and a great soul), the work itself (a text that must be composed of dignified and elevated diction while simultaneously disposing the reader to high thoughts), and the reader's response (the reaction of a learned audience largely determines the value or worth of any given text), Longinus's critical method foreshadows New Criticism, reader-oriented criticism, and other schools of twentieth-century criticism.

PLOTINUS (204–270 C.E.)

Born in Egypt in 204 C.E., Plotinus, the founder of neo-Platonism, traveled to Alexandria in his mid-twenties, where he was taught by Longinus's teacher, Ammonius Saccas. Ammonius sparked Plotinus's inextinguishable love for philosophy, and in 244 C.E., Plotinus left Ammonius in an attempt to discover Persian and Indian wisdom first hand. Accompanying the Emperor Gordian on an expedition to Persia, Plotinus hoped to engage Persia's leading philosophers in dialogue. Plotinus never reached Persia because Emperor Gordian was assassinated. Plotinus then traveled to Rome, where he taught philosophy for the next 20 years. Urged on by his most famous student, Porphyry, Plotinus began to write his own treatises in an attempt, he believed, to articulate clearly other scholars' garbled misinterpretations of Plato, whom he declared to be the ultimate authority on all philosophical matters. At the time of his death in 270 C.E., Plotinus had authored 54 treatises, all of which were collected, edited, and then named *The Enneads* by his student and friend Porphyry.

Through dialogues with his students, especially Porphyry, Plotinus developed and clearly articulated the most pivotal concept stemming from the teachings of Plato: The One. Plato mentions The One only briefly in *Parmenides*, also referring to parts of this concept, such as the Good, in *The Republic*. Simultaneously, The One is "unique and absolutely uncomplex" but also "absolutely transcendental." Both to and from The One all things flow, and it is the complete origin of everything. Humanity's goal, both Plato and Plotinus believed, was to achieve unity with The One through contemplation and study.

Because unity with The One is the goal of humanity, Plotinus asserts that humanity exists in other forms of being: intelligence (*nous*), Soul (*psyche*), and Matter (*physis*)—which are separate from The One, but which also stem from it. Intelligence corresponds with Plato's realm of ideas. In this mode, people comprehend ideas and concepts through the intellect, not the senses. Within this level of intellect emerges cognitive identity. By thinking and conceptualizing, Intelligence also conceptualizes itself. This dimension Plotinus refers to as "the realm of number," giving this name to the next domain, the Soul. In Plotinus's philosophic system, the Soul refers to the overarching Soul that runs through not only humanity but also the entire creation. According to Plotinus, all souls form only one Soul; such unity allows all souls to inter-communicate by extrasensory means. The Soul, however, has a selfish desire to possess itself, resulting in Matter, the third or lowest mode of being. For Plotinus, matter is at first praiseworthy because creation is able to know The One only because of its overflow into matter. But matter is also fallen because it is the lowest form of existence, one that is more frequently than not separate from The One.

Plotinus's complex philosophy becomes pivotal to literary criticism because of its adoption and adaptation by thinkers throughout the subsequent centuries. Immediately after Plotinus, Porphyry of Tyre and his contemporaries continued the journey toward transcendence. In the fourth century, St. Augustine, accompanied by Boethius in the fifth century, blended Plotinus's concepts of Neoplatonism with Christianity. This blending of Neoplatonism and Christianity eventually influenced medieval scholars such as St. Thomas Aquinas and Meister Eckhard. And not surprisingly, centuries later, the American transcendentalists Ralph Walso Emerson and Henry David Thoreau borrowed and amended some of Plotinus's key concepts.

Alongside Plato and Aristotle, many scholars consider Plotinus one of the greatest philosophers of antiquity because the writings and teaching of Plotinus form much of the Western perception of Plato and his works.

DANTE ALIGHIERI (1265–1321)

Born in Florence, Italy, during the Middle Ages, Dante is one of the most significant contributors to literary criticism since Longinus and Plotinus and the appearance of their texts *On the Sublime* and *The Enneads*, approximately 1000 years earlier. Similar to Longinus, Dante's concern is the proper language for poetry.

Banished from his native Florence for political reasons, Dante wrote many of his works in exile, including his masterpiece, *Commedia* (c. 1310–1321), later named *La Divina Commedia*, or *The Divine Comedy*. Written in three parts—*Inferno* (c. 1314), *Purgatorio* (c. 1319), and *Paradiso* (c. 1321)—*The Divine Comedy* (and the world depicted in it) mirrors Dante's contemporary world and his concept of the Christian God. Even before the third part of *The Divine Comedy* was published, Dante was already being heralded as Tuscany's greatest poet. As an introduction to the *Paradiso*, the third and last section of the *Commedia*, Dante wrote a letter to Can Grande della Scala explaining his literary theory. Known today as *Letter to Can Grande della Scala*, this work states that the language spoken by the people (the vulgar tongue or the vernacular) is an appropriate and beautiful language for writing.

Until the publication of Dante's works, Latin was the universal language, and all important works—such as histories, Church documents, and even government decrees—were written in this official Church tongue. Only frivolous or popular works appeared in the vulgar language of the common people. But in his *Letter*, Dante asserts and establishes that the vernacular is an excellent vehicle for works of literature.

In the *Letter*, Dante also notes that he uses multiple levels of interpretation or symbolic meaning in *The Divine Comedy*. Since the time of St. Augustine and throughout the Middle Ages, the Church theologians, writers, and priests had followed a tradition of **allegoric reading** of Scripture that interpreted many of the Old Testament laws and stories as symbolic representations (allegories) of Christ's actions. Such a **semiotic interpretation**—reading of signs—had been applied only to Scripture. Until Dante's *Commedia*, no secular work had used these principles of symbolic interpretation.

Praising the lyric poem and ignoring a discussion of genres, Dante established himself as the leading critic of the Middle Ages. Because he declared the common tongue an acceptable vehicle of expression for literature, literary works found an ever-increasing audience.

GIOVANNI BOCCACCIO (1313–1375)

Born the illegitimate son of a wealthy merchant from Florence, Italy, in 1313, little is known of Boccaccio's early life. In his late teens, he moved to Paris, where he pursued his studies of the new humanistic literature appearing on the scene. In Paris, he wrote some of his first vernacular poetry and was exposed to the works of Petrarch. Dante was Boccaccio's "poet–hero," and like Dante, Boccaccio often wrote in the vernacular. He eventually returned to Florence, where he and most other Europeans experienced the Black Death of 1348 (a disease that killed about 25 million Europeans), writing about events of this time in his most famous work, *Decameron* (1358). By 1360, Boccaccio was the center of Florentine culture, being one of the founders of the Renaissance. In 1373, he delivered the now famous *lecturae Dantis*, the first lecture series ever dedicated to a European vernacular text.

Boccaccio's most influential scholarly work is his *De Genealogia Deorum Gentilium* or *On the Genealogy of the Gods of the Gentiles* (1374), a collection of classical myths and legends. This work serves as a window into literary criticism of the 1300s. Throughout this mammoth encyclopedia of myths, Boccaccio successfully maneuvers through the scholasticism of the late medieval ages and the humanism of the dawning Renaissance, a shift of focus from God and the afterlife to the present moment, focusing primarily on the problem of the human condition. For Boccaccio, myths reflect both truth and reality while simultaneously having moral and religious value.

Particularly in books 14 and 15 of *The Genealogy of the Gods*, Boccaccio defends poetry and classical myth, arguing that the purpose of poetry is to improve life by revealing both truth and God, thereby disavowing Plato's beliefs that poetry is useless or full of lies. Poetry comes from "the bosom of God" and "moves the minds of a few men from on high to a yearning for the eternal." Poets, argues Boccaccio, are similar to philosophers, who seek truth through contemplation rather than reason. In similar fashion, poets are equal to theologians, who seek knowledge about God Himself. And the truth found by the poet in poetry or literature lies in allegory, revealing its truthfulness "in a fair and fitting garment of fiction." Even Christ Himself, points out Boccaccio, used stories or literature to reveal truth.

Boccaccio's defense of poetry had an immediate and lasting impact on literary theory and criticism, especially throughout the Renaissance. Boccaccio's concerns, critical writings, and collection of myths continued to appear in texts for the next several centuries, including those of Chaucer, Spenser, Jonson, Milton, and Shelley, to name a few. And Boccaccio's defense of poetry paves the way for one of the most famous defenses of all, Sir Philip Sidney's *Defense of Poesy*.

SIR PHILIP SIDNEY (1554–1586)

The paucity of literary criticism and theory during much of the Middle Ages is more than made up for by the abundance of critical activity during the Renaissance. One critic of this period far excels all others, Sir Philip Sidney. The representative scholar, writer, and gentleman of Renaissance England, Sidney is usually considered to be the first great English critic–poet. His work *An Apology for Poetry* (published 1595; originally *Defense of Poesy*) is the definitive formulation of Renaissance literary theory and the first influential piece of literary criticism in English history. With Sidney begins the English tradition and history of literary criticism.

As evidenced in *An Apology for Poetry*, Sidney is eclectic, borrowing and often amending the theories of Plato, Aristotle, Horace, and a few of his contemporary Italian critics. He begins his criticism by quoting from Aristotle: "Poesy therefore is an art of imitation, for so Aristotle termeth it in his word **mimesis**, that is to say, a representing, counterfeiting, or figuring forth." Eight words later, however, he adds a Horatian note, declaring poesy's chief end to be "to teach and delight." Similar to Aristotle, Sidney values poetry over history, law, and philosophy; but he takes Aristotle's idea one step further in declaring that poetry, above all the other arts and sciences, embodies truth. Poetry alone, he declares, is a teacher of virtue, moving the mind and spirit to both teach and desire to be taught. And the poet "is the most persuasive advocate of virtue, and none other exposes vice so effectively."

Unlike critics before him, Sidney best personifies the Renaissance period when he dictates his literary precepts. After ranking the different literary genres and declaring all to be instructive, he proclaims that poetry excels all because poetry is "the noblest of all works of [humankind]." He mocks other genres (e.g., tragicomedy) and adds more dictates to Aristotelian tragedy by insisting on unity of action, time, and place.

Throughout *An Apology for Poetry*, Sidney stalwartly defends poetry against those who view it as a mindless or immoral activity. For Sidney, creative poetry is akin to religion because both guide and accomplish their purpose by stirring the emotions of the reader. Poets, says Sidney, not only affirm morality, but by engaging the reader's emotions, blend truth with symbolism, delighting "every sense and faculty of the whole being." By the essay's end, a passionate and somewhat platonically inspired poet places a curse on all those who do not love poetry. He concludes, "I conjure you all . . . no more to scorn the sacred mysteries of Poesy . . . Thus doing, your name shall flourish in the printer's shops . . . you shall dwell upon superlatives." England did indeed rise up and take notice because in the 25 years after *An Apology for Poetry*, thirty-seven new works of drama and poetry took England by storm. And echoes of Sidney's emotionality reverberate throughout the centuries in English literature, especially in British Romantic writings of the early 1800s.

JOHN DRYDEN (1631–1700)

More than any other English writer, John Dryden—poet laureate, dramatist, and critic—embodies the spirit and ideals of the Neoclassical period, the literary age that follows Sidney and the Renaissance. Dr. Samuel Johnson attributes to Dryden "the improvement, perhaps the completion of our meter, the refinement of our language, and much of the correctness of our sentiments." The most prolific writer of the Restoration (the name given to the period of English literature from 1660 to 1700), Dryden excelled in almost all genres, including literary criticism. In effect, says one critic, Dryden "brought literary criticism out of the church and into the coffee house." And T. S. Eliot, the great twentieth-century poet and essayist, asserts that Dryden wrote "the first serious literary criticism in English by an English poet." Dryden's lasting contribution to literary criticism, *An Essay of Dramatic Poesy* (1668), highlights his genius.

The structure of Dryden's *An Essay of Dramatic Poesy* reflects his brilliance: During a naval battle between the English and the Dutch, four men are floating down a barge on the Thames River, each supporting a different aesthetic theory among those prominently espoused in Renaissance and Neoclassical literary criticism. The Platonic and Aristotelian debate concerning the nature or inherent condition of art as an imitation of nature itself begins the discussion. Nature, argues one debater, must be imitated directly. Another declares that writers should imitate the classical authors such as Homer because such ancient writers were the best imitators of nature. Through the voice of Neander, Dryden presents the benefits of both positions.

A lengthy discussion then ensues over the Aristotelian concept of the three unities of time, place, and action within a drama. Should the plot of a drama take place during one 24-hour cycle (time)? And in one location (place)? Should it be only a single plot, with no subplots (action)? The position that a drama must keep the three unities unquestionably wins the debate. Other concerns center on the following:

1. The language or diction of a play, with the concluding emphasis being placed on "proper" speech
2. Issues of decorum—that is, whether violent acts should appear on the stage, with the final speaker declaring it would be quite "improper"
3. The differences between the English and French theaters, with the English drama winning out for its diversity, its use of the stage, and its Shakespearian tradition
4. The value of rhymed as opposed to blank verse in the drama, with rhymed verse the victor—although Dryden later recanted this position and wrote many of his tragedies in blank verse. A reflection of his age in his life and works, Dryden sides with politesse (i.e., courteous formality), clarity, order, decorum, elegance, cleverness, and wit controlling characteristics of literary works.

Overall, Dryden's contribution to literary criticism is immense. First, he develops the study of literature in and of itself, not obsessing over its moral and theological worth. Second, he creates a natural, simple prose style that still guides and affects modern criticism and writing in general. Third, by making use of a variety of critical perspectives—from Greek to French—Dryden brings all of these critical perspectives' best insights into the new discipline of English literary criticism. And finally, Dryden advocates for the establishing of objective principles of criticism while simultaneously moving the emphasis of criticism away from simply the construction of a work into its more modern emphasis on how readers and critics appreciate texts.

JOSEPH ADDISON (1672–1719)

Essayist Joseph Addison was born on May 1, 1672. Working alongside other critics such as John Dryden and Alexander Pope, Addison highlights the concept of the "greatness of literature" in his essays and newspaper articles, appealing to the common readers of England. Educated at Magdalen College, Oxford, England, Addison was a Latin poet and a classical scholar.

His classical training served him well throughout his life, fostering his reading and criticism of literature. His literary criticism first appeared in the newspaper, *The Tatler*, that he started with Richard Steele and then *The Tatler*'s successor, *The Spectator*. Although his critical essays were sparse in *The Tatler*, Addison's critical commentaries blossomed in *The Spectator*, filling the newspaper with classical and contemporary readings, but tempering the readings' tone, diction, and content for popular readers, making his writing "polite."

Throughout his essays, Addison more frequently than not acknowledges the superority of the ancient critics compared with the modern ones, paying homage to Aristotelian and Longinian ideas, among others. In *Spectator 25*, he writes: "It is impossible for us who live in the later Ages of the World, to make Observations in Criticism, Morality, or in any Art or Science, which has not been touched upon by others." In short, the past critics have already said all there is to say, and to write after them is to expound upon and justify their past criticism.

Believing that "philosophy was the elegant common sense apt to mould [humankind]," Addison became known as the "British Virgil," and "the suave and homely Marcus Aurelius" bringing "philosophy out of closets and libraries, schools and colleges, to dwell in clubs and assemblies, at tea-tables and coffee-houses" (*Spectator 10*). Avoiding lofty or pious language in his criticism, his literary goal was "to endeavor to enliven morality with wit and to temper wit with morality" (*Spectator 10*). And his audience, he believed, was the common person, especially the women of England because he notes, "there are none to whom this paper will be more useful" (*Spectator 10*). Whereas other English criticism of the time focuses on the author and the rules of literature, Addison highlights the *sublime* or what he calls the *greatness* of literature: "By *greatness* I do not mean only the Bulk of any single Object, but the Largeness of the whole View, considered as one entire Piece" (*Spectator 412*). For Addison, greatness in literature is not mechanical superiority but the prowess to display the immensity of life in a way that transcends imagination. Greatness, or the sublime, comes from both "great ideas and vehement passions." The aim of literary critics, attests Addision, is not to dissect the writer of genius but to look at what occurs in the interaction of literature and its audience. Our curiosity, says Addison, is one of the strongest and most lasting appetites implanted in us. Because of such curiosity, a critic's writings must be necessarily broad, touching on politics, sciences, arts, society, and any other concern pertinent to humanity. And the audience of such writings should be the general public, enlightening ordinary people with well-written prose combined with wit while simultaneously introducing them to the study of genius, the sublime, greatness, and audience response over the mechanics of a text.

Unlike his contemporary critics and authors such as John Dryden and Alexander Pope, Addison aimed to enlighten common British citizens by giving to them the writings of the classical authors presented in simple, clear prose that could and would be discussed in the coffee houses and at the tea tables throughout Great Britain.

ALEXANDER POPE (1688–1744)

Born into a Roman Catholic family in a Protestant-controlled England, born a healthy infant but soon disabled by spinal tuberculosis, and born at the beginning of the Neoclassical age (English literature from 1660 to 1798) and becoming its literary voice by age 20, Alexander Pope embodies in his writings eighteenth-century thought and literary criticism. His early poems such as *The Rape of the Lock* (1712), "Eloisa to Abelard," and "Pastorals" establish him as a major British poet, but with the publication of his *Essay on Criticism* (1711), he becomes for all practical purposes the "literary pope" of England.

In this essay, Pope, unlike previous literary critics and theorists, directly addresses critics rather than poets, because he undertakes to codify Neoclassical literary criticism. Toward the end of the essay, however, he does speak to both critics and poets.

According to Pope, the golden age of criticism is the classical age, the age of Homer, Aristotle, Horace, and Longinus. Those writers discovered the truth about "unerring Nature." It is the critic and the poet's task first to know and then to copy these authors and not nature because "To copy nature is to copy them [the classical authors]."

Pope asserts that the chief requirement of a good poet is natural genius, coupled with a knowledge of the classics and an understanding of the rules of poetry (literature). Such knowledge must be tempered with politeness and grace because "Without good breeding truth is disapproved/That only makes superior sense beloved."

Natural genius and good breeding being established, the critic or poet must then give heed to certain rules, says Pope. To be a good critic or poet, one must follow the established traditions as defined by the ancients. Not surprisingly, Pope spells out what these rules are and how they should be applied to eighteenth-century verse. Great concern for poetic diction, the establishment of the heroic couplet as a standard for verse, and the personification of abstract ideas, for example, became fixed standards, but emotional outbreaks and free verse were *extraordinaire* and considered unrefined.

Governed by rules, restraint, and good taste, poetry, as defined by Pope, seeks to reaffirm truths or absolutes already discovered by the classical writers. The critic's task is clear: to validate and maintain classical values in the ever-shifting flux of cultural change. In effect, the critic becomes the custodian and defender of good taste and cultural values.

By affirming the imitation of the classical writers and through them of nature itself and by establishing the acceptable or standard criteria of poetic language, Pope grounds his criticism in both the **mimetic** (imitation) and **rhetoric** (patterns of structure) literary theories. By the end of the 1700s, however, a major shift in literary theory occurs.

WILLIAM WORDSWORTH (1770–1850)

By the close of the eighteenth century, the world had witnessed several major political rebellions, among them the American and French Revolutions, along with extreme social upheavals and prominent changes in philosophical thought. During this age of rebellion, a paradigmatic shift occurred in how people viewed the world. Whereas the eighteenth century valued order and reason, the emerging nineteenth-century worldview emphasized intuition as a proper guide to truth. The eighteenth-century mind likened the world to a great machine, with all its parts operating harmoniously, but in the nineteenth century, the world was perceived as a living organism that was always growing and eternally becoming. The city housed the centers of art and literature and set the standards of good taste for the rationalistic mind of the eighteenth century. In contrast, emerging nineteenth-century citizens saw rural places as fundamental, as the setting in which a person could discover the inner self. Devaluing the empirical and rationalistic methodologies of the previous century, nineteenth-century thinkers believed that truth could be attained by tapping into the core of our humanity or our transcendental natures, best sought in our original or natural setting.

Such radical changes found their spokesperson in William Wordsworth. Born in Cockermouth, Cumberlandshire, and raised in the Lake District of England, Wordsworth completed his formal education at St. John's College, Cambridge, in 1791. After completing his grand tour of the Continent, he published *Descriptive Sketches* and then met one of his literary admirers and soon-to-be friends and coauthors, Samuel T. Coleridge. In 1798, Wordsworth and Coleridge published *Lyrical Ballads*, a collection of poems that heralded the beginning of British Romanticism. In the ensuing 15-year period, Wordsworth wrote most of his best poetry, including *Poems in Two Volumes*, *The Excursion*, *Miscellaneous Poems*, and *The Prelude*. But *Lyrical Ballads* ushers in the Romantic age in English literature.

In an explanatory preface written as an introduction to the second edition of *Lyrical Ballads*, Wordsworth espouses a new vision of poetry and the beginnings of a radical change in literary theory. His purpose, he notes, is "to choose incidents and situations from common life, and . . . describe them in language really used by [people] in situations . . . the manner in which we associate ideas in a state of excitement." Similar to Aristotle, Sidney, and Pope, Wordsworth concerns himself with the elements and subject matter of literature, but he changes the emphasis: Common men and women people his poetry rather than kings, queens, and aristocrats because in "humble and rustic life" the poet finds that "the essential passions of the heart find a better soil in which they can attain their maturity, are less under restraint, and speak a plainer and more emphatic language."

Not only does Wordsworth suggest a radical change in subject matter, but he also dramatically shifts the focus of poetry's "proper language." Unlike Pope and his predecessors, Wordsworth chooses "language really used by [people]"—everyday speech, not the inflated poetic diction of heroic couplets, complicated rhyme schemes, and convoluted figures of speech placed in the mouths of the typical eighteenth-century character. Wordsworth's rustics, such as Michael and Luke in his poetic narrative "Michael," speak in the simple, everyday diction of their trade.

In addition to reshaping the focus of poetry's subject and language, Wordsworth redefines poetry itself: "For all good poetry is the spontaneous overflow of powerful feelings." Unlike Sidney, Dante, and Pope, who decree that poetry should be restrained, controlled, and reasoned, Wordsworth now highlights poetry's emotional quality. Imagination, not reason or disciplined thought, becomes poetry's core.

In altering poetry's subject matter, language, and definition, Wordsworth redefines the role of the poet. The poet is no longer the preserver of civilized values or proper taste, but "he is a man speaking to men: a man . . . endowed with more lively sensibility, more enthusiasm and tenderness, who has a greater knowledge of human nature and a more comprehensive soul than are supposed to be common among mankind." Wordsworth's poet "has acquired a greater readiness and power in expressing what he thinks and feels, and especially those thoughts and feelings which, by his own choice, or from the structure of his own mind, arise in him without immediate external excitement." Such a poet need no longer follow a prescribed set of rules because this artist may freely express his or her own individualism, valuing and writing about feelings that are peculiarly the artist's.

Because he defines poetry as "the spontaneous overflow of powerful feelings . . . [taking] its origin from emotion recollected in tranquility," Wordsworth's new kind of poet crafts a poem by internalizing a scene, circumstance, or happening and "recollects" that occasion with its accompanying emotions at a later time when the artist can shape the remembrance into words. Poetry, then, is unlike biology or the other sciences because it deals not with something that can be dissected or broken down into its constituent parts, but primarily with the imagination and feelings. Intuition, not reason, reigns.

What then of the reader? What part does the audience play in such a process? Toward the end of the Preface to *Lyrical Ballads*, Wordsworth writes, "I have one request to make of my reader, which is, that in judging these poems he would decide by his own feelings genuinely, and not by reflection upon what will probably be the judgement of others." Wordsworth apparently hopes that his readers' responses to and opinions of his poems will not depend on critics who would freely dispense their evaluations. Wordsworth wants his readers to rely on their own feelings and their own imaginations because they grapple with the same emotions the poet felt when he first saw and then later "recollected in tranquility" the subject or circumstances of the poem itself. Through poetry, declares Wordsworth, the poet and the reader share such emotions.

This subjective experience of sharing emotions leads Wordsworth away from the preceding centuries' mimetic and rhetorical theories of criticism and toward a new development in literary theory: the **expressive school**, which emphasizes the individuality of the artist and the reader's privilege to share in this individuality. By expressing such individuality and valuing the emotions and the imagination as legitimate concerns in poetry, Wordsworth lays the foundation for English Romanticism and broadens the scope of literary criticism and theory for both the nineteenth and twentieth centuries.

PERCY BYSSHE SHELLEY (1792–1822)

One of the strongest and most vocal voices of British Romanticism (1798–1832), Percy Shelley was born in Sussex, England in 1792, the eldest child of a wealthy country squire. Educated at an academy in London, Shelley attended Oxford University, where he found intellectual companionship with Thomas Jefferson Hogg (1792–1862), who became a lifelong friend. After mastering the works of Plato and the writings of William Godwin (1756–1836), especially *Political Justice*, Shelley and Hogg authored a pamphlet titled *The Necessity of Atheism*, an act that resulted in Hogg and Shelley's expulsion from Oxford. Ironically, Shelley was not an atheist but wanted to establish the right to debate the beliefs of Christianity.

Such disputes and quarrels with the establishment of both Church and state followed Shelley the remainder of his life, including an unhappy marriage to Harriet Westbrook, an elopement with Mary Wollstonecraft Godwin, and other such events esteemed disgraceful by Britain's citizenry. Yet Shelley produced some of the best known Romantic poems, including "Ozymandias" (1817), "Ode to the West Wind" (1819), and "Adonais" (1821), to name a few. He also wrote a pivotal text of literary criticism, *A Defence of Poetry* (1821), written in response to a whimsical attack on Romantic poetry by Thomas Love Peacock (1785–1866), a good friend of Shelley's and a poet, essayist, and scholar in his own right.

Of all the Romantic poets, Shelley, by far, is the greatest devotee of Plato, embracing Plato's beliefs and establishing himself as the voice of neo-Platonism in British Romanticism. In *A Defence of Poetry*, Shelley's indebtedness to Plato quickly becomes obvious. Shelley, for example, embraces Plato's concept of the Ideal Forms, the belief that all things around us are merely representations or shadows of the Truth, of the Ideal world, of spiritual reality—what Plato names The One. Shelley blends Plato's concept of spiritual reality with his own understanding, asserting that poetry is by far the best way to gain access to the Forms and to ultimate truth. Disavowing Neoclassicism's emphasis on order and reason, Shelley emphasizes the individual and the imagination. For Shelley, Plato's Forms intertwine with the Romantic ideal of the imagination. Poetry, then, is less concerned with reason and rationality and more concerned with the spiritual and the transcendental. Now the imagination and the emotions, not didactic structural elements, become center stage in interpreting a text because Shelley redefines poetry as "the expression of the imagination." For Shelley, "poetry is . . . that from which all spring, and that which adorns all; and that which if blighted, denies the fruit and the seed, and withholds from the barren world the nourishment and succession of the scions of the tree of life." Poetry is not only an outstanding art form but also a teacher and a guide to Truth, one embodied in nature and the individual, not in science, reason, or philosophy. Shelley believes that philosophy and history stem from poetry, with poetry occupying a superior place to these disciplines. And poets, the crafters of poetry, are found in all walks of life: architects, painters, musicians, teachers, and even lawmakers. If true to their craft, poets will lead people toward Truth—the Truth of the spiritual nature of ultimate reality, Plato's The One—opening the minds of their readers to the unseen beauty all around them.

For Shelley, nothing is more sacred and perfect than poetry. Above all other kinds of artists, the poet is the greatest because the poet alone can see the future in the present and, as Shelley notes, "participates in the eternal, the infinite, and the one," becoming more than just an ordinary person. Shelley's passion for both the poet and poetry and their role in the world as teacher and prophet who can lead us to ultimate truth represents a paradigmatic shift in thought from the Age of Reason or Neoclassicism to Romanticism, a new direction in literary criticism that cannot be simply dismissed or ignored by modern-day theorists.

HIPPOLYTE ADOLPHE TAINE (1828–1893)

Wordsworth's Romanticism, with its stress on intuition as a guide to learning ultimate truth and its belief that emotions and the imagination form the core of poetry's content, dominated literature and literary criticism throughout the first three decades of the nineteenth century, and its influence still continues today. With the rise of the Victorian era in the 1830s, reason, science, and a sense of historical determinism began to supplant Romantic thought. The growing sense of historical and scientific determinism finally found its authoritative voice and culminating influence in Charles Darwin and his text *On the Origin of Species*, published in 1859. Humankind was now demystified because we finally knew our origins and understood our physiological development. Science, it seemed, had provided us with the key to our past and an understanding of the present and would help us determine our future if we relied on the scientific method in all our human endeavors.

Science's methodology, philosophical assumptions, and practical applications found an admiring adherent and a strong voice in French historian and literary critic Hippolyte Taine. Born in Vouziers, France, Taine was a brilliant but unorthodox student at the École Normale Supérieure in Paris. After finishing his formal education, he taught in various schools throughout France, continuing his investigations in both aesthetics and history. During the 1850s, he published various philosophical and aesthetic treatises, but his chief contribution to literary criticism and history is *The History of English Literature*, published in 1863. In this work, Taine crystallizes what is now known as the historical approach to literary analysis.

In the introduction to *The History of English Literature*, Taine uses a scientific simile to explain his approach to literary criticism:

> What is your first remark on turning over the great, stiff leaves of a folio, the yellow sheets of a manuscript—a poem, a code of laws, a declaration of faith? This, you say was not created alone. It is but a mould, like fossil shell, an imprint, like one of those shapes embossed in stone by an animal which lived and perished. Under the shell there was an animal, and behind the document there was a man. Why do you study the shell, except to represent to yourself the animal? So do you study the document only in order to know the [person].

For Taine, a text is similar to a fossil shell that naturally contains the likeness of its inhabiter, who, in this case, is the author. To study only the text (e.g., discovering its date of composition or the accuracy of its historical references or allusions) without considering the author and his or her inner psyche would, therefore, result in an incomplete analysis. An investigation of both the text and the author, Taine believed, would result in an accurate understanding of the literary work.

Taine asserts that to understand any literary text, we must examine the environmental causes that joined together in its creation. He divides such influences into four main categories: race, milieu, moment, and dominant faculty. By race, Taine posits that authors of the same race, or those born and raised in the same country, share peculiar intellectual beliefs, emotions, and ways of understanding. By examining each author's inherited and learned personal characteristics, Taine believes we will then be able to understand more fully the author's text. In addition, we must also examine the author's milieu or surroundings. English citizens, he believed, respond differently to life than do French or Irish citizens. Accordingly, by examining the culture of the author, Taine proposes that we would understand more fully the intellectual and cultural concerns that inevitably surface in an author's text. Further, Taine maintains that we must investigate an author's epoch or moment—that is, the time period in which the text was written. Such information reveals the dominant ideas or worldview held by people at that particular time, therefore helping us identify and understand the literary characters' actions, motivations, and concerns more fully than if we did not have such information. Finally, Taine decrees we must examine each author's individual talents that make him or her different from others who share similar characteristics of race, milieu, and moment. For Taine, a work of art is "the result of given causes" and can best be represented by using the following formula: race + milieu + moment + dominant faculty = work of art. Taine argues that we cannot appreciate art as it "really" is without considering all four of his stated elements.

Ultimately, for Taine, the text becomes a literary object that can be dissected to discover its meaning. By examining the actual text itself, the circumstances of place and race, the historical times in which the text was written, and each author's individual talents, we will realize, Taine asserts, that no text is written in a vacuum, but is instead the result of its history.

MATTHEW ARNOLD (1822–1888)

In the Preface to *Lyrical Ballads*, Wordsworth declares that "poetry is the breath and finer spirit of all knowledge; it is the impassioned expression which is the countenance of all science." Such a lofty statement concerning the nature and role of poetry finds an advocate in Matthew Arnold, the self-appointed voice for English Victorianism, the literary epoch immediately occurring after Wordsworth and Shelley's Romanticism.

Born during the Romantic era, Matthew Arnold was the son of an English educator. Following in his family's tradition, Arnold attended Oxford. After graduation, he accepted a teaching position at Oriel College. He spent most of his professional life (nearly 35 years) as a government school inspector. By age 35, he had already written the majority of his poetry, including "Dover Beach," "The Scholar-Gipsy," and "Sohrab and Rustum," some of his most famous poems.

During Arnold's early career, reactions against Romanticism and its adherents began to occur. Writers, philosophers, and scientists began to give more credence to empirical and rationalistic methods for discovering the nature of their world rather than to Romantic concepts of emotion, individualism, and intuition as pathways to truth. With the publication of Charles Darwin's *On the Origin of Species* in 1859 and the writings of philosopher and sociologist Herbert Spencer (1820–1903) and German theologian and philosopher David Friedrich Strauss (1808–1874), science seemingly usurped the place of Romanticism's "religion of nature" and the beliefs of most other traditional religions. At the same time, however, philosophy became too esoteric and, therefore, less relevant as a vehicle for understanding reality for the average Victorian. Into this void stepped Arnold, proclaiming that poetry can provide the necessary truths, values, and guidelines for society.

Fundamental to Arnold's literary criticism is his reapplication of classical criteria to literature. Quotes and borrowed ideas from Plato, Aristotle, Longinus, and other classical writers pepper his criticism. From Aristotle's *Poetics*, for example, Arnold adapts his idea that the best poetry is of a "higher truth and seriousness" than history—or any other human subject or activity, for that matter. Similar to Plato, Arnold believes that literature reflects the society in which it is written and thereby heralds its values and concerns. Similar to Longinus, Arnold attempts to define a classic and decrees that such a work belongs to the "highest" or "best class." And in attempting to support many of his other ideas, Arnold also cites the later "classical" writers such as Dante, Shakespeare, and Milton.

For Arnold, poetry—not religion, science, or philosophy—is humankind's crowning activity. He notes, "More and more [human]kind will discover that we have to turn to poetry to interpret life for us, to console us, to sustain us. Without poetry, our science will appear incomplete; and most of what now passes with us for religion and philosophy will be replaced by poetry." And in the best of this poetry, he declares, we find "in the eminent degree, truth and seriousness." Equating "seriousness" with moral excellence, Arnold asserts that the best poetry can and does provide standards of excellence, a yardstick by which both Arnold and his society should judge themselves.

In his pivotal essays "The Study of Poetry" and "The Function of Criticism at the Present Time," Arnold crystallizes his critical position. Similar to Plato's critic, Arnold reaffirms but slightly amends the social role of criticism: creating "a current of true and fresh ideas." To accomplish this goal, the critic must avoid becoming embroiled in politics or any other activity that would lead to a form of bias, because the critic must view society disinterestedly, keeping aloof from the world's mundane affairs. In turn, such aloofness benefits all of society because the critic will be able to pave the way for high culture—a prerequisite for the poet and the writing of the best poetry.

How then may the best poetry be achieved or discovered? This may be done by establishing objective criteria whereby we can judge whether any poem contains or achieves, in Aristotelian terms, "higher truth or seriousness." The critic's task is "to have always in one's mind lines and expressions of the great masters, and to apply them as a touchstone to other poetry." By comparing the newly written lines to classical poems that contain elements of the "sublime," the critic will instantly know whether a new poem is good or bad.

In practice, such apparent objectivity in criticism becomes subjective. Whose judgments, for example, shall we follow? Shall lines written by Homer and Dante be considered excellent? How about Sidney's or even Aristophanes's? Need the critic rank all past poets in an attempt to discover who is great and who is not in order to create a basis for such comparisons and value judgments? And whose moral values shall become the yardstick with which we judge poetry? Arnold's only?

Such "objective" **touchstone theory** redefines the task of the literary critic and introduces a subjective approach in literary criticism. No longer just being the interpreter of a literary work, the critic now functions as an authority on values, culture, and tastes. This new literary "watchdog" must guard and defend high culture and its literature while simultaneously defining what high culture and literature really are.

Decreeing the critic to be the preserver of society's values and poetry to be its most important activity, Arnold became the recognized spokesperson for Victorian England and its literature. Even modern-day literary criticism remains peppered with some of his distinct phrases: "a disinterested effort to learn and propagate the best that has been known and thought" "to see the object as in itself it really is," "culture and anarchy," and "a criticism of life," to cite a few. By taking Wordsworth's concept of the poet one step further, Arnold separated both the critic and the poet from society in order to create a type of poetry and criticism that could supposedly rescue society from its baser elements and preserve its most noble characteristics. Opposed by some modern critics whose analyses stop short of considering literary criticism of the previous two centuries, Arnold's criticism serves as either a rallying point or as a standard of opposition by which theorists can now measure their own critical statements. More than any other critic, Arnold helped establish "culture," particularly literature, as the highest object of veneration among civilized people.

HENRY JAMES (1843–1916)

While Arnold was decreeing how poetry would rescue humanity from its baser elements and help lead us to truth, literary works were also being written in other genres, particularly the novel. Throughout both the Romantic and Victorian eras, for example, people in England and America were reading such works as *Wuthering Heights*, *Vanity Fair*, *The House of the Seven Gables*, and *Great Expectations*. Few, however, were providing for either the writers or the readers of this genre a body of criticism comparable to that continually being formulated for poetry. As Henry James notes in his critical essay "The Art of Fiction" (1884), the English novel "had no air of having a theory, a conviction, a consciousness of itself behind it—of being the expression of an artistic faith, the result of choice and comparison." It was left to James himself to provide us with such a theory.

Born in New York City in 1843, Henry James enjoyed the privileges of education, travel, and money. Throughout his early life, he and his family (including his brother William, the founder of American pragmatic philosophy) traveled to the capitals of Europe, visiting the sites and meeting the leading writers and scholars of the day. Having all things European injected early into his life and thoughts, James believed he wanted to be a lawyer and enrolled in Harvard Law School. He quickly discovered that writing, not law, captivated him, and he abandoned law school for a career in writing. By 1875, the early call of Europe on his life had to be answered, and James, a bachelor for life, settled permanently in Europe and began in earnest his writing career.

Noted for his short stories—"The Real Thing," "The Beast in the Jungle," and "The Jolly Corner," to name a few—and his novels—*The American*, *The Portrait of a Lady*, *The Bostonians*, and *The Turn of the Screw*, among others—James's favorite theme is the conflict he perceives between Europe and America. The seasoned aristocracy with its refined manners and taste is often infiltrated in his stories by the naive American who seemingly lacks refined culture and discernment. Though a very involved practicing writer, James was also concerned with developing a theory of writing, particularly for the novel. Indeed, in his critical essay "The Art of Fiction," he provides us with the first well-articulated theory of the novel in English literature.

In "The Art of Fiction," James states that "a novel is in its broadest definition a personal, a direct impression of life: that, to begin with, constitutes its value, which is greater or less according to the intensity of the impression." Furthermore, "the only obligation to which in advance we may hold a novel, without incurring the accusation of being arbitrary, is that it be interesting. The ways in which it is at liberty to accomplish this result [are] innumerable." From the start, James's theory rejects the romantic notion of either Wordsworth or Coleridge that the reader suspend disbelief while reading a text. For James, a text must first be realistic, a representation of life as it is and one that is recognizable to its readers. Bad novels, declares James, are either romantic or scientific; good novels show us life in action and, above all else, are interesting.

Bad novels, James continues, are written by bad authors, whereas good novels are written by good authors. Unlike weak authors, good writers are good thinkers who can select, evaluate, and imaginatively use the "stuff of life" (i.e., the facts or pictures of reality) in their work. These writers also recognize that a work of art is organic. The work itself is not simply the amassing of realistic data from real-life experiences but has a life of its own that grows according to its own principles or themes. The writer must acknowledge this fact and distance him- or herself from directly telling the story. Shunning the omniscient, third-person narrator as a vehicle for telling a story, James asserts that a more indirect point of view is essential so that the author shows characters, actions, and emotions to readers rather than telling us about them. By showing rather than telling us about his characters and their actions, James believes that he creates a greater illusion of reality than if he were to present his story through one point of view or one character. Ultimately, however, the reader must decide the worth of the text, and "nothing of course, will ever take the place of the good old fashion liking of a work of art or not liking it: the most improved criticism will not abolish that primitive, that ultimate test."

Thanks to Henry James, the genre of the novel became a respectable topic for literary critics. With his emphasis on realism and "the stuff of life," James formulated a theory of fiction that is still discussed and debated today.

MIKHAIL BAKHTIN (1895–1975)

Perhaps more than any other modern-day literary theorist, Mikhail Bakhtin exemplifies present-day literary theory because Bakhtin himself represents diverse academic disciplines and interests. Bakhtin has been dubbed a linguist, a historian, a philosopher, a writer, an artist, a Formalist critic, a Marxist critic, a literary historian, an ethicist, and a cultural critic. Without question, he is one of the most original thinkers of the twentieth century.

Ironically, Bakhtin received little attention during his lifetime, except perhaps in his later years. Born in Oriel, Russia, to a middle-class family, Bakhtin grew up in Vilnius and Odessa before moving to Petrograd to study at the University of St. Petersburg in 1913. Leaving the university without completing his studies, he then moved first to Nevel and then to Vitebsk, where he worked as a teacher. At Vitebsk, he was surrounded by a group of intellectuals who addressed the social and cultural influences of the Russian Revolution and its rule under Joseph Stalin. Today, this group of scholars, including Bakhtin, P.N. Medvede, and V.N. Voloshinov, is known as the **Bakhtin Circle**. By 1924, the group had moved to Leningrad, where Bakhtin struggled financially as his illness (osteomyelitis in his leg) and his lack of proper political credentials prevented him from finding work. In 1929, he was arrested for supposedly participating in the underground Russian Orthodox Church. Sentenced to exile in Siberia for 10 years, he appealed his sentence because of his weakening physical condition and was then sentenced to 6 years of internal exile in Kazakhstan.

Throughout the 1930s, Bakhtin worked as a bookkeeper and then as a teacher at Mordovia State Teacher's College in Saransk, moving often to escape further imprisonment during various political purges. In 1938, his osteomyelitis advanced, causing his right leg to be amputated. Although he was plagued with pain for the rest of his life, his scholarly work dramatically improved after the amputation. In 1946, he successfully defended his doctoral dissertation on Rabelais and his world. From the late 1940s until his retirement in 1961, Bakhtin taught at the Mordov Pedagogical Institute, now the University of Saranak. In the latter part of the 1950s, Russian academics and scholars were again interested in his work and were more than surprised to discover that he was still alive. Producing a new edition of his 1929 study of Dostoevsky along with additional works on Rabelais and the Renaissance culture, Bakhtin quickly became the "poster scholar" for Russian scholarship. After his death in 1975, a variety of his manuscripts became available, with a few edited by the author himself. By the 1980s and 1990s, Bakhtin was regarded as one of the most profound scholars of the twentieth century.

His most reknown academic writings include his first work, *Problems of Dostoyevsky's Poetics* (1929; 2nd ed., 1963); his doctoral dissertation, *Rabelais and His World*, which was successfully defended in 1946, but not published until 1968; and *The Dialogic Imagination: Four Essays by M.M. Bakhtin* (edited, translated, and published in 1981). Since Bakhtin's death in 1975, many more of his speeches and essays have been translated and published, but the core of his linguistic and literary theories can be discovered from the earlier works.

Central to Bakhtin's critical theory is the concept of the **dialogic**. According to Bakhtin, all language is a dialogue in which a speaker and a listener form a relationship. Language is always the product of at least two people in a dialogue, not a monologue. And it is language that defines us as individuals. Our personal consciousness consists of the inner conversations we have only in our heads, conversations with a variety of voices that are significant for us. Each of these voices can respond in new and exciting ways, developing who we are and helping shape who we become. In one very real sense, no individual can ever, then, be completely understood or fully known. The idea that any person always has the capability to change or never fully be known in this world Bakhtin calls **unfinalizability**.

Because Bakhtin posits that all language is a dialogue, not a monologue, he employs the term **heteroglossia** (a translation of the Russian word *raznorecie*, meaning "other or different tongues") to demonstrate the multiplicty of languages that operate in any given culture, language not being defined only as the spoken tongue of a given, cultural people. For Bakhtin, all the forms of social speech that people use in their daily activities constitute heteroglossia. Professors speak one way while lecturing to their classes, another to their spouses, another to their friends, another to the clerk at the store, another to the server at a restaurant, and another to the police officer who gives the professor a speeding ticket. Each individual speech act is a **dialogic utterance** that is oriented toward a particular listener or audience, demonstraing the relationship that exists between the speaker and listener.

In his essay "Discourse in the Novel," Bakhtin applies his ideas directly to the novel. He believes that the novel is characterized by **dialogized heteroglossia**. Within the novel, multiple worldviews and a variety of experiences continually dialogue with each other, resulting in multiple interactions, some of which are real and others which are imagined. Although the characters' utterances are, indeed, important, the commenting narrator's dialogic utterances, Bakhtin asserts, are the most important. Through these utterances, diverse voices and complex interactions and relationships form, creating a complex unity. Whatever meaning the language of the text possesses, says Bakhtin, resides not in the intention of the speaker nor in the text but somewhere between the speaker or writer or between the listener or reader. Such dialogized heteroglossia continually occurs because within a single utterance, two different languages clash, a process Bakhtin calls **hybridization**.

Bakhtin believes that some novels, especially those written by Dostoevsky, are **polyphonic**. In nonpolyphonic novels, the author knows the ending of the novel while writing the novel's beginning. The writer knows all the characters' actions and choices, and the author also knows the work's entire structure. In this kind of novel, the author's understanding of truth is what is exhibited in the work. In a polyphonic novel, there is no overall outlined structure or prescribed outcome, nor is the novel a working out of the author's worldview or understanding of truth. The truth of the polyphonic novel is an active creation in the consciousnesses of the author, the readers, and the characters, allowing for genuine surprises for all concerned. All participants—author, reader, and characters—participate as equals in creating the novel's "truth," because truth requires a plurality of consciousnesses.

For Bakhtin, the polyphonic nature of the novel implies that there are many truths, not one. Each character speaks and thinks his or her own truth. Although one truth may be preferred to others by a character, a reader, or the author, no truth is particularly certain. Readers watch as one character influences another, and readers listen to the multitude of voices heard by each character as these voices shape those who hear them. What develops, says Bakhtin, is a **carnivalistic** atmosphere, a sense of joyful relativity. This sense of **carnival** is one of Bakhtin's most significant contributions to literary theory and helps describe the novel's polyphonic style, especially the novels of Dostoevsky. Polyphonic novels, asserts Bakhtin, have a carnival sense of the world, a sense of joyful abandonment where many voices are simultaneously heard and directly influence their hearers. Each participant tests both the ideas and the lives of other participants, creating a somewhat seriocomic environment.

Bakhtin's interest in language, culture, literature, religion, and politics encompasses much of contemporary literary theory and criticism. His ideas have become starting points for conversations and dialogues between competing and often conflicting voices in contemporary cultural theory.

MODERN LITERARY CRITICISM

Matthew Arnold's death in 1888 (and to a lesser degree, Henry James's death in 1916) marked a transitional period in literary criticism. Similar to Dryden, Pope, and Wordsworth before him, Arnold was the recognized authority and leading literary critic of his day, and his theories and criticism embody the major ideas of his era. With the passing of Arnold, the predominance of any one person or set of ideas representing a broad time period or literary movement ends, although Bakhtin's concerns and voice vie for prominence. After Arnold, literary theory and criticism become splintered and more diversified, with no one voice speaking *ex cathedra* and no one theory tenaciously held by all. At the end of the nineteenth century, most critics emphasized either a biographical or a historical approach to a text. Using Taine's historical interests in a text and Henry James's newly articulated theory of the novel, many critics investigated a text as if it were the embodiment of its author or a historical artifact. No single, universally recognized voice dominates literary theory in the years that follow Arnold or James. Instead, many distinctive literary voices give rise to a host of differing and exciting ways to examine a text.

What follows in the twentieth century is a variety of schools of criticism, with each school asking legitimate, relevant but different questions about a text. Most of these schools abandon the **holistic approach** to literary study, which investigates, analyzes, and interprets all elements of the artistic situation in favor of concentrating on one or more specific aspects. For example, modernism (and, in particular, the New Criticism, the first critical movement of the twentieth century) wishes to break from the past and seemingly disavow cultural influences that may affect a work of literature. The text, these critics declare, will interpret the text. On the other hand, Cultural Poetics or New Historicism, a school of criticism that first appeared in the late 1970s and continues to develop its underlying assumptions and methodologies to the present day, argues that most critics' historical consciousness must be reawakened because, in reality, the fictional text and its historical and cultural milieu are amazingly similar. For these critics, a reader can never fully discern the truth about a historical or a literary text since truth itself is perceived differently from one era to another. The text-only criticism of the early and mid–twentieth century therefore appears biased and incomplete to those espousing the principles of Cultural Poetics.

The remaining chapters of this book examine the most prominent schools of twentieth-century interpretation. For each of these diverse schools, we will note the tenets of the philosophy underlying their literary theory. Most, if not all, have borrowed ideas, principles, and concerns from the literary critics and theories already discussed. We will examine closely what they borrow from these past schools of criticism, what they amend, and what concepts they add. We will also note each school's historical development, examining how new schools of criticism often appear as a reaction to previously existing ones.

After explaining each school's historical development, working assumptions, and methodology, we will then examine a student-written essay that interprets a text from the point of view of the particular school of criticism under discussion. A close examination of such essays will allow us to see how the theories of the various schools of criticism can be applied directly to a text and, simultaneously, to evaluate the different emphases of each critical school.

In becoming acquainted with these schools of criticism, we also undertake to examine our own theory of interpretation and to articulate our own principles of criticism. We will then come to realize that there is no such thing as an innocent reading of a text, because all readings presuppose either a conscious or unconscious, articulated and well-informed or piecemeal and uninformed reading of a literary work. An informed and intelligent reading is by far the better option.

FURTHER READING

Adams, Hazard, ed. *Critical Theory Since Plato*, 3rd ed. New York: Harcourt, 2004.

Adams, Hazard, and Leroy Searle, eds. *Critical Theory Since 1965*. Parkland, FL: University Press of Florida, 1986.

Atkins, G. Douglas, and Laura Morrow, eds. *Contemporary Literary Theory*. Amherst, MA: University of Massachusetts Press, 1989.

Bauerlein, Mark. *Literary Criticism: An Autopsy*. Philadelphia, PA: University of Pennsylvania Press, 1997.

Childers, Joseph W., and Gary Hentzi. *The Columbia Dictionary of Modern Literary and Cultural Criticism*. New York: Columbia University Press, 1995.

Con Davis, Robert, and Ronald Schleifer, eds. *Contemporary Literary Criticism and Theory: Literary and Cultural Studies*, 4th ed. Boston: Addison-Wesley, 1998.

Cuddon, J.A., and Claire Preston. *A Dictionary of Literary Terms and Literary Theory*, 4th ed. Oxford: Blackwell, 2000.

Groden, Michael, ed. *The Johns Hopkins Guide to Literary Theory and Criticism*, 2nd ed. Baltimore: Johns Hopkins University Press, 2005.

Harland, Richard. *Literary Theory From Plato to Barthes: An Introductory History*. New York: Palgrave, 1999.

Hutner, Gordon, ed. *The American Literary History Reader*. Oxford: Oxford University Press, 1995.

Leitch, Vincent B., ed. *The Norton Anthology of Theory and Criticism*. New York: Norton, 2001.

Murray, Penelope, trans. *Classical Literary Criticism*. New York: Penguin, 2001.

Rice, Philip, and Patricia Waugh, eds. *Modern Literary Theory: A Reader*, 4th ed. London: Edward Arnold, 2001.

Russell, D.A., and Michael Winterbottom. *Classical Literary Criticism. Oxford World Classics*. Oxford: Oxford University Press, 1998.

Selden, Raman. *Cambridge History of Literary Criticism: From Formalism to Poststructuralism*, vol. 1. Cambridge: Cambridge University Press, 2006.

Selden, Raman, Peter Widdowson, and Peter Brooker. *A Reader's Guide to Contemporary Literary Theory*. New York: Longman, 2005.

Wolfreys, Julian. *Literary Theories: A Reader's Guide*. New York: New York University Press, 1999.

WEB SITES FOR EXPLORATION

http://press/jhu.edu/
   The Johns Hopkins Guide to Literary Theory on the web; an excellent source for historical information on most literary critics and theorists

http://www.questia.com
   Declares itself to be the world's largest online library; provides a survey of most classical literary critics

http://www.kristisiegel.com/thoery.htm
   A detailed overview of the various schools of twentieth-century criticism

http://www.library.utoronto.ca/utel/glossary/headerindex.htm
   A useful glossary of literary theory

http://andromeda.rutgers.edu/~jlynch/lit/theory.htm
   Contains many useful literary theory and criticism links

3

RUSSIAN FORMALISM
AND NEW CRITICISM

To incriminate the poet with ideas and feelings is just as absurd as the behavior of the medieval public that beat up the actor who played Judas.

Roman Jakobson, *Modern Russian Poetry*

B y the end of the nineteenth century, no single school of criticism dominated literary studies. For the most part, literary criticism was not even considered an academic activity. Academic research was more frequently than not governed by psychological or sociohistorical principles that attempted to show that a literary work was a social or political product encased in a particular history. Some scholars who rejected this view espoused a theory that exulted the author, claiming a text to be the personal impressions and visions of its creator, a place where the author and the reader can imaginatively revel in the text and perhaps communicate with each other. And still others declared that a literary work should be read biographically, seeing the author's life and private concerns peeping throughout the text. But in the early part of the twentieth century, a radical break occurred in these traditional ways of interpretation with the emergence of a group of Russian scholars who articulated a set of interpretive principles known as **Russian Formalism**.

RUSSIAN FORMALISM

In the middle of the second decade of the twentieth century, two distinct groups of Russian scholars emerged in Moscow and Petrograd (St. Petersburg) who radically changed the direction of literary theory and criticism. Founded in 1915, the Moscow Linguistic Circle included Roman Jakobson, Jan Mukarovsky, Peter Bogatyrev, and G.O. Vinokur. The following year in Petrograd, the Society for the Study of Poetic Language (OPOYAZ) was formed, including in its membership Victor Shklovsky, Boris Eichenbaum, and Victor Vinogradov. Although the adherents of both groups often disagreed about the principles of literary interpretation, they were united in their rejection of many nineteenth-century assumptions of textual analysis, especially the belief that a work of literature was the expression of the author's worldview and their dismissal of psychological and biographical criticism as being irrelevant to interpretation. These Russian scholars boldly declared the autonomy of literature and poetic language, advocating a scientific approach to literary interpretation. Literature, they believed, should be investigated as its own discipline, not merely as a platform for discussing religious, political, sociological, or philosophical ideas. By radically divorcing themselves from previous literary approaches and advocating new principles of hermeneutics, these members of the Moscow Linguistic Circle and OPOYAZ are considered the founders of modern literary criticism, establishing what is known as Russian Formalism.

Coined by opponents of the movement to deprecate Russian Formalism's supposedly strict methodological approach to literary interpretation, the terms **Formalism** and **Formalist** were first rejected by the Russian Formalists themselves because they believed that their approach to literature was both dynamic and evolutionary, not a "formal" or dogmatic one. Nevertheless, the terms ultimately became the battle cry for the establishment of what they dubbed a science of literature.

The first task of the Russian Formalists was to define their new science. Framing their theory on the work of Ferdinand de Saussure, the French linguist and founder of modern linguistics, the Formalists emphasized the autonomous nature of literature. The proper study of literature, they declared, is literature itself. To study literature is to study **poetics**, which is an analysis of a work's constituent parts—its linguistic and structural features—or its **form**. Form, they asserted, included the internal mechanics of the work itself, especially its poetic language. These internal mechanics—or what the Formalists called **devices**—comprise the artfulness and literariness of any given text, not a work's subject matter or content. Each device or compositional feature possesses peculiar properties that can, as in any science, be analyzed. For the Formalists, this new science of literature became an analysis of the literary and artistic devices that the writer manipulates to create a text.

The Formalists' chief focus of literary analysis was the examination of a text's **literariness**, the language used in the text. Literary language, they asserted, is different from everyday language. Unlike everyday speech, literary language **foregrounds** itself, shouting, "Look at me! I am special; I am unique." Through structure, imagery, syntax, rhyme scheme, paradox, and a host of other devices, literary language identifies itself as deviations from every day speech patterns, ultimately producing the defining feature of literariness, **defamiliarization**. Coined by the Russian Formalist Victor Shklovsky, defamiliarization is the process of making strange (**ostranenie**) the familiar, of putting the old in new light, what Shklovsky called a "sphere of new perception." By making strange the familiar, defamiliarization (or what some Russian Formalists call **estrangement**) slows down the act of perceiving everyday words or objects, forcing the listener or reader to reexamine the image. For example, when we read in a poem the words "dazzling darkness," our attention is caught by the unusual pairing of these words. Our ordinary experience of every day language is slowed down because we must now unpack the meaning of the author's choice of language. When we do so, poetry, with its accompanying poetic diction, has called attention to itself as poetry and to its literariness, allowing its listeners or readers to experience a small part of their world in a new way by intensifying the act of perception.

In addition to examining the constituent devices present in poetry, Shklovsky also analyzed narrative prose and declared that the structure of a narrative has two aspects: **fabula** (story) and **syuzhet** (plot). Fabula is the raw material of the story and can be considered somewhat akin to the writer's working outline. This outline contains the chronological series of events of the story. The syuzhet is the literary devices the writer uses to transform a story (the fabula) into plot. By using such techniques as digressions, surprises, and disruptions, the writer dramatically alters the fabula, making it a work of literature that now has the potential to provoke defamiliarization, "to make strange" the language of the text and render a fresh view of language, the reader's world, or both.

Russian Formalism contributed to the study of literature and literary theory a reevaluation of the text itself. Bringing a scientific approach to literary studies, the Formalists redefined the meaning of a **text** as a unified collection of various literary devices and conventions that can be objectively analyzed. Literature is not, they declared, the vision of an author or authorial intent. Using linguistic principles, the Formalists asserted that literature, like all sciences, is a self-enclosed, law-governed system. To study literature is to study its form and only incidentally its content. For the Formalists, form is superior to content.

As a group, the Russian Formalists were suppressed and disbanded in 1930 by the Soviet government because they were unwilling to view literature through the Stalinist regime's political and ideological perspectives. Their influence, however, continued to flourish in Czechoslovakia through the work of the Prague Linguistic Circle (founded in 1926, its leading figure being Roman Jakobson) and through the work of the Russian folktale scholar Vladimir Propp. Fortunately for the advancement of literary theory and criticism, Russian Formalism resurfaced in the 1960s in French and American structuralism (see Chapter 5).

BRIDGING THE GAP BETWEEN RUSSIAN FORMALISM AND NEW CRITICISM

Russian Formalism is sometimes paired with the first modern school of Anglo-American criticism: the New Criticism. Dominating both American and British criticism from the 1930s to the 1950s, New Criticism, at best, can be considered a second cousin of Russian Formalism. Although both schools use some similar terminology and are identified as types of Formalism, no direct relationship exists between them. New Criticism has its own unique history and development in Great Britain and the United States. Interestingly, however, in the 1940s, two leading Russian Formalists, Roman Jakobson and Réne Wellek, came to the United States and actively participated in the scholarly discussions of the New Critics. The interaction of these two Russian Formalists with the New Critics does evidence itself in some of the Russian Formalism's ideas being mirrored in New Critical principles.

APPLYING RUSSIAN FORMALISM TO A LITERARY TEXT

Read carefully the following poem by the contemporary American poet John Leax. After reading the text several times, be able to apply, discuss, and demonstrate how the following terms from Russian Formalism can be used in developing an interpretation of this text:

- poetics
- form
- devices
- literariness
- foregrounding of literary language
- defamiliarization.

Sacramental Vision[1]

Sometimes in my dream
he is still alive.
We stand at the fence
talking about the garden.
"Plant kohlrabi," he says,   5
and I remember the way
he'd slice white wafers
from the bulb, offering
them to me balanced
on his knife blade.   10

[1]Copyright © 1985 by John Leax. Reprinted with the permission of Zondervan Publishing House.

I would eat again
that sharp sacrament
and join myself
to that good world
he walks, but I wake   15
in time
and know my flesh is one
with frailty. The garden
I must tend is dark
with weeping, grown up   20
in widow's weeds.

John Leax, *The Task of Adam*, 1985

NEW CRITICISM

If Leax's poem "Sacramental Vision" were taught in many high school or introductory-level college literature courses, the instructor would probably begin the discussion with a set of questions that contains most, if not all, of the following:What is the meaning of the title? What is the title's relationship to the rest of the poem? Who is the *he* in line 2? What is *kohlrabi*? What is a *sacrament*? Are there other words in the text that need to be defined? What words connote sharpness? How are these words related to the garden discussed in the poem? Is Leax discussing any particular garden or all gardens in general? Is the word *garden* an allusion to some other garden in the canon of Western literature? Is Leax establishing any other relationships between words or concepts in the text? What of the poem's physical structure? Does the arrangement of the words, phrases, or sentences help establish relationships among them? What is the poem's tone? What tensions does Leax create in the poem? What ambiguities? Does Leax successfully resolve these tensions by the poem's end? Based on the answers to all of these questions, what does the poem mean? In other words, what is the poem's form or its overall meaning?

Upon close examination of these discussion questions, a distinct pattern or methodology quickly becomes evident. This interpretive model begins with a close analysis of the poem's individual words, including both denotative and connotative meanings, and then moves to a discussion of possible allusions within the text. After this discussion, the teacher or critic searches for any patterns developed through individual words, phrases, clauses, sentences, figures of speech, and allusions. The critic's sharp eye also notes any **symbols** (either **public** or **private**) that represent something else. Other elements for analysis include point of view, tone, and any other poetic device that will help the reader understand the dramatic situation. After ascertaining how all the above information interrelates and finally coalesces in the poem, the critic can then declare what the poem means. The poem's overall meaning or form depends solely on the text in front of the reader. No library research, no studying of the author's life and times, and no other extratextual information is needed; the poem itself contains all the necessary information to discover its meaning.

This method of analysis became the dominant school of thought during the first two-thirds of the twentieth century in most high school and college literature classes and in both British and American scholarship. Known as **New Criticism**, this approach to literary analysis provides readers with a formula for arriving at the correct interpretation of a text using—for the most part—only the text itself. Such a formulaic approach gives both beginning students of literature and academicians a seemingly objective approach for discovering a text's meaning. Using New Criticism's clearly articulated methodology, any intelligent reader, say its adherents (called **New Critics**), can uncover a text's hitherto so-called "hidden meaning."

New Criticism's theoretical ideas, terminology, and critical methods are, more often than not, disparaged by many present-day critics who themselves are introducing new ideas concerning literary theory. Despite its current unpopularity, New Criticism stands as one of the most important English-based contributions to literary critical analysis. Its easily repeatable principles, teachability, and seemingly undying popularity in literature classrooms and in some scholarly journals have enabled New Criticism to enrich theoretical and practical criticism while helping generations of readers to become **close readers** of texts.

The term *New Criticism* came into popular use to describe this approach to understanding literature with the 1941 publication of John Crowe Ransom's *The New Criticism*, which contained Ransom's personal analysis of several of his contemporary theorists and critics. Ransom himself was a Southern poet, a critic, and one of the leading advocates of this evolving movement. While teaching at Vanderbilt University in the 1920s, Ransom, along with several other professors and students, formed the Fugitives, a group that believed in and practiced similar interpretative approaches to a text. Other sympathetic groups, such as the Southern Agrarians (also in Nashville, Tennessee), soon formed. In *The New Criticism*, Ransom articulates the principles of these various groups and calls for an **ontological critic**, one who will recognize that a **poem** (used as a synonym in New Criticism for any literary work) is a concrete entity, as is Leonardo da Vinci's *Mona Lisa* or the score of Handel's *Messiah* or any chemical element, such as iron or gold. Similar to these concrete objects, a poem can be analyzed to discover its true or correct meaning independent of its author's intention or of the emotional state, values, or beliefs of either its author or reader. Because this claim rests at the center of the movement's critical ideas, it is not surprising that the title of Ransom's book quickly became the official name for this approach to literary analysis.

Called *modernism, Formalism, aesthetic criticism, textual criticism,* or *ontological criticism* throughout its long and successful history, New Criticism, like all schools of criticism, does not represent a coherent body of critical theory and methodology espoused by its followers. At best, New Criticism and its adherents (i.e., New Critics) are an eclectic group, each challenging, borrowing, and changing terminology, theory, and practices from one another while asserting a common core of basic ideas. Their ultimate unity stems from their opposition to the prevailing methods of literary analysis found in academia in the first part of the twentieth century.

HISTORICAL DEVELOPMENT

At the beginning of the twentieth century (often said to mark the start of **modernism** or the modernist period), historical and biographical research dominated literary scholarship. Criticism's function, many believed, was to discover the historical context of a text and to ascertain how authors' lives influenced their writings. Such **extrinsic analysis** (examining elements outside the text to uncover the text's meaning) became the norm in the literature departments of many American universities and colleges. Other forms of criticism and interpretation were often intermingled with this prominent emphasis on history and biography. For example, some critics believed readers should appreciate texts for their beauty. For these **impressionistic critics**, how readers feel and what they personally see in a work of art are what really matters. Others were more philosophical, arguing a naturalistic view of life that emphasizes the importance of scientific thought in literary analysis. For advocates of **naturalism**, human beings are animals that are caught in a world that operates on definable scientific principles and that respond somewhat instinctively to their environment and internal drives. Still other critics, the **New Humanists**, valued the moral qualities of art. Declaring that human experience is basically ethical, these critics demanded that literary analysis be based on the moral values exhibited in a text. Finally, remnants of nineteenth-century **Romanticism** asserted themselves. For the Romantic scholar, literary study concerns itself with the artists' feelings, attitudes, and personal visions exhibited in their work. Known as the **expressive school**, this view values the individual artist's experiences as evidenced in a text.

Along with impressionism, the New Humanism, and naturalism, this Romantic view of life and art was rejected by the "New" Critics—and thus their name: critics who reacted again these "old" forms of criticism. In declaring the objective existence of the poem, the New Critics assert that only the poem itself can be objectively evaluated, not the feelings, attitudes, values, and beliefs of the author or the reader. Because they concern themselves primarily with an examination of the work itself and not its historical context or biographical elements, the New Critics belong to a broad classification of literary criticism called **Formalism**. Similar to the Russian Formalists, the New Critics espouse what many call the "text and text alone" approach to literary analysis. Both schools of criticism believe that every text and all literature is a complex, rule-governed system of forms (literary devices) that are analyzable. Such an analysis reveals with considerable objectivity the text's meaning.

New Criticism's approach to textual criticism automatically leads to multiple and divergent views about the elements that constitute what the New Critics call the poem. Because many of the practitioners of this Formalistic criticism disagree with each other concerning the various elements that make up the poem and hold differing approaches to textual analysis, it is difficult to cite a definitive list of critics who consider themselves New Critics. We can, however, group together critics who hold to some of the same New Critical assumptions of poetic analysis. Among this group are John Crowe Ransom, René Wellek, William K. Wimsatt, R.P. Blackmur, I.A. Richards Robert Penn Warren, and Cleanth Brooks. Thanks to the publication of the 1938 college text *Understanding Poetry: An Anthology for College Students* by Brooks and Warren, New Criticism emerged in American universities as the leading form of textual analysis throughout the late 1930s until the early 1960s.

Although New Criticism emerged as a powerful force in the 1940s and 1950s, its roots stem from the early 1900s. Two British critics and authors, T.S. Eliot and I.A. Richards, helped lay the foundation for this form of Formalistic analysis. From Eliot, New Criticism borrows its insistence that criticism be directed toward the poem, not the poet. The poet, declares Eliot, does not infuse the poem with his or her personality and emotions, but uses language in such a way as to incorporate within the poem the impersonal feelings and emotions common to all humankind. Poetry is not, then, the freeing of the poet's emotions, but an escape from them. Because a poem is an impersonal formulation of common feelings and emotions, a successful poem unites the poet's impressions and ideas with those common to all humanity, producing a text that is not simply a reflection of the poet's personal feelings.

The New Critics also borrow Eliot's belief that the reader of poetry must be instructed in literary technique. Eliot maintains that a good reader perceives the poem structurally, resulting in good criticism. Such a reader must necessarily be trained in reading good poetry (especially the poetry of the Elizabethans, John Donne, and other metaphysical poets) and be well acquainted with established poetic traditions. A poor reader, on the other hand, simply expresses his or her personal emotions and reactions to a text. Such a reader is untrained in literary technique and craftsmanship. Following Eliot's lead, the New Critics declare that there are both good and bad readers and good and bad criticism. A poor reader and poor criticism, for example, may argue that a poem can mean anything its reader or its author wishes it to mean. On the other hand, a good critic and good criticism will assert that only through a detailed structural analysis of a poem can the correct interpretation arise.

Eliot also lends New Criticism some of its technical vocabulary. Thanks to Eliot, for example, the term **objective correlative** has become a staple in poetic jargon. According to Eliot, the only way of expressing emotion through art is by finding an objective correlative, or a set of objects, a situation, a chain of events, or reactions that can effectively awaken in the reader the emotional response the author desires without being a direct statement of that emotion. When the external facts are thus presented in the poem, they somehow coalesce (correlate), immediately evoking an emotion. The New Critics readily adopted and advanced this indirect or impersonal theory of the creation of emotions in poetry.

From Eliot's British contemporary I.A. Richards, a psychologist and literary critic, New Criticism borrows a term that has become synonymous with its methods of analysis, **practical criticism**. In an experiment at Cambridge University, Richards distributed to his students copies of poems minus such information as the authors, dates, and oddities of spelling and punctuation, and asked them to record their responses. From these data he identified the difficulties that poetry presents to its readers, including matters of interpretation, poetic techniques, and specific meanings. From this analysis, Richards then devised an intricate system for arriving at a poem's meaning, including a minute scrutiny of the text. This close scrutiny or **close reading** of a text has become synonymous with New Criticism.

From Eliot, Richards, and other critics, New Criticism borrows, amends, and adds its own ideas and concerns. Although few of its advocates would agree on many tenets, definitions, and techniques, a core of assumptions does exist, which allows us to identify adherents of this critical approach.

ASSUMPTIONS

New Criticism begins by assuming that the study of imaginative literature is valuable; to study poetry or any literary work is to engage oneself in an **aesthetic experience** (i.e., the effects produced on an individual when contemplating a work of art) that can lead to truth. The truth discoverable through an aesthetic experience, however, is distinguishable from the truth that science provides. Science speaks propositionally, telling us whether a statement is demonstrably either true or false. Pure water, in the language of science, freezes at 32 degrees Fahrenheit, not 30 or 31. Poetic truth, on the other hand, involves the use of the imagination and intuition, a form of truth that, according to the New Critics, is discernable only in poetry. In the aesthetic experience alone we are cut off from mundane or practical concerns, from mere rhetorical, doctrinal, or propositional statements. Through an examination of the poem itself, we can ascertain truths that cannot be perceived through the language and logic of science. Both science and poetry, then, provide different but valid sources of knowledge.

Similar to many other critical theories, New Criticism's theory begins by defining its object of concern—in this case, a poem. (New Critics use the word *poem* synonymously with *work of art*; however, their methodology works most efficiently with poetry rather than any other genre.) New Critics assert that a poem has ontological status—that is, it possesses its own being and exists like any other object. In effect, a poem becomes an artifact, an objective, self-contained, autonomous entity with its own structure. As Wimsatt declares, a poem becomes a "verbal icon."

Having declared a poem an object in its own right, New Critics then develop their objective theory of art. For them, the meaning of a poem must not be equated with its author's feelings or stated or implied intentions. To believe that a poem's meaning is nothing more than an expression of the private experiences or intentions of its author is to commit a fundamental error of interpretation, which the New Critics call the **Intentional Fallacy**. According to Wimsatt and Monroe C. Beardsley, the New Critics who coined this term, the design or intent of the author is neither available nor desirable as a standard for judging a literary work. Along with many other New Critics, Wimsatt and Beardsley believe that the poem is an object. Any literary work is a public text that can only be understood by applying the standards of public discourse, not simply the private experience, concerns, and vocabulary of its author. In their widely read New Critical text *Understanding Poetry*, Brooks and Warren temper the dogmatism of the Intentional Fallacy, asserting that understanding the origin of a poem may enhance its appreciation. They still insist, however, that a poem's origin or historical setting must not be confused with a close reading of the actual poem itself.

That the poem is somehow related to its author cannot be denied. In his essay "Tradition and the Individual Talent," Eliot states the New Critical position on the relationship between the author and his or her work. The basis of Eliot's argument is an analogy. We all know, he says, that certain chemical reactions occur in the presence of a **catalyst**, an element that causes, but is not affected by, the reaction. For example, if we place hydrogen peroxide, a common household disinfectant, in a clear bottle and expose it to the sun's rays, we will no longer have hydrogen peroxide. Acting as a catalyst, the sun's rays will cause a chemical reaction to occur, breaking down the hydrogen peroxide into its various parts, while the sun's rays remain unaffected.

Similarly, the poet's mind serves as a catalyst for the reaction that yields the poem. During the creative process, the poet's mind, serving as the catalyst, brings together the experiences of the author's personality (not the author's personality traits or attributes) into an external object and a new creation: the poem. It is not the personality traits of the author that coalesce to form the poem, but the experiences of the author's personality. In apparently distinguishing between the personality and the mind of the poet, Eliot asserts that the created entity, the poem, is about the experiences of the author that are similar to all of our experiences. By structuring these experiences, the poem allows us to examine them objectively.

Dismissing the poet's stated or supposed intentions as a means of discovering the text's meaning, the New Critics give little credence to the biographical or contextual history of a poem. If the Intentional Fallacy is correct, then unearthing biographical data will not help us ascertain a poem's meaning. Likewise, trying to place a poem in its social or political context will tell us much social or political history about the time when the poem was authored. Although such information may indeed help in understanding the poem's sociological or historical context, its real meaning cannot reside in this extrinsic or outside-the-text information.

Of particular importance to the New Critics is the etymology of individual words. Because the words of a poem sometimes change meaning from one historical period to another, the critic often needs to conduct historical research, discovering what individual words meant at the time the poem was written. For example, if a fifteenth-century poet called some a "nice person," the New Critics would investigate the meaning of the world *nice* in the fifteenth century, discovering that at that time *nice* meant foolish. The *Oxford English Dictionary* (a dictionary that cites a word's multiple historical meanings chronologically) becomes one of the New Critic's best friends.

Placing little emphasis on the author, the social context, or a text's historical situation as sources for discovering a poem's meaning, the New Critics assert that a reader's emotional response to the text is neither important nor equivalent to its interpretation. Such an error in judgment, called the **Affective Fallacy**, confuses what a poem *is* (its meaning) with what it *does*. If we derive our standard of criticism, say the New Critics, from the psychological effects of the poem, we are then left with impressionism or, worse yet, relativism (i.e., believing that a poem has innumerable valid interpretations).

Where, then, can we find the poem's meaning? According to the New Critics, the meaning does not reside in the author, in the historical or social context of the poem, or even in the reader. Because the poem itself is an artifact or an objective entity, its meaning must reside within its own structure, within the poem itself. Like all other objects, a poem and its structure can be analyzed scientifically. Accordingly, careful scrutiny reveals that a poem's structure operates according to a complex series of laws. By closely analyzing this structure, the New Critics believe they have devised a methodology and a standard of excellence that we can apply to all poems to discover their correct meaning. The critic's job, they conclude, is to ascertain the structure of the poem, to see how it operates to achieve its unity, and to discover how meaning evolves directly from the poem itself.

New Criticism sees the poet as an organizer of the content of human experience. Structuring the poem around the often confusing and sometimes contradictory experiences of life, the poet crafts the poem in such a way that the text stirs its readers' emotions and causes its readers to reflect on the poem's contents. As an artisan, the poet is most concerned with effectively developing the poem's structure because the artist realizes that the meaning of a work emerges from its structure. The poet's chief concern, maintain the New Critics, is how meaning is achieved through the various and sometimes conflicting elements operating in the poem itself.

The chief characteristic of the poem—and therefore of its structure—is coherence or interrelatedness. Borrowing their ideas from the writings of Samuel T. Coleridge, the New Critics posit the **organic unity** of a poem—that is, all parts of a poem are necessarily interrelated, with each part reflecting and helping to support the poem's central idea. Such organic unity allows for the harmonization of conflicting ideas, feelings, and attitudes and results in the poem's oneness. Superior poetry, declare the New Critics, achieves such oneness through **paradox**, **irony**, and **ambiguity**. Because such tensions are necessarily a part of everyone's life, it is only fitting and appropriate, say the New Critics, that superior poetry present these human experiences while at the same time showing how these tensions are resolved within the poem to achieve its organic unity.

Because the poem's chief characteristic is its oneness, New Critics believe that a poem's form and content are inseparable. For the New Critics, however, **form** is more than the external structure of a poem; a poem's form encompasses and simultaneously rises above the usual definition of poetic structure (i.e., whether or not the poem is a Shakespearian or Petrarchan sonnet, or a lyric, or any other poetic structure having meter, rhyme, or some other poetic pattern). In New Criticism, form is the overall effect the poem creates. Because all the various parts of the poem combine to create this effect, each poem's form is unique. When all the elements of a poem work together to form a single, unified effect—the poem's form—New Critics declare that the poet has written a successful poem, one that possesses organic unity.

Because all good and successful poems have organic unity, it would be inconceivable to try to separate a poem's form and its content, maintain the New Critics. How can we separate what a poem says from how it says it? Because all the elements of a poem, both structural and aesthetic, work together to achieve a poem's effect or form, it is impossible to discuss the overall meaning of a poem by isolating or separating form and content.

To the New Critic, it is therefore inconceivable to believe that a poem's interpretation is equal to a mere paraphrased version of the text. Labeling such an erroneous belief the **Heresy of Paraphrase**, New Critics maintain that a poem is not simply a statement that is either true or false, but a bundle of harmonized tensions and resolved stresses, more like a ballet or musical composition than a statement of prose. No simple paraphrase can equal the meaning of the poem because the poem itself resists through its inner tensions any prose statement that attempts to encapsulate its meaning. Paraphrases may help readers in their initial understanding of the poem, but such prose statements must be considered working hypotheses that may or may not lead to a true understanding of the poem's meaning. In no way should paraphrased statements about a poem be considered equivalent to the poem's structure or form, insist the New Critics.

METHODOLOGY

Believing in the thematic and structural unity of a poem, New Critics search for meaning within the text's structure by finding the tensions and conflicts that must eventually be resolved into a harmonious whole and inevitably lead to the creation of the poem's chief effect. Such a search first leads New Critics to the poem's diction or word choice. Unlike scientific discourse with its precision of terminology, poetic diction often has multiple meanings and can immediately set up a series of tensions within the text. For example, many words have both a **denotation**, or dictionary meaning, and **connotations**, or implied meanings. A word's denotation may directly conflict with its connotative meaning determined by the context of the poem. In addition, it may be difficult to differentiate between the various denotations of a word. For example, if someone writes that "a *fat* head enjoys the *fat* of the land," the reader must note the various denotative and connotative differences of the word *fat*. At the start of poetic analysis, then, conflicts or tensions exist by the very nature of poetic diction. New Critics call this tension **ambiguity**, or language's capacity to sustain multiple meanings. At the heart of literary language or discourse, claim the New Critics, is ambiguity. At the end of a close reading of a text, however, all such ambiguities must be resolved.

Even a surface level of understanding or upon a first reading, a poem, from a New Critic's perspective, is a reconciliation of conflicts, of opposing meanings and tensions. The poem's form and content are indivisible, so the critic's job is to analyze the poetic diction to ascertain such tensions. Although various New Critics give a variety of names to the poetic elements that make up a poem's structure, all agree that the poem's meaning is derived from the oscillating tensions and conflicts that are brought to the surface through the poetic diction.

For example, Brooks claims that the chief elements in a poem are **paradox** and **irony**, two closely related terms that imply that a word or phrase is qualified or even undercut by its context. By definition, a paradox is a seemingly self-contradictory statement that must be resolved on a higher metaphysical level. The New Critics broaden this definition, maintaining that by its very nature, literary language is ambiguous. Literary discourse, unlike normal or every day language, is able to sustain multiple meanings. For Brooks, the discourse of poetry is "the language of paradox." Similarly, the New Critics enhance the meaning of the word *irony*. Irony is a figure of speech in which the words express a meaning that is often the direct opposite of the intended meaning. In New Criticism, irony is the poet's ability to recognize incongruities, and it becomes New Criticism's master **trope** because it is essential for the production of paradox and ambiguity. Some New Critics use the word **tension** to describe the opposition or conflicts operating within a text. For these critics, tension implies the conflicts between a word's denotation and its connotation, between a literal detail and a figurative one, and between an abstract and a concrete detail.

Because conflict, ambiguity, or tension controls the poem's structure, the meaning of the poem can be discovered only by contextually analyzing the poetic elements and diction. Furthermore, because context governs meaning, meanings of individual words or phrases are, therefore, context related and unique to the poem in which they occur. The critic's job is to unravel the various apparent conflicts and tensions within each poem and ultimately to show that the poem has organic unity, thereby showing that all parts of the poem are interrelated and support the poem's chief paradox. This paradox, which New Critics often call *form* or overall effect, can usually be expressed in one sentence that contains the main tension and the resolution of that tension. All other elements of the poem must relate to this "key idea."

Although most New Critics would agree that the process of discovering the poem's form is not necessarily linear (because advanced readers often see ambiguities and ironies when first reading a text), New Criticism provides readers with a distinct methodology to help uncover the paradox or chief tension. These guided steps allow both novices and advanced literary scholars together to enter the discussion of a text's ultimate meaning, each contributing to the poem's interpretation. From a New Critical perspective, a reader begins the journey of discovering a text's correct interpretation by reading the poem several times and by carefully noting the work's title (if it has one) and its relationship to the text. Then, by following the prescribed steps listed here, the reader can ascertain the text's meaning. The more practice a reader has at following this methodology and the more opportunities he or she has to be guided by an advanced reader and critic, the more adept he or she will undoubtedly become at textual analysis:

Step 1:   Examine the text's diction. Consider the denotations, connotations, and etymological roots of all words in the text.

Step 2:   Examine all allusions found within the text by tracing their roots to the primary text or source, if possible.

Step 3:   Analyze all images, symbols, and figures of speech within the text. Note the relationships, if any, among the elements, both within the same category (e.g., between images) and among the various elements (e.g., between an image and a symbol).

Step 4:   Examine and analyze the various structural patterns that appear within the text, including the technical aspects of **prosody**. Note how the poet manipulates metrical devices, grammatical constructions, tonal patterns, and syntactic patterns of words, phrases, or sentences. Determine how these various patterns interrelate with each other and with all elements discussed in steps 1 to 3.

Step 5:   Consider such elements as tone, theme, point of view, and any other element—dialogue, foreshadowing, narration, parody, setting, and so forth—that directly relates to the text's dramatic situation.

Step 6:   Look for interrelationships of all elements, noting where tensions, ambiguities, or paradoxes arise.

Step 7:   After carefully examining all of the above, state the poem's chief, overarching tension and explain how the poem achieves its dominant effect by resolving this tension.

Because all poems are unique, the process of uncovering a poem's chief tension is unique. By using the prescribed methodology of New Criticism, New Critics believe that readers will be able to justify their interpretations of a text with information gleaned from the text alone while enjoying the aesthetic process that allows them to articulate the text's meaning.

According to such New Critical principles, a **good critic** examines a poem's structure by scrutinizing its poetic elements, rooting out and showing its inner tensions, and demonstrating how the poem supports its overall meaning in reconciling these tensions into a unified whole. By implication, **bad critics** are those who impose extrinsic evidence, such as historical or biographical information, on a text to discover its meaning. These critics fail to realize that the text itself elicits its own meaning. More frequently than not, they also fail to discuss or examine the definitive aspects of a work of art: irony, paradox, and ambiguity. They therefore flounder in their analysis, declare the New Critics, because such unskilled critics believe more often than not that a text can have multiple meanings.

Asserting that a poem has ontological status, the New Critics believe that a text has one and only one correct interpretation and that the poem itself provides all the necessary information for revealing its meaning. By scrutinizing the text and giving it a **close reading** and by providing readers with a set of norms that will assist them in discovering the correct interpretation of the text, New Criticism provides a teachable, workable framework for literary analysis.

QUESTIONS FOR ANALYSIS

To apply the assumptions and methodology of New Criticism to a given text, one can begin by asking the following questions:

- If the text has a title, what is the relationship of the title to the rest of the poem? Before answering this question, New Critical theory and practice assume that the critic has read the text several times.
- What words, if any, need to be defined?
- What words and their etymological roots need to be scrutinized?
- What relationships or patterns do you see among words in the text?
- What are the various connotative meanings words in the text may have? Do these various shades of meaning help establish relationships or patterns in the text?
- What allusions, if any, are found in the text? Trace these allusions to their appropriate sources and explore how the origins of the allusions help elucidate meaning in this particular text.
- What symbols, images, and figures of speech are used? What is the relationship between any symbol or image? Between an image and another image? Between a figure of speech and an image? A symbol?
- What elements of prosody can you note and discuss? Look for rhyme, meter, and stanza patterns.
- What is the tone of the work?
- From what point of view is the content of the text being told?
- What tensions, ambiguities, or paradoxes arise within the text?
- What do you believe is the chief paradox or irony in the text?
- How do all the elements of the text support and develop the text's chief paradox?

CRITIQUES AND RESPONSES

With the emergence of New Criticism in the 1940s came the birth and growth of literature departments in colleges and universities across America. Its methodological and somewhat scientific approach to literature gained enormous support as monies for academic research expanded and as soldiers came back to America from the fields of Europe after World War II. As the influence of English literature expanded, there arose a practical need for a consistent and a convenient form of literary criticism. Brooks and Warren's *Understanding Poetry* provided such consistency. College professors could now focus on a single text (particularly poetry) that could be easily studied and analyzed by following the prescribed "formula" as developed by the New Critics. No longer did students have to know the sociohistorical background of any given text because the text itself was the object of examination.

Such a formulaic approach to literary analysis, which excludes external evidence from its analytic methodology, readily opens up itself to criticism. Some critics assert that different perspectives for understanding a text's meaning do, indeed, exist and help broaden what constitutes literature. Examining authors' lives can illuminate their works. Psychology, sociology, and history do impact both individual writers and their works, helping to fill a vacuum created by examining only the text. Without such analyses, argue many critics, we miss out on some meanings and purposes. By dismissing such external-text analyses, the New Critics may, indeed, be contradicting their own claims that the meaning of a text is context bound. For example, a work's sociohistorical context, assert New Criticism's challengers, is part of its context and, therefore, its meaning. Other critics argue that the methodology espoused by New Criticism is elitist. To arrive at the so-called "correct" interpretation of a text, a reader must first learn the vocabulary and then the correct procedures for analysis. Do no feelings or ideas of an actual reader who has not mastered New Criticism's theory matter at all? Does the interpretation of a text always have to be so objective? Can the New Critic's search for a text's organic unity blind the critic to elements that do not contribute to such unity? Despite New Criticism's insistence on the objective nature of literary interpretation, individual readers who may or may not be trained in New Critical methodology will most certainly find a variety of ways to make meaning of a particular text.

Despite these and other criticisms, the influence of New Criticism on twentieth- and twenty-first-century literary analyses remains. All schools of criticism, for example, espouse a close reading of texts. New Criticism's terminology and its understanding of a literary work of art have influenced—either directly or indirectly—all modern schools of literary criticism.

What other advantages or disadvantages do you see in using the principles of New Criticism to critique a literary work?

FURTHER READING

Brooks, Cleanth. "My Credo: Formalist Critics." *Kenyon Review* 13 (1951):72–81.

———. *Understanding Fiction*, 3rd ed. Upper Saddle River, NJ: Pearson, 1998.

———. *The Well Wrought Urn: Studies in the Structure of Poetry*. New York: Harcourt, 1956.

Brooks, Cleanth, and Robert Penn Warren, eds. *Understanding Poetry*, 4th ed. New York: Heinle, 1976.

Empson, William. *Seven Types of Ambiguity*, 3rd ed. New York: New Directions, 1990.

Ransom, John Crowe. *The New Criticism*. New York: Greenwood, 1979.

Richards, I.A. *Practical Criticism: A Study of Literary Judgment*. New York: Harcourt, 1929.

———. *Principles of Criticism*, 2nd ed. New York: Taylor and Francis, 2001.

Steiner, Peter. *Russian Formalism: A Metapoetics*. Ithaca, NY: Cornell University Press, 1984.

Wellek, René, and Austin Warren. *Theory of Literature*, rev. ed. New York: Harcourt, 1977.

Wimsatt, W.K., and Monroe C. Beardsley. *The Verbal Icon: Studies in the Meaning of Poetry*. Lexington, KY: University of Kentucky Press, 1954.

Winters, Yvor, and Kenneth Fields, eds. *In Defense of Reason*. Denver: Swallow Press, 1993.

WEB SITES FOR EXPLORATION

http://www.lawrence.edu/dept/english/courses/60A/newcrit.html
A good introduction to New Criticism, including terminology and definition of critical terms used by New Critics

http://www.ipl.org/ref/litcrit/
The Internet Public Library's (IPL) *Online Literary Criticism Collection* links 745 critical and biographical Web sites about authors and their works. One of the best research tools on the Web, it can be searched by author name, title, nationality, or literary period

http://litguide.press.jhu.edu
The Johns Hopkins Guide to Literary Theory and Criticism. This online source provides some of the best essays on both classical and modern literary criticism

http://130.179.92.25/arnason_de/new_criticism.html
Another good working definition of New Criticism

http://www.sou.edu/english/hedges/sodashop/rcenter/theory/explaind/ncritexp.htm
An excellent explanation of New Criticism

http://en.wikipedia.org/wiki/New_Critics
New Criticism defined in the Wikipedia, the free encyclopedia on the world wide web

Sample Essay

The following student essay highlights the theoretical assumptions and practical methodology of New Criticism. Because John Keats's poem "On First Looking into Chapman's Homer" is often viewed as the archetypal Petrarchan sonnet, the student author specifically chose this sonnet for her New Critical analysis. By so doing, all student readers will be able to use their understanding of the Petrarchan sonnet and their knowledge of poetry as they analyze both Keats's poem and the following essay. Such knowledge would, of course, be presupposed by the New Critics before beginning their

analysis of Keats's poem. Similarly, student readers will be able to participate fully in a New Critical reading of the poem.

After carefully reading this essay, be able to answer each of the following
questions:

- Is this a successfully written New Critical essay? To answer this question, review
  the sections of this chapter on assumptions and methodology of New Criticism.
  Does this author use New Critical assumptions and practices within the essay
  itself?
- What are the strengths of the essay? What are its weaknesses? Be specific in your
  answers, pointing out concrete examples.

Student Essay

Controlled Passion[2]

John Keats's "On First Looking into Chapman's Homer" gains much of its
power from the effective use of the structure of the Petrarchan sonnet and
metaphors filled with imagery, exemplifying Keats's mastery of the poetic
craft. Keats harnesses his speaker's passion by confining himself to the
boundaries inherent in a sonnet, the refined form providing a framework
that best displays the speaker's emotions. In the octave, the poet presents a
narrative and states a proposition; the sestet then drives home the narrative
by applying the proposition. Utilizing the pattern established in the tradition
of the Petrarchan sonnet and creating unique metaphors to capture the
speaker's emotion, Keats powerfully and effectively communicates the
speaker's awe-inspiring revelation and quiet joy at the discovery of Homer's
writings. While the strict rhyme scheme and the development of the octave
and the sestet limit the poet's word choices, Keats embraces the structure of
the sonnet and creates a poem that magnificently expresses the speaker's
emotions upon "[f]irst [l]ooking into Chapman's Homer."

Keats wrote "On First Looking into Chapman's Homer" in October of
1816, after he and a childhood friend spent a night joyfully exploring and
immersing themselves in Chapman's rich and fluid translation of Homer.
Ironically, Keats chooses to use the strict pattern of the Italian sonnet for his
description of Chapman's translation of Homer, the very elitism of which
ought to appeal to an educated audience; scholars who were firmly rooted in
the intelligentsia or the academy, however, would have never needed a
translation to experience the depth and breadth of Homer, thereby creating
tension for the reader who does not know the Greek language.

Keats dramatically establishes the narrative with the arresting first line,
drawing the reader into the overarching metaphor that encompasses the

[2]Reprinted by permission of Hilary S. Brautigam.

poem. "Much have I travell'd in the realms of gold," the speaker reveals, introducing the motif of exploration and discovery (1). From this first line, the speaker characterizes himself as traveler, a person on a journey through the "realms of gold" (1). Capturing the imagination, "realms of gold" connotes a rich and illustrious world. The realms of gold to which he refers are not literal, of course, because "bards in fealty to Apollo" hold the kingdoms of this world. When referring to Apollo, the god of the arts, as ruling these kingdoms, Keats established that this "realm of gold" is that of the arts. The speaker has traveled throughout the world of art, visiting "many goodly states and kingdoms" (2). "Goodly" implies not only a "notable or considerable number" but also that the object is "of good quality, admirable, splendid," and even "excellent" (OED). Having encountered much superb art, the speaker had ventured to navigate around "western island . . . / which bards in fealty to Apollo hold" (3–4). The lordship of these islands lies with epic poets, whose duty, in turn, lies with Apollo, the Greek god of the arts. More specifically, the term "western islands" refers to ancient poets who are foundational to Western literature, as indicated by the speaker's reference to Apollo.

This initial metaphor—using exploration and navigation of the world to connect to the journey throughout the realm of art—becomes more focused in the following lines: "Oft of one wide expanse had I been told / That deep-brow'd Homer rules as his demesne" (5–6). By using the phrase "wide expanse," the reader becomes aware of a highly regarded but not easily accessible area of this realm which the speaker has yet to explore. The use of the passive voice adds an air of mystery to the vast unexplored territory which Homer—whose brow is furrowed in deep thought—possesses. Homer's territory, undoubtedly his epics the *Iliad* and the *Odyssey*, remains elusive for the speaker because he is unable to partake in a bit of the refreshing calm that his wide expanse of literature seemingly offers.

By choosing the word "serene" when writing "Yet never did I breathe its pure serene" (7), Keats creates ambiguity. The Oxford English Dictionary defines "serene" as "of the weather, air, sky: clear, fine and calm" as well as "pure, clear, bright," or "suggestive of repose." At times, it is "jocularly applied to anything appertaining to a person" designated as a member of royalty. Choosing the words "pure" and "serene" emphasizes the pristine splendor of this land, and Keats chooses to play upon the additional definition of serene. A beautiful vista could be descriptively elaborated upon as "serene majesty," as were members of royalty. Not only does Keats refer to the calm atmosphere but he also alludes to the greater ruler of this land, Homer himself.

The speaker is able to breathe deeply of the serene when he hears "Chapman speak out loud and bold" (8). In the years between 1612 and 1615, George Chapman released vibrant translations of Homer's great works, the *Iliad* and the *Odyssey*, and clearly the speaker embraces these powerful translations. This strong line ends the octave boldly and forcefully while at the same time providing a continuation of the theme that allows the poet to make a clear transition into the next section of the poem, the sestex. Continuing to employ the overarching metaphor of discovery, the speaker explains that he feels "like some watcher of the skies / When a new planet swims into his ken" (9–10). Imagining the excitement of a newly sighted planet, the discovery alters and expands the speaker's view of the cosmos. The word "ken" has not only the denotation of being newly discovered but also of being fully comprehended or understood (OED). The speaker has more than just skimmed Chapman's translation of Homer's works; he has steeped himself in their complexity, attempting to understand them in their fullness, even upon his first reading.

Echoing and complementing the first metaphor, the speaker then offers another figurative statement in the following lines: he feels "like stout Cortez when with eagle eyes / He star'd at the Pacific" (11–12). The persona incorrectly attributes the discovery of the Pacific Ocean to Cortez, but regardless, the lines capture a sense of awestruck wonder at the vastness of the land opened by Chapman's translations. Keats notes that, "all his men / Look'd at each other with a wild surmise," while the speaker stares silently at a formerly closed territory, standing atop "a peak in Darien" (12–14). This metaphor draws attention to the singularity of feeling, apparent through the actions of the explorers. While Cortez gazes out at the Pacific, his men are caught up conjecturing about this new wonder. The speaker thus relates a feeling of almost lonely exhilaration that stems from immersing himself in Chapman's translation of Homer. The metaphor also indicates a new perspective for the speaker: just as Cortez stands on the peak of Darien and overlooks the newly discovered Pacific, the speaker himself stands in awe, intently studying the freshly revealed literature.

Expanding the situation related in the octave, the sestet is the culmination and resolution of the persona's set of circumstances. Dividing the sonnet, the octave presents the overarching metaphor that governs the poem, with a declaratory first line and a transitive ending line, while the sestet provides the culmination of the octave's proposition. Helping to provide the framework for the situation introduced in the octave, the octave's last line shifts the focus of the poem from the situation of pedantic traveling to the act of surprising and awe-inspiring discovery. Keats strictly adheres to the rules of sonnets, embracing the sonnet's boundaries and yet fully expressing the emotion of the speaker. The metaphors employed and the word choice inherent in their creation also create a tone that moves from one of familiar comfort with the world of art to an awed and dumbstruck state. As the speaker grasps the vastness of the world of art, Keats chooses to write in a form of poetry that significantly limits his freedom inherent in discovery.

Unique metaphors and the tradition of the Petrarchan sonnet aid Keats in his attempt to communicate the speaker's new perspective upon discovering Homer's writings. Effectively revealing the speaker's hushed joy, Keats's "On First Looking into Chapman's Homer" gains much of its power from the effective use of the Italian sonnet and metaphors filled with imagery, exemplifying Keats's mastery of the poetic craft. Unfortunately, his highly honed poetry reached an audience who scoffed at the need for a translation in order to grapple with Homer's classics, thereby creating tension for the modern observant reader.

HILARY S. BRAUTIGAM

4

READER-ORIENTED CRITICISM

The house of fiction has in short not one window, but a million—a number of possible windows not to be reckoned, rather; every one of which has been pierced, or is still pierceable, in its vast front, by the need of the individual vision and by the pressure of the individual will.

Henry James, Preface to the New York Edition of *Portrait of a Lady*

Imagine, for a moment, that you and three of your closest friends are once again 8 years old. All of you have been invited to a birthday party at another friend's house three blocks away. For 4 weeks, you have been eagerly anticipating the big event. Unlike you and your three friends, the birthday party celebrant is the child of millionaires and lives in a mansion containing thirty-four rooms, and has let it be known that the party would be the biggest and best you have ever attended. Not surprisingly, rumors that the celebration would include a circus with clowns and animals dressed in human clothes and accompanied by a host of costumed people and the full trappings of a Barnum and Bailey production have been circulating among the four of you for weeks. But today is Saturday, the day of the big event.

Meeting at your house at 9:30 A.M., you and your friends walk excitedly the three blocks to the birthday house. Upon arrival, you see that the front door is completely covered with red aluminum foil with no doorknob visible. Even the doorbell is shielded from view by the bright foil covering. Quickly, one of your friends dashes to the back of the house, hoping to gain access through the back door. With head hung low, this friend returns in about a minute with the news that the back door is also covered with red foil.

Being the nearest to the front window to the right of the door, you peek into the house—and what a sight you see! On the tile near the fireplace sleeps a lion. To the left of the lion is a cage containing a leopard licking a block of ice. And directly below the window is the longest snake you have ever seen. You scream for your friends to come and see the animals, but they too have each discovered their own view into the house. To your right, one of your friends is standing on a ladder and is peering through a porthole window. Through this opening, the den is clearly visible, but no one is there—no decorations, no movement, no signs of any party. It all looks a bit gloomy and most certainly uninhabited. But another friend has found a ladder and placed it to the left of the house's front door. Climbing up the ladder, this friend looks into the second-story window and sees at least fifteen laughing children playing pin the tail on the donkey while they are drinking purple punch and eating cookies, chips, and cake. But the fourth child has discovered another view into the party house: running around the back, this friend peeks into the kitchen window and sees a mountain of presents wrapped in funny-looking paper, some with big bows, other with little ones, and still others with none at all.

The door being barred, all four children have discovered a way to see into the same house, each of the openings being of a different size and shape, with each opening providing a different view. Where one child is surprised by joy at the sight of the mountain of presents, another is saddened by the apparent emptiness of the house. Another, however, is eager to gain entrance and join the many children eating and playing, and the last friend is longing to pet the lion, the leopard, and the snake. The same house, but different views. The same house, but different reactions to each view into its contents.

According to the nineteenth-century novelist, essayist, literary critic, and short story writer Henry James (1843–1916), this house represents the literary form—a story, a novel, a poem, or an essay—with each window being an individual reader's distinct impression of that literary work. Similar to the four children peering into the house's windows and seeing different views, readers read the same text but "see" unique scenes, coming away from the text with different impressions and interpretations. Each person most certainly reads the same text, but all will gain entrance into the meaning of that text through different apertures and come away with a variety of differing impressions.

Now imagine that you and other members of your college-level, introductory literature class have been asked to read Chapter 31 of Mark Twain's *Adventures of Huckleberry Finn* (1885), part of which reads as follows:

> Once I said to myself it would be a thousand times better for Jim to be a slave at home where his family was, as long as he'd *got* to be a slave, and so I'd better write a letter to Tom Sawyer and tell him to tell Mis Watson where he was. But I soon give up that notion, for two things: she'd be mad and disgusted at his rascality and ungratefulness for leaving her, and so she'd sell him straight down the river again; and if she didn't, everybody naturally despises an ungrateful nigger, and they'd make Jim feel it all the time, and so he'd feel ornery and disgraced. And then think of *me*! It would get all around that Huck Finn helped a nigger to get his freedom; and if I was to ever see anybody from that town again I'd be ready to get down and lick his boots for shame. That's just the way: a person does a low-down thing, and then he don't want to take no consequences of it. Thinks as long as he can hide it, it ain't no disgrace. That

was my fix exactly. The more I studied about this the more my conscience went to grinding me, and the more wicked and low-down and ornery I got to feeling. And at last, when it hit me all of a sudden that here was the plain hand of Providence slapping me in the face and letting me know my wickedness was being watched all the time up there in heaven, whilst I was stealing a poor old woman's nigger that hadn't ever done me no harm, and now was showing me there's One that's always on the lookout, and ain't agoing to allow no such miserable doings to go only just so fur and no further, I most dropped in my tracks I was so scared. Well, I tried the best I could to kinder soften it up somehow for myself by saying I was brung up wicked, and so I warn't so much to blame; but something inside of me kept saying, "There was the Sunday school, you could a gone to it; and if you'd a done it they'd a learn't you there that people that acts as I'd been acting about that nigger goes to everlasting fire."

It made me shiver.

Several class members are now voicing their interpretations of this portion of Twain's novel. Student A declares that Huck Finn's struggle is obvious: He is simply debating whether he should listen to his feelings and keep Jim's whereabouts a secret or listen to his conscience, which dictates that he must report the slave's location to Miss Watson, Jim's lawful owner. This chapter, asserts Student A, illustrates the novel's unifying theme: Huck's struggle to obey his innately good feelings versus his obeying the abstract commandments of an institutionalized system, his society. What unites all the chapters in the text and is now highlighted and climaxed in this chapter, maintains Student A, is Huck's realization that his inner feelings are correct and his society-dominated conscience is wrong. He accordingly opts for declaring Jim's humanity and thus tears up the letter he has written to Miss Watson.

Student B objects, declaring that Student A's interpretation is not relevant for the twenty-first century. Student A is correct, claims Student B, when she notes that Huck chooses to obey his conscience and disavow his allegiance to society's dictates. This is indeed Twain's chief purpose in *Huckleberry Finn*. The novel's significance, however, rests in how it can be applied today. Prejudice, she contends, still exists in our college town. We, like Huck, must see the humanness in all our citizens.

Student C affirms that although both Student A and Student B have made valid criticisms, they have overlooked the change that takes place in Huck himself. No longer will we see, maintains Student C, a Huck who will play dirty tricks on Jim or even consider hurting him in any way. We now have a Huck who has positioned himself against his society and will not retreat from his stance. In the rest of the novel, declares Student C, we will observe this more mature and directed Huck as he responds to Jim's personal needs.

With a quiver in his voice, Student D remarks that Huck reminds him of his friend George. One day when he and George were walking down the hall of their high school on their way to their eleventh-grade biology class, they passed a group of students who began cursing and throwing milk cartons at them. "Go home, Jap," "USA all the way," and other derogatory comments came their way. Then George retorted, "Cut it out, guys. Pete has feelings, too. Should we call some of you towheads, carrot tops, or other names because of how you look and because of your ancestors?" Like George, says Student D, Huck hates prejudice no matter where he finds it. Being on the side of the oppressed, he chooses to guard his friend's dignity and self-worth, therefore destroying the letter to Miss Watson and eventually helping Jim obtain his freedom.

Each of these four students sees something slightly different in Twain's passage, peeking into the text from different windows and thus seeing different scenes, receiving different impressions, and coming away from their reading with different interpretations. Consciously or unconsciously, each of their interpretations rests upon different theoretical assumptions with their corresponding interpretative methodologies. Of the four interpretations, Student A's is the most theoretically distinct approach to the passage. Seeing an overall textual unity, this student presupposes that the text is autonomous; it must interpret itself with little or no help from historical, societal, or any other extrinsic factors, with all its parts relating back to its central theme. Using the tenets of New Criticism, Student A posits the organic unity of the text. For this student, learning and applying literary terminology and searching for the correct interpretation are of utmost importance.

Unlike Student A, who applies a given set of criteria to the text in an attempt to discover its meaning, Students B, C, and D become participants in the interpretive process, actively bringing their own experiences to bear upon the text's meaning. Student B's interpretation, for example, highlights the theoretical difference between a text's meaning (the author's intentions) and its significance or relevance to present-day readers. Student C's approach begins filling in the gaps in the text, hypothesizing how Huck Finn will act in the pages yet unread based on Huck's decision not to write to Jim's owner. Whether Student C is correct or not and whether she will have to alter some of her presently held ideas about Jim remain open questions. Student D's theoretical framework objectifies the text and its meaning based on the reader's personal experiences with prejudice.

Although Students B, C, and D differ in their various approaches, none view the text as an objective entity that contains its own meaning (as does Student A). For these students, the text does not and cannot interpret itself. To determine a text's meaning, these students believe they must become active readers and participants in the interpretive process. The various theoretical assumptions and methodologies they used to discover the text's meaning exemplify **reader-response criticism**, now frequently referred to as **reader-oriented criticism**.

HISTORICAL DEVELOPMENT

Although reader-oriented criticism rose to prominence in the United States in the early 1970s and still influences much contemporary criticism, its historical roots can be traced to the 1920s and 1930s. Such precise dating, however, is artificial, because readers have obviously been responding to what they have read and experienced since the dawn of literature itself. Even the classical writers Plato and Aristotle were aware of and concerned about the reader's (or viewer's) reactions. Plato, for example, asserts that watching a play could so inflame the passions of the audience that the viewers would forget that they were rational beings and allow passion, not reason, to rule their actions. Similarly, in the *Poetics*, Aristotle voices concern about the effects a play will have on the audience's emotions. Will it arouse the spectators' pity or fear? Will these emotions purge the viewer? Will they cleanse a spectator of all emotions by the play's end? Interest in audience response to artistic creation dominates much present-day literary criticism. Critics who emphasize such audience response frequently involve themselves in **rhetorical criticism**, focusing on the strategies, devices, and techniques authors use to elicit a particular reaction or interpretation of a text.

Underlying both Plato and Aristotle's concerns about audience response—as well as the concern of many critics who follow in their paths—is the assumption that the audience (or the reader) is passive. As if watching a play or reading a book were a spectator sport, readers sit passively, absorbing the contents of the artistic creation and allowing it to dominate their thoughts and actions. From this point of view, readers bring little to the play or text. The text provides all that is needed to interpret itself.

From Plato's time until the beginning of the Romantic movement in British literature in the early 1800s, such a passive view of the reader existed. Although many critics recognized that a text did, indeed, have an effect on its readers, criticism concerned itself primarily with the text. With the advent of British Romanticism, emphasis shifted from the text to the author. The author now became the genius who could assimilate truths that were unacknowledged or unseen by the general populace. And as the nineteenth century progressed, concern for the author continued, with literary criticism stressing the importance of the author's life, times, and social context as chief aids in textual analysis.

By the beginning of the twentieth century, emphasis in textual analysis again shifted to the text. With the advent of the New Criticism, the text became autonomous—an objective entity that could be analyzed and dissected. If studied thoroughly, the New Critics believed, the text would reveal its own meaning. Extrinsic factors, such as historical or social context, mattered little. Now considered a verbal icon, the text itself, declared the New Critics, contains what is needed to discover its meaning. We need only master the technical vocabulary and the correct techniques to unlock it.

While positing the autonomy of the text and declaring it to be an **autotelic artifact**, the New Critics did acknowledge the effects a text could have on its readers. Studying the effects of a literary work, they decreed, was not the same as studying the text itself. This emphasis on the objective nature of the text again created a passive reader who did not bring personal experiences or private emotions to bear when engaged in textual analysis.

autotelic artifact - something complete within itself. Written for its own sake

I.A. Richards

In the midst of New Criticism's rise to dominance in the field of textual analysis—a dominance that would last for more than 30 years—one of its two early pioneers, I.A. Richards (T.S. Eliot being the other) became interested in the reading process itself. Unlike many of his Formalist friends who disavowed any relationship between a reader's personal feelings and a text's interpretation, Richards set about to investigate such a relationship. Using a decidedly reader-response approach to textual analysis, Richards distributed to his classes at Cambridge University copies of short poems of widely diverse aesthetic and literary value, without citing their authors and titles and with various editorial changes that updated spelling and pronunciation. He then asked his students to record their free responses to and evaluations of each of these short texts. What surprised Richards was the wide variety of seemingly incompatible and contradictory responses.

After collecting and analyzing these responses, Richards published his findings, along with his own interpretations of the short texts, in *Principles of Literary Criticism* (1925). Underlying Richards's text is his assumption that science, not poetry or any other literary genre, leads to truth—that is, science's view of the world is the correct one. Poems, on the other hand, can produce only "pseudo-statements" about the nature of reality. But such pseudo-statements, declares Richards, are essential to the overall psychological health of each individual. In fact, according to Richards, human beings are basically bundles of desires called **appetencies**. In order to achieve psychic health, one must balance these desires by creating a personally acceptable vision of the world. Richards observes that religion was once able to provide this vision but has now lost its effectiveness to do so. Borrowing from the thoughts of the nineteenth-century poet Matthew Arnold, Richards decrees that poetry, above all other art forms, can best harmonize and satisfy humankind's appetencies and thereby create a fulfilling and intellectually acceptable worldview.

After creating this substantially affective system of analysis, which gives credence to a reader's emotional response to a text, Richards then abandons this same reader-oriented approach in his analysis of his students' responses. Similar to the New Critics who were to follow him in the next several decades, he asserts that "the poem itself" contains all the necessary information to arrive at the "right" or "more adequate" interpretation. Through textual analysis—that is, by closely examining the poem's diction, imagery, and overall unity—Richards believes a reader can arrive at a better (i.e., more correct) interpretation of a poem than one derived from personal responses to a text.

Despite this seemingly complete departure from his initial reader-oriented methodology, Richards does recognize the contextual nature of reading poems: In his text *Practical Criticism* (1929), he acknowledges that a reader brings to the text a vast array of ideas amassed through life's experiences, including previous literary experiences, and applies such information to the text. These life experiences provide a kind of reality check for the reader, either validating or negating the authenticity of the experiences as represented in the text. By so doing, the reader is no longer the passive receiver of knowledge but is instead an active participant in the creation of a text's meaning.

Louise M. Rosenblatt

In the 1930s, Louise M. Rosenblatt, literary theorist, author, scholar, and professor of literacy, further developed Richards's earlier assumptions concerning the contextual nature of the reading process. In her text *Literature as Exploration* (1938), Rosenblatt asserts that both the reader and the text must work together to produce meaning. Unlike the New Critics, she shifts the emphasis of textual analysis away from the text alone and views the reader and the text as partners in the interpretative process. For Rosenblatt, a text is not an autotelic artifact, and there are no generic literary works or generic readers who must master the Formalists' methodology with its accompanying complex and often dense terminology in order to gain the one and only correct interpretation of any text. Instead, there are millions of potential individual readers of the potential millions of individual texts. Readers bring their individual personalities, their memories of past events, their present concerns, their particular physical condition, and all of their personhood to the reading of a text. Disavowing New Criticism's Affective Fallacy and other such tenets, Rosenblatt asserts the validity of multiple interpretations of a text shaped not only by the text but also by the reader.

In the late 1930s, however, Rosenblatt's ideas seemed revolutionary, too abstract, and simply off the beaten, critical path. Although New Criticism dominated literary practice for the next 30 years or so, Rosenblatt continued to develop her ideas, publishing in 1978 *The Reader, the Text, the Poem*. This work became a pivotal force in helping to cause a paradigm shift in the teaching of literature by changing the focus from the text alone to a reader's individual response to a text as a key element in the interpretive process. In this work, Rosenblatt clarifies her earlier ideas and presents what has become one of the main critical positions held by many theorists and practical critics today.

According to Rosenblatt, the reading process involves both a reader and a text. The reader and the text participate in or share a **transactional experience:** The text acts as a stimulus for eliciting various past experiences, thoughts, and ideas from the reader, those found in both our everyday existence and in past reading experiences. Simultaneously, the text shapes the reader's experiences by functioning as a blueprint, selecting, limiting, and ordering those ideas that best conform to the text. Through this transactional experience, the reader and the text produce a new creation, a poem. For Rosenblatt and many other reader-oriented critics, a **poem** is defined as the result of an *event* that takes place during the reading process, or what Rosenblatt calls the "aesthetic transaction." No longer synonymous with the word *text*, a poem is created each time a reader transacts with a text, whether that transaction is a first reading or any one of countless rereadings of the same text.

For Rosenblatt, readers can and do read in one of two ways: *efferently* or *aesthetically*. When we read for information—for example, when we read the directions for heating a can of soup—we are engaging in **efferent reading** (from the Latin *effere*, "to carry away"). During this process, we are interested only in newly gained information that we can "carry away" from the text, not in the actual words as words themselves. When we read efferently, we are motivated by specific needs to acquire information. When we engage in **aesthetic reading**, we experience the text. We note its every word, its sounds, its patterns, and so on. In essence, we live through the transactional experience of creating the poem. Of primary importance is our engagement or our unique "lived-through" experience with the text. Rosenblatt adds, however, that at any given moment in the reading process, a reader may shift back and forth along a continuum between an efferent and an aesthetic mode of reading.

When reading aesthetically, says Rosenblatt, we involve ourselves in an elaborate give-and-take encounter with the text. Although the text may allow for many interpretations by eliciting and highlighting different past experiences of the reader, it simultaneously limits the valid meanings the poem can acquire. For Rosenblatt, a poem's meaning is not a smorgasbord of infinite interpretations; rather, it is a transactional experience in which several different yet probable meanings emerge in a particular social context and thereby create a variety of "poems."

What differentiates Rosenblatt's and all reader-oriented critics from other critical approaches (especially New Criticism) is their purposive shift in emphasis away from the text as the sole determiner of meaning and toward the significance of the reader as an essential participant in the reading process and the creation of meaning. Such a shift negates the Formalists' assumption that the text is autonomous and can, therefore, be scientifically analyzed to discover its meaning. No longer, then, is the reader passive, merely applying a long list of learned, poetic devices to a text in the hope of discovering its intricate patterns of paradox and irony, which, in turn, supposedly leads to the one correct interpretation. For reader-oriented critics, the reader is an active participant along with the text in creating meaning. It is from the **literacy experience** (an event that occurs when a reader and print transact), they believe, that meaning evolves.

ASSUMPTIONS

Similar to most approaches to literary analysis, reader-oriented criticism does not provide us with a unified body of theory or a single methodological approach for textual analysis. What those who call themselves reader-response critics, reader-oriented critics, reader–critics, or audience-oriented critics share is a concern for the reader. Believing that a literary work's interpretation is created when a reader and a text interact or transact, these critics assert that the proper study of textual analysis must consider both the reader and the text, not simply a text in isolation. For these critics,

$$\text{Reader} + \text{Text} = \text{Poem (Meaning)}$$

Only in context, with a reader actively involved in the reading process with the text, can meaning emerge.

Meaning, declare reader-oriented critics, is context dependent and intricately associated with the reading process. Similar to literary theory as a whole, several theoretical models and their practical applications exist to explain the reading process—or how we make sense of printed material. Using these models, we can group the numerous approaches to the literacy experience into three broad categories. Each category emphasizes a somewhat different philosophy, a body of assumptions, and a methodology to explain what these various critics believe happens when a reader interacts or transacts with printed material.

Although each model espouses a different approach to textual analysis, all hold to some of the same presuppositions and concerns and ask similar questions. All, for example, focus directly on the reading process. What happens, they ask, when a person picks up printed material and reads it? Put another way, their chief interest is what occurs when a text and a reader interact or transact. During this exchange, reader-oriented critics investigate and theorize whether the reader, the text, or some combination finally determine the text's interpretation. Does the reader manipulate the text, they ponder, or does the text manipulate the reader to produce meaning? Does some word, phrase, or image trigger in the reader's mind a specific interpretation, or does the reader approach the text with a conscious or unconscious collection of learned reading strategies that systematically impose an interpretation on the text? Is the reading process linear or nonlinear, and is it predictable? Can texts deliberately try to mislead the reader, thereby causing readers to make predictable mistakes? And are readers' responses predictable?

Such questions then lead reader-oriented critics to a further narrowing and developing of terminology. They ask, for example, what is a text? Is it simply the words or symbols on a page? How, they ask, can we differentiate between what is actually in the text and what is in the mind of the reader? And who is this reader, anyway? Are there various kinds of readers? Is it possible that different texts presuppose different kinds of readers?

In addition, what about a reader's response to a text? Are the responses equivalent to the text's meaning? Can one reader's response, they speculate, be more correct than another reader's, or are all responses of equal validity? Although readers respond to the same text in a variety of ways, why is it, they ask, that often many readers individually arrive at the same conclusions or interpretations of the same text?

Reader-oriented critics also ask questions about another person, the author. What part, if any, does the author play in a work's interpretation? Can the author's attitudes toward the reader, they wonder, actually influence a work's meaning? And if a reader knows the author's clearly stated intentions for a text, does this information have any part in creating the text's meaning, or should an author's intentions for a work simply be ignored?

The concerns, then, of reader-oriented critics can best be summarized in one question: What is and what happens during the reading process? The answer to this question, however, is perplexing because it involves investigating such factors as:

- The reader, including his or her view of the world, background, purpose for reading, knowledge of the world, knowledge of words, and other such factors
- The text, with all its various linguistic elements
- Meaning, or how the text and the reader interact or transact so that the reader can make sense of the printed material

How reader-oriented critics define and explain each of these elements determines their approach to textual analysis. Furthermore, their definitions and explications also help determine what constitutes a valid interpretation of a text for each critic.

Although many reader-oriented critics allow for a wide range of legitimate responses to a text, most agree that reader-oriented criticism does not mean that any and all interpretations are valid or of equal importance. The boundaries and restrictions placed on possible interpretations of a text vary, depending on how the critic defines the multiple elements of the reading process. These definitions and assumptions allow us to group reader-oriented critics into several broad subgroups.

METHODOLOGY

Although reader-oriented critics use a wide variety of critical approaches—from those espousing their own particular and modified form of New Criticism to postmodern practitioners such as deconstructionists—most adherents of reader-oriented theory and practice fall into three distinct groups. Although members within each group may differ slightly, each group espouses its own distinct theoretical and methodological concerns. Student B's interpretation at the beginning of this chapter represents the focus of the first group.

Similar to all reader-oriented critics, this group believes that the reader must be an active participant in the creation of meaning. But for these critics, the text has more control over the interpretative process than does the reader. A few of these critics lean toward New Critical theory, asserting that some interpretations are more valid than others, while still other critics differentiate between a text's meaning and its significance. For all these critics, the text's meaning can be synonymous with its author's intention, yet its significance can change from one context or historical period to another. Notwithstanding these variations, the majority of critics in this first group belong to a school of criticism known as **structuralism.**

Structuralism

Basing their ideas on the writings of Ferdinand de Saussure, the founder of modern linguistics, structuralists often approach textual analysis as if it were a science. The proponents of structuralism—Roland Barthes, Gerard Genette, Roman Jakobson, Claude Lévi-Strauss, Gerard Prince, and Jonathan Culler in his early works—look for specific codes within the text that allow meaning to occur. These codes or signs embedded in the text are part of a larger system that allows meaning to occur in all facets of society, including literature. For example, when we are driving a car and we see a red light hanging above an intersection, we have learned that we must stop our car. Or when we hear a fire engine or an ambulance siren, we have learned that we must drive our car to the side of the road. Both the red light and the sirens are signs or codes in our society that provide us with ways of interpreting and ordering our world.

According to structuralist critics, a reader brings to the text a predetermined system for ascertaining meaning (a complex system of signs or codes similar to the sirens and the red light) and applies this sign system directly to the text. The text becomes important because it contains signs or signals to the reader that have preestablished and acceptable interpretations. Many structuralists are therefore more concerned about the overall system of meaning a given society has developed (called **langue** by linguists) than with textual analysis itself; they concentrate on what a reader needs to know about interpreting any sign (e.g., a road sign or a word) in the context of acceptable societal standards. Because of this emphasis, structuralists seem to push both the text and the reader to the background and concentrate their attention on a linguistic theory of communication and interpretation. Because structuralism has become a springboard for many other modern theories of literary criticism, its significance to literary theory and practical criticism are explored at length in the next chapter. Meanwhile, the ideas of one leading structuralist, Gerard Prince, illustrate the methodology of structuralism.

In the 1970s, Gerard Prince helped develop a specific kind of structuralism known as **narratology,** the process of analyzing a story using all the elements involved in its telling, such as narrator, voice, style, verb tense, personal pronouns, audience, and so forth. Prince noted that critics often ask questions about the story's point of view—omniscient, limited, first person, and so on—but rarely ask about the person to whom the narrator is speaking, the **narratee.** Usually, the narratee is not the actual person reading the text; Prince argues that the narrative itself—that is, the story—produces the narratee. By first observing and then analyzing various signs in the text, such as pronoun reference; direct address ("Dear reader"); gender, race, and social class references; and writing style, Prince believes it is possible not only to identify the narratee but also to classify stories based on the different kinds of narratees created by the texts themselves. Such narratees may include the **real reader** (person actually reading the book), the **virtual reader** (the reader to whom the author believes he or she is writing), and the **ideal reader** (the one who explicitly and implicitly understands all the nuances, terminology, and structure of the text).

Although such an approach relies heavily on textual analysis, Prince's concerns about the reader place him in the reader-oriented school of criticism. Other structuralists such as Jonathan Culler who distance themselves from Prince and this kind of close reliance on the text to generate meaning are discussed in Chapter 5.

Phenomenology

Student C who interpreted Twain's Huckleberry Finn represents the second major group of reader-oriented critics. For the most part, these theorists follow Rosenblatt's assumption that the reader is involved in a transactional experience when interpreting a text. Both the text and the reader, they declare, play somewhat equal parts in the interpretative process. For them, reading is an event that culminates in the creation of the poem.

Many adherents in this group—George Poulet, Wolfgang Iser, Hans Robert Jauss, Roman Ingarden, and Gaston Bachelard—are often associated with phenomenology. **Phenomenology** is a modern philosophical tendency that emphasizes the perceiver. Objects can have meaning, phenomenologists maintain, only if an active consciousness (a perceiver) absorbs or notes their existence. In other words, objects exist if, and only if, we register them in our consciousness. Rosenblatt's definition of a poem directly applies this theory to literary study. The true poem can exist only in the reader's consciousness, not on the printed page. When a reader and text transact, the poem and, therefore, meaning are created; they exist only in the consciousness of the reader. Reading and textual analysis now become an aesthetic experience, in which both the reader and the text combine in the consciousness of the reader to create the poem. Similar to Student C's interpretation at the beginning of the chapter, the reader's imagination must work, filling in the gaps in the text and conjecturing about characters' actions, personality traits, and motives. The ideas and practices of two reader-oriented critics, Jauss and Iser, serve to illustrate phenomenology's methodology.

Hans Robert Jauss Writing toward the end of the 1960s, the German critic Hans Robert Jauss emphasizes that a text's social history must be considered when interpreting the text. Unlike New Critical scholars, Jauss declares that critics must examine how any given text was accepted or received by its contemporary readers. Espousing a particular kind of reader-oriented criticism known as **reception theory**, Jauss asserts that readers from any given historical period devise for themselves the criteria whereby they will judge a text. Using the term **horizons of expectation** to include all of a historical period's critical vocabulary and assessment of a text, Jauss points out that how any text is evaluated from one historical period to another (e.g., from the Age of Enlightenment to the Romantic period), necessarily changes. For example, Alexander Pope's poetry was heralded as the most nearly perfect poetry of its day because heroic couplets and poetry that followed prescribed forms were judged superior. During the Romantic period, however, with its emphasis on content, not form, the critical reception of Pope's poetry was not as great.

Accordingly, Jauss argues that because each historical period establishes its own horizons of expectation, the overall value and meaning of any text can never become fixed or universal; readers from any given historical period establish for themselves what they value in a text. A text, then, does not have one and only one correct interpretation because its supposed meaning changes from one historical period to another. A final assessment about any literary work thus becomes impossible.

For Jauss, the reader's reception or understanding and evaluation of a text matter greatly. Although the text itself remains important in the interpretive process, the reader, declares Jauss, plays an essential role.

Wolfgang Iser The German phenomenologist Wolfgang Iser borrows and amends Jauss's ideas. Iser believes that any object—for example, a stone, a house, or a poem—does not achieve meaning until an active consciousness recognizes or registers this object. Thus, it is impossible to separate what is known (i.e., the object) from the mind that knows it (i.e., human consciousness). Using these phenomenological ideas as the basis for his reader-oriented theory and practice, Iser declares that the critic's job is not to dissect or explain the text because as soon as a text is read, the object and the reader (the perceiver) are essentially one. Instead, the critic's role is to examine and explain the text's effect on the reader.

Iser, however, differentiates two kinds of readers. The first is the **implied reader**, who "embodies all those predispositions necessary for a literary work to exercise its effect—predispositions laid down, not by an empirical outside reality but by the text itself. Consequently, the implied reader . . . has his or her roots firmly planted in the structure of the text" (Iser, 1978). In other words, the implied reader is the reader implied by the text, one who is predisposed to appreciate the overall effects of the text. On the other hand, the **actual reader** is the person who physically picks up the text and reads it. This reader, as opposed to the implied reader, comes to the text shaped by particular cultural and personal norms and prejudices. By positing the implied reader, Iser affirms the necessity of examining the text in the interpretive process; at the same time, by acknowledging the actual reader, Iser declares the validity of an individual reader's response to the text.

Similar to Jauss, Iser disavows the New Critical stance that a text has one and only one correct meaning and asserts that a text has many possible interpretations. For Iser, texts, in and of themselves, do not possess meaning. When a text is **concretized** (i.e., the phenomenological concept whereby the text registers in the reader's consciousness), the reader automatically views the text from his or her personal worldview. However, because texts do not tell the reader everything that needs to be known about a character, a situation, a relationship, or other such textual elements, readers must automatically fill in these "gaps," using their own knowledge base, grounded as it is in a worldview. In addition, each reader creates his or her own **horizons of expectation**—that is, expectations about what will or may or should happen next. (Note the variation in meaning Iser gives this term compared with Jauss, who coined it.) These horizons of expectation change frequently because at the center of all stories is conflict or dramatic tension, often resulting in sudden loss, pain, unexpected joy or fear, and at times great fulfillment. Such changes cause a reader to modify his or her horizons of expectation to fit a text's particular situation. For example, in Chapter 31 of the *Adventures of Huckleberry Finn*, when Huck declares that he will not write a letter to Miss Watson telling her the location of Jim, Huck openly chooses to side with Jim against the precepts of Huck's society. A reader may then assume that Huck will treat Jim differently because now Jim, the slave, has a chance to become a free person. According to Iser, the reader has now established horizons of expectation. When, however, in just a few short chapters, Tom Sawyer talks Huck into chaining Jim to a table, the reader may reformulate his or her horizons of expectation because Huck is not treating Jim as a free man but once again as a slave.

In making sense of the text, in filling in the text's gaps, and in continually adopting new horizons of expectation, the reader uses his or her own value system, personal and public experiences, and philosophical beliefs. According to Iser, each reader makes "concrete" the text; each concretization is, therefore, personal, allowing the new creation—the text's meaning and effect on the reader—to be unique.

For Iser, the reader is an active, essential player in the text's interpretation, writing part of the text as the story is read and concretized and, indispensably, becoming its coauthor.

Subjective Criticism

Student D represents the third group of reader-oriented critics who place the greatest emphasis on the reader in the interpretative process. For these psychological or subjective critics, the reader's thoughts, beliefs, and experiences play a greater part than the actual text in shaping a work's meaning. Led by Norman Holland and David Bleich, these critics assert that readers shape and find their self-identities in the reading process.

Norman Holland Using Freudian psychoanalysis as the foundation for his theory and practices formulated in the early 1970s, Norman Holland believes that at birth we receive from our mothers a primary identity. We personalize this identity through our life's experiences, transforming it into our own individualized **identity theme** that becomes the lens through which we see the world. Textual interpretation becomes a matter of working out our own fears, desires, and needs to help maintain our psychological health.

Similar to Rosenblatt, Holland asserts that the reading process is a transaction between the text and the reader. The text is indeed important because it contains its own themes, unity, and structure. A reader, however, transforms a text into a private world, a place where the reader works out (through the ego) his or her fantasies, which are actually mediated by the text so that they will be socially acceptable.

For Holland, all interpretations are subjective. Unlike New Criticism, his reader-oriented approach asserts that no "correct interpretation" exists. From his perspective, there are as many valid interpretations as there are readers because the act of interpretation is a subjective experience in which the text is subordinated to the individual reader.

David Bleich The founder of "subjective criticism," David Bleich agrees with Holland's psychological explanation of the interpretive process, but Bleich devalues the role the text plays, denying its objective existence.

Meaning, Bleich argues, does not reside in the text but is *developed* when the reader works in cooperation with other readers to achieve the text's collective meaning (what Bleich calls "the interpretation"). When each reader is able to articulate his or her individual responses about the text within a group, then—and only then—can the group, working together, negotiate meaning. Such communally motivated negotiations ultimately determine the text's meaning.

For Bleich, the starting point for interpretation is the reader's responses to a text, not the text itself. Bleich states, however, that these responses do not constitute the text's meaning because meaning cannot be found within a text or within responses to the text. Rather, a text's meaning must be *developed* from and out of the reader's responses, working in conjunction with other readers' responses and with past literary and life experiences. In other words, Bleich differentiates between the reader's responses to a text (which for Bleich can never be equated to a reader's interpretation) and the reader's interpretation or meaning, which must be developed communally in a classroom or similar setting.

For Bleich and his adherents, the key to developing a text's meaning is the working out of one's responses to a text so that these responses will be challenged, amended, and then accepted by one's social group. Subjective critics such as Bleich assert that when reading a text, a reader may respond to something in the text in a bizarre and personal way. Through discussion, these private responses are pruned away by members of the reader's social group. Finally, the group decides on the acceptable interpretation of the text. As in Student D's interpretation cited at the beginning of this chapter, the reader responds personally to some specific element in the text, seeks to objectify this personal response, and then declares it to be an interpretation of the text. Only through negotiations with other readers and other texts— **intertextuality**—however, can one develop the text's meaning.

A Two-Step Methodology

Although reader-oriented critics all believe the reader plays a part in discovering a text's meaning, just how small or large a part is debatable. Espousing various theoretical assumptions, these critics have different methodologies for textual analysis. According to the contemporary critic Steven Mailloux, reader-oriented critics all share a two-step procedure, which they then adapt to their own theories. These critics all show that a work gives a reader a task or something to do, and they represent the reader's response or answer to that task.

Returning, for example, to Student D: At the beginning of the chapter, Student D's argument shows that he saw something in the text that triggered his memories of his friend George. His task is to discover what in the text triggered his memory and why. He moves, then, from the text to his own thoughts, memories, and past experiences. These personal experiences temporarily overshadow the text, but he realizes that his personal reactions must in some way become acceptable to his peers; therefore, he compares George to Huck and himself to Jim and thereby objectifies his personal feelings while at the same time having his interpretation deemed socially respectable in his **interpretive community**—a term coined by the reader-oriented critic Stanley Fish to designate a group of readers who share the same interpretive strategies.

Stanley Fish (1938–), a contemporary reader-oriented critic, has coined the term **affective stylistics** or **reception aesthetics** to describe his reading strategy. Similar to other theorists, Fish's approach to texts has developed through time, with Fish periodically appending his theoretical and practical concerns. Presently, Fish argues that meaning inheres in the reader, not the text. More pointedly, however, a text's meaning resides in the reading community to which a reader belongs, or what Fish calls the *interpretive community*—a group of people defined by a distinct epistemology. The interpretation of a text therefore depends on a reader's subjective experience in one or more of these interpretive communities. This community (or these communities) ultimately invests meaning. Unlike the New Critics, Fish declares that the objectivity of a text is an illusion because the text is a *tabula rasa*, a blank slate upon which the reader, while engaged in the reading process, writes the actual text. For Fish, the text being held by the reader is like a Rorschach blot on which the reader projects his or her understanding as filtered through cultural assumptions held by one or more interpretive communities. In effect, the reader determines the form and content of the text. Gone is New Criticism's assumption that the text is a self-enclosed system or structure that determines its own meaning. For Fish, the reader, not the text, is preeminent.

Because the term *reader-oriented criticism* allows for so much divergence in theory and methods, many present-day schools of criticism, such as deconstruction, feminism, Marxism, and cultural poetics, declare their membership in this broad classification. Each of these approaches to textual analysis provides its own ideological basis to reader-oriented theory and develops its unique methods of practical criticism. Such an eclectic membership denotes the continued growth and ongoing development of reader-oriented criticism.

QUESTIONS FOR ANALYSIS

Because reader-oriented critics use a variety of methodologies, no particular listing of questions can encompass all their concerns. Nevertheless, by asking the following questions of a text, one can participate in both the theory and practice of reader-oriented criticism:

- Who is the actual reader?
- Who is the implied reader?
- Who is the ideal reader?
- Who is the narratee?
- What are some gaps you see in the text?
- Can you list several horizons of expectations and show how they change from a particular text's beginning to its conclusion?
- Using Jauss's definition of horizons of expectation, can you develop (first on your own and then with your classmates) an interpretation of a particular text?
- Can you articulate your identity theme as you develop your personal interpretation of a particular text?
- Using Bleich's subjective criticism, can you state the difference between your response to a text and your interpretation?
- In a classroom setting, develop your class's interpretive strategies for arriving at the meaning of a particular text.
- As you interpret this text, can you cite the interpretive community or communities to which you, the reader, belong?

CRITIQUES AND RESPONSES

Similar to most schools of criticism that have emerged since the 1960s, reader-oriented theory is a collective noun embodying a variety of critical positions. Unlike New Criticism's "text and text alone" approach to interpretation that claims the meaning of a text is enclosed in the text itself, reader-oriented critics emphasis the reader of a text, declaring that the reader is just as much (or more) a producer of meaning as the text itself. To varying degrees, the reader helps create the meaning of any text. In approaching a work, the reader brings to the interpretative process his or her **forestructure**, which includes his or her accrued life experiences, memories, beliefs, values, and any other quality or characteristics that make an individual unique. In making sense of the text—what we call the interpretation—the elements of the reader's forestructure interact, transact, or intermingle (depending on the reader's theoretical stance), producing the actual interpretation. Because all reader-oriented critics agree (to varying degrees) that the individual reader creates the text's meaning, reader-orientated criticism declares that there can be no one correct meaning for any text; instead, many valid interpretations are possible. What the reading process is and how readers read are major concerns for all reader-oriented critics. Their answers to these and similar questions, however, are widely divergent.

Reader-oriented criticism has been harshly critiqued by some scholars, who believe that the text, not the reader creates meaning. If multiple interpretations of the same text can exist side by side, how can we ever say what a text means? Can a text actually mean anything a reader says it means? Are there no clearly delineated guidelines for interpretation? Are there no fixed values in any text? If the reader is the producer of meaning, then the reader's physical or mental condition while reading a text will directly influence the interpretation, producing an array of bizarre and, more frequently than not, misguided and pointless interpretations. In response, reader-oriented critics provide a wide range of answers, including Iser's gap theory, Rosenblatt's transactional theory, and Fish's rather relativistic assumption that no text can exist until either the reader or an interpretive community creates it.

Reader-oriented criticism is not as popular today as it was in the 1960s or 1970s. Although its theoretical assumptions and critical theorists—Rosenblatt, Bleich, Jauss, Iser, and Holland—still influence literary criticism and, in all probability, will continue to do so for decades, many reader-oriented critics now emphasize how certain groups read, asking such questions as: Do African-Americans read differently from European Americans? How do women read? How do men read? How do gays and lesbians read? In other words, different schools of literary criticism such as feminism, gender studies, and queer theory have embraced the principles of reader-oriented criticism, again turning the attention of theorists and critics to the reading process and the reader.

FURTHER READING

Bleich, David. *Subjective Criticism*. Baltimore, MD: Johns Hopkins University Press, 1978.

Fish, Stanley. *Is There a Text in This Class? The Authority of Interpretive Communities*. Cambridge, MA: Harvard University Press, 1982.

Holland, Norman N. *5 Readers Reading*. New Haven, CT: Yale University Press, 1975.

———. *Holland's Guide to Psychoanalytic Psychology and Literature*. Oxford: Oxford University Press, 1990.

Iser, Wolfgang. *The Act of Reading: A Theory of Aesthetic Response*. Baltimore, MD: Johns Hopkins University Press, 1980.

———. *The Implied Reader: Patterns of Communication in Prose Fiction from Bunyan to Beckett*. Baltimore, MD: Johns Hopkins University Press, 1979.

Jauss, Hans Robert. *Aesthetic Experience and Literary Hermeneutics*. Minneapolis, MN: University of Minnesota Press, 1982.

Machor, James. *Reception Study: From Literary Theory to Cultural Studies*. London: Routledge, 2000.

Mailloux, Steven. "Learning to Read: Interpretation and Reader-Response Criticism." *Studies in the Literary Imagination* 12 (1979):93–108.

McGregor, Graham, and R.S. White, eds. *Reception and Response: Hearer Creativity and the Analysis of Spoken and Written Texts*. London: Routledge, 1990.

Rosenblatt, Louise M. *Literature as Exploration*, 5th ed. New York: Noble, 1996.

———. *Making Meaning with Texts: Selected Essays*. New York: Reed-Elsevier, 2005.

———. *The Reader, the Text, the Poem*. Carbondale, IL: Southern Illinois University Press, 1994.

———. "Towards a Transactional Theory of Reading." *Journal of Reading Behavior* 1 (1969):31–47.

Suleiman, Susan, and Inge Crosman, eds. *The Reader in the Text: Essay on Audience and Interpretation*. Princeton, NJ: Princeton University Press, 1990.

Tompkins, Jane, ed. *Reader-Response Criticism: From Formalism to Post-Structuralism*. Baltimore, MD: Johns Hopkins University Press, 1980.

WEB SITES FOR EXPLORATION

http://litguide.press.jhu.edu
   The Johns Hopkins Guide to Literary Theory and Criticism. This site provides a wide range of essays on all aspects of literary theory and criticism

http://www.questia.com/library/literature/reader_response_criticismjsp
   A solid online library that provides working definitions of reader-oriented criticism and links to other site

http://www.cnr.edu/home/bmcmanus/readercrit.html
   A good overview of reader-response criticism plus excellent links to other sites

http://en.wikipedia.org/wiki/Reader-response-criticism/
   Essay from Wikipedia on all aspects of literary theory and criticism. Wikipedia is known as the free encyclopedia

http://bac.bedfordstmartins.com
   Provides working definitions for various schools of criticism, including reader-oriented criticism

http://www.geocities.com/Athens/Academy14573/Readerresponse/
readerresponse2.html
   "A Paradigm of Reader-response Criticism" giving a personal interpretation of this school of criticism

Sample Essay

The following student essay uses the principles of reader-oriented criticism in its analysis of Flannery O'Connor's short story "A Good Man Is Hard to Find." The student author specifically chose this short story for analysis because of the multiple reactions readers usually have to this text. As you read the essay, ask yourself the following questions:

- How does this essay demonstrate reader-oriented principles of literary analysis?
- What are the strengths of the essay? Weaknesses? Be specific, citing places in the essay that support your answers.
- On the continuum of reader-oriented criticism, is this essay developed using the ideas espoused by the phenomenological critics? By transactional critics? By subjective critics? Cite concrete examples from the essay to support your statements.
- Who is the narrate? The implied reader? The ideal reader?
- What personal strategies or moves does the author makes to arrive at his interpretation?
- Can you identify the interpretive community to which the author belongs? Does the author belong to more than one interpretive community?
- From what point of view does the author write the essay? Why?
- How does the author establish tone, and do you believe the essay's tone is effective?

Student Essay

The Child Grandmother[1]

When I was first told that Flannery O'Connor's short story "A Good Man Is Hard to Find" is about an elderly grandmother, I wondered how captivating such a story could be. After all, I thought, how interesting are senior citizens. Little did I realize that my pre-conceived assumptions and ideas concerning senior citizens and family-member interactions were about to be shattered. After reading and re-reading the story, I came to realize the irony and absurdity of my initial reactions and ideas toward O'Connor's character the grandmother and her family. This grandmother is, by no means, a typical grandmother. Bewildered by this unexpected difference, I was soon keenly aware that I would have to change my ideas of the elderly as my horizons of expectation for both the grandmother and the entire story itself dramatically changed with each reading of the text. At first the story itself was a monotonous bore, but after engaging the text numerous times, I now realize that O'Connor's tale is, in actuality, both a depiction and a revelation about how I should live and interact with everyone.

When I began reading and then simultaneously thinking about the Grandmother in O'Connor's tale, I immediately thought of my own grandmother who is a kind, gentle, and soft spoken woman. Such an image quickly became blurred and then vanished when I was confronted with the

[1]Reprinted by permission of Ian J. Galloway.

stubbornly independent and outspoken grandmother portrayed in the story. Almost from the start, I disliked her. Her undying attempts to dissuade the family from going to Florida—no matter how reasonable her argument— began to irritate me. In the end, it was her selfish scheming to see a house in the country and her stubborn unwillingness to leave her cat behind that became the causes of the car wreck, leaving her ironically dependent on three strangers.

The grandmother's tone also caught me off guard concerning my usual expectations of elderly women. At first I sympathized with Bailey as his mother gave him driving advice as if he were still learning to drive: ". . . she cautioned Bailey that the speed limit was fifty-five miles an hour and that the patrolmen hid themselves behind billboards and small clumps of trees and sped out after you before you had a chance to slow down." I grimaced at these words, placing myself in Bailey's seat as the words rang familiarly in my own head, hearing the voices of my parents on similar occasions. Although such "advice" was intended to be cautionary and welcomed, such words are degrading, as if saying to Bailey—and to me—that he is both stupid and an inept driver. Connecting myself to Bailey's situation, I understood his situation, my dislike of the grandmother becoming stronger and more concrete.

Regal, proper, and a lady, the grandmother and her opinion stands in sharp contrast to her actual life which caused even further frustration for me. Remembering my own grandmother, I recalled that she too keenly noticed changes around her, both in people's physical characteristics and their material possessions. At times, her alertness would be wearisome, her giving the impression that only a person's material wealth or physical appearance was all that mattered. O'Connor's Grandmother takes this tendency to an extreme with her "friend" Edgar Atkins Teagarden. In this relationship and her memories about it, the Grandmother is blind to the discontinuity that exists in her understanding of people and appearances. To the Grandmother, Mr. Teagarden is only an object, a means to wealth, not a person in his own right.

Such an appearance-driven life also evidences itself in what the Grandmother wears. Her belief that if she dressed like a lady she would therefore be a lady did not impress me as she might have hoped it would; in actuality, such an idea caused resentment to rise in me. When the narrator first informed me about this particular ill-formed and illogical belief held by the Grandmother, I remembered the first time I traveled to Honduras as a young and rather naïve teen, not knowing what to expect or for what I should prepare. The greatest surprise for me was the Honduran people themselves. Despite the tragedies of Hurricane Mitch and the ever-present state of poverty, the Hondurans were always willing to help, always willing to give of their material possessions, and always willing to give of their time and energy. By looking at their outward appearance and their material possessions, my first impressions of them shouted "lazy" or "apathetic" or "heartless," but that certainly was not the case. Unfortunately, for the Grandmother first impressions were the only impressions, as evidenced in her comments about a young African American boy sitting on the side of the road during the family's road trip. This judgmental attitude coupled with her know-it-all tone compounded my negative feelings for her, feelings that began to fester like a thorn lodged under the skin. I wondered what great flaw would appear next in her character.

The appearance of the Misfit into the story came like a cold, refreshing shower taken after I had played hours of soccer in the afternoon of a hot summer's day. Finally, a multi-layered character emerged, and with his entrance into the story came a sense of reality. The Misfit serves as a foil to the grandmother, not only as a realistic character but also in his personality. Whereas the Grandmother is motivated by a cynical selfishness, the Misfit counters her personality with his need to murder, seemingly he notes, from necessity. And the Grandmother's ladylike appearance is exposed by a rather translucent criminal, one who at least can articulate his feelings honestly. In addition, the Grandmother's apathetic attitude toward her family is countered by the Misfit's respect for the Grandmother when he apologizes to her on her son's behalf for Bailey's harsh, offensive words.

What was even more shocking was my reaction to the final events of the story. Because the Misfit's appearance in the story provided me with a genuine sense of a "real" character possessing a multi-faceted personality, I was all too soon cheering for him, siding with his character, not the Grandmother and her family. Even more revolting to me was what I felt when the Grandmother discovered grace immediately preceding her death. When I read these words, ". . . her legs crossed under her like a child's and her face smiling up at the cloudless sky," memories of Sunday school popped into my head, remembering words like "Let the little children come to me, and do not hinder them, for the kingdom of God belongs to such as these."

Astonishingly, this self-righteous, know-it-all, arrogant woman receives grace in her dying moment! While her sudden transformation should have been a positive note in an otherwise bleak ending, I was left questioning the validity of her salvation, her moment of grace. Thoughts about youth meetings where I saw dozens of teens stand and promise to change their ways flooded my thoughts. Only days after these meetings, however, when the music, the speakers, and the electric environment were now silent, these same teens continued living their lives as they had done before the meeting. And if the Grandmother had lived, I doubted whether her life would have changed even a tad from what it was before her encounter with the Misfit.

But my own epiphany was soon to come. As I read and contemplated O'Connor's story, I realized that, over time, I began to loathe the Grandmother. In actuality, however, I was in fact being caught up in the same faults for which I was condemning her! She was judgmental; similarly,

I was becoming increasingly judgmental of her, looking intently for her next fault that I could embellish with my own thoughts and memories. I was all too quickly dismissing the grace that was given her moments before her death. Then I realized that I had summarily rejected the Misfit's words that Jesus had thrown everything off balance as the unintelligible ramblings of a criminal, a social misfit. Suddenly, his words rang true for me. It was his words that held a deeper truth I had not seen before. The scales were decidedly tilted against the grandmother, but because Jesus did throw everything off balance, the Grandmother could now receive grace. Like the grandmother who finally saw the truth—that the Misfit was indeed one of her babies—I too realized that I was like the Grandmother more than I had ever thought. Like her, I too need to learn to give and to receive grace daily before someone holds a gun to my head.

IAN J. GALLOWAY

5

MODERNITY AND POSTMODERNISM: STRUCTURALISM AND DECONSTRUCTION

Of all social institutions, language is least amenable to initiative. It blends with the life of society, and the latter, inert by nature, is a prime conservative force.

Ferdinand de Saussure, *Course in General Linguistics*

To pretend, I actually do the thing: I have therefore only pretended to pretend.

Jacques Derrida, Interview

MODERNITY

For many historians and literary theorists, the Enlightenment (or the Age of Reason in the 18th century) is synonymous with **modernity** (from the Latin word *modo*, meaning "just now"). That its roots predate this time period is unquestioned, with a few scholars even dating its beginnings to 1492, coincident with Columbus's journeys to the Americas, and its overall spirit lasting until the middle of the twentieth century. At the center of this view of the world lie two prominent features: a belief that reason is humankind's best guide to life and that science, above all other human endeavors, could lead humanity to a new promised land. Philosophically, modernity rests on the foundations laid by René Descartes (1596–1650), a French philosopher, scientist, and mathematician. Ultimately, declares Descartes, the only thing one cannot doubt is one's own existence. Certainty and knowledge begin with the self. "I think, therefore I am" thus becomes the only solid foundation upon which knowledge and a theory of knowledge can be built. For Descartes, the rational essence freed from superstition, human passions, and one's often irrational imagination allows humankind to discover truth about the physical world.

Whereas Descartes's teachings elevated to new heights the individual's rational essence and humankind's ability to reason, the scientific writings and discoveries of both Francis Bacon (1561–1626) and Sir Isaac Newton (1642–1727) allowed science to be likewise coronated. Thanks to Bacon, the scientific method has become part of everyone's elementary and high school education. It is through experimentation, conducting experiments, making inductive generalizations, and verifying the results that one can discover truths about the physical world. And thanks to Newton, the physical world is no longer a mystery but a mechanism that operates according to a system of laws that can be understood by any thinking, rational human being who is willing to apply the principles of the scientific method to the physical universe.

Armed with an unparalleled confidence in humankind's capacity to reason—the ability to inquire and grasp necessary conditions essential for seeking out such undoubtable truths as provided by mathematics—and the assurance that science can lead the way to a complete understanding of the physical world, the Enlightenment (i.e., modern) scholar was imbued with a spirit of progress. Anything the enlightened mind set as its goal, these scholars believed, was attainable. Through reason and science, all poverty, ignorance, and injustice would finally be banished.

Of all Enlightenment thinkers, Benjamin Franklin (1706–1790) may best exemplify the characteristics of modernity. Gleaned from self-portraits contained in his *Autobiography*, Franklin is the archetypal modern philosopher-scientist. Self-assured, Franklin declares that he "pulled himself up by his own bootstraps," overcoming poverty and ignorance through education to become America's first internationally known and respected philosopher-scientist-diplomat. Believing in the power and strength of the individual mind, he delighted in the natural world and decided early in life to know all possible aspects of his universe. Accordingly, he abandoned superstitions and myths and placed his trust in science to lead him to truths about his world. Through observations, experiments, and conclusions drawn upon the data discovered by using the scientific method, Franklin believed he could obtain and know the necessary truths for guiding him through life.

Similar to Descartes, Franklin does not abandon religion and replace it with science. Holding to the tenets of deism, he rejects miracles, myths, and much of what he calls religious superstitions. He does not reject, however, a belief in the existence of God. He asserts that God leaves it to humanity, to each individual, to become the master of his or her own fate. According to Franklin, individuals must find salvation within themselves. By using one's God-given talent for reason and joining these rational abilities to the principles of science, every person, declares Franklin, can experience and enjoy human progress.

For Franklin and other enlightened minds, truth is to be discovered scientifically, not through the unruly and passionate imagination or through one's feelings or intuition. Indeed, what is to be known and discovered via the scientific method is reality: the physical world. All people, declares Franklin, must know this world objectively and must learn how to investigate it to discover its truths.

Self-assured, self-conscious, and self-made, Franklin concludes that all people possess an essential nature. It is humanity's moral duty to investigate this nature contained within ourselves and also to investigate our environment through rational thinking and the methods of science so that we can learn and share the truths of the universe. By devoting ourselves to science and to the magnificent results that will necessarily follow, Franklin proclaims that human progress is inevitable and will usher in a new golden age.

Franklin and modernity's spirit of progress permeated humankind's beliefs well into the twentieth century. For several centuries, modernity's chief tenets—that reality can be known and investigated and that humanity possesses an essential nature characterized by rational thought—became the central ideas upon which many philosophers, scientists, educators, and writers constructed their worldviews. Briefly put, modernity's core characteristics are as follows:

- The concept of the self is a conscious, rational, knowable entity.
- Reality can be studied, analyzed, and known.
- Objective, rational truth can be discovered through science.
- The methodology of science can and does lead to ascertaining truth.
- The yardstick for measuring truth is reason.
- Truth is demonstrable.
- Progress and optimism are the natural results of valuing science and rationality.
- Language is referential, representing the perceivable world.

In particular, writers and literary theoreticians—New Critics, structuralists, and others—believed that texts possess some kind of objective existence and therefore could be studied and analyzed, with appropriate conclusions to follow from such analyses. Whether a text's actual value and meaning were intrinsic or extrinsic was debatable; nevertheless, an aesthetic text's meaning could be discovered and articulated. Such a basic assumption concerning a text's meaning was soon to be challenged by principles espoused by what has been dubbed postmodernism.

POSTSTRUCTURALISM OR POSTMODERNISM

What is truth? How can truth be discovered? What is reality? Is there an objective reality on which we can all agree? If so, how can we best investigate this reality so that all humanity can understand the world in which we live and prosper from such knowledge? Until the late 1960s (with a few notable exceptions), the worldview espoused by modernity and symbolized by Benjamin Franklin provided acceptable and workable answers to these questions. For Franklin and other modern thinkers, the primary form of discourse is like a map. The map itself is a representation of reality as known, discovered, and detailed by humanity. By looking at a map, a traveler who holds to these assumptions can see a delineated view of the world and an accurate picture of reality itself: the mountains, rivers, plains, cities, deserts, and forests. By placing his or her trust in this representation of reality, the traveler can then plot a journey, feeling confident in the accuracy of the map and its depictions. For the modern mind, objective reality as pictured on the map was knowable and discoverable by any intelligent person who wished to do so.

With the inception of deconstruction, in Jacques Derrida's poststructural view of the world in the mid-1960s, however, modernity's understanding of reality is challenged and turned on its head by **postmodernism**, meaning "after modernity" or "just after now," from its Latin root meaning "just now." For Derrida and other postmodernists, there is no such thing as objective reality. For these thinkers, all definitions and depictions of truth are subjective, simply creations of human minds. Truth itself is relative, depending on the nature and variety of cultural and social influences in one's life. Because these poststructuralist thinkers assert that many truths exist, not *the* truth, they declare that modernity's concept of one objective reality must be disavowed and replaced by many different concepts, each a valid and reliable interpretation and construction of reality.

Postmodernist thinkers reject modernity's representation of discourse (the map) and replace it with a collage. Unlike the fixed, objective nature of a map, a collage's meaning is always changing. Whereas the viewer of a map relies on and obtains meaning and direction from the map itself, the viewer of a collage actually participates in the production of meaning. Unlike a map, which allows one interpretation of reality, a collage permits many possible meanings: the viewer (or "reader") can simply juxtapose a variety of combinations of images, constantly changing the meaning of the collage. Each viewer, then, creates his or her own subjective picture of reality.

To say postmodernism popped onto the American literary scene with the coming of Derrida to the United States in 1966 would, of course, be inaccurate. Although historians disagree about who actually coined the term *postmodernism*, there is general agreement that the word first appeared in the 1930s. Its seeds, however, had already germinated far earlier in the writings of Friedrich Nietzsche (1844–1900). As Zarathustra, the protagonist of Nietzsche's *Thus Spake Zarathustra* (1891), proclaims the death of God, simultaneously the death knell begins to sound for the demise of objective reality and ultimate truth. World Wars I and II, a decline in the influence of Christianity and individualism, and the appearance of a new group of theologians led by Thomas Altizer, who in the 1950s echoed Nietzsche's words that God is dead, all contributed to the obsolescence of objective reality and of the autonomous scholar who seeks to discover ultimate reality.

Beginning in the 1960s and continuing to the present, the voices of the French philosopher Jacques Derrida, the French cultural historian Michel Foucault, the aesthetician Jean-Francois Lyotard, and the ardent American pragmatist Richard Rorty, professor of humanities at the University of Virginia, declare univocally the death of objective truth. These leading articulators of postmodernism assert that modernity failed because it searched for an external point of reference—God, reason, science, among others—on which to build a philosophy. For these postmodern thinkers, there is no such point of reference because there is no ultimate truth or inherently unifying element in the universe and thus no ultimate reality.

According to postmodernists, all that is left is difference. We must acknowledge, they say, that each person shapes his or her own concepts of reality. Reality, then, becomes a human construct that is shaped by each individual's dominant social group. There exists no center, nor one all-encompassing objective reality, but as many realities as there are people. Each person's interpretation of reality will necessarily be different. No one has a claim to absolute truth; therefore, tolerance of each other's points of view becomes the postmodern maxim.

Because postmodern philosophy is constantly being shaped, reshaped, defined, and articulated by its adherents, no single voice can adequately represent it or serve as an archetypal spokesperson, as Franklin can for modernity. However, by synthesizing the beliefs of Derrida, Foucault, Lyotard, and Rorty, we can hypothesize what this representative postmodern thinker would possibly espouse:

> I believe, like my forebears before me, that we, as a race of people, will see progress, but only if we all cooperate. The age of the lone scholar, working diligently in the laboratory, is over. Cooperation among scholars from all fields is vital. Gone are the days of individualism. Gone are the days of conquest. Now is the time for tolerance, understanding, and collaboration.
>
> Because our knowledge always was and always will be incomplete, we must focus on a new concept: holism. We must realize that we all need each other, including all our various perspectives on the nature of reality. We must also recognize that our rationality (i.e., our thinking processes) is only one of many avenues that can lead to an understanding of our world. Our emotions, our feelings, and our intuition can also provide us with valid interpretations and guidelines for living.
>
> And we have finally come to realize that no such thing as objective reality exists; there is no ultimate truth because truth is perspectival, depending on the community and social group in which we live. Since many truths exist, we must learn to accept each other's ideas concerning truth, and we must learn to live side by side in a pluralistic society, learning from each other while celebrating our differences.
>
> We must stop trying to discover the undiscoverable—absolute truth— and openly acknowledge that what may be right for one person may not be

right for another. Acceptance, not criticism; openmindedness, not closed-mindedness; tolerance, not bigotry; and love, not hatred, must become the guiding principles of our lives. When we stop condemning ourselves and others for "not having truth," then and only then will we be able to spend more time interpreting our lives and giving them meaning, as together we work and play.

When such principles are applied to literary interpretation, the post-modernist realizes that no such thing as *the* meaning—or, especially, the *correct* meaning—of an aesthetic text exists. Like looking at a collage, meaning develops as the reader interacts with the text, for meaning does not reside within the text itself. And because each reader's view of truth is perspectival, the interpretation of a text that emerges when a reader interacts with a text will necessarily be different from every other reader's interpretation. For each text, then, there exists an almost infinite number of interpretations or at least as many interpretations as there are readers.

Overall, postmodernism's core characteristics can be stated as follows:

- A skepticism or rejection of grand metanarratives to explain reality
- The concept of the self as ever-changing
- No objective reality, but many subjective interpretations
- Truth as subjective and perspectival, dependent on cultural, social, and personal influences
- No "one correct" concept of ultimate reality
- No metatheory to explain texts or reality
- No "one correct" interpretation of a text

MODERNITY TO MODERNISM

Rooted in the philosophy and ideals of the Enlightenment, modernity, with its accompanying philosophical, political, scientific, and ethical ideas, provides much of the basis for intellectual thought from the 1700s to the midpoint of the twentieth century. World War I, however, marks a dramatic shift, especially in the arts. Growing out of the devastation of the war, the arts began to reflect society's concerns, emphasizing decay, loss, and disillusionment. The term **modernism** is given to this aesthetic movement dated from 1914 to 1945 that questioned the ideals of British Victorianism and reflected both the material and the psychological devastation of two world wars. Writers such as W.H. Auden, T.S. Eliot, Virginia Woolf, Ezra Pound, W.B. Yeats, George Bernard Shaw, and many others began to question some of modernity's core beliefs such as the objective status of reality and the fixed nature of aesthetic forms. Using unconventional stylistic techniques such as stream of consciousness and multiple-narrated stories, artists and writers emphasized the subjective, highlighting how "seeing" or "reading" actually occurs rather than investigating the actual object being seen or read. Characterized by a transnational focus, literary artists blurred the established distinctions among the various genres, rejecting previously established aesthetic theories, choosing to highlight unconscious or subconscious elements in their works by using the psychoanalytic theories of Sigmund Freud and Carl Jung. Decentering the individual and introducing ambiguity and fragmentation, modernism began to see life as a collage rather than a map.

Partly in answer to the growing skepticism and the rising sense of meaningless of both life and art, a new way of examining reality and language arose in France in the 1950s: **structuralism**, a term coined in 1929 by the **Russian Formalist** Roman Jakobson. Structuralism asserts an overall unity and significance to every form of communication and social behavior. Grounded in structural linguistics, the science of language, structuralism uses the techniques, methodologies, and vocabulary of linguistics, offering a scientific view of how we achieve meaning not only in literary works but also in every cultural act.

To understand structuralism, we must trace its historical roots to the linguistic writings and theories of Ferdinand de Saussure, a Swiss professor and linguist of the late nineteenth and early twentieth centuries. It is his scientific investigations of language and language theory that provide the basis for structuralism's unique approach to literary analysis.

HISTORICAL DEVELOPMENT OF STRUCTURALISM

Pre-Saussurean Linguistics

Throughout the nineteenth and early twentieth centuries, philology, not linguistics, was the science of language. Its practitioners, philologists, described, compared, and analyzed the languages of the world to discover similarities and relationships. Their approach to language study was **diachronic**—that is, they traced language change throughout long expanses of time, discovering, for example, how a particular phenomenon, such as a word or sound, in one language had changed etymologically or phonologically over several centuries and whether a similar change could be noted in other languages. Using a cause-and-effect relationship as the basis for their research, the philologists' main emphasis was the historical development of languages.

Such an emphasis reflected the nineteenth-century philologists' theoretical assumptions concerning the nature of language. Language, they believed, mirrored the structure of the world it imitated and therefore had no structure of its own. Known as the **mimetic theory of language,** this linguistic hypoth-esis asserts that words (either spoken or written) are symbols for things in the world, each word having its own **referent**—the object, concept, or idea that is represented or symbolized by that word. According to this theory, the symbol (a word) equals a thing:

$$\text{Symbol (word)} = \text{Thing}$$

Saussure's Linguistic Revolution

In the first decade of the 1900s, a Swiss philologist and teacher named Ferdinand de Saussure (1857–1913) began questioning these long-held ideas and, by so doing, triggered a reformation in language study. Through his research and innovative theories, Saussure changed the direction and subject matter of linguistic studies. His *Course in General Linguistics*, a compilation of his 1906 to 1911 lecture notes published posthumously by his students, is one of the seminal works of modern linguistics and forms the basis for struc-turalist literary theory and practical criticism. Through the efforts of this pio-neer of modern linguistics, nineteenth-century philology evolved into the more multifaceted science of twentieth-century linguistics.

Saussure began his linguistic revolution by affirming the validity and necessity of the diachronic approach to language study used by such nineteenth-century philologists as the Grimm brothers and Karl Verner. Using this diachronic approach, these linguists discovered the principles governing consonantal pronunciation changes that occurred in Indo-European languages (the language group to which English belongs) over many centuries. While not abandoning a diachronic examination of language, Saussure introduced the **synchronic** approach, a method that proceeds by focusing on a language at one particular time—a single moment—and that emphasizes the whole state of a particular language at that time. Attention focuses on how the language and its parts function, not on tracing the historical development of a single element, as would occur in a diachronic analysis. By highlighting the activity of the language system and how it operates rather than its evolution, Saussure drew attention to the nature and composition of language and its constituent parts. For example, along with examining the phonological antecedents of the English sound *b*, as in the word *boy* (a diachronic analysis), Saussure opened a new avenue of investigation, asking how the *b* sound is related to other sounds in use at the same time by speakers of Modern English (a synchronic analysis). This new concern necessitated a rethinking of language theory and a reevalua-tion of the aims of language research, and it finally resulted in Saussure's articulating the basic principles of modern linguistics.

Unlike many of his contemporary linguists, Saussure rejected the mimetic theory of language structure. In its place, he asserted that language is primarily determined by its own internally structured and highly systematized rules. These rules govern all aspects of a language, including the sounds its speakers identify as meaningful, the grouping of various combinations of these sounds into words, and the arrangement of these words to produce meaningful communication within a given language.

The Structure of Language

According to Saussure, all languages are governed by their own internal rules that do not mirror or imitate the structure of the world. Emphasizing the systematized nature of language, Saussure asserts that all languages are composed of basic units called **emes**. The task of a linguist is to identify these units (sometimes called *paradigms* or *models*) and/or identify their relationships among symbols—like the letters of the alphabet, for example—in a given language. This task becomes especially difficult when the emes in the linguist's native language and those in an unfamiliar language under investigation differ. According to Saussure, the basic building block or unit of language is the **phoneme**—the smallest, meaningful (significant) sound in a language. The number of phonemes differs from language to language, with the least number of total phonemes for any one language being around nine and the most in the mid-sixties. American English, for example, consists of approximately forty-three to forty-five phonemes, depending on the specific dialect being spoken. Although native speakers of American English are capable of producing phonemes found in other languages, it is these forty-five distinct sounds that serve as the building blocks of American English. For example, the first sound heard in the word *pin* is the /p/ phoneme, the second /I/, and the last /n/. A phoneme is identified in writing by enclosing the **grapheme**—the written symbol that represents the phoneme's sound—in virgules or diagonal lines.

Although each phoneme makes a distinct sound that is meaningful and recognizable to speakers of a particular language, actually, a phoneme is composed of a family of nearly identical speech sounds called **allophones**. For instance, in the word *pit*, the first phoneme is /p/, and in the word *spin*, the second phoneme is also /p/. Although the /p/ appears in both words, its pronunciation is slightly different. To validate this statement, simply hold the palm of your hand about 2 inches from your mouth and pronounce the word *pit* followed immediately by the word *spin*. You will quickly note the difference. These slightly different pronunciations of the same phoneme are two different allophones of the phoneme /p/.

Telling the difference among sounds, knowing when any alternation in the pronunciation of a phoneme changes the meaning of a group of phonemes (i.e., a word), or knowing when a simple variation in a phoneme's pronunciation is linguistically insignificant (an allophone) can, at times, be difficult. For example, in English, the letter *t* represents the sound /t/, but is there one distinct pronunciation for this sound whenever and wherever it appears in an English word? Is the *t* in the word *tip*, for instance, pronounced the same as the *t* in *stop*? Obviously not—the first *t* is **aspirated**, or pronounced with a greater force of air, than the *t* in *stop*. In either word, however, a speaker of English could still identify the /t/ as a phoneme or a distinct sound. If we replace the *t* in *tip* with a *d*, we now have *dip*, the difference between the two words being the sounds /t/ and /d/. Upon further analysis, we find that these sounds are pronounced in the same location in the mouth, but with one difference: whereas /d/ is **voiced**, or pronounced with the vocal cords vibrating, /t/ is **unvoiced**, with the vocal cords remaining basically still. This difference between the sounds /t/ and /d/ allows us to say that /t/ and /d/ are phonemes or distinct sounds in English. Whether the eme is a sound, or a minimal unit of grammar such as the adding of an *s* in English to form most plurals or any other distinct category of a language, Saussure's basic premise operates: within each eme, distinctions depend on differences.

How phonemes and allophones arrange themselves to produce meaningful speech in any language is not arbitrary but is governed by a prescribed set of rules developed through time by the speakers of a language. For example, in Modern American English (1755–present), no English word can end with the two phonemes /m/ and /b/. In Middle English (1100–1500), these phonemes could combine to form the two terminal sounds of a word, resulting, for example, in the word *lamb*, in which the /m/ and /b/ were both pronounced. Over time, the rules of spoken English have changed so much that when *lamb* appears in Modern English, /b/ has lost its phonemic value. The study of the rules governing the meaningful units of sound in a linguistic system is called **phonology**, and the study of the production of these sounds is known as **phonetics**.

In addition to phonemes, another major building block of language is the **morpheme**, the smallest part of a word that has lexical or grammatical significance. **Lexical** refers to the base or root meaning of a word; **grammatical** refers to the elements of language that express relationships between words or groups of words, such as the **inflections** {-ed}, {-s}, and {-ing} that carry tense, number, gender, and so on. (Note that in print, morphemes are placed in braces.) Similar to the phoneme, the number of lexical and grammatical morphemes varies from language to language. In American English, the number of lexical morphemes far outdistances the relatively handful of grammatical morphemes (ten or so). For instance, in the word reaper, {reap} is a lexical morpheme, meaning "to ripple flax," and {-er} is a grammatical morpheme, meaning "one who." All words must have a lexical morpheme (hence their great number), but not every word needs to have a grammatical morpheme. How the various lexical and grammatical morphemes combine to form words is highly rule governed and is known in modern linguistics as the study of **morphology**.

Another major building block in the structure of language is the actual arrangement of words in a sentence—its **syntax**. Just as the placement of phonemes and morphemes in individual words is a rule-governed activity, so is the arrangement of words in a sentence. For example, although native speakers of English would understand the sentence "John threw the ball into the air," such speakers would have difficulty ascertaining the meaning of "Threw the air into the ball John." Why? Native speakers of a language have mastered which strings of morphemes are permitted by syntactic rules and which are not. Those that do not conform to these rules do not form English sentences and are called **ungrammatical**. Those that do conform to the established syntactic structures are called **sentences** or **grammatical sentences**. In most English sentences, for example, the subject ("John") precedes the verb ("threw"), followed by the complement ("the ball into the air"). Although this structure can sometimes be modified, such changes must follow tightly prescribed rules of syntax if a speaker of English is to be understood.

Having established the basic building blocks of a sentence—phonemes, morphemes, words, and syntax—language also provides us with one additional body of rules to govern the various interpretations or shades of meaning such combinations of words can evoke: **semantics**. Unlike morphemes (the meanings of which can be found in the dictionary) and unlike the word stock of a language—its **lexicon**—the **semantic features** (i.e., the properties of words that show facets of meaning) are not so easily defined. Consider, for example, the following sentences:

"Brandon is a nut."

"I found a letter on Willard Avenue."

"Get a grip, Anna."

To understand each of these sentences, a speaker or reader needs to understand the semantic features that govern an English sentence because each of the above sentences has several possible interpretations. In the first sentence, the speaker must grasp the concept of metaphor; in the second, lexical ambiguity; and in the third, idiomatic structures. Unless these semantic features are consciously or unconsciously known and understood by the reader or listener, problems of interpretation may arise. As with the other building blocks of language, an understanding of semantics is necessary for clear communication in any language.

Langue and Parole

By age 5 or 6, native speakers of English or any other language have consciously and unconsciously mastered their language's complex system of rules or its **grammar**—the language's phonology, morphology, syntax, and semantics—which enables them to participate in language communication.

They have not, however, mastered such advanced elements as all the semantic features of their language, nor have they mastered its **prescriptive grammar**. This type of grammar consists of prescriptive rules of English usage often invented by eighteenth- and nineteenth-century purists who believed that there were certain constructions that all educated people should know and employ, such as using the nominative form of a pronoun after an intransitive linking verb as in the sentence, "It is I." What these 5- or 6-year-old native speakers of a language have learned Saussure dubs **langue**, the structure of the language that is mastered and shared by all its speakers.

Although langue emphasizes the social aspect of language and an understanding of the overall language system, Saussure calls an individual's actual speech utterances and writing **parole**—that is, linguistic features such as loudness or softness that are overlaid on language's structure, its langue. For example, two speakers can utter the same sentence: "I see a rat." One speaker shouts the words while another whispers them. Both utterances are examples of parole and how individuals personalize language. Speakers can generate countless examples of individual utterances, but all are governed by the language's system, its langue. It is the task of the linguist, Saussure believes, to infer a language's langue from the analysis of many instances of parole. In other words, for Saussure, the proper study of linguistics is the system (langue), not the individual utterances of its speakers (parole).

Saussure's Redefinition of a Word

Having established that languages are systems that operate according to verifiable rules and that they need to be investigated both diachronically and synchronically, Saussure then reexamined philology's definition of a word. Rejecting the long-held belief that a word is a symbol that equals a thing (its **referent**), Saussure proposed that words are **signs** made up of two parts: the **signifier** (a written or spoken mark) and a **signified** (a concept):

$$\text{Sign} = \frac{\text{Signifier}}{\text{Signified}}$$

For example, when we hear the sound *ball*, the sound is the signifier, and the concept of a ball that comes to our minds is the signified. Like the two sides of a sheet of paper, the linguistic sign is the union of these two elements. As oxygen combines with hydrogen to form water, Saussure says, so the signifier joins with the signified to form a sign that has properties unlike those of its parts. Accordingly, for Saussure a word does not represent a referent in the objective world but a sign. Unlike previous generations of philologists who believed that we perceive things (word = thing) and then translate them into units or meaning, Saussure revolutionizes linguistics by asserting that we perceive signs.

Furthermore, the linguistic sign, declares Saussure, is arbitrary: the relationship between the signifier (*ball*) and the signified (the concept of *ball*) is a matter of convention. The speakers of a language have simply agreed that the written or spoken sounds or marks represented by *ball* will equal the concept *ball*. With few exceptions, proclaims Saussure, there is no natural link between the signifier and the signified, nor is there any natural relationship between the linguistic sign and what it represents.

If, as Saussure maintains, there is no natural link between the linguistic sign and the reality it represents, how do we know the difference between one sign and another? In other words, how does language create meaning? We know what a sign means, says Saussure, because it differs from all other signs. By comparing and contrasting one sign with other signs, we learn to distinguish each individual sign. Individual signs, then, can have meaning (or signify) only within their own langue.

For Saussure, meaning is therefore relational and a matter of difference. Within the system of sound markers that comprise our language, we know *hill*, for instance, because we differentiate it from *hall*, *pill*, and *mill*. Likewise, we know the concept "bug" because it differs from the concepts "truck," "grass," and "kite." As Saussure declares, "In language there are only differences."

Because signs are arbitrary, conventional, and differential, Saussure concludes that the proper study of language is not an examination of isolated entities but the system of relationships among them. He asserts, for example, that individual words cannot have meaning by themselves. Because language is a system of rules governing sounds, words, and other components, individual words obtain their meaning only within that system. To know language and how it functions, he declares, we must study the system (langue), not individual utterances (parole) that operate according to the rules of langue.

For Saussure, language is the primary sign system whereby we structure our world. Language's structure, he believes, is similar to any other sign system of social behavior, such as fashion, table manners, and sports. Like language, all such expressions of social behavior generate meaning through a system of signs. Saussure proposed a new science called **semiology** to study how we create meaning through these signs in all our social behavioral systems. Since language was the chief and most characteristic of all these systems, Saussure declared, it was to be the main branch of semiology. The investigation of all other sign systems would be patterned after language, because like language's signs, the meaning of all signs is arbitrary, conventional, and differential.

Although semiology never became the important new science Saussure envisioned, a similar science was being proposed in the United States almost simultaneously by philosopher and teacher Charles Sanders Peirce (1839–1914). Called **semiotics**, this science borrowed linguistic methods used by Saussure and applied them to all meaningful cultural phenomena. Meaning in society, this science of signs declares, can be systematically studied by investigating how meaning occurs and by understanding the structures that allow it to operate. Distinguishing among the various kinds of signs, semiotics continues to develop today as a particular field of study. Because it uses structuralist methods borrowed from Saussure, *semiotics* and *structuralism* are terms often used interchangeably, although the former denotes a distinct field of study and the latter is more an approach and method of analysis.

ASSUMPTIONS OF STRUCTURALISM

Borrowing the linguistic vocabulary, theory, and methods from Saussure and to a smaller degree from Peirce, structuralists—their studies being variously called structuralism, semiotics, **stylistics**, and **narratology**, to name a few— believe that codes, signs, and rules govern all human social and cultural practices, including communication. Whether that communication is the language of fashion, sports, education, friendships, or literature, each is a systematized combination of codes (signs) governed by rules. Structuralists want to discover these codes, which they believe give meaning to all our social and cultural customs and behavior. The proper study of meaning— and therefore, reality—they assert, is an investigation of the system behind these practices, not the individual practices themselves. Their aim is to discover how all the parts fit together and function.

Structuralists find meaning in the relationship among the various components of a system. When applied to literature, this principle becomes revolutionary. For the structuralists, the proper study of literature involves an inquiry into the conditions surrounding the act of interpretation itself (how literature conveys meaning), not an in-depth investigation of an individual work. Since an individual work can express only those values and beliefs of the system of which it is a part, structuralists emphasize the system (**langue**) whereby texts relate to each other, not an examination of an isolated text (**parole**). They believe that a study of the system of rules that govern literary interpretation becomes the critic's primary task.

Such a belief presupposes that the structure of literature is similar to the structure of language. Like language, say the structuralists, literature is a self-enclosed system of rules that is composed of language. Literature, like language, needs no outside referent except its own rule-governed, but socially constrained, system. Before structuralism, literary theorists discussed the literary conventions—that is, the various genres or types of literature, such as the novel, the short story, or poetry. Each genre, it was believed, had its own conventions or acknowledged and acceptable way of reflecting and interpreting life. For example, in poetry, a poet could write in nonsentences, using symbols and other forms of figurative language to state a theme or to make a point. For these prestructuralist theorists, the proper study of literature was an examination of these conventions and of how either individual texts used applicable conventions to make meaning or how readers used these same conventions to interpret the text. Structuralists, however, seek out the system of codes that they believe convey a text's meaning. For them, how a text convenes meaning rather than what meaning is conveyed is at the center of their interpretative methodology—that is, how a symbol or a metaphor, for example, imparts meaning is of special interest. For instance, in Nathaniel Hawthorne's short story "Young Goodman Brown," most readers assume that the darkness of the forest equates with evil and that images of light represent safety. Of particular interest to the structuralist is *how* (not *that*) darkness comes to represent evil. A structuralist would ask why darkness more frequently than not represents evil in any text and what sign system or code is operating that allows readers to interpret darkness as evil intertextually or in all or most texts they read. To structuralists, how a symbol or any other literary device functions is of chief importance, not how literary devices imitate reality or express feelings.

In addition to emphasizing the system of literature and not individual texts, structuralism claims it demystifies literature. By explaining literature as a system of signs encased in a cultural frame that allows that system to operate, say the structuralists, a literary work can no longer be considered a mystical or magical relationship between the author and the reader, the place where author and reader share emotions, ideas, and truth. A scientific and objective analysis of how readers interpret texts, not a transcendental, intuitive, or transactional response to any one text, leads to meaning. Similarly, an author's intentions can no longer be equated to the text's overall meaning because meaning is determined by the system that governs the writer, not an individual author's own quirks. And no longer can the text be autonomous, an object whose meaning is contained solely within itself. All texts, declare structuralists, are part of the shared system of meaning that is **intertextual**, not text specific; in other words, all texts refer readers to other texts. Meaning, claim the structuralists, can therefore be expressed only through this shared system of relations, not in an author's stated intentions or the reader's private or public experiences.

Declaring both isolated text and author to be of little importance, structuralism attempts to strip literature of its magical powers or so-called hidden meanings that can only be discovered by a small, elite group of highly trained specialists. Meaning can be found, it declares, by analyzing the system of rules that comprise literature itself.

METHODOLOGIES OF STRUCTURALISM

Similar to all other approaches to textual analysis, structuralism follows neither one methodological strategy nor one set of ideological assumptions. Although most structuralists use many of Saussure's ideas in formulating their theoretical assumptions and foundations for their literary theories, how these assumptions are used when applied to textual analysis vary greatly. A brief examination of five structuralists or subgroups will help highlight structuralism's varied approaches to textual analysis.

Claude Lévi-Strauss

One of the first scholar–researchers to implement Saussure's principles of linguistics to narrative discourse in the 1950s and 1960s was the French anthropologist Claude Lévi-Strauss (1908–). Attracted to the rich symbols in myths, Lévi-Strauss spent years studying myths from around the world. Myth, he assumed, possessed a structure like language. Each individual myth was therefore an example of parole. What he wanted to discover was myth's langue, its overall structure that allows individual examples (parole) to function and have meaning. In his work "The Structural Study of Myths," Lévi-Strauss presents his structural analysis of why myths from different cultures from all over the world seem similar. These myths' similarities reside, he asserts, at the level of structure.

After reading countless myths, Lévi-Strauss identified recurrent themes running through all of them. Such themes transcended culture and time, speaking directly to the minds and hearts of all people. These basic structures, which he called **mythemes**, are similar to the primary building blocks of language, the phonemes. Similar to phonemes, mythemes find meaning in and through their relationships within the mythic structure. And like phonemes, such relationships often involve oppositions. For example, the /b/ and /p/ phonemes are similar in that they are pronounced by using the lips to suddenly stop a stream of air. They differ or oppose one another in only one aspect: whether the air passing through the wind pipe does or does not vibrate (voiced and unvoiced, respectively) the vocal cords; during actual speech, vibrating vocal cords produce /b/ and nonvibrating /p/. Similarly, a mytheme finds its meaning through opposition. Hating or loving one's parents, falling in love with someone who does or who does not love you, and cherishing or abandoning one's children all exemplify the dual or opposing nature of mythemes. The rules that govern how these mythemes may be combined constitute myth's structure or grammar. The meaning of any individual myth depends on the interaction and order of the mythemes within the story. Out of this structural pattern comes the myth's meaning.

When applied to a specific literary work, the intertextuality of myth becomes evident. For example, in Shakespeare's *King Lear*, King Lear overestimates the value and support of children when he trusts Regan and Goneril, his two oldest daughters, to take care of him in his old age. He also underestimates the value and support of children when he banishes his youngest and most-loved daughter, Cordelia. Like the binary opposition that occurs between the /b/ and /p/ phonemes, the binary opposition of underestimating versus overestimating love automatically occurs when reading the text, for such mythemes have occurred in countless other texts and immediately ignite emotions within readers.

Like our unconscious mastery of our language's langue, we also master myth's structure. Our ability to grasp this structure, says Lévi-Strauss, is innate. Like language, myths are simply another way we classify and organize our world.

Roland Barthes

Researching and writing in response to Lévi-Strauss was his contemporary, the eminent French structuralist Roland Barthes (1915–1980). Barthes's contribution to structuralist theory is best summed up in the title of his most famous text, *S/Z*. In Balzac's *Sarrasine*, Barthes noted that the first *s* is pronounced as the *s* in *snake* and the second as the *z* in *zoo*. Both phonemes, /s/ and /z/ respectively, are a **minimal pair**—that is, both are produced by using the same articulatory organs and in the same place in the mouth, the difference being that /s/ is unvoiced (no vibration of vocal cords) and /z/ is voiced (vibration of vocal cords when air is blowing through the breath channel). Like all minimal pairs—/p/and /b/, /t/ and /d/, and /k/ and /g/, for example—this pair operates in what Barthes calls **binary opposition**. Even within a phoneme, binary opposition exists because a phoneme is, as Saussure reminded us, a class of nearly identical sounds called allophones, which differ phonetically—that is, by slightly changing the pronunciation but not altering the recognizable phoneme. Borrowing and further developing Saussure's work, Barthes declares that all language is its own self-enclosed system based on binary operations (i.e., difference).

Barthes then applies his assumption that meaning develops through difference to all social contexts, including fashions, familial relations, dining, and literature, to name a few. When applied to literature, an individual text is simply a message—a parole—that must be interpreted by using the appropriate codes or signs or binary operations that form the basis of the entire system, the langue. Only through recognizing the codes or binary operations within the text, says Barthes, can the message encoded within the text be explained. For example, in Nathaniel Hawthorne's "Young Goodman Brown," most readers intuitively know that Young Goodman Brown will come face to face with evil when he enters the forest. Why? Because one code or binary operation that we all know is that light implies good and dark implies evil. Brown thus enters the dark forest and leaves the light of his home, only to find the "false light" of evil emanating from the artificial light—the fires that light the baptismal service of those being baptized into Satan's fellowship. By finding other binary oppositions within the text and showing how these oppositions interrelate, the structuralist can then decode the text and explain its meaning.

Such a process abandons or dismisses the importance of the author, any historical or literary period, or particular textual elements or genres. Rather than discovering any element of truth within a text, this methodology shows the process of decoding a text in relationship to the codes provided by the structure of language itself.

Vladimir Propp and Narratology

Expanding Lévi-Strauss's linguistic model of myths, a group of structuralists called **narratologists** began another kind of structuralism: **structuralist narratology**, the science of narrative. Like Saussure and Lévi-Strauss, these structuralists illustrate how a story's meaning develops from its overall structure, its langue, rather than from each individual story's isolated theme. Narratology's overriding concern is the narrative structure of a text. What is the interrelationship of a narrative's constituent parts, ask narratologists, and how are these parts constructed to shape the narrative itself? What are the "rules" that govern the formation of plot? Of point of view? Of narrator? Of audience?

Like other critics, narratologists amend and borrow ideas from other reading strategies to help shape their ideas. Narratology borrows elements from both the French structuralists such as Lévi-Strauss and from Russian Formalist critics such as Vladimir Propp (1895–1970). In his influential text *Morphology of the Folk Tale* (1928), Propp investigates Russian fairy tales to decode their langue. According to his analysis, all folk or fairy tales are based on thirty-one fixed elements, or what Propp calls **narrative functions**, that occur in a given sequence. Each function identifies predictable patterns or functions that central characters, such as the hero, the villain, or the helper, enact to further the plot of the story. Any story may use any number of these elements, such as "accepting the call to adventure," "recognizing the hero," and "punishing the villain," among others, but each element occurs in its logical and proper sequence. Other critics, notably Paul Vehvilainen, have simplified Propp's thirty-one functions into a five-point system that, like Propp's, always occurs in the same order:

- A *lack* of something exists.
- This lack forces the hero to go on a *quest* to eliminate this lack.

- During the quest, the hero encounters a *magical helper*.
- This helper is subjected to one or more *tests*.
- After passing the test(s), the hero receives a *reward*.

Like Propp's thirty-one functions, these simplified five basic functions can be applied to most fairy tales.

Applying Propp's narratological principles to specific literary works is both fun and simple. For example, in Mark Twain's **Adventures of Huckleberry Finn**, Huck, the protagonist or hero, is given a task to do: free Jim. His evil enemy (the villain)—society—tries to stop him. But throughout the novel, various helpers appear to propel the plot forward, until the hero's task is completed and Huck successfully frees Jim and then "lits out" from society.

Tzvetan Todorov and Gerard Genette

Another narratologist, the Bulgarian theorist and philosopher Tzvetan Todorov (1939–), declares that all stories are composed of grammatical units. For Todorov, the syntax of narrative—how the various grammatical elements of a story combine—is essential. By applying a rather intricate grammatical model to narrative—dividing the text into semantic, syntactic, and verbal aspects—Todorov believes he can discover the narrative's langue and establish a grammar of narrative. He begins by asserting that the grammatical clause, and in turn, the subject and verb, is the basic interpretative unit of each sentence and can be linguistically analyzed and further dissected into a variety of grammatical categories to show how all narratives are structured. An individual text (parole) interests Todorov as a means to describe the overall properties of literature in general (langue).

Other narratologists such as the French theorist Gerard Genette (1930–) have also developed methods of analyzing a story's structure to uncover its meaning, each building upon the former work of another narratologist (and in some cases, Russian Formalists) and adding an additional element or two. Genette is responsible for reintroducing a host of rhetorical terms into literary theory and criticism. For example, he believes that **tropes** or figures of speech require a reader's special attention. Genette's four-part work *Figures* (a series written from 1967 to 1999) and particularly his text *Narrative Discourse: An Essay on Method* (1979) have influenced structuralism's vocabulary and methodology, both in the United States and France.

Although these narratologists provide us with various approaches to texts, all furnish us with a **metalanguage**—words used to describe language—so that we can understand *how* a text means, not *what* it means.

Jonathan Culler

By the mid-1970s, Jonathan Culler (1944–) became the voice of structuralism in the United States and took structuralism in yet another direction. In his work *Structuralist Poetics* (1975), Culler declared that abstract linguistic models used by narratologists tended to focus on parole, spending too much time analyzing individual stories, poems, and novels. What was needed, he believed, was a return to an investigation of langue, Saussure's main premise.

According to Culler, readers, when given a chance, somehow make sense out of the most bizarre text because readers possess **literary competence**. Through experiences with texts, Culler asserts, readers have internalized a set of rules that govern their acts of interpretation. Instead of analyzing individual interpretations of a work, we must spend our time, Culler insists, on analyzing the act of interpretation itself. We must shift the focus from the text to the reader. How, asks Culler, does interpretation occur in the first place? What system underlies the very act of reading that allows any other system to operate?

Unlike other structuralists, Culler presents a theory of reading. What, he asks, is the internalized system of literary competence readers use to interpret a work? In other words, how do they read? What system guides them through the process of interpreting the work, of making sense of the spoken or printed word?

Culler asserts that every reader holds to three underlying assumptions when reading and interpreting texts:

- A text should be unified.
- A text should be thematically significant.
- This significance can take the form of reflection.

Accordingly, Culler then seeks to establish the system, the langue, that undergirds the reading process. By focusing on the act of interpretation itself to discover literature's langue, Culler believes he is returning structuralism to its Saussurean roots.

A Model of Interpretation

Although structuralist theories abound, a core of structuralists believe that the primary signifying system is best found as a series of binary oppositions that the reader organizes, values, and then uses to interpret the text. Each binary operation can be pictured as a fraction, the top half (the numerator) being what is more valued than its related bottom half (the denominator).

Accordingly, in the binary operation light/dark, the reader has learned to value light over dark, and in the binary operation good/evil, the reader has similarly valued good over evil. How the reader maps out and organizes the various binary operations and their interrelationships found within the text but already existing in the mind of the reader determines for that particular reader the text's interpretation.

No matter what its methodology, structuralism emphasizes form and structure, not the actual content of a text. Although individual texts must be analyzed, structuralists are more interested in the rule-governed system that underlies texts rather than the texts themselves. *How* texts mean—not *what* they mean—is their chief interest.

DECONSTRUCTION THEORY: FROM STRUCTURALISM TO POSTSTRUCTURALISM

Throughout much of the 1950s and 1960s, structuralism dominated European and American literary theory and criticism. Although the application of structuralist principles varies from one theorist to another, all believe that language is the primary means of **signification** (i.e., how we achieve meaning through linguistic signs and other symbols) and that language comprises its own rule-governed system to achieve such meaning. Although language is the primary sign system, it is not the only one. Fashions, sports, dining, and other activities all have their own language or codes whereby the participants know what is to be expected of them in a particular situation. When dining at an elegant restaurant, for example, connoisseurs of fine dining know that it is inappropriate to drink from the finger bowl. Similarly, football fans know that it is appropriate to shout and scream to support their team.

From a structuralist perspective, such expectations highlight that all social and cultural practices are governed by rules or codes. Wishing to discover these rules, structuralists declare that the proper study of reality and meaning is the system behind such individual practices, not the individual practices themselves. Like attending a football game or dining at a fine restaurant, the act of reading is also a cultural and a social practice that contains its own codes. Meaning in a text resides in these codes that the reader has mastered before he or she even picks up an actual text. For the structuralist, the proper study of literature is an inquiry into the conditions surrounding the act of interpretation itself, not an investigation of an individual text.

In the mid-1960s, however, this structuralist assumption that meaning can be discovered through an examination of its structural codes was challenged by the maxim of **undecidability**: a text has many meanings and, therefore, no definitive interpretation. Rather than providing answers about the meaning of texts or a methodology for discovering how a text means, a new approach to reading, **deconstruction theory**, asks a different set of questions, endeavoring to show that what a text claims it says and what it actually says are discernibly different. By casting doubt on most previously held theories, deconstruction declares that a text has an almost infinite number of possible interpretations. Furthermore, declare some deconstructionists, the interpretations themselves are just as creative and important as the text or texts being interpreted.

With the advent of deconstruction and its challenge to structuralism and other prior theories, a paradigmatic shift occurs in literary theory and criticism. Before deconstruction, literary critics—New Critics, some reader-oriented theorists, structuralists, and others—found meaning *within* the literary text or the codes of the various sign systems within the world of the text and the reader. The most innovative of these theorists, the structuralists, provided new and exciting ways of discovering meaning, but nonetheless, these theorists maintained that meaning could be found. Underlying all the predeconstructionist suppositions about the world is a set of philosophical, ethical, and scientific assumptions we dub **modernity** that provided the bases for the beliefs held by Western culture for about 300 years. With the emergence of deconstruction, however, these long-held beliefs were challenged by **poststructuralism**, a new basis for understanding and guiding humanity (its name denoting that it historically comes after or *post* structuralism). Often, historians, anthropologists, literary theorists, and other scholars use the term **postmodernism** synonymously with deconstruction and poststructuralism, although the term *postmodernism* was coined in the 1930s and has broader historical implications outside the realm of literary theory than do the terms *poststructuralism* or *deconstruction*.

DECONSTRUCTION: HISTORICAL DEVELOPMENT

Beginnings

The term *deconstruction* first emerged on the American literary stage in 1966 when Jacques Derrida (1930–2004), a French philosopher and teacher, read his paper "Structure, Sign, and Play in the Discourse of the Human Sciences" at a Johns Hopkins University symposium. In the essay, Derrida questioned and disputed the metaphysical assumptions held to be true by Western philosophy since the time of Plato and thus inaugurated what many critics believe to be the most intricate and challenging method of textual analysis yet to appear.

Derrida himself, however, would not want deconstruction construed as a critical theory, a school of criticism, a mode or method of literary criticism, or a philosophy. Nowhere in Derrida's writings does he state the encompassing tenets of his critical approach, nor does he ever present a codified body of deconstructive theory or a practical methodology. Although he gives his views in bits and pieces throughout his canon, Derrida believes that he cannot develop a formalized statement of his "rules for reading, interpretation, and writing." Unlike a unified treatise, Derrida claims that his approach to reading and literary analysis is more a "strategic device" than a methodology, more a strategy or approach to literature than a school or theory of criticism. Such theories of criticism, he believes, must identify with a body of knowledge that adherents decree to be true or to contain truth. It is this assertion—that truth or a core of metaphysical ideals actually exists and can be believed, articulated, and supported—that Derrida wishes to dispute and "deconstruct." His device is deconstruction.

Because deconstruction uses previously formulated theories from other schools of criticism, coins many words for its newly established ideas, and challenges beliefs long held in Western culture, many students, teachers, and even critics avoid studying its ideas, fearing the supposed complexity of its analytical apparatus. By organizing deconstruction and its assumptions into three workable areas of study rather than plunging directly into some of its complex terminology, we can begin to grasp this approach to textual analysis.

First, we will briefly examine what Derrida borrows and then amends from structuralism, the starting point for his deconstructive strategy. Then we will investigate the proposed radical changes Derrida makes in Western philosophy and metaphysics. Such changes, Derrida readily admits, literally turn Western metaphysics on its head. Finally, we must master the new terminology, coupled with the new philosophical assumptions and their corresponding methodological approaches to textual analysis, of deconstruction in order to understand and use this approach to interpreting a text.

Derrida's Starting Place: Structuralism

Derrida begins formulating his strategy of reading by critiquing Ferdinand de Saussure's *Course in General Linguistics*. Derrida accepts Saussure's primary belief that language is a system of rules and that these rules govern every aspect of language. In addition, Derrida affirms Saussure's assumption that the linguistic sign (Saussure's linguistic replacement for the word *word*) is both arbitrary and conventional. For example, most languages have different words for the same concept. The English word *man*, for example, is *homme* in French. And in English we know that the meaning of the word *pit* exists not because it possesses some innate acoustic quality but because it differs from *hit*, *wit*, and *lit*. In other words, the linguistic sign is composed of two parts: the **signifier**, which is the spoken or written constituent such as the sound /t/ and the orthographic (written) symbol *t*, and the **signified**, which is the concept signaled by the signifier. Saussure maintains that this relationship between the signifier (e.g., the word *dog*) and the signified (the concept or the reality behind the word *dog*) is arbitrary and conventional. The linguistic sign is thus defined by differences that distinguish it from other signs, not by any innate properties.

Believing that our knowledge of the world is shaped by the language that represents it, Saussure is insistent about the arbitrary relationship between the signifier and the signified. In establishing this principle, he undermines the long-held belief that some natural link exists between the word and the thing it represents. Saussure argues, however, that it is only *after* a signifier and the signified are linked that some kind of relationship exists between these two linguistic elements, although the relationship itself is both arbitrary and conventionalized. Ultimately, meaning in language for Saussure resides in a systematized combination of sounds that rely chiefly on the differences among these signs, not on any innate properties within the signs themselves. It is this concept that meaning in language is determined by the differences among the language signs that Derrida borrows from Saussure as a key building block in the formulation of deconstruction.

Derrida's Interpretation of Saussure's Sign

Derridean deconstruction begins with and emphatically affirms Saussure's decree that language is a system based on differences. Derrida agrees with Saussure that we can know the meaning of signifiers through and because of their relationships and their differences among themselves. Unlike Saussure, Derrida also applies this reasoning to the signified. Like the signifier, the signified can also be known only through its relationships and its differences among other signifieds. Furthermore, declares Derrida, the signified cannot orient or make permanent the meaning of the signifier because the relationship between the signifier and the signified is both arbitrary and conventional. Accordingly, signifieds often function as signifiers. For example, in the sentence *I filled the glass with milk*, the spoken or written word *glass* is a signifier; its signified is the concept of a *container* that can be filled. However, in the sentence *The container was filled with glass*, the spoken or written word *container*, a signified in the previous sentence, is now a signifier, its signified being the concept of an object that can be filled.

DECONSTRUCTIONS' ASSUMPTIONS

Transcendental Signified

Believing that signification is both arbitrary and conventional, Derrida now begins his process of turning Western philosophy on its head: He boldly asserts that the entire history of Western metaphysics from Plato to the present is founded on a classic, fundamental error. The great error is in searching for what Derrida calls a **transcendental signified**, an external point of reference upon which one may build a concept or philosophy. Once found, this transcendental signified would provide ultimate meaning because it would be the origin of origins, reflecting itself and, as Derrida says, providing a "reassuring end to the reference from sign to sign." It would, in essence, guarantee to those who believe in it that they do exist and have meaning. For example, if we posit that *I* or *self* is a transcendental signified, then the concept of *self* becomes the unifying principle upon which I structure my world. Objects, concepts, ideas, or even people only take on meaning in my world if I filter them through my unifying, ultimate signified: *self*.

Unlike other signifieds, the transcendental signified would have to be understood without comparing it with other signifieds or signifiers. In other words, its meaning would originate directly with itself, not differentially or relationally, as does the meaning of all other signifieds or signifiers. Thus, a transcendental signified functions as or provides the *center* of meaning, allowing those who believe in one or more of them to structure their ideas of reality around such centers of truth. By definition, a center of meaning could not subject itself to structural analysis because by so doing, it would lose its place as a transcendental signified to another center. For example, if I declare the concept *self* to be my transcendental signified and then learn that my mind or self is composed of the id, the ego, and the superego, I could no longer hold the *self* or *I* to be my transcendental signified. In the process of discovering the three parts of my conscious and unconscious mind, I have both structurally analyzed and "decentered" *self*, thus negating it as a transcendental signified.

Logocentrism

According to Derrida, Western metaphysics has invented a variety of terms that function as centers: *God, reason, origin, being, essence, truth, humanity, beginning, end*, and *self*, to name a few. Each can operate as a concept that is self-sufficient and self-originating and can serve as a transcendental signified. Derrida names this Western proclivity for desiring a center **logocentrism**, the belief that an ultimate reality or center of truth exists and can serve as the basis for all our thoughts and actions.

Derrida readily admits that we can never totally free ourselves from our logocentric habit of thinking and our inherited concept of the universe. To "decenter" any transcendental signified is to be caught up automatically in the terminology that allows that centering concept to operate. For example, if the concept *self* functions as my center and I then discover my unconscious self, I automatically place in motion what Derrida calls a "binary opposition" (two opposing concepts): the *self* and the *unconscious self*. By decentering and questioning the *self*, I cause the *unconscious self* to become the new center. By questioning the old center, I establish a new one.

Such logocentric thinking, declares Derrida, has its origin in Aristotle's principle of noncontradiction: A thing cannot both have a property and not have a property. Thanks to Aristotle, maintains Derrida, Western metaphysics has developed an "either/or" mentality or logic that inevitably leads to dualistic thinking and to the centering and decentering of transcendental signifieds. The process of logocentric thinking, asserts Derrida, is natural, but problematic, for Western readers.

Binary Oppositions

Because establishing one center of unity automatically means that another is decentered, Derrida concludes that Western metaphysics is based on a system of **binary operations** or conceptual oppositions. For each center, an opposing center (e.g., God/humankind) exists. In addition, Western philosophy decrees that in each of these binary operations or opposing centers, one concept is superior and defines itself by its opposite or inferior center. We know *truth*, for instance, because we know *deception*; we know *good* because we know *bad*. Derrida objects to the creation of these hierarchal binaries as the basis for Western metaphysics.

Phonocentrism

Derrida believes that establishing such conceptually-based binary oppositions as the basis for believing what is really real (one's world view) is problematic at best. He therefore wishes to dismantle or deconstruct the structure such binary operations have created. Derrida asserts that the binary oppositions on which Western metaphysics has been constructed since the time of Plato are structured so that one element will always be **privileged** (be in a superior position) and the other **unprivileged** (in an inferior position). In this way of thinking, the first or top elements of the pairs in the following list of binary oppositions are privileged: man/woman, human/animal, soul/body, good/bad. Key for Derrida is his assertion that Western thought has long privileged speech over writing. This privileging of speech over writing Derrida calls **phonocentrism**.

In placing speech in the privileged position, phonocentrism treats writing as inferior. We value, says Derrida, a speaker's words more than the speaker's writing because words imply presence. Through the vehicle of spoken words, we supposedly learn directly what a speaker is trying to say. From this point of view, writing becomes a mere copy of speech, an attempt to capture the idea that was once spoken. Whereas speech implies presence, writing signifies absence, thereby placing into action another binary opposition: presence/absence.

Since phonocentrism is based on the assumption that speech conveys the meaning or direct ideas of a speaker better than writing (a mere copy of speech), phonocentrism assumes a logocentric way of thinking, that the self is the center of meaning and can best ascertain ideas directly from other selves through spoken words. Through speaking, the self declares its presence, its significance, and its being or existence.

Metaphysics of Presence

Accordingly, Derrida coins the phrase **metaphysics of presence** to encompass those ideas such as logocentrism, phonocentrism, the operation of binary oppositions, and other notions that Western thought posits in its conceptions of language and metaphysics. His objective is to demonstrate the shaky foundations upon which such beliefs have been established. By deconstructing the basic premises of metaphysics of presence, Derrida believes he provides a strategy for reading that opens up a variety of new interpretations heretofore unseen by those who are bound by the restraints of Western thought.

METHODOLOGY

Acknowledging Binary Operations in Western Thought

The first stage in a deconstructive reading is to recognize the existence and the operation of binary oppositions in our thinking. According to Derrida, one of the most "violent hierarchies" derived from Platonic and Aristotelian thought is speech/writing, with speech being privileged. Consequently, speech is awarded presence, and writing is equated with absence. Because it is the inferior of the two, writing becomes simply the symbols of speech, a secondhand representation of ideas.

Once any of these hierarchies is recognized and acknowledged, Derrida proposes that we can readily reverse its elements. Such a reversal is possible because truth is ever elusive; we can always decenter the center if any is found. By reversing the hierarchy, Derrida does not wish to merely substitute one hierarchy for another and involve himself in a negative mode. When the hierarchy is reversed, says Derrida, we will be able to examine the values and beliefs that give rise to both the original hierarchy and the newly created one. When Derrida examines each value or belief in the hierarchy, he is putting these elements under a process he calls **erasure**—he is assuming, for the moment, that each of the signifiers is clear and definitive. He realizes, however, that he is involving himself in a reading strategy because each value or belief is, according to Derrida, absent of any definitive meaning. Such an examination will reveal how the meaning of terms arises from the differences between them.

Arche-writing

In *Of Grammatology* (1967/1974), Derrida spends much time explaining why the speech/writing hierarchy can and must be reversed. **Grammatology** is Derrida's term for the science of writing and his investigation of the origin of language itself. In short, he argues for a redefinition of the term *writing* that will allow him to assert that writing is actually a precondition for and prior to speech. According to Derrida's metaphysical reasoning, language then becomes a special kind of writing, which he calls **arche-writing** or **archi-écriture**.

Using traditional Western metaphysics that is grounded in phonocentricism, Derrida begins his reversal of the speech/writing hierarchy by noting that both language and writing share common characteristics. Both, for example, involve an encoding or inscription. In writing, this coding is obvious because the written symbols represent various phonemes. In language or speech, a similar encoding exists. As Saussure has already shown, an arbitrary relationship exists between the signifier and the signified (between the spoken word *cat* and the concept of cat itself). There is, then, no innate relationship between the spoken word and the concept, object, or idea it represents. Nevertheless, as soon as a signifier and a signified join to form a sign, some kind of relationship then exists between these components of the sign. For example, some kind of inscription or encoding has taken place between the spoken word *cat* (the signifier) and its concept (the signified).

For Derrida, both writing and language are means of signification, and each can be considered a signifying system. Traditional Western metaphysics and Saussurean linguistics equate speech (language) with presence because speech is accompanied by the presence of a speaker. The presence of the speaker necessarily links sound and sense and therefore leads to understanding—one usually comprehends the spoken word. Writing, on the other hand, assumes an absence of a speaker. Such absence can produce misunderstanding because writing is a depersonalized medium that separates the actual utterance of the speaker and his or her audience. This absence can lead to misunderstanding of the signifying system.

All the more reason, Derrida asserts, that we broaden our understanding of writing. Writing, he declares, cannot be reduced to letters or other symbols inscribed on a page. Rather, writing is directly related to what Saussure believed to be the basic element of language: difference. We know one phoneme or one word because each is different from another, and we know that there is no innate relationship between a signifier and its signified. The phoneme /b/, for example, could have easily become the symbol for the phoneme /d/, just as the coined word *bodt* could have become the English word *ball*. It is this free play or "undecidability" in any system of communication that Derrida calls writing. The quality of play with the various elements of signification in any system of communication eludes a speaker's awareness when using language because the speaker falsely assumes a position of supposed master of his or her speech.

By equating writing with the free play or the element of undecidability at the center of all systems of communication, Derrida declares that writing actually governs language, thereby negating the speech/writing hierarchy of Western metaphysics. Writing now becomes privileged and speech unprivileged because speech is a kind of writing called arche-writing.

Derrida then challenges Western philosophy's concept that human consciousness gives birth to language. Without language (or arche-writing), argues Derrida, there can be no consciousness because consciousness presupposes language. Through arche-writing, we impose human consciousness upon the world.

Supplementation

The relationship between any binary hierarchy, however, is always unstable and problematic. It is not Derrida's purpose simply to reverse all binary oppositions that exist in Western thought; rather he wants to show the fragile basis for the establishment of such hierarchies and the possibility of inverting these hierarchies to gain new insights into language and life. Derrida uses the term **supplement** to refer to the unstable relationship between elements in a binary operation. For example, in the speech/writing opposition, writing supplements speech and actually takes the place of speech (arche-writing). **Supplementation** exists in all binary oppositions. In the truth/deception hierarchy, for example, Western thought would assert the supremacy of truth over deception, attributing to deception a mere supplementary role. The logocentric way of thinking asserts the purity of truth over deception. Upon examination, deception more frequently than not contains at least some truth, and who is to say, asks Derrida, when truth has been spoken, achieved, or even conceived? Purity of truth may simply not exist. In all human activity, then, supplementation operates.

Différance

By realizing that supplementation operates in all binary operations of Western metaphysics and by inverting the privileged and unprivileged elements, Derrida begins to develop his reading strategy of deconstruction. After he "turns Western metaphysics on its head," he asserts his answer to logocentrism and other Western elements by coining a new word and concept: **différance**. The word itself is derived from the French word *différer*, meaning "to defer, postpone, or delay," and "to differ, to be different from." Derrida deliberately coins his word to be ambiguous, taking on both meanings simultaneously. And in French, the word is a pun because it exists only in writing. In speech, there is no way to tell the difference between the French word *différence* and Derrida's coined word *différance*.

Understanding what Derrida means by différance is one of the basic keys to understanding deconstruction. Basically, *différance* is Derrida's "What if?" question. What if no transcendental signified exists? What if there is no presence in whom we can find ultimate truth? What if all our knowledge does not arise from self-identity? What if there is no essence, being, or inherently unifying element in the universe? What then?

The presence of such a transcendental signified would immediately establish the binary operation presence/absence. Because Western metaphysics holds that presence is supreme or privileged and absence unprivileged, Derrida suggests that we temporarily reverse this hierarchy, making it now absence/presence. With such a reversal, we can no longer posit a transcendental signified. No longer is there an absolute standard or coherent unity from which knowledge proceeds and develops. All human knowledge and all self-identity must now spring from difference, not sameness; from absence, not presence.

When a reversal of this pivotal binary operation occurs, two dramatic results follow: First, human knowledge becomes referential—that is, we can only know something because it differs from some other bit of knowledge, not because we can compare this knowledge to any absolute or coherent unity (a transcendental signified). Human knowledge must now be based on difference. We know something because it differs from something else to which it is related. By the reversal, nothing can be studied or learned in isolation because all knowledge becomes context related. Second, we must also forgo closure—because no transcendental signified exists, all interpretations concerning life, self-identity, and knowledge are possible, probable, and legitimate.

But what is the significance of *différance* when reading texts? If we, like Derrida, assert that *différance* operates in language and therefore also in writing (Derrida sometimes equates *différance* and arche-writing), what are the implications for textual analysis? The most obvious answer is that texts lack presence. As soon as we do away with the transcendental signified and reverse the presence/absence binary operation, texts can no longer have presence: In isolation, texts cannot possess meaning. Because all meaning and knowledge are now based on differences, no text can simply mean one thing. Texts become intertextual. The meaning of a text cannot be ascertained by examining only that particular text; instead, a text's meaning *evolves* from that derived from the interrelatedness of one text to an interrelatedness of many texts. Like language itself, texts are caught in a dynamic, context-related interchange. Never can we state a text's definitive meaning, for it has no "one" correct or definitive interpretation. No longer can we declare one interpretation to be right and another wrong, for meaning in a text is always illusive, dynamic, and transitory.

The search, then, for the text's "correct" meaning or the author's so-called intentions becomes meaningless. Since meaning is derived from differences in a dynamic, context-related, ongoing process, all texts have multiple meanings or interpretations. If we assert, as does Derrida, that no transcendental signified exists, then there can exist no absolute or pure meaning conveyed supposedly by authorial intent or professorial dictates. Meaning evolves as we, the readers, interact with the text, with both the readers and the text providing social and cultural context.

DECONSTRUCTIVE SUPPOSITIONS FOR TEXTUAL ANALYSIS

A deconstructor begins textual analysis by assuming that a text has multiple interpretations and that it allows itself to be reread and thus reinterpreted countless times. Denying the New Critical stance that a text possesses a special ontological status and has one and only one correct interpretation, deconstructors assert that the great joy of textual analysis resides in discovering new interpretations each time a text is read and reread. Ultimately, a text's meaning is undecidable because each reading or rereading can elicit different interpretations.

When beginning the interpretative process, deconstructors seek to override their own logocentric and inherited ways of viewing a text. Such revolutionary thinking decrees that they find the binary oppositions at work in the text itself. These binary oppositions, they believe, represent established and accepted ideologies that more frequently than not posit the existence of transcendental signifieds. These binary operations, then, restrict meaning because they already assume a fixed interpretation of reality. They assume, for instance, the existence of truth and falsehood, reason and insanity, good and bad. Realizing that these hierarchies presuppose a fixed and a biased way of viewing the world, deconstructors search for the binary oppositions operating in the text and reverse them. By reviewing these hierarchies, deconstructors wish to challenge the fixed views assumed by such hierarchies and the values associated with such rigid beliefs.

The technique of identifying the binary operations that exist in a text allows deconstructors to expose the preconceived assumptions on which most of us base our interpretations. We all, for example, declare some activity, being, or object to be good or bad, valuable or worthless, significant or insignificant. These kinds of values or ideas automatically operate when we write or read any text. In the reversal of hierarchies that form the basis of our interpretations, deconstructors wish to free us from the constraints of our prejudiced beliefs. Such freedom, they hope, will allow us to see a text from exciting new perspectives that we have never before recognized.

These various perspectives cannot be simultaneously perceived by the reader or even the writer of a text. In Nathaniel Hawthorne's "Young Goodman Brown," for example, many readers believe that the 50-year-old character who shepherds Goodman Brown through his night's visit in the forest is Satan and therefore necessarily an evil character. Brown's own interpretation of this character seems to support this view. According to deconstructionist ideas, at least two binary operations are at work here: good/evil and God/Satan. But what if we reverse these hierarchies? Then the sceptral figure may not be Satan and therefore may not be evil! Such a new perspective will dramatically change our interpretation of the text.

Deconstructors say that we cannot simultaneously see both of these perspectives in the story. To discover where the new hierarchy Satan/God or evil/good will lead us in our interpretation, we must suspend our first interpretation. We do not, however, forget it because it is locked in our minds. For the time being, we simply shift our allegiance to another perspective.

The process of oscillating between interpretations, levels, or perspectives allows us to see the impossibility of ever choosing a correct interpretation because meaning is an ongoing activity that is always in progress, always based upon *différance*. By asking what will happen if we reverse the hierarchies that frame our preconceived ways of thinking, we open ourselves to a never-ending process of interpretation, one that decrees that no hierarchy or binary operation is right and no other is wrong.

Deconstruction: A New Reading Strategy

Deconstructors do not want, then, to set up a new philosophy, a new literary theory of analysis, or a new school of literary criticism. Instead, they present a new reading strategy, one that allows us to make choices concerning the various levels of interpretation we see operating in a text. All levels, they maintain, have validity. Deconstructors also believe that their approach to reading frees the reader from ideological allegiances that restrict the comprehension of meaning in a text.

Because meaning, they believe, emerges through interpretation, even the author does not control a text's interpretation. Although writers may have clearly stated intentions concerning their texts, such statements should and must be given little credence. Like language itself, texts have no outside referents or transcendental signifieds. What an author thinks he or she says or means in a text may be quite different from what is actually written. Deconstructors therefore look for places in the text where the author **misspeaks** or loses control of language and says what was supposedly not meant to be said. These slips of language often occur in questions, figurative language, and strong declarations. For example, suppose we read the following words: "Important Seniors Meeting." Although the author thinks that readers will interpret these words to mean that it is important that all seniors be present at this particular meeting, the author may have misspoken; these words can actually mean that only important seniors should attend this meeting. By examining such slips and the binary operations that govern them, deconstructors are able to demonstrate the **undecidability** of a text's meaning.

At first glance, a deconstructionist reading strategy may appear to be linear—that is, having a clearly delineated beginning, middle, and end. If this is so, then to apply this strategy to a text, we must do the following:

- Discover the binary operations that govern a text.
- Comment on the values, concepts, and ideas beyond these operations.
- Reverse these present binary operations.
- Dismantle previously held worldviews.
- Accept the possibility of various perspectives or levels of meaning in a text based on the new binary inversions.
- Allow meaning of the text to be undecidable.

Although all these elements do operate in a deconstructionist reading, they may not operate in this exact sequence. Since we all tend toward logocentrism when reading, we may not note some logocentric binary operations functioning in the text until we have reversed some other obvious binary oppositions and are interpreting the text on several levels. In addition, we must never declare such a reading to be completed or finished since the process of meaning is ongoing, never allowing us to pledge allegiance to any one view.

Such a reading strategy disturbs most readers and critics because it is not a neat, completed package, whereby if we follow steps A through Z, we arrive at *the* reading of the text. Because texts have no external referents, their meanings depend on the close interaction of the text, the reader, and social and cultural elements, as does every reading or interpretative process. Denying the organic unity of a text, deconstructors declare the free play of language in a text. Language, they assert, is reflexive, not mimetic. We can therefore never stop finding meaning in a text, whether we have read it once or a hundred times.

Overall, deconstruction solicits an ongoing relationship between the interpreter (the critic) and the text. By examining the text alone, deconstructors hope to ask a set of questions that will continually challenge the ideological positions of power and authority that dominate literary criticism. Furthermore, in the process of discovering meaning in a text, deconstructors declare that criticism of a text is just as valuable as the text being read, thereby inverting the text/criticism hierarchy.

American Deconstructors

After Derrida's introduction of deconstruction to his American audience in 1966, the philosopher found several sympathetic listeners who soon became loyal adherents and defenders of his new reading strategy: notably, the Romantic scholar Paul de Man (*Blindness and Insight*, 1971), the rhetorical deconstructor Hayden White (*Tropics of Discourse*, 1978), the sometimes terse metaphysical deconstructor Geoffrey Hartman (*Criticism in the Wilderness*, 1980), the strong voice of Barbara Johnson (*The Critical Difference*, 1980), and the phenomenological critic turned deconstructor J. Hillis Miller (*Fiction and Repetition: Seven English Novels*, 1982). These critics assured that deconstruction would have a voice and an established place in American literary theory and criticism. Although the voices of other poststructural theories, such as Cultural Poetics and Postcolonialism, now clamor to be heard, deconstruction's philosophical assumptions and practical reading strategies form the basis of many postmodern literary practices.

QUESTIONS FOR ANALYSIS

Structuralism

When examining any text through the lens of structuralism, ask yourself the following questions:

- What are the tensions—the binary oppositions—highlighted in the text?
- Is each of these tensions minor or major ones?
- What do you believe is the major or pivotal tension in the work?

- Can you explain the intertextuality of all the discovered binaries?
- Does this work contain any mythemes? If so, what are they, and how do they help you discover the text's structure?

The following questions apply your understanding of structuralism:

- What are the various binary oppositions or operations that operate in Edgar Allan Poe's short story "Ligiea"? Which of these binaries control the story's structure? What is the chief binary?
- What mythemes are evident in Poe's "Ligiea"? How do these mythemes show the intertextuality of this particular text with other literary texts you have read?
- How do the various semantic features contained in a text of your choosing directly relate to the codes, signs, or binary oppositions you find in the text?
- Using a text of your choice, apply at least three different methods of structuralism to arrive at how the text achieves meaning. In the final analysis, is there a difference among the three methodologies in how the text achieves its meaning?
- Choose another sign system—sports, music, classroom etiquette—and explain the codes that generate meaning.

Deconstruction

When examining any text through the lens of deconstruction theory and practice, ask yourself the following questions:

- What are the binary operations or oppositions that govern the text?
- What ideas, concepts, and values are being established by these binaries?
- By reversing the elements in each of the binaries, can you challenge the previously held value system posited by the original binary?
- After reversing one or more binaries in a given text, can you dismantle your original interpretation of that text?
- Can you cite three different interpretations for a text of your choosing by flipping a series of three major binaries contained in that text?

The following questions apply your understanding of deconstruction theory:

- Write an interpretation for any one of the aesthetic texts located at the back of this text. After you have completed your interpretation, cite the binary operations that function both within your chosen text and within your thinking to allow you to arrive at your perspective.
- Using the same text and interpretation you used for question one, reverse one of the binary operations and reinterpret the text. When you are finished, reverse two additional binaries and reinterpret the story. What differences exist between the two interpretations?
- Using a poem of your choice, demonstrate either how the author misspeaks or where the text involves itself in paradox, sometimes called **aporia**. Be specific. Be able to point to lines, figurative speech, or imaginative language to support your statements.

- Using the poem you read for the above exercise, cite at least four dramatically different interpretations, all based on a deconstructive reading.

- Reread the student-generated essay found at the end of Chapter 4, "Reader-Oriented Criticism." What elements of the story does the author simply ignore or dismiss? Consider how Derrida's concept of supplementation is operating in this critic's analysis.

- Using the structuralist student essay found at the end of this chapter, state the binary operations that control the critic's interpretation of the text. From these binaries, cite the ideological positions of the critic and note what elements in the story he must ignore to arrive at his conclusions. In other words, deconstruct the structuralist essay.

- Read the student essay located at the end of Chapter 6 based on Edgar Allan Poe's short story "Ligeia." Using the principles of Derrida and deconstruction theory, write an essay in which you deconstruct this student essay.

CRITIQUES AND RESPONSES

Structuralism

By the mid-1960s, structuralism became a dominant theory in both the United States and Europe. Borrowing and blending elements of Ferdinand de Saussure's linguistics, the textual concerns of Russian Formalism, the psychoanalysis of both Sigmund Freud and Jacques Lacan, the epistemological concerns of Michel Foucault, the Marxist concerns of the French theorist Louis Althusser, and the multiple ideas of the narratologists, structuralism seemingly embraced all disciplines and offered a unifying approach not only to literary theory but also to life itself. Applying its "objective" and "scientific" analyses to texts and culture, it provided a new lens through which to see the world, a lens that promised to demystify literature and life. Its basic premise—that no element, situation, or text has significance in isolation but must be first integrated and then analyzed by examining the overall structure of which it is a part—asserts that all life, including literary texts, is constructed—that is, based on a series of interrelated systems. These systems and the study of them—rather than individual actions or an isolated text—are ultimately important.

Overall, structuralism is less important today than it was in the 1960s. Other theories that take into account the cultural significance of both people and texts have outpaced structuralism for several reasons. First, structuralism's greatest strength—its study of the systems or codes that shape meaning—is also its greatest weakness. In highlighting the various systems of meaning, structuralism deemphasizes personhood and individual texts. Critics argue that structuralism is thus deterministic (favoring systems over events or an individual) and is ahistorical. It does not account for human individuality or for any independent acts, nor does it address the dynamic aspects of culture.

Individual texts, assert structuralism's critics, do matter. The changing faces of culture that are simultaneously reflected in isolated texts also matter. Texts, like people, are at times illogical, breaking from tradition and systems of belief.

With the advent of postmodernism and its emphases on the incredulity of the grand metanarratives and the slippery nature of language, structuralism, with its logical, objective study of systems, structure, and language, began to lose popularity. Although some structuralists—particularly the narratologists—continue to contribute to literary theory and criticism, literary theories grounded in the philosophy and methodology of postmodernism currently receive prime attention.

Deconstruction

Rushing onto the literary stage in the latter half of the 1960s, deconstruction theory entered academic and cultural studies at a time when questioning the status quo was both academically and culturally acceptable, becoming, as some would argue, the norm. The first word of Derrida's inauguration speech for deconstruction's introduction in America ("Structure, Sign, and Play in the Discourse of the Human Sciences" presented at Johns Hopkins University in 1966) was "perhaps," a word that successfully encapsulates the basic idea underlying deconstruction theory. Perhaps, said Derrida, we cannot make either positive or negative definitive statements. Disavowing the existence of a transcendental signified, deconstruction questioned Western humanity's proclivity toward logocentrism and its valuing of other elements and ideas encompassed by Derrida's concept of metaphysics of presence. Derrida dared to ask the "What if?" question: What if no transcendental signified exists? What if there is no such entity as objective truth? What if, indeed, all is based on difference and différance? And what if language is arbitrary and differential?

With the emergence of deconstruction theory and postmodernism began a questioning of the grand metanarratives upon which humanity had previously structured its existence. All was now open to question. The exact meaning of a text could never be definitively stated because texts have multiple meanings and language itself is elusive and slippery. Indeed, all writers misspeak, often revealing not what they thought they said, but almost what they were afraid to say. And all interpretation is really a form of play, with each participant handling slippery texts whose meanings are often illusive.

Although some critics thought Derrida's philosophy and literary theory would destroy the very foundations upon which Western philosophy rests, deconstruction theory did not do so. Instead, deconstruction theory provides an energetic and rigorous reading of texts, not only by questioning all previous readings but also by questioning the nature of reading itself. Some of its critics, however, point out both deconstruction and postmodernism's seemingly internal inconsistencies. By questioning the validity of the grand metanarratives (or positing an incredulity toward such narratives), deconstruction is itself essentially establishing a metanarrative, one based on incredulity and doubt. In questioning the validity and existence of objective truth, it creates its own yardstick by which its own concept of truth can be measured. In advocating its antitheoretical position, it thereby establishes one of its own and involves itself in circular reasoning. And while advocating for intertextuality, it more frequently than not treats texts in isolation.

Overall, deconstruction's vocabulary and methodology have been appropriated by other disciplines and continue to elicit debate among literary theorists and educators alike. Some of its adherents have brought deconstruction's analysis into politics and cultural events and concerns. After almost four decades of being an active participant on the literary stage, deconstruction theory remains a significant force in literary theory and practice.

FURTHER READING

Structuralism

Barthes, Roland. *Critical Essays*. Howard, Richard (trans). Evanston, IL: Northwestern University Press, 1972.

———. *Mythologies*. Lavers, Annette (trans). New York: Hill and Wang, 1972.

Culler, Jonathan. *Structuralist Poetics: Structuralism, Linguistics, and the Study of Literature*, 2nd ed. New York: Routledge, 1990.

Genette, Gerard. *Narrative Discourse: An Essay in Method*. Lewin, Jane (trans). Ithaca, NY: Cornell University Press, 1983.

Hawkes, Terence. *Structuralism and Semiotics*, 2nd ed. New York: Routledge, 2003.

Jakobson, Roman. Linguistics and poetics. In *Style in Language*. Thomas Sebeok. Cambridge: MIT Press, 1960:350–77.

Jameson, Fredric. *The Prison House of Language: A Critical Account of Structuralism and Russian Formalism*. Princeton: Princeton University Press, 1975.

Lévi-Strauss, Claude. *Structural Anthropology*. Jacobson, Claire and Schoepf, Brooke (trans). New York: Basic Books, 2000.

Propp, Vladimir. *The Morphology of the Folktale*. Scott, Laurence (trans). Austin, TX: University of Texas Press, 1968.

Saussure, Ferdinand de. *Course in General Linguistics*. New York: Open Court, 1986.

Scholes, Robert. *Semiotics and Interpretation*. New Haven, CT: Yale University Press, 1982.

———. *Structuralism in Literature: An Introduction*. New Haven, CT: Yale University Press, 1974.

Todorov, Tzvetan. *The Fantastic: A Structural Approach to a Literary Genre*. Howard, Richard (trans). Ithaca, NY: Cornell University Press, 1977.

Deconstruction

Atkins, G. Douglas. *Reading Deconstruction: Deconstructive Reading*. Lexington, KY: University Press of Kentucky, 1983.

Bloom, Harold. *A Map of Misreading*. New York: Oxford University Press, 1975.

Butler, Christopher. *Postmodernism: A Very Short Introduction*. A Very Short Introduction Series. New York: Oxford University Press, 2002.

Cantor, Norman, F. *Twentieth Century Culture: Modernism to Deconstruction*. New York: Peter Lang, 1988.

Caputo, John D. The good news about alterity: Derrida and theology. *Faith and Philosophy* 10.4(Oct 1993):453–70.

Culler, Jonathan. *On Deconstruction: Theory and Criticism after Structuralism*. Ithaca, NY: Cornell University Press, 1982.

de Man, Paul. *Blindness and Insight: Essays in the Rhetoric of Contemporary Criticism*. New York: Oxford University Press, 1971.

———. *The Rhetoric of Romanticism*. New York: Columbia University Press, 1984.

Derrida, Jacques. "Structure, sign, and play in the discourse of the human sciences." In *Writing and Différence*. Bass, Alan (trans). Chicago: University of Chicago Press, 1978.

———. "The Time is Out of Joint." *Deconstruction Is? In America*. Haverkamp, Anslem (trans). New York: New York University Press, 1995:14–38.

Ellis, John M. *Against Deconstruction*. Princeton, NJ: Princeton University Press, 1989.

Gasche, Rodolphe. Deconstruction as criticism. *Glyph Textual Studies* 6(1979):177–215.

Hartman, Geoffrey. *Saving the Text: Literature/Derrida/Philosophy*. Baltimore: Johns Hopkins University Press, 1981.

Johnson, Barbara. *The Critical Difference: Essays in the Contemporary Rhetoric of Reading*. Baltimore: Johns Hopkins University Press, 1980.

Johnson, Christopher. *Derrida: The Scene of Writing*. New York: Routledge, 1999.

Miller, J. Hillis. *Tropes, Parables, and Performatives: Essays on Twentieth-Century Literature*. Hemel Hempstead, UK: Harvester Wheatsheaf, 1990.

Norris, Christopher. *Deconstruction: Theory and Practice*. London: Methuen, 1982.

———. *The Deconstructive Turn: Essays in the Rhetoric of Philosophy*. London: Methuen, 1983.

Rajnath, ed. *Deconstruction: A Critique*. London: Macmillan, 1989.

WEB SITES FOR EXPLORATION

www.philospher.org.uk/poststr.htm
An overview of poststructuralism, including a discussion of postmodernism, Michel Foucault's *Genealogy of Knowledge*, and Jacques Derrida and deconstruction

http://www.indiana.edu/~reading/ieo/digests/d104.html
Poststructuralism in theory and practice in the English classroom; includes a good discussion of the beginnings of poststructuralism and a working definition

http://www.brocku.ca/english/courses/4F70/struct.html
A review of the basic elements of structuralism and its application to literary theory; also includes a summary of Gerard Genette's "Structuralism and Literary Criticism"

http://www.colorado.edu/English/ENGL2012Klages/1derrida.html
A comparative essay of structuralism and poststructuralism

http://www.colorado.edu/English/ENGL2012Klages/saussure.html
A solid essay delineating the elements of structuralism and Saussure

http://www.as.ua.edu/ant/Faculty/murphy/436/struct.htm
An excellent structuralist website; includes structuralism's premises, key works, leading figures, methodologies, criticisms, and sources

http://www.brocku.ca/english/courses/4F70/deconstruction.html
Some key assumptions made by Derrida

http://www.hydra.umn.edu/derrida/content.html
An excellent overview of key links for deconstruction on the Internet

http://130.179.92.25/Arnason_DE/Derrida.html
A solid essay on Derrida and deconstruction

http://www.arts.gla.ac.uk/SESLL/EngLit/ugrad/hons/theory/Ten%20Ways.htm
Ten ways of thinking about deconstruction

Sample Essays

The following two essays highlight the theoretical assumptions and practical methodologies of structuralism (essay I) and deconstruction (essay II). In the structuralist essay titled "A Disconnect of Appearance and Reality: The Binaries of 'Rappaccini's Daughter,'" the student author of the essay specifically chose Nathaniel Hawthorne's short story "Rappaccini's Daughter" to analysis from a structuralist perspective. Being an American Romantic writer, Hawthorne sees the interconnectedness of reality and humanity. In addition, without question, he posits the intertextuality of his tales, qualities that a structuralist would admire. After noting how Hawthorne uses binaries to structure his short story "Rappaccini's Daughter," the student author of this essay believes it will become clearer to all readers how Hawthorne uses some of these same binaries to structure his other tales.

After reading the structuralist essay, be able to answer each of the following questions:

• Is this a successfully written structuralist essay? To answer this question, review the sections on structuralism's assumptions and methodology in this chapter. What assumptions and practices does this student author use within his essay?

- What do you perceive to be the strengths of this essay? What are its weaknesses? Be specific in your answers, pointing out concrete examples.

In the student essay using deconstruction theory and practice, "Choosing Between Two Roads: Deconstructing 'The Road Not Taken,'" the student author believed it would be profitable and fun to deconstruct one of the most famous Frost poems so that the readers could enjoy this familiar text from a new perspective. After reading this celebration of freeplay within a text, ask yourself the following questions:

- Is this a successfully written essay using the theory and practice of deconstruction? Before you answer this question, review the sections on assumptions and methodology of deconstruction in this chapter.
- What do you perceive to be the strengths of this essay? Its weaknesses? Be specific in your answers, pointing out concrete examples from the student's essay.

Student Essay I (Structuralist Approach)

A Disconnect of Appearance and Reality: The Binaries of "Rappaccini's Daughter"[1]

Nathaniel Hawthorne's "Rappaccini's Daughter" is the story of two lovers caught in the machinations of a pair of contending doctors. Throughout the tale, Hawthorne questions the discrepancy between the characters' inner nature and outward appearance through several key binary oppositions: youth/old age, naïveté/experience, physical/spiritual, light/dark, good/evil, isolation/inclusion, appearance/reality, and interior worlds/exterior worlds. Of these binaries, three—natural/artificial, isolation/inclusion, and appearance/reality—form the crux of the story, with one—appearance/reality—being the all-encompassing binary and overarching metaphor.

At the beginning of the story, Giovanni, the youthful protagonist, looks down from his apartment window into the garden of his neighbor, Dr. Rappaccini, the Faustian scholar. As Giovanni examines this interior world from the safety of his window, he observes Rappaccini within the garden interacting with the plants as if they were "savage beasts, or deadly snakes or evil spirits." Unlike her cautious father, Beatrice interacts with the plants with unafraid affection. The characters' differing reactions introduce the minor binary of caution/ease which in turn leads to the first major binary of the story: natural/artificial. This controlling binary becomes more obvious when Giovanni enters the garden, leaving behind the outer world

[1]Reprinted by permission of Matthew G. Hepler.

and entering one governed by Rappaccini. Because Giovanni enters the garden alone, he first examines the vegetation, describing it as "fierce, passionate, and even unnatural . . . the adultery of various vegetable species." This description contrasts with his previous hope that the garden in the midst of the city would serve "as a symbolic language to keep him in communication with Nature." Instead of furthering Giovanni's communion with Nature, the opposite actually occurs. The plants are the creation of Rappaccini's scientific experimentations, the tampering and crossbreeding of natural flowers. In essence, this vegetation is an artificial construct which seems beautiful and exotic from afar, but upon closer observation is unnatural and disturbing. Furthermore, the plants exude deadly poisons that have affected and infiltrated Beatrice, causing her to become a deadly poison herself. Beatrice mirrors the flowers, which look beautiful and natural from afar, but actually repel when Giovanni looks closer. The beauty which attracts also conceals her father's poison, killing a lizard, several flowers, and flying insects that come into her presence.

The second controlling binary of the tale stems from the natural/artificial binary and centers on the figure of Rappaccini himself. In Giovanni's conversation with Dr. Baglioni, the counterpart of Dr. Rappaccini, Rappaccini is described as willing to sacrifice anything "for the sake of adding so much as a grain of mustard seed to the great heap of his accumulated knowledge." This binary of isolation/inclusion helps structure much of the Hawthorne canon, most evidently in the story of Ethan Brand who commits the Unpardonable Sin by severing all ties with humanity in order to further his own pursuit of knowledge, breaking his link in "the magnetic chain of humanity." The opposition predominantly manifests itself in the relationship between Beatrice and Rappaccini. Though Giovanni and Baglioni see Rappaccini outside his garden walking through the streets of the city, the practices by which he experiments lack regard for human life, even his own. Rappaccini tyrannically controls Beatrice, confining her within their house and the garden, allowing her no other human interaction until Giovanni is allowed into the garden by the Dame Lisabetta, who smiles a disfiguring smile through the whole episode. When the reader remembers that laughter and smiling are often signifiers in the Hawthorne canon for evil, the episode takes on a darker shroud, evidence that Rappaccini is manipulating events to sever Giovanni from humanity even as he had severed Beatrice. Later in the story when Giovanni learns that he too has become a deadly poison through his interactions with Beatrice, Rappaccini declares of the two lovers, "He now stands apart from common men, as thou dost, daughter of my pride and triumph, from ordinary women." Because Giovanni and Beatrice's poisonous natures separate them from the world, Rappaccini declares his experiment a success. In his glorification of their physical separation, Rappaccini demonstrates that he too is isolated, though his isolation is more profound than that he had inflicted; it is of a spiritual rather than a physical nature. It is also self-inflicted rather than inflicted by an outside agent.

When viewed together, the natural/artificial and isolation/inclusion binaries function integrally in the story's plot and are interconnected with several minor binaries that help structure the text: interior/exterior worlds and physical/spiritual binaries, among others. The binary of appearance/ reality, however, forms the overarching thematic polarity that shapes this entire network of binaries. From the beginning, Hawthorne uses language which introduces doubt into the narrative: the plants of the garden "seemed" to have been subject to great care, the light of the central flower "seemed" enough to illuminate the whole garden, Rappaccini masked his mouth "as if" the flowers concealed a deadly malice. When being especially concerned with things viewed from Giovanni's external world, the narrator rarely makes definitive statements but hedges descriptions in uncertainty and distrust.

Similarly, the characters' physical countenances are contradictory to their actions and inward character, as if they wear their faces as masks. The narrator's description of Dr. Rappaccini paints him as "tall, emaciated, sallow, and sickly looking"; these adjectives elicit a response of dislike and indicate an evil, sickened creature. Later, the narrator claims that his visage was marked by such a "piercing and active intellect that an observer might easily have overlooked the merely physical attributes and seen only this wonderful energy." The narrator then describes Rappaccini's foil, Baglioni, in far different terms: "of elderly personage, apparently of genial nature and habits that might almost be called jovial." The astute reader, however, will notice that Baglioni's description contains carefully inserted qualifiers— *apparently* and *might almost be called*—which produce the same distrust as evidenced earlier. Though Baglioni seems to have Giovanni's best interests in view, the character's power play against Rappaccini ultimately results in the death of Beatrice. Finally, the narrator describes the character of Beatrice in lofty terms: her beauty "so brilliant, so vivid . . . that she glowed amid the sunlight, and . . . positively illuminated the more shadowy intervals." Over and again, she is described as the archetypal woman, the one all men would pursue. Yet, her beauty hides her tragic flaw: that by the manipulations of her father she is condemned to an almost solitary existence, her mere presence a deadly poison.

Through the lens of the appearance/reality binary, all the other binaries invert from their usual denotations to unsuspected connotations. For instance, the garden of Rappaccini, while looking fair from a distance, becomes the infernal Eden, playground for evil. Likewise, the youthful beauty of Beatrice becomes a mask for the deadly femme fatale while the benevolent maturity of Baglioni becomes a façade for a manipulative schemer. Instead of the wisdom and knowledge generally associated with old age and the rank of a professor in the academy, the figure of Rappaccini becomes a fallen creature whose quest for knowledge results in depravity. Similarly, the positive signifier, light, becomes negative when emanating from the unnatural vegetation, much like the fires of the Witches' Sabbath in "Young Goodman Brown." Finally, though Rappaccini appears in public while Beatrice remains in solitude, he voluntarily isolates himself through his disregard for humanity while she has no control over the poisons he instilled within her body.

The tale of Rappaccini imparts a basic truth about the nature of reality and humanity's interactions: appearances do not always convey the reality of an object or a person. An apple can look perfect, much like Beatrice, but could be rotten inside or infested with worms. A tree can look healthy, much like Baglioni, yet be rotten in its center and spread its rottenness to others. Hawthorne's use of binaries both consciously and unconsciously conveys his belief that being human necessitates interaction and connection. To be true to reality and humanity is to interact with others while keeping the outward portrayal true to the inward nature; to be false is to fall into the Faustian trap. Though the signifiers used to convey these ideas violate their usual interpretation, the binaries control the story and assist the reader in arriving at this viable interpretation.

MATTHEW G. HEPLER

Student Essay II (Deconstructive Approach)

Choosing Between Two Roads: Deconstructing Robert Frost's "The Road Not Taken"[2]

Robert Frost's poem "The Road Not Taken" tells of a traveler deciding between two roads splitting in the woods and the choice the traveler eventually makes. A conventional interpretation of this text may conclude that the poem is concerned about choices made in life and the importance of choosing the right path. This right path is of the unknown and of experiencing new horizons, for the final lines of the poem state, "I took the one less traveled by, / And that has made all the difference," implying that life has been richer as a result of the traveler's choice. The traveler about whom the poem speaks privileges adventure or the unknown over the familiar or known. The poet, however, ultimately misspeaks, showing that he in fact does not view the unknown as privileged. In addition, the author also privileges fair or fresh over wear and tear, but misspeaks as well, showing that he actually privileges the old over the new. As the text dismantles or deconstructs itself through the reversal of binaries, the freeplay of the text reveals the infinite possibilities within Frost's poem that are indeed off the worn path.

[2]Reprinted by permission of Danielle M. Bowers.

Upon a first reading of the text, several binaries surface: the road taken/the road not taken; traveling/staying; and fair/used. By closely examining these binaries, we note the emergence of a major binary opposition: adventure or the unknown/the familiar and the known. The traveler decides to take the lesser, worn road because of the potential for adventure and excitement. The poet, however, misspeaks in line 15 with the word "doubted." This word implies that although the traveler takes the road "less traveled by," he is skeptical that he is making the right decision. He questions his decision and wonders if he should have taken the other road after all.

The poem also misspeaks in line 16 with the use of the word "sigh." A sigh may be a signal of contentedness, but it may also signal regret, discontentment, and sorrow for having chosen the lesser-worn path. Is the traveler really content with his decision to travel the unknown path? The unknown, he undoubtedly knows, is not always better than the known, for within the unknown lies the potential for danger and heartbreak. Is adventure, then, more desirable than staying on the path that is both known and familiar? At this point the text dismantles the center of embracing the unknown, revealing that the unknown isn't what is desirable after all.

While privileging traveling over staying, the author once again misspeaks in line 12, stating, "In leaves no step had trodden black." By noting the travel/staying binary, one's initial interpretation may be that travel is privileged. In stating that stepping along the paths makes the leaves black, the poet once again misspeaks, and in actuality portrays traveling as undesirable. The word "trodden" means walking, but it also conjures images of imprisonment. This walk is both subjugated and broken. Blackness is the result of destruction—the leaves were perhaps green or golden, but with travel they will become black, destroyed. The poet views taking the unknown path as robbing him of tranquility, perhaps a destruction of the tranquility, peace, and comfort of staying at home and of embracing the goodness of the familiar.

A third privileging occurs in the text: that of fair and fresh over what is worn and old. In line 6, the poet declares that both roads are "fair," but the less traveled road is better for him because it is not as traveled or used (although both are nearly equal). In line 8, the poet misspeaks again when he uses the word "wanted," saying, "Because it was grassy and wanted wear." The word "wanted" implies a need, a desire, or a yearning. If the poet believes that a fresh path—one that has not had much traffic or is new—is a better path to follow, why, then, does he "want" a path with wear? A path with wear is perhaps more desirable for a traveler, for it means that others have traveled the path, and it is potentially safe. A path that has no sign of wear may not or should not be trusted. The persona appears to privilege the fresher path, but in actuality privileges a path with more use, yearning for the comfort a worn path brings. The text thus continues to dismantle itself, allowing for multiple interpretations.

One of the chief images of the poem, the juxtaposition of the two roads—one traveled upon and slightly worn, the other not trodden by any number of travelers—allows for an interesting reversal of binaries and a continued examination of the freeplay of the text. What would happen in interpreting this text if the binary of the two roads were inverted? The worn and traveled upon road then becomes the road the traveler takes, and "the road not taken" literally becomes the road that is not taken by any travelers. Would the traveler have regretted taking the more familiar path? If the poet privileges experience over the unknown, the poem would then be an account of a traveler who briefly pondered taking a risky path, but decided to remain among the safe and familiar. The poem would then be about the importance of following what is stable and comforting, and the difference that such comfort and stability would make in one's life.

"Two roads diverged in a yellow wood" writes the poet. And the traveler takes the "one less traveled by." By noting where the poet misspeaks, we can observe that the traveler regrets his decision. The freeplay of the text and much misspeaking add to the enjoyment of a work that successfully dismantles itself. Frost's poem is indeed a celebration of the seemingly infinite possibilities of interpretation when employing Jacques Derrida's reading strategy of deconstruction.

DANIELLE M. BOWERS

6

PSYCHOANALYTIC CRITICISM

We have not even to risk the adventure alone; for the heroes of all time have gone before us; the labyrinth is thoroughly known; we have only to follow the thread of the heropath.

Joseph Campbell, *The Hero With a Thousand Faces*

Our dreams fascinate, perplex, and often disturb us. Filled with bizarre twists of fate, wild exploits, and highly sexual images, our dreams can bring us pleasure or terrorize us. Sometimes they cause us to question our feelings, contemplate our unspoken desires, and even doubt the nature of reality itself. Do dreams, we wonder, contain any degree of truth? Do they serve any useful function?

The chemist Friedrich August Kekule answers in the affirmative. For years, Kekule investigated the molecular structure of benzene. One night, he saw in a dream a string of atoms shaped like a snake swallowing its tale. Upon awakening, he drew this serpentine figure in his notebook and realized it was the graphic structure of the benzene ring he had been struggling to decipher. When reporting his findings at a scientific meeting in 1890, he stated, "Let us learn to dream, gentlemen, and then we may perhaps find the truth."

Giuseppe Tartini, an Italian violinist of the eighteenth century, similarly discovered the value of dreams. One night, he dreamed the devil came to his bedside and offered to help him finish a rather difficult sonata in exchange for his soul. Tartini agreed, whereupon the devil picked up Tartini's violin and completed the unfinished work. On awakening, Tartini jotted down from memory what he had heard in his dream. Titled *The Devil's Trill Sonata*, this piece is Tartini's best known composition.

Like numerous scientists and composers, many writers have claimed that they, too, have received some of their best ideas from their dreams. Robert Louis Stevenson, for example, maintained that many of his ideas for *Dr. Jekyll and Mr. Hyde* came directly from his nightmares. Similarly, Dante,

Goethe, Blake, Bunyan, and a host of others owed much of their writings, they claimed, to their world of dreams. Still others, such as Poe, DeQuincey, and Coleridge, borrowed from their drug-induced dreams the content of some of their most famous works.

That our dreams and those of others fascinate us cannot be denied. Whether it is their bizarre and often erotic content or their seemingly prophetic powers, dreams cause us to question and explore that part of our minds over which we have ostensibly little control, the unconscious.

Without question, the foremost investigator of the unconscious and its activities is the Vienna neurologist and psychologist Sigmund Freud. Beginning with the publication of *The Interpretation of Dreams* in 1900, Freud lays the foundation for a model of how our minds operate. Hidden from the workings of the conscious mind, the unconscious, he believes, plays a large part in how we act, think, and feel. According to Freud, the best avenue for discovering the content and the activity of the unconscious is through our dreams. In the interaction of the conscious and unconscious working together, argues Freud, we shape both ourselves and our world.

Developing both a body of theory and a practical methodology for his science of the mind, Freud became the leading pioneer of psychoanalysis, a method of treating emotional and psychological disorders. During psychoanalysis, Freud had his patients talk freely in a patient–analyst setting about their early childhood experiences and dreams. When we apply these same methods to our interpretations of works of literature, we engage in psychoanalytic criticism.

Unlike some other schools of criticism, **psychoanalytic criticism** exists side by side with any other critical method of interpretation. Because this approach attempts to explain the how's and why's of human actions without developing an aesthetic theory—a systematic, philosophical body of beliefs about how meaning occurs in literature and other art forms—Marxists, feminists, and New Historicists, for example, use psychoanalytic methods in their interpretations without violating their own **hermeneutics**. Psychoanalytic criticism may best be called an approach to literary interpretation rather than a particular school of criticism.

Although Freud is unquestionably the founder of this approach to literary analysis, psychoanalytic criticism has continued to develop throughout the twentieth century. Carl Jung, Freud's rebellious student, borrowed some of Freud's ideas but rejected many others. Jung branched out into new theories and concerns and established **analytical psychology**. Using some of Jung's ideas, Northrop Frye, an English professor and literary theorist, developed symbolic or archetypal criticism in the mid-1950s that changed the direction of twentieth-century literary analysis. In the 1960s, the French neo-Freudian psychoanalyst Jacques Lacan revised and expanded Freud's theories in light of new linguistic and literary principles, thereby revitalizing psychoanalytic criticism and ensuring its continued influence on literary criticism today. Many present-day feminist critics such as Julia Kristeva, Luce Irigaray, and E. Ann Kaplan turn to psychoanalytic criticism as well, using the ideas of Freud, Jung, Lacan and others like them as the basis of their critical methodology.

HISTORICAL DEVELOPMENT

Sigmund Freud

The theories and practice of Sigmund Freud (1856–1939) provide the foundation for psychoanalytic criticism. While working with patients whom he diagnosed as hysterics, Freud theorized that the root of their problems was psychological, not physical. His patients, he believed, had suppressed incestuous desires that they had unconsciously refused to confront. Suffering from his own neurotic crisis in 1887, Freud underwent self-analysis. Results from his self-analysis, together with his research and analyses of patients, led Freud to posit that fantasies and wishful thinking, not actual experiences, play a large part in the onset of neuroses.

Models of the Human Psyche: Dynamic Model   Throughout his lifetime, Freud developed various models of the human psyche, which became the changing bases of his psychoanalytic theory and his practice. Early in his career, he posited the **dynamic model**, asserting that our minds are a dichotomy consisting of the conscious (the rational) and the unconscious (the irrational). The conscious, Freud argued, perceives and records external reality and is the reasoning part of the mind. Unaware of the presence of the unconscious, we operate consciously, believing that our reasoning and analytical skills are solely responsible for our behavior. Nevertheless, Freud is the first to suggest that the unconscious, not the conscious, governs a large part of our actions.

This irrational part of our psyche, the unconscious, receives and stores our hidden desires, ambitions, fears, passions, and irrational thoughts. Freud, however, did not coin this term; this honor goes to C.G. Carus. Carus and many of Freud's other contemporaries viewed the unconscious as a static system that simply collects and maintains our memories. Freud dramatically redefined the unconscious, believing it to be a dynamic system that not only contains our biographical memories but also stores our suppressed and unresolved conflicts. Freud believed that the unconscious houses humanity's two basic instincts: **eros**, or the **sexual instinct** (later referred to by Freud as **libido**), and the **destructive** or **aggressive instinct**. Although these two instincts can work harmoniously, they often act as enemies, working against each other. Whatever the case, asserts Freud, these two basic instincts influence all we do.

For Freud, the unconscious is also the storehouse of disguised truths and desires that want to be revealed in and through the conscious. These disguised truths and desires inevitably make themselves known through our so-called mistakes of speech or actions. Freud calls such mistakes **parapraxes** or **Freudian slips**. Through seemingly innocuous actions, such as accidental slips of the tongue, failures of memory, the misplacing of objects, or the misreading of texts, Freud believes we consciously bring to our conscious minds our unconscious wishes and intentions. It is especially in our dreams, our art, our literature, and our play that these parapraxes reveal our true intentions or desires.

Economic Model Freud's second model of the human psyche enlarges upon but retains most of the ideas he posits in the dynamic model. In both models, the conscious and the unconscious battle for control of a person's actions, and in both models, a person's unconscious desires force their way to the conscious state. In the **economic model**, however, Freud introduces two new concepts that describe and help govern the human psyche: the pleasure principle and the reality principle. According to Freud, the **pleasure principle** craves only pleasures and instantaneous satisfaction of instinctual drives, ignoring moral and sexual boundaries established by society. Freud calls an individual's instinctual and psychic energy **cathexes**, its chief aim being to maximize pleasure because the pleasure principle's goal is immediate relief from all pain or suffering. The pleasure principle is usually not allowed free reign in an individual's psyche because it is held in check by what Freud dubs the **anti-cathexes** or an anti-charge of energy governed by the **reality principle**, that part of the psyche that recognizes the need for societal standards and regulations on pleasure. Freud believed that both of these principles are at war within the human psyche.

Typographical Models Over his long career, Freud developed yet another model of the human psyche known as the **typographical model**. In an earlier version of this model, Freud separates the human psyche into three parts: the conscious, preconscious, and unconscious. The **conscious** is the mind's direct link to external reality; it perceives and reacts with the external environment, allowing the mind to order its outside world. The **preconscious** is the storehouse of memories that the conscious part of the mind allows to be brought to consciousness without disguising these memories in some form or another. As in his previously devised models, Freud contends that the third part of the psyche, the **unconscious**, holds the repressed hungers, images, thoughts, and desires of human nature. Because these desires are not housed in the preconscious, they cannot be directly summoned into the conscious state. These repressed impulses must travel in disguised forms to the conscious part of the psyche and surface in their respective disguises in our dreams, our art, and in other unsuspecting ways in our lives.

The most famous model of the human psyche, however, is Freud's revised version of the typographical model, the **tripartite model** sometimes referred to at the **structural model**. This model divides the psyche into three parts: the id, ego, and superego. The irrational, instinctual, unknown, and unconscious part of the psyche Freud calls the **id**. Containing our secret desires, darkest wishes, and most intense fears, the id wishes only to fulfill the urges of the pleasure principle. In addition, it houses the **libido**, the source of all our psychosexual desires and all our psychic energy. Unchecked by any controlling will, the id operates on impulse, wanting immediate satisfaction for all its instinctual desires.

The second part of the psyche Freud names the **ego**, the rational, logical, waking part of the mind, although many of its activities remain in the unconscious. Whereas the id operates according to the pleasure principle, the ego operates in harmony with the reality principle. It is the ego's job to regulate the instinctual desires of the id and allow these desires to be released in nondestructive ways.

The third part of the psyche, the **superego**, acts like an internal censor, causing us to make moral judgments in light of social pressures. In contrast to the id, the superego operates according to the **morality principle** and serves primarily to protect society and us from the id. Representing all of society's moral restrictions, the superego serves as a filtering agent, suppressing the desires and instincts forbidden by society and thrusting them back into the unconscious. Overall, the superego manifests itself through punishment. If allowed to operate at its own discretion, the superego will create an unconscious sense of guilt and fear.

It is left to the ego to mediate between the instinctual (especially sexual) desires of the id and the demands of social pressure issued by the superego. What the ego deems unacceptable it suppresses and deposits in the unconscious, and what it has most frequently repressed in all of us is our sexual desires of early childhood.

Freud's Pre-Oedipal Developmental In addition to his various models of the human psyche, Freud proposed several phases or stages of human development that he believed are important to the healthy growth of one's psyche. According to Freud, in our early childhood, all of us go through three overlapping phases: the oral, anal, and phallic stages. As infants, we experience the **oral phase**: When we suck our mother's breast to be fed, our sexuality (or libido) is activated. Through this activity, our mouths develop into an erotogenic zone that will later cause us to enjoy sucking our thumbs and, still later in life, kissing. In the second, or **anal stage** (sometimes referred to as the **sadistic-anal phase**) the anus becomes an object of pleasure when children learn the delights of defecation and, simultaneously, realize that they are independent persons who are separate from their mothers. During this stage, the anus becomes an erotogenic zone because children become sadistic, expelling and destroying through defecation as a means of expressing both their anger and their excitement in discovering their independence from their mothers. By withholding feces, children also learn that they can control others. In the final phase, the **phallic stage**, a child's sexual desires, or libido, are directed toward the genitals when the child learns the pleasure that results from stimulating one's sexual organs.

At this point in a child's development, Freud asserts that the pleasure principle basically controls the child. Being self-centered, sadistic, and assertive, the child cares for nothing but his or her own pleasure. If a child, however, is to grow up as a normal adult, he or she must develop a sense of sexuality, a sense of his maleness or her femaleness. Freud maintains that this awareness can be achieved by a successful handling of either the Oedipus or the Electra complex.

The Oedipus, Castration, and Electra Complexes The formulation of the **Oedipus complex** is one of Freud's most significant contributions not only to psychoanalytic criticism but also to literary criticism in general. Freud borrows the name from the play *Oedipus Rex*, written by the Greek dramatist Sophocles. In this play, Oedipus, the protagonist, is prophesied to kill his father and marry his mother. His attempts to abort the prophecy fail, and the once-foretold events occur as predicted. According to Freud, the essence of Oedipus's story becomes universal human experience, illustrating a formative stage in each individual's psychosexual development when the child transfers his love object from the breast (the oral phrase) to the mother.

Using Sophocles's plot as the basis for his Oedipus complex, Freud asserts in his *Introductory Lectures (Twenty-first Lecture)* that during the late **infantile stage** (somewhere between ages 3 and 6), all infant males possess an erotic attachment to their mother. Unconsciously, the infant desires to engage in sexual union with his mother, but he recognizes a rival for his mother's affection: the father. Already in the **phallic stage** and therefore sexually aware of his own erogenous organs, the child perceives the father's attention to the mother as sexual.

If a child's sexual development is to proceed normally, Freud maintains, each must then pass through the **castration complex**. From observing themselves, their mothers, and perhaps their sisters, little boys know they have a penis like their fathers, while their mothers and sisters do not. What prevents the male child from continuing to have incestuous desires for his mother is fear of castration by his father. The child therefore represses his sexual desire, identifies with his father, and hopes someday to possess a woman as his father now possesses his mother. Unconsciously, the boy has now successfully made the transition to manhood.

Whereas a boy must successfully negotiate the Oedipus complex in order to become a normal man, a girl must successfully negotiate the **Electra complex** if she is to make the transition from a girl to a normal woman. Like a boy, a young girl is also erotically attracted to her mother, and like a boy, she too recognizes a rival for her mother's affection: the father. Unconsciously, the girl realizes that she is already castrated as is her mother. Because she knows her father possesses that which she desires, a penis, she turns her desires to him and away from her mother. After the seduction of her father fails, she turns back toward the mother and identifies with her. Her transition into womanhood being completed, the girl realizes that one day she, too, like her mother, will possess a man. Through her relationships with a man, her unfulfilled desire for a penis (**penis envy**) will be mitigated, and her sense of lack will be somewhat appeased.

The process of becoming a man or a woman, Freud maintained, may be long and difficult, but necessary. For within this process, the child passes from basing his or her life on the **pleasure principle** under which all decisions are grounded in the immediate gratification of pleasure, to the **reality principle**, under which societal needs and the operation of the superego guide decisions. During this stage, Freud believed that a child's moral sensibility and conscience appear for the first time.

The Significance of Dreams   According to Freud, even though the passage into manhood or womanhood may be successful, every adult has stored many painful memories of repressed sexual desires, anger, rage, and guilt in his or her unconscious. Because the conscious and the unconscious are part of the same psyche, the unconscious, with its hidden desires and repressed wishes, continues to affect the conscious in the form of inferiority feelings, guilt, irrational thoughts and feelings, and dreams and nightmares.

In his magnum opus, *The Interpretation of Dreams* (1900), Freud asserts that the unconscious expresses its suppressed wishes and desires. Even though the conscious mind has repressed these desires and has forced them into the unconscious, such wishes may be too hard for the conscious psyche to handle without producing feelings of self-hatred or rage. The unconscious then redirects and reshapes these concealed wishes into acceptable social activities, presenting them in the form of images or symbols in our dreams or our writings. In the process, the psyche creates a window to the id by allowing these softened and socially acceptable desires to seep into the conscious state.

The psyche may create this window to the id in a variety of ways. Through the process of **displacement**, for example, the unconscious may switch a person's hatred for someone named Mr. Appleby onto a rotting apple in a dream. Or through **condensation**, the psyche may consolidate one's anger toward a variety of people and objects into a simple sentence.

Whatever the case, through symbols and images, but not directly, the unconscious continually asserts its influence over our motives and behavior.

When certain repressed feelings or ideas cannot be adequately released through dreams, jokes, or other methods, the ego must act and block any outward response. In so doing, the ego and id become involved in an internal battle Freud calls **neurosis**. From a fear of heights to a pounding headache, neurosis can assume many physical and psychological abnormalities. Freud says it is the job of psychoanalysts to identify these unresolved conflicts that give rise to a patient's neurosis. Through psychoanalytic therapy and dream analysis, psychotherapists attempt to return the patient to a state of well-being or normalcy.

Literature and Psychoanalysis For Freud, the unresolved conflicts that give rise to any neurosis constitute the stuff of literature. A work of literature, he believes, is the external expression of the author's unconscious mind. Accordingly, the literary work must then be treated like a dream, applying psychoanalytic techniques to the text to uncover the author's hidden motivations, repressed desires, and wishes.

Carl G. Jung

Freud's most famous pupil is Carl Gustav Jung (1875–1961), a Swiss physician, psychiatrist, philosopher, and psychologist. Selecting Jung as his favorite "son," Freud appointed him his successor. Toward the end of their 7-year, teacher–disciple relationship (1912), however, Jung prophetically wrote to Freud, quoting from Nietzsche's *Thus Spake Zarathustra*, "One repays a teacher badly if one remains only a pupil." A year later, the pupil broke away from his master and eventually became one of the leading forces in the psychoanalytic movement.

Jung's dissatisfaction with some elements of Freudian psychoanalysis arose from theoretical differences with Freud concerning the interpretation of dreams and the model of the human psyche. According to Freud, all human behavior, including dreams, is fundamentally sexual because it is driven by an individual's sensual or sexual energy, what Freud calls the **libido**. Freud interpreted dreams almost exclusively in sexual terms, linking most of them to the Oedipus or Electra complexes. Jung disagreed with Freud's basic premise that all human behavior is sexually driven; Jung argued that more than sexual imagery appears in dreams. In 1912, Jung published his seminal work, *Symbols of Transformation*, which ultimately led to his separation from Freud. In this work, Jung asserts that dreams include mythological images as well as sexual ones. Jung's ideas caused him to be banished from the psychoanalytic community for the next 5 years. During this time, he formulated his own model of the human psyche, which would become his most important contribution to psychology and literary criticism.

In forming his model of the human psyche, Jung accepts Freud's assumption that the unconscious exists and that it plays a major role in our conscious decisions, but he rejects Freud's analysis of the contents of the unconscious. For Jung, the human psyche consists of three parts: the personal conscious, personal unconscious, and collective unconscious. The personal conscious and personal unconscious comprise the individual psyche. The **personal conscious** or waking state is that image or thought of which we are aware at any given moment. Similar to a slide show, every moment of our lives provides us with a new slide. As we view one slide, the previous slide vanishes from our personal consciousness because nothing can remain in the personal conscious. Although these vanished slides are forgotten by the personal consciousness, they are stored and remembered by the **personal unconscious**. Jung asserts that all conscious thoughts begin in the personal unconscious. Because each person's moment-by-moment slide show is different, everyone's personal unconscious is unique.

In the depths of the psyche and blocked off from human consciousness lies the third part of Jung's model of the psyche: the **collective unconscious**, the part of the psyche that is more impersonal and universal than the personal conscious or the personal unconscious. This part of the psyche houses the cumulative knowledge, experiences, and images of the entire human species. According to Jung, people from all over the world respond to certain myths or stories in the same way, not because everyone knows and appreciates the same story but because lying deep in our collective unconscious are the species' memories of humanity's past. According to Jung, this collective unconscious is "a second psychic system of collective, univeral, and impersonal nature which is identical in all individuals." This universal psychic aspect is an inherited receptable of deep, powerful human themes and commonalities. These memories exist in the form of **archetypes**, which are patterns or images of repeated human experiences—such as birth, death, rebirth, the four seasons, and motherhood, to name a few—that express themselves in our stories, dreams, religions, and fantasies. Archetypes are not ready-made ideas but are predispositions, causing us to respond to stimuli in certain ways. In addition, they are inherited genetically (a psychic, not a biological, inheritance), making up an identical collective unconsciousness for all humankind. Jung states that the archetypes "give form to countless typical experiences of our ancestors [and are] the psychic residue of innumerable experiences of the same type, of joys and sorrows that have been repeated countless times in our ancestral history." Occurring in literature in the form of recurrent plot patterns, images, or character types, the archetypes stir profound emotions that are similar in all readers because they awaken images stored in the collective unconscious and produce feelings or emotions over which readers initially have little control.

Jung was the first to suggest that such archetypes directly affect the way we respond to external elements. For example, when we see or read about an infant in diapers surrounded by a litter of puppies licking the baby's face, feelings of contentment, warmth, and love seemingly overwhelm most of us. These somewhat uncontrollable emotions, Jung would claim, are the results of the stirring of an archetype.

Many anthropologists would argue that archetypes are inherited cultural responses, which are passed down from one generation to the next in a particular social group. Eventually, such social phenomena become myths or stories that help give meaning and significance to people's lives. Jung would strongly disagree, asserting that myths are "symbolic expressions of the inner, unconscious drama of the psyche." Both myths and modern stories often portray the archetypal symbols over and over, proving their thematic importance. Through repetition of such symbols, the archetype—the **anima** (the feminine in the male), the **animus** (the masculine in the female), the mother, and rebirth, to name a few—may then be applied to the interpretive process in order to understand the underlying meanings of human stories and experiences. Because the unconscious mind continually uses symbols from the collective psychic pool to make sense of life, such symbols help us to delve more deeply into the archetypes and commonalities of life. For Jung, stories and myths are the means by which archetypes evidence themselves not only in our dreams but also in the personal conscious.

Throughout the 1920s and until his death in 1961, Jung continued developing his methods of **analytical psychology**. When we apply his theories and methods to literature, we engage in **archetypal criticism**. Unquestionably, the foremost archetypal critic of the twentieth century is Northrop Frye.

Northrop Frye

With the publication of his work *Anatomy of Criticism* in 1957, Northrop Frye (1912–1991) became the primary advocate of the principles of **archetypal criticism**. Although he never declares allegiance to Jung's concept of the collective unconscious, Frye borrows Jung's ideas about myths and archetypes and develops a systematic approach to interpretation called **archetypal** or **mythic criticism**. Divorcing a text from its social history, Frye maintains that there exists an overall structure or mythic development that explains both the structure and the significance of all texts. All literature, he argues, is on a sliding scale, ranging from the most explicitly allegorical to the most anti-allegorical and anti-explicit. The archetypal symbols found within literature help to emphasize and portray the allegory and "deeper" story every author is telling. The overall structural principles of literature, declares Frye, are to be derived from archetypal criticism because this kind of criticism presupposes a larger context for literature as a whole. The most elemental form and structure in literature is myth because myth possesses the deepest imagery and most abstract meaning of any kind of literature. Above all other forms of literature, myth is the most profoundly allegorical and is most directly related through symbols.

Frye believes that all of literature comprises one complete and whole story called the **monomyth**. This monomyth can best be diagramed as a circle containing four separate phases, with each phase corresponding to a season of the year and to peculiar cycles of human experiences. The **romance phase**, located at the top of the circle, is our summer story. In this story, all our wishes are fulfilled, and we can achieve total happiness. At the bottom of the circle is winter, or the **anti-romance phase**. The opposite of summer, this phase tells the story of bondage, imprisonment, frustration, and fear. Midway between romance and anti-romance and to the right of the middle of the circle is the **spring phase**, or comedy. This phase relates the story of our rise from anti-romance and frustration to freedom and happiness. Correspondingly, across the circle is tragedy, or the **fall phase**, narrating our fall from the romance phase and from happiness and freedom to disaster. According to Frye, all stories can be placed somewhere on this diagram.

What Frye provides for us is a schematic of all possible kinds of stories. Such a structural framework furnishes the context whereby we can identify stories based on their particular genre, kinds of symbolization, themes, points of view, and other literary elements. In addition, Frye's schematic supplies the background and context for his form of literary criticism and allows us to compare and contrast stories on the basis of their relationship among themselves.

With the advent of archetypal criticism and Frye's schematics in the 1950s, few critics used Freudian analysis in their practical criticism. But in the 1960s, the French psychoanalyst, neo-Freudian, and poststructuralist critic Jacques Lacan helped revive Freudian criticism and through his work, rescued it from its overwhelmingly **phallocentric** or a male-dominated position.

Jacques Lacan

Similar to Freud, Jacques Lacan (1901–1981) believes that the unconscious greatly affects our conscious behavior. Unlike Freud, who pictures the unconscious as a chaotic, unstructured, bubbling cauldron of dark passions, hidden desires, and suppressed wishes, Lacan asserts that the unconscious is structured, like the structure of language. Like language, this highly structured part of the human psyche can be systematically analyzed. What we will learn from such an analysis, claims Lacan, is that all individuals are fragmented; no one is whole. The ideal concept of a wholly unified and psychologically complete individual is just that, an abstraction that is simply not attainable.

Lacan's Model of the Human Psyche   Similar to Freud, Lacan devises a three-part model of the human psyche. In Freud's model, the interactions of the id, ego, and superego greatly determine our behavior. Underlying Lacan's model, however, is the basic assumption that language shapes and ultimately structures our unconscious and conscious minds and shapes our self-identity.

For Lacan, the human psyche consists of three parts or, as Lacan names them, orders: the imaginary order, the symbolic order, and the real order. As in Freud's tripartite model, each of the orders interacts with the others. From our birth until somewhere around 6 months, we function primarily in the **imaginary order**—that is, in the part of the psyche that contains our wishes, our fantasies, and most importantly, our images. In this phase of our psychic development, we are joyfully united as one with our mother, receiving our food, our care, and all our comfort from her. In this preverbal state, we rely on images as a means of perceiving and interpreting the world. Consequently, our image of ourselves is always in flux because we are not able to differentiate where one image stops and another begins.

Somewhere between the age of 6 and 18 months, we enter what Lacan calls the looking-glass or **mirror stage**. In this stage, we literally see ourselves in a mirror while metaphorically seeing ourselves in our mother's image. Observing this mirror image permits us to perceive images that have discrete boundaries, allowing us to become aware of ourselves as independent beings who are separate from our mothers. This mirror image of ourselves as a whole and complete being is an ideal, an illusion because unlike the actual mirror image, we are not in full control of ourselves. We cannot, for example, move our bodies as we want or eat when we desire.

During the mirror stage, we come to recognize certain objects—what Lacan calls **objet petit a**—as being separate images from ourselves. These objects include eliminating bodily wastes, our mother's voice and breasts, and our own speech sounds. When these objects or sounds are not present, we yearn for them. Lacan says such objects become for us symbols of lack, and this sense of lack will continue to plague us for the rest of our lives.

While we are passing through the imaginary order, one great consuming passion dominates our existence: the desire for our mother. Mother, we believe, can fulfill all our wishes just as we can fulfill all of hers. But we, like our mothers before us, must learn that we are separate entities who can never be totally unified with our mothers. Lacan says that such total unity and wholeness are an illusion.

Once we learn that we are individual beings who are separate from our mothers, we are ready to enter Lacan's second developmental phase, the

symbolic order. Whereas the mother dominates the imaginary order, the father dominates the symbolic order. In this phase, we learn language. Lacan would argue that in actuality language masters us because he believes that language shapes our identity as separate beings and molds our psyches. Using linguistic principles formulated by the founder of modern linguistics, Ferdinand de Saussure, Lacan declares that we differentiate between individual sounds and words on the basis of difference. We know the word *might*, for example, because it is different from *sight*, and we know *hill* because it differs from *bill*. Knowing and mastering this concept of difference enables us to enter and to pass through the symbolic order successfully.

Lacan contends that in the symbolic order, we learn to differentiate between male and female. This process of learning gender identity is based on difference and loss. Whereas in the imaginary order, we delighted in the presence of our mother, in the symbolic order, we learn that our father comes to represent cultural norms and laws. He stands between us and our mother, and he enforces cultural rules by threatening to castrate us if we do not obey. Because the castration complex is obviously different for boys and girls, the process of completing the symbolic order successfully is different for each sex.

For Lacan, what sex we are is biologically determined, but our gender or our sexuality is culturally created. Society decrees, for example, that little boys should play with cars and little girls with dolls. The father, the power symbol, enforces these cultural rules and ensures that we follow them. Both sexes come to understand their own sexuality by observing what they are not, a boy noting that he does not do the things a girl does and vice versa. Each must recognize that he or she will forever be a splintered self, never again able to experience the wholeness and joy of being one with his or her mother in the imaginary order.

For the boy, entry into the symbolic order dictates that he identifies and acknowledges the father as the symbol of society's power and as the object that blocks his desire for sexual union with his mother. For the girl, entry into the symbolic order decrees that she, too, acknowledge the father or the male as the symbol of power in society and as her personal superior. Like the boy, she wishes to return to the happy state of union with her mother in the imaginary order. Unlike the boy, she maintains more access than he to this pre-Oedipal stage as she grows up.

Lacan maintains that entering the symbolic order is a form of castration for both sexes. In Lacan's view, castration is symbolic, not literal, and represents each person's loss of wholeness and his or her acceptance of society's rules. For the male, it means accepting the father, the power symbol who possesses a phallus or penis. Likewise, the female must not only accept the father figure as dominant but also accept her lack of a phallus. Similar to his differentiation between sex and gender, Lacan distinguishes between the penis, the actual biological organ, and the **phallus**, what becomes for Lacan, in poststructural terms, the **transcendental signified**—the object that gives meaning to all other objects. In other words, for Lacan, the phallus is the ultimate symbol of power. Although neither males nor females can ever possess the phallus and can never be complete or whole, males do have a penis, giving them a slight claim to such power.

Lacan and Textual Analysis At the heart of Lacan's theory and his understanding of the human psyche are lack and fragmentation. All of us have longings for love, physical pleasure, and countless objects, but nothing can fulfill our desire to return to the imaginary order and be at one with our mother. This fragmentation or divided self concerns Lacan when he examines a literary text. For Lacan, literary texts hold the possibility of capturing, at least for a moment, our desire to return to the imaginary order and to regain that sense of pure joy when we were once whole and united with our mothers.

In examining a text, Lacan also looks for elements of the third and most remote and unreachable part of the human psyche, the **real order**. On the one hand, the real order consists of the physical world, including the material universe and everything in it; on the other hand, the real order also symbolizes all that a person is not. Or as Lacan would say, the real order contains countless objet petit a, objects that continually function for us as symbols of primordial lack. Because these objects and, indeed, the entire physical universe are and can never be parts of ourselves, we can never experience or really know them except through language. In addition, as Lacan contends, language causes our fragmentation in the first place. In Lacan's theory, literature has the particular ability to capture **jouissance**—that is, to call up a brief moment of joy or terror or desire that somehow arises from deep within our unconscious psyche and reminds us of a time of perfect wholeness when we were incapable of differentiating among images from the real order. More frequently than not, these experiences are sexual, although other images and experiences such as birth or death can serve this function. Lacan frequently finds such moments of joy in the writings of Poe, Shakespeare, and Joyce.

THE PRESENT STATE OF PSYCHOANALYTIC CRITICISM

Thanks primarily to Lacan, psychoanalytic criticism has enjoyed new popularity. In particular, feminist critics such as Sandra Gilbert and Susan Gubar (*Madwoman in the Attic*, 1979), Julia Kristeva (*Powers of Horror*, 1982; *Revolution in Poetic Language*, 1984), and Luce Irigaray (*An Ethics of Sexual Difference*, 1993), and others continue to adapt both Freud's and Lacan's theoretical models to show the psychological conflicts and concerns encountered by female writers in a male-dominated world. Other critics such as Felix Guattari continue to challenge both Freud's and Lacan's ideas, devising their own models of the human psyche. Although many present-day critics reject Freud's phallic-centered sexual theories, preferring a less sexually centered system, some still embrace Freud's dream work and the linguistic, symbolically interpretive methods of this original psychoanalyst.

ASSUMPTIONS

The foundation for most forms of psychoanalytic criticism belongs to Freud and his theories and techniques developed during his psychiatric practice. Whether any practicing psychoanalytic critic uses the ideas of Jung, Frye, Lacan, or any other psychoanalyst, all acknowledge Freud as the intellectual center of this form of criticism.

Central to psychoanalytic criticism is Freud's assumption that all artists, including authors, are neurotic. Unlike most other neurotics, the artist escapes many of the outward manifestations and end results of neurosis, such as madness or self-destruction, by finding a pathway back to saneness and wholeness in the act of creating his or her art.

Freud says that an author's chief motivation for writing any story is to gratify some secret desire, some forbidden wish that probably developed during the author's infancy and was immediately suppressed and dumped in the unconscious. The outward manifestation of this suppressed wish becomes the literary work itself. Freud declares that the literary work is indeed the author's dream or fantasy. By using Freud's psychoanalytic techniques developed for dream therapy, psychoanalytic critics believe we can "unlock" the hidden meanings contained within the story and housed in symbols. Only then can we arrive at an accurate interpretation of the text.

Because Freud believes that the literary text is really an artist's dream or fantasy, the text can and must be analyzed like a dream. For Freud, this means that we must assume that the dream is a disguised wish. All of our present wishes, Freud believes, originated in some way during infancy. As an infant, we longed to be both sensually and emotionally satisfied. The memory of these satisfied infantile desires provides fertile ground for our present wishes to occur. All present wishes are therefore recreations of a past infantile memory—especially elements of the Oedipal phase—brought to the surface of our unconscious and conscious states through sensations, emotions, and other present-day situations.

But the actual wish is often too strong and too forbidden to be acknowledged by the mind's censor, the ego. Accordingly, the ego distorts and hides the wish or **latent content** of the dream, thereby allowing the dreamer to remember a somewhat changed and oftentimes radically different dream. The dreamer tells the dream analyst about this changed dream or **manifest content** of the dream. In turn, the dream analyst must strip back the various layers of the patient's conversation and carefully analyze the multiple layers of the dream. The analyst's job is similar to that of an archaeologist who painstakingly uncovers a valued historical site layer by layer. Like the archaeologist, the analyst must peal back the various layers of a dream until the true wish is uncovered.

Like the dream analyst, the psychoanalytic critic believes that any author's story is a dream that on the surface, reveals only the manifest content of the true tale. Hidden and censored throughout the story on various levels lies the latent content of the story, its real meaning or interpretation. More frequently than not, this latent content directly relates to some element and memory of the Oedipal phase of our development. By directly applying the techniques used in Freudian dream analysis, the psychoanalytic critic believes the actual, uncensored wish can be brought to the surface, revealing the story's true meaning.

Psychoanalysts do not all agree with Freud's basic assumptions, as noted earlier in this chapter. For example, Jung believes that mythological as well as sexual images appear in our dreams, and Frye borrows this assumption from Jung and develops a schematic for interpreting all dreams and stories. Lacan, on the other hand, disavows Freud's assumption that the unconscious is a cauldron of boiling passions and announces that the unconscious is as highly structured as language itself. By analyzing this structure, Lacan declares that no one can achieve wholeness because we are all and will always remain fragmented individuals who are seeking completeness. Nevertheless, all of these theorists with their accompanying theories relate in some way to Freud's presuppositions.

METHODOLOGIES

First introduced to literary studies in the 1920s and 1930s, Freud's psychoanalytic criticism still survives today. Although its methods have been challenged, revised, and supplemented, psychoanalytic criticism provides a stimulating approach to literary analysis that decrees that we humans are complex yet somewhat understandable creatures who often fail to note the influence of the unconscious on both our motivations and our everyday actions.

For several decades after its introduction, psychoanalytic criticism focused mainly on the author. Known as **psychobiography**, this method of analysis begins by amassing biographical information about an author through biographies, personal letters, lectures, and any other document related in some way to the author. Using these data and the author's **canon** (collected works), psychoanalytic critics believed they could theoretically construct the author's personality, with all its idiosyncrasies, internal and external conflicts, and more importantly, neuroses. In turn, such a devised theory, they believed, could illuminate an author's individual works, giving rise to the latent content in the author's texts. By gaining an in-depth understanding of the author, these critics assumed they would be better able to interpret an author's canon. Of particular interest to them were the lives and works of Edgar Allan Poe, William Blake, and Leonardo da Vinci.

In the 1950s, psychoanalytic critics turned their attention away from psychobiography to character analysis, studying the various aspects of characters' minds found in an author's canon. Such a view gave rise to a more complex understanding of a literary work. Individual characters within a text now became the focus. Believing that the author had in mind a particular personality for his or her characters, critics also noted that readers develop their own conceptions of each character's personality. A character's motivations and actions, then, became more complex than simply attributing them to the author's ideas. How readers interpreted characters now became an integral part of the text's interpretation. Whereas the author creates a character, a reader recreates the same character, bringing to the text and to an individual character all the reader's past experiences and knowledge. The character simultaneously becomes the creation of the author and of the reader. In order to interpret the story, a psychoanalytic analysis of the author and the reader were therefore necessary.

Today, many psychoanalytic critics realize that the reader plays a major role in interpreting a work. Understanding ourselves from a Freudian point of view as well as the context in which we live is considered essential if we are to interpret a text.

One of the most controversial psychoanalytic techniques used today involves applying Freud's key assumption—that all human behavior is sexually driven—directly to a text. In the hands of novice critics, who are often ill- or misinformed about Freud's psychoanalytic techniques, everything in a text more frequently than not becomes a sexual image. For these critics, every concave image, such as a flower, cup, cave, or vase, is a **yonic symbol** (female), and any image whose length exceeds its diameter, such as a tower, sword, knife, or pen, becomes a **phallic symbol** (male). Consequently, a text containing a dance, a boat floating into a cave, or a pen being placed within a cup is interpreted as a symbol of sexual intimacy. From this perspective, all images and actions within a text must be traced to the author's id because everything in a text is ultimately the hidden wishes of the author's libido.

Another psychoanalytic approach is archetypal criticism, first developed by Jung and then later by Frye. In this form of analysis, critics examine a text to discover the various archetypes that they observe in the text itself. From Jung's view, these archetypes have the same meaning for all readers. The color red, for example, signifies danger just as water symbolizes life. By showing where and how these archetypes appear in the text, and whether or not they form recognizable patterns, the archetypal critic believes that he or she will be able to discover the text's meaning. To apply this method accurately, a critic must have a complete grasp of Jung's rather complex theories and terminology.

In some modern archetypal approaches to literature, critics focus on the mythic concepts within texts. One such critic is Joseph Cambell (1904–1987), a critic and scholar who has written extensively within the field of mythology and literature concerning the ways that archetypal symbols portray human experience. In his seminal work *The Hero with a Thousand Faces* (1949), Campbell focuses on the journey of the archetypal hero in myths and in all literature as a whole. He asserts that psychoanalysts such as "Freud, Jung, and their followers have demonstrated irrefutably that the logic, the heroes, and the deeds of myth survive into modern times." Accordingly, Campbell argues that the human psyche and modern literature directly relate to the ancient, primordial myths and themes. Because of this relationship, we must probe literature for such themes. By understanding the ancient stories and themes, seeing their relationship to modern stories, and applying archetypal psychoanalysis, Campbell believes that we may better understand not only our world but also each other, and even our own inner psyches. Other psychoanalysts such as David Leeming and James Hillman use Jung's and Campbell's ideas and theories in their works, spanning psychology, mythology, and literature.

Another type of psychoanalytic criticism used today is based on ideas developed by Jacques Lacan. A Lacanian critic would attempt to uncover how a text symbolically represents elements of the real, imaginary, and symbolic orders. By identifying the symbolic representations of these orders within the text, the critic would then examine how each of these symbols demonstrates the fragmentary nature of the self. Such a demonstration would show the reader that all individuals are actually splintered selves. The overall purpose of a Lacanian analysis is to teach us that a fully integrated and psychologically whole person does not exist and that we must all accept fragmentation.

One of the most current and productive directions of psychoanalysis is being used by feminist critics. Using some of Freud's concerns but "rescuing" Freud from his male-dominated culture and understanding are psychoanalytic critics such as Julia Kristeva. Kristeva borrows and amends concepts from Freud, Lacan, anthropology, philosophy, linguistics, and phenomenology, developing a new science, **semanalysis**. Elaborating on the Lacanian idea of the mirror stage, Kristeva posits that during a **pre-mirror stage** (a stage that she argues Lacan ignores), a child experiences a lack or separation from the mother that shapes meaning or significance, moving from this lack or need to desire. An emotional force that is tied to our instincts thus develops, what she calls the **semiotique**. The semiotique exists not in symbols, as noted by Lacan, but in the prosody of language itself. This process of signification is an ever-ongoing one that uses a variety of Freudian, Lacanian, and linguistic concepts. In her most contemporary writings, Kristeva continues to explore the intersection of language, culture, and the written word through psychoanalysis.

Whichever psychoanalytic method a critic may choose to use, he or she must master the psychoanalytic theories and practices of Freud and his pupils in order to borrow, amend, and devise an interpretation that is credible and clear. Although mastering such complex theory and its appropriate applications may be difficult, the result is a rewarding discovery of the truths that lie within each of us.

QUESTIONS FOR ANALYSIS

- Because psychoanalytic criticism is based on various models of the mind rather than on an aesthetic theory, this critical approach to textual analysis can use the methodology of a variety of schools of criticism. Explain how the critical methods of New Criticism, reader-oriented criticism, and deconstruction can be used in a psychoanalytic reading of a text. What similarities do these schools of criticism have in common with psychoanalysis?

- Using Hawthorne's short story "Young Goodman Brown,"analyze the protagonist from each of the following perspectives: Freudian, Jungian, and Lacanian.

- Apply Freud's theories to a poem of your choice, and articulate a psychoanalytic interpretation of this poem.

- Using a short story or poem of your choice, identify the different images and structural patterns that occur in the text. Then using your understanding of psychoanalytic criticism, explain the presence of these images and patterns and analyze how each relates to an overall psychoanalytic interpretation of the text itself.

- Investigate the life of Edgar Allan Poe and apply the principles of psychobiography to his short story "Ligeia." When your psychobiographical analysis is completed, apply the theories of Freud to one of Poe's poems, such as "The Raven" or "The Bells."

CRITIQUES AND RESPONSES

In the past several decades, much "Freud bashing" has occurred, growing from simply being an argument against Freud and his theories to a movement. Whereas Freud was once declared a genius, nowadays he is often dubbed a "very troubled man," with his technique of psychoanalysis being declared a pseudoscience by many psychologists, physicians, linguists, epistemologists, and literary theorists and critics. Be that as it may, Freud remains a central figure in both general psychology and literature. Thanks largely to Freud, few, if any, question the influence of the human unconscious upon our everyday actions. And thanks to Freud, we understand, at least in part, that our minds create more than we can grasp and that the search for meaning in our lives can be painful—but search we do. And thanks to Freud's theories and his founding of psychoanalysis, psychoanalytic criticism continues to explore the workings of the human psyche through the writings of Jacques Lacan, Joseph Campbell, Julia Kristeva, Gilles Deleuze, Felix Guattari, and a host of others interested in the relationship among the human psyche, culture, society, politics, and the arts.

Although Freud's theories have provided for present-day scholars and theorists a springboard for a myriad of ways to examine the human psyche and the making of meaning, Freud has been criticized for multiple reasons. First, to use successfully and therefore accurately Freud's psychoanalytic methodology in literary analysis, a critic must master a seemingly insurmountable mountain of theoretical knowledge. Second, by emphasizing such an extensive body of theory before a text can be analyzed, some critics argue that psychoanalytic criticism detracts from what should be a critic's first concern: the text itself. Third, many critics believe that psychoanalytic criticism reduces a text to a collection of sexual and sensual urges, thereby denying the aesthetic qualities that are inherent in a literary work and should receive a critic's attention. Fourth, Freud is particularly masculine in his interpretation, asserting the predominance of the male, giving only a secondary nod to the female. His theories, critics assert, are sexually unbalanced. Although some may argue that Freud was a "male product" of his masculine times, it took the work of Lacan and other present-day psychoanalytic critics to "rescue" Freud from his masculine bias. Fifth, some argue that psychoanalysis is too simplistic in its attempt to understand the human psyche in all its complexities. Such arguments, however, can be made for most models of the human psyche because, after all, they are simply models. And last, many declare that as a science, psychoanalysis is not objective or scientific. Freud himself was unshakeable in declaring the scientific validity of his own work, but even he was concerned about the "narrative" quality of many of his case histories.

That Freud pioneered new avenues of exploration of the human psyche remains unquestioned. The fact that literary theorists and critics continue to accept, reject, borrow, or amend his theories and their applications stands as a testament to Freud's continued importance, not only from a historical perspective but also from a practicing critic's point of view.

FURTHER READING

Evans, Dylan. *An Introductory Dictionary of Lacanian Psychoanalysis*. New York: Routledge, 1996.

Freud, Sigmund. *The Interpretation of Dreams*. New York: Avon, 1936.

———. *The Freud Reader*. New York: Norton, 1995.

Frye, Northrop. *Anatomy of Criticism*. Princeton, NJ: Princeton University Press, 2000.

Holland, Norman N. *The Dynamics of Literary Response*. New York: Columbia University Press, 1989.

Jung, Carl. *The Archetypes and the Collective Unconscious. Vol. 9, Part I of Collected Works*, 2nd ed. Adler, Gerhard (ed). Princeton, NJ: Princeton University Press, 1980.

Meisel, Perry, ed. Freud: *A Collection of Critical Essays*. Englewood Cliffs, NJ: Prentice Hall, 1981.

Rabaté, Jean-Michel. *The Cambridge Companion to Lacan*. Cambridge: Cambridge University Press, 2003.

Slavrj, Zizek. *Looking Awry: An Introduction to Jacques Lacan through Popular Culture*. Cambridge: MIT Press, 1992.

Wright, Elizabeth. *Psychoanalytic Criticism: A Reappraisal*, 2nd ed. New York: Taylor and Francis, 1998.

WEB SITES FOR EXPLORATION

http://www.lawrence.edu/dept/english/courses/60a/psycho.html
    An introduction to psychoanalyis and a good selection of suggested readings

http://faculty.washington.edu/divya/rge2-8-05.htm
    A review of basic terms used in psychoanalytic theory

http://web.olivet.edu/english/rbelcher/lit310/310psy.htm
    A good review of Freudian principles and the concepts of Jacques Lacan and Julia Kristeva

http://www.neiu.edu/~edepartm/dep/profs/scherm/html/psychcrit.htm
    An overview of psychoanalysis and with a comparison to other literary schools of criticism

http://www.soloved.org/eng/critic.htm
    An introduction to psychoanalysis, including questions to ask of a text to use a psychoanalytic interpretation and model essays

http://www.sou.edu/English/IDTC/timeline/uslit.htm
    A timeline of major critical theories in the United States

http://en.wikipedia.org/wiki/psychoanalysis
    A solid overview of psychoanalysis

http://www.cla.purdue.edu/academic/eng/theory/index.htm
    An introductory guide to critical theory, including psychoanalysis

Sample Essay

In the student essay that follows, note carefully how the author applies Jungian psychoanalytic terminology and methodology to arrive at his interpretation. After briefly reviewing the basic elements of Jungian analysis presented in this chapter, be prepared to discuss how the critic/writer demonstrates in his essay Jung's three-part understanding of the human psyche. In addition, examine carefully how the author employs an understanding of the workings of archetypes and symbols within Poe's story to arrive at a working interpretation. Overall, what do you see as the major strengths and weaknesses of this Jungian interpretation of Poe's short story "Ligeia"?

Student Essay

Anima and Reality in Poe's "Ligeia"[1]

Edgar Allan Poe is a master of the genre of horror, the psychological, and the detective story. Because his canon deals with the psychological aspects of humanity—both in and through the characters as well as the readers—his literature is often studied through the lens of archetypal criticism. In his tales, archetypal symbols of the psyche abound. One such story portraying major psychological elements is "Ligeia," the strongest of such elements being the conflict between the anima and reality itself.

Perhaps the most prominent symbol in "Ligeia" is the Lady Ligeia herself. She is, after all, the central character, and a representative symbol from the initial paragraph to the last sentence of the text. Ligeia foremost represents Carl Jung's anima concept. Jung states that "every man carries a woman within himself,"[2] describing the anima as the feminine aspect present within the male mind, an archetype of the dual nature or syzygy of the psyche (syzygy being the contrasexual opposites yoked together in the mind). The anima is frequently exemplified by "an angel of light, a psychopomp who points the way to the highest meaning."[3] Poe describes Ligeia as possessing a "placid cast of beauty," "free spirit," and "holy light"—all descriptions that evoke the thoughts of a wisdom-filled, goddess-like figure. Possessing such characteristics, this symbolic representation is clearly a parallel to Jung's anima.

Poe's text allows us to assume that Ligeia's spiritual aspect represents Jung's psychological anima: "She came and departed as a shadow" and her "beauty passed into my spirit, there dwelling as in a shrine." These passages speak not only of the goddess nature but also of the unconscious spiritual nature of the lady. In addition to the descriptions of Ligeia, the narrator (who by the end of the story has gone insane from the unconscious welling up to overtake his psyche) speaks of the lady as if she may be a creature of illusion,

[1]Reprinted by permission of Brandon W. Hawk.
[2]Jung, C. G., ed., *Man and His Symbols* (New York: Dell, 1964) 17.
[3]Jung, C. G., *The Archetypes and the Collective Unconscious*, Volume 9, Part I of *Collected Works*, 2nd ed., Trans. R. F. C. Hull (Princeton: Princeton UP, 1968) 29.

relating that he remembers her as "the radiance of an opium-dream," and says that he was "habitually fettered in the shackles of the drug [opium]," a psychoactive drug that breaks down the barriers between the conscious and the unconscious mind. Ligeia is not merely a lady of angelic attributes but a psycho-spiritual figure within the recesses of the narrator's mind.

Although Ligeia may be overtly portrayed as a deific feminine character, she also represents the feature of the anima that Jung calls the "chaotic urge to life" (*Archetypes* 30). In her death and rebirth, she evokes fear and chaos. Within Ligeia's final words, those of a gothic poem, she recites a story "much of Madness and more of Sin / And Horror the soul of the plot." Upon the rebirth of the lady, the narrator says, "There was a mad disorder in my thoughts," and an "inexpressible madness seized me." Poe also describes the reborn Ligeia's appearance as having "disheveled hair" and "wild eyes." With the symbolic anima's entrance from the unconscious to the conscious, a sort of madness and chaos issues forth. The anima is indeed an angel of the mind, but it also exists as a product and the very reason for part of the tension within the psyche.

All of Ligeia's attributes and symbolic representations may be closely contrasted with the attributes and symbolic representations of Rowena. Unlike Ligeia, Rowena is not a character with a forgotten origin or one lacking a paternal name: she is a well known, definite, physical person, as "the fair-haired and blue-eyed Lady Rowena Trevanion, of Tremaine." This new Lady opens the mind from the unconscious anima to the reality of the outside world, with only memories remaining of the once lost Ligeia. In further relation to the anima and reality, the narrator names his first love not merely as "Lady Ligeia," but as "the lady," whereas he names Rowena as "Lady" only in title. Never is she called a lady otherwise. To the narrator, Rowena is not the feminine, but a convention of society. As a foil to Ligeia (the anima), Rowena (reality) is a reminder that the inner self and the outer world are ever in tension within the mind.

Poe presents to us yet another major archetypal symbol: that of death and rebirth. Several cycles of death and rebirth are apparent in the story, the most prominent representations exemplified through the Lady Ligeia and the Lady Rowena. Death, for example, is a prevalent symbol portrayed through the deaths of both Ligeia and Rowena, symbolizing earthly death, spiritual death, and the end of marriage with the narrator, respectively. There is also a rebirth. As the narrator sits beside the bed of the dying Rowena, the harrowing onset of death begins, and in the final paragraph, the narrator watches as Ligeia returns to life. While this episode may be a sign of the narrator's insanity, it also depicts the depths of the unconscious rising to consciousness. In Ligeia's reappearance comes the surfacing of the feminine shadow (anima) within the male psyche. This rebirth is a resurrection of all that the narrator once held dear: the deific, adored, perfect (yet, as the reader knows, ultimately shadowy and darkened) Lady Ligeia, the symbol of the anima. It is, in effect, the death of the rational Lady Rowena, representing reality, and the rebirth of the overwhelming unconscious psyche within the narrator.

Just as the whole of "Ligeia" encompasses a death and rebirth cycle, smaller cycles also present themselves throughout the work. At the story's end, the resurrected Ligeia represents the new birth sprouting from the death of Rowena. Yet, with her appearance, Rowena too represents a sort of new birth, sprouting from the first death of Ligeia—as the narrator says, "the successor of the unforgotten Ligeia." She is the birth of practicality, reason, and the sanity of reality. Even the change in setting—to "fair England" and the solace of an abbey—serves as a new life, with the narrator leaving the old behind. Yet here too is a mini-cycle of rebirth because the narrator seeks the solace of the former spiritual side of life in the setting. The setting itself contains a turret with "semi-Gothic, semi-Druidical" characteristics. While the narrator has moved away from the unknown world in which he once lived with Ligeia, that turret serves as a rebirth and return to the old life.

Still one more cycle of death and rebirth pervades Poe's "Ligeia": the slow, agonizing death of Rowena. Lying on her death-bed, Rowena falls into a series of illnesses, several times resulting in the recurrence of seeming death and the "hideous drama of revivication." The narrator notes that "each terrific relapse was only into sterner and apparently more irredeemable death," and each time, she was revived by some other force. Each of these episodes serves as a mini death, and consequently a mini rebirth for Rowena, until the final major rebirth not of Rowena, but of the Lady Ligeia. Such a cycle is representative of the psyche's wish to hold onto reality and reconcile it with the unconscious desires and aspects of the anima. As the anima rises into the fully conscious mind (which is becoming steadily more unstable and neurotic), there may be no reconciliation. In the end, there is only the death of the symbolic reality in Rowena and the rebirth of the symbolic anima in Ligeia.

From the two overarching archetypes of the anima and the cycle of death and rebirth, we can draw yet another parallel. According to Jung, the mind is in continual tension between interior and exterior forces. Within "Ligeia," Poe vividly portrays the tension of the psyche, through the tensions between the attributes and the characters of Ligeia and Rowena, as well as the brooding underlying settings. Throughout the story a conflict exists between apocalyptic (paradisiacal) and demonic (wasteland) imagery. The acute descriptions of Ligeia as a heavenly and paradisiacal creature show the initial apocalyptic aspect. Ligeia's death and her prophetic poem, however, present the onset of a descent into demonic imagery, followed by the narrator's life with Rowena characterized by chambers, halls, and the dark interior of the closed-off abbey. The finale of the story culminates in the most shadowy imagery in the death of Rowena and the rebirth of Ligeia.

More specific than the foils of apocalyptic and demonic imagery, much of the climactic action of the story takes place during night, and often during autumn. For Jung, night and autumn pose strong symbolic representations of death as well as uncertainty. Night lies outside of the daylight hours when most common stories occur, and autumn lies on the twilight of the seasons, just before the earth plunges into the full wasteland of winter. Neither night nor autumn connect to the concepts of day (light) and spring (life) that are traditionally privileged, and both display mythic properties of limbo and tension. The deaths of Ligeia and Rowena occur in the shadowy realm of night: Rowena's illness is described specifically as occurring "one night, near the closing of September," and the final death of Rowena and rebirth of Ligeia "must have been close to midnight." Such symbols represent the deep unknown of the psyche and open the way for the final tension between anima and reality. These clashes of imagery in the settings—between apocalyptic and demonic imagery as well as the climax of night and autumnal setting—point to the psychic turmoil also apparent within the story.

Although Poe's horror tales evoke strong psychological responses within readers, more meaningful psychological concepts present themselves in the deeper layers of Poe's illusions. "Ligeia" is no exception. Pervading the whole of the story is the contrast of the inner anima of the psyche and the conflicting reality of the outer world. These two opposing forces of the mind find external symbols through the characters of Ligeia and Rowena. The tension between the two also surfaces through the symbolically apocalyptic and demonic settings. In addition, the struggle of the psyche is depicted through the symbolic cycles of death and rebirth. Through the archetypal symbols in "Ligeia," Poe creates not only a fascinating story of the gothic macabre but also a tale full of the struggle found in every psyche: the necessary struggle for reconciliation with the world, lest insanity overcomes the mind.

BRANDON W. HAWK

7

FEMINISM

To emancipate woman is to refuse to confine her to the relations she bears to man.

Simone de Beauvoir, *The Second Sex* (1949)

In the inaugural edition of one of the earliest American newspapers owned and operated by women, the *Woman's Chronicle* of Little Rock, Arkansas, Kate Cunningham, the editor, penned and published these words on Saturday, March 24, 1888:

> No one is so well calculated to think for woman kind as woman herself. In the province of administering to the wants of her sex, no one can be so well adapted as she. Her advancement is in no better way proven than by her progress in medicine and literature, to say nothing of the reform movements which she is steadily carrying on for the benefit of her sex.

More than 100 years later, another Arkansas woman and "first lady" of both Arkansas and the United States of America, Senator Hillary Rodham Clinton of New York, spoke these words in September 2005 at the United Nations Fourth World Conference on Women held in Beijing, China: "It is no longer acceptable to discuss women's rights as separate from human rights." That Senator Clinton voiced these words more than a century after Cunningham's newspaper proclamation is indeed telling. Were not Cunningham's words embraced by Americans in the latter part of the 1800s? And why need Clinton be assuring women of the twenty-first century that their rights and the rights of all humanity are one in the same? Are not twenty-first century women and men equal in all respects? Feminist studies, feminist theorists, and feminist critics all answer in one accord: No!

As one of the most significant developments in literary studies in the second half of the twentieth century, feminist literary criticism advocates equal rights for all women (indeed, all peoples) in all areas of life: socially, politically, professionally, personally, economically, aesthetically, and psychologically. Emerging in the 1960s, feminist criticism is one strand of feminist studies. Informed by feminist literary theory and scholarship, **feminist criticism** is an umbrella term for a variety of approaches to culture and literature that are of particular interest to women. Central to the diverse aims and methods of feminist criticism is its focus on **patriarchy**, the rule of society and culture by men. In her 1980 essay titled "Dancing through the Minefield"—one of the first works to articulate the theoretical assumptions of feminist theory and to survey its methodology—Annette Kolodny, a contemporary feminist critic, articulates feminist criticism's chief tenet:

> What unites and repeatedly invigorates feminist literary criticism . . . is neither dogma nor method but an acute and impassioned attentiveness to the ways in which primarily male structures of power are inscribed or (encoded) within our literary inheritance [and] the consequences of that encoding for women— as characters, as readers, and as writers.

These male structures of power embrace **phallocentrism**, the belief that identifies the **phallus** as the source of power in culture and literature, with its accompanying male-centered and male-dominated patriarchal assumptions. In her landmark essay "Feminist Literary Criticism," Toril Moi, another leading feminist theorist and critic, defines feminist criticism as "a specific kind of political discourse, a critical and theoretical practice committed to the struggle against patriarchy and sexism." According to Moi, one of feminist criticism's chief aims is to challenge and critique this patriarchal vision established in both culture and literature, denouncing and rejecting all phallocentric assumptions. Judith Fetterley, another leading feminist theorist and critic, agrees with Moi's definition. In the introduction to Fetterley's seminal text *The Resisting Reader: A Feminist Approach to American Fiction*, Fetterley asserts that "feminist criticism is [also] a political act whose aim is not simply to interpret the world but to change it by changing the consciousness of those who read and their relation to what they read." According to Fetterley, the first act of a feminist critic is "to become a resisting rather than an assenting reader and, by this refusal to assent, to begin the process of exorcising the male mind that has been implanted in us."

How has the male mind, with its accompanying phallocentric belief system, been implanted in us? Through its literature and its acclaimed writers, philosophers, and scholars, most of whom are male. A brief historical survey of comments made and beliefs held by canonical male writers lends support to feminist criticism's belief that a patriarchal vision has been established in the Western literary canon:

> *Do not let a woman with a sexy rump deceive you with wheedling and coaxing words; she is after your barn. The man who trusts a woman trusts a deceiver.*

> Hesiod, poet 8th century B.C.E.

> *Plato thanks the gods for two blessings: that he had not been born a slave and that he had not been born a woman.*

> Plato (c. 427–c. 347 B.C.E.)

Silence gives the proper grace to women.

Sophocles (497–406 B.C.E.)

The male is by nature superior, and the female inferior; and the one rules and the other is ruled.
Woman "is matter, waiting to be formed by the active male principle. . . . Man consequently plays a major part in reproduction; the woman is merely the passive incubator of his seed."

Aristotle (384–322 B.C.E.)

Frailty, thy name is woman.

Shakespeare (1564–1616)

Most women have no character at all.

Alexander Pope (1688–1744)

Women, women! Cherished and deadly objects that nature has embellished to torture us . . . whose hatred and love are equally harmful, and whom we cannot either seek or flee with impunity.

Jean-Jacques Rousseau (1702–1778)

Mary Wollstonecraft is a "hyena in petticoats."

Horace Walpole, author of one of the earliest Gothic novels,
The Castle of Otranto (1717–1797)

Nature intended women to be our slaves. . . . They are our property. . . . What a mad idea to demand equality for women!

Napoleon Bonaparte (1769–1821)

Literature cannot be the business of a woman's life, and it ought not to be. The more she is engaged in her proper duties, the less leisure will she have for it, even any . . . recreation.

Robert Southey, poet laureate (1774–1843)

Woman is a slave whom we must be clever enough to set upon a throne.

Honoré de Balzac (1799–1850)

Jane Austen's novels are "vulgar in tone, sterile in artistic invention . . . without genius, wit or knowledge of the world. Never was life so pinched and narrow."

Ralph Waldo Emerson (1803–1882)

Women writers are a "damned mob of scribbling women" who only write anything worth reading if the devil is in them.

Nathaniel Hawthorne (1804–1864)

The woman author does not exist. She is a contradiction in terms. The role of the woman in letters is the same as in manufacturing; she is of use when genius is no longer required.

Pierre-Joseph Proudhon (1809–1865)

Woman is natural, that is, abominable.

Charles-Pierre Baudelaire (1821–1867)

Jane Austen is entirely impossible to read. It seems a great pity that they allowed her to die a natural death.

Mark Twain (1835–1910)

The very idea of womanhood is a storm of hair . . . with a greedy little mouth somewhere behind the mirage of beauty.

Friedrich Nietzsche (1844–1900)

An artist's most essential quality is "masterly execution, which is a kind of male gift, and especially marks off men from women, the begetting of one's thoughts on paper. . . . The male quality is the creative gift."

Gerard Manley Hopkins (1844–1889)

Feminism is a political mistake. Feminism is a mistake made by women's intellect, a mistake which her instinct will recognize.

Valentine de Saint-Point (1875–1953)

Educating a woman is like pouring honey over a fine Swiss watch. It stops working.

Kurt Vonnegut, Jr. (1922–)

Feminist literary criticism challenges such patriarchal statements with their accompanying male-dominated, philosophical assumptions and such gender-biased criticism. Feminist criticism argues that literature should be free from such biases because of race, class, or gender, and provides a variety of theoretical frameworks and approaches to interpretation that values each member of society.

HISTORICAL DEVELOPMENT

According to feminist criticism, the roots of prejudice against women have long been embedded in Western culture. The ancient Greeks abetted gender discrimination, declaring the male to be the superior and the female the inferior. Women, they maintained, lure men away from seeking after truth, preventing them from attaining their full potential. In the centuries that follow, other philosophers and scientists continue such gender discrimination. For example, in *The Descent of Man* (1871), Charles Darwin (1809–1882) announces that women are of a "characteristic of . . . a past and lower state of civilization." Such beings, he notes, are inferior to men, who are physically, intellectually, and artistically superior.

Century after century, male voices continue to articulate and determine the social role and cultural and personal significance of women. Some scholars believe that the first major work of feminist criticism challenging these male voices was that authored by Christine de Pisan in the fourteenth century, *Epistre au Dieu D'amours* (1399). In this work, Pisan critiques Jean de Meun's biased representation of the nature of woman in his text *Roman de La Rose*. In another work, *La Cite des Dames* (1405), Pisan declares that God created men and women as equal beings.

But it was not until the late 1700s that another voice arose in opposition to patriarchal beliefs and statements. Influenced by the French revolution and believing that women along with men should have a voice in the public arena, Mary Wollstonecraft (1759–1797) authored *A Vindication of the Rights of Women* (1792), the first major published work that acknowledges an awareness of women's struggles for equal rights. Women, she maintains, must define for themselves what it means to be a woman. Women themselves must take the lead and articulate who they are and what role they will play in society by rejecting the patriarchal assumption that women are inferior to men.

It was not until the Progressive Era of the early 1900s, however, that major concerns of feminist criticism took root. During this time, women gained the right to vote and became prominent activists in the social issues of the day, such as health care, education, politics, and literature, but equality with men in these arenas still remained outside their grasp.

Virginia Woolf

In 1919, the British scholar and teacher Virginia Woolf (1882–1941) developed and enlarged Mary Wollstonecraft's ideas, laying the foundation for present-day feminist criticism in her seminal work *A Room of One's Own* (1929). In this text, Woolf declares that men have and continue to treat women as inferiors. Men define what it means to be female and determine who controls the political, economic, social, and literary structures. Agreeing with Samuel T. Coleridge, one of the foremost nineteenth-century literary critics, that great minds possess both male and female characteristics, Woolf hypothesizes the existence of Shakespeare's sister, one who is equally as gifted a writer as Shakespeare himself. Shakespeare's sister's gender, however, prevents her from having "a room of her own." Because she is a woman, she cannot obtain an education or find profitable employment. Because she cannot economically afford a room of her own, her innate artistic talents will never flourish. Being able to afford her own room would symbolize the solitude and autonomy needed to seclude herself from the world and its social constraints in order to find time to think and write. In Woolf's text, Shakespeare's sister dies alone without any acknowledgment of her personal genius. Even her grave plot does not bear her name; she is buried in a unmarked grave because she is female.

Such a loss of artistic talent and personal worth, argues Woolf, is the result of society's opinion of women: They are seen as intellectually inferior to men. Women, Woolf declares, must reject the social construct of female-ness and establish and define for themselves their own identity. To do so, they must challenge the prevailing, false cultural notions about their gender identity and develop a female discourse that will accurately portray their relationship "to the world of reality and not to the world of men." If women accept this challenge, Woolf believes that Shakespeare's sister can live once again in and through women living today, even those who may be "washing up the dishes and putting the children to bed" right now. Societal and world calamities such as the Great Depression of the 1930s and World War II in the 1940s, however, changed the focus of humankind's attention and delayed the advancement of these feminist ideals.

Simone de Beauvoir

After World War II and the 1949 publication of *The Second Sex* by the French writer Simone de Beauvoir (1908–1986), feminist concerns once again surfaced. Heralded as the foundational work of twentieth-century feminism, Beauvoir's text asserts that French society (and Western societies in general) are **patriarchal**, controlled by men. Like Woolf before her, Beauvoir believes that men define what it means to be human, including what it means to be female. Since the female is not male, Beauvoir maintains, she becomes the **Other**, an object whose existence is defined and interpreted by the dominant male. Being subordinate to the male, the female discovers that she is a secondary or nonexistent player in the major social institutions of her culture, such as the church, government, and educational systems. Beauvoir believes that women must break the bonds of their patriarchal society and define themselves if they wish to become a significant human being in their own right, and they must defy male classification as the Other. Women must ask themselves, "What is a woman?" Beauvoir insists that a woman's answer must not be "mankind" because such a term once again allows men to define women. Beauvoir rejects this generic label, believing that such labeling assumes that "humanity is male and man defines woman not as herself but as relative to him."

Beauvoir insists that women must see themselves as autonomous beings. Women, she maintains, must reject the societal construct that men are the subject or the absolute and women are the Other. Embedded in this erroneous statement is the assumption that men have the power to control the dominant **discourse** and the power to define cultural terms and roles. Accordingly, women must define themselves, articulate their own social constructs of what it means to be a woman, and reject being labeled as the Other.

Kate Millett

With the advent of the 1960s and with its political activism and social concerns, feminist issues found new voices, such as Mary Ellmann (*Thinking About Women*, 1968) and Kate Millett. With Millett's publication of *Sexual Politics* in 1969, a new wave of feminism begins. Millett is one of the first to challenge the ideological characteristics of both the male and the female. She argues that a female is born, but a woman is created. In other words, one's sex is determined at birth, but one's gender is a social construct created by cultural norms. Consciously or unconsciously, women and men conform to the societal constructs established by society. Boys, for example, should be aggressive, self-assertive, and domineering, but girls should be passive, meek, and humble. Such cultural expectations are transmitted through media, including television, movies, songs, and literature. Conforming to these prescribed sex roles dictated by society is what Millett calls **sexual politics**, or the operations of power relations in society. In the West, institutional power rests with males, forcing the subordination of women. Women, Millett maintains, must disenfranchise the power center of their culture: male dominance. By so doing, women will be able to establish female social conventions as defined by females, not males, and in the process, they themselves will shape and articulate female discourse, literary studies, and feminist theory.

FEMINISM IN THE 1960s, 1970s, AND 1980s

In 1963, two works help bring feminist concerns into the public arena: *American Women*, edited by Frances Bagley Kaplan and Margaret Mead, and *The Feminine Mystique* by Betty Freidan. *American Women* was the culminating work of 2 years of investigation by the President's Commission on the Status of Women commissioned by President John F. Kennedy. This work details the great inequality between men and women in the workplace, education, and society as a whole. Armed with verifiable evidence of their inequality, women asserted political pressure in Congress and state legislative houses across America for reforms. As women began to enter the political arena and articulate their concerns, a freelance writer, Betty Friedan (1921–2006), published *The Feminine Mystique*. Friedan articulated and helped popularize two central questions of feminist criticism that soon became popular: "A woman has got to be able to say, and not feel guilty, '*Who am I*, and *What do I want out of life*?' She mustn't feel selfish and neurotic if she wants goals of her own, outside of husband and children." By 1966, Friedan was elected president of the newly formed National Organization for Women (NOW) whose platform argued for equal opportunity for women "under the law," including educational and employment reforms; the right of choice concerning abortion; and a host of other social, political, and personal issues.

During this time and throughout the 1970s, feminist theorists and critics began to examine the traditional literary canon, discovering copious examples of male dominance and prejudice that supported Beauvoir's and Millett's assertion that males consider the female "the Other." Stereotypes of women abounded in the canon: Women were sex maniacs, goddesses of beauty, mindless entities, or old spinsters. In addition, although Charles Dickens, William Wordsworth, Nathaniel Hawthorne, Henry David Thoreau, Mark Twain, and a host of other male authors found their way into the established canon, few female authors achieved such status. Those who did appear, such as Mary E. Wilkins Freeman or Sarah Orne Jewett, were referred to as "local color writers," implying their secondary or minor position in the canon. Similarly, the roles of female, fictionalized characters were often limited to minor characters whose chief traits reinforced the male's stereotypical image of women. Female theorists, critics, and scholars such as Woolf and de Beauvoir were simply ignored, their writings seldom, if ever, referred to by the male crafters of the literary canon.

Feminist theorists and critics of this era declared that male authors who created and enjoyed such a place of prominence within the canon had assumed that their ideal readers were all men. Women reading such works could easily be duped into reading like a man. In addition, because most of the university professors were men, more frequently than not, female students were being trained to read literature as if they, too, were men. The feminist critics of the 1960s, 1970s, and 1980s announced the existence of a female ideal reader who was affronted by the male prejudices abounding in the canon. Questions now arose concerning the male *and* female qualities of literary form, style, voice, theme, and other aesthetic elements of texts.

Throughout the 1970s, books that defined women's writings in feminine terms flourished. Having successfully highlighted the importance of gender, feminist theorists uncovered and rediscovered a body of works authored by women that their male counterparts had decreed inferior and unworthy to be part of the canon. In America, for example, Kate Chopin's late nineteenth-century novel *The Awakening* (1899) served as the archetypal, rediscovered feminist text of this period. In England, Doris Lessing's *The Golden Notebook* (1962) and in France, Monique Wittig's *Les Guérillères* (1969) fulfilled these roles. Throughout the universities and in the reading populace, many readers now turned their attention to historical and current works authored by women. Simultaneously, works that helped define the feminine imagination, categorize and explain female literary history, and articulate a female aesthetic became the focus of feminist critics.

Feminist concerns were supported in print by the establishment of the Feminist Press in 1972 and journals such as *Signs, Women's Studies Quarterly*, and *Feminist Studies*, to name a few. Texts such as Annette Kolodny's *The Lay of the Land* (1975); Arlyn Diamond and Lee R. Edwards's *The Authority of Experience* (1977); Judith Fetterley's *The Resisting Reader* (1978); Nina Baym's *Women's Fiction: A Guide to Novels by and About Women in America, 1820–1870* (1978); Sandra M. Gilbert and Susan Gubar's edited work *Shakespeare's Sisters: Feminist Essays in Women Poets* (1979); and Gilbert and Gubar's *The Madwoman in the Attic* (1979) helped shape the ongoing concerns and direction of feminist theory and criticism, providing public venues for these discussions.

Elaine Showalter

A leading voice of feminist criticism throughout the late 1970s and through the next several decades is that of Elaine Showalter. In her text *A Literature of Their Own* (1977), Showalter chronicles three historical phases of female writing: the **feminine phase** (1840–1880), the **feminist phase** (1880–1920), and the **female phase** (1970–present). During the "feminine" phase, writers such as Charlotte Brontë, George Eliot, and George Sand accepted the prevailing social constructs that defined women. Accordingly, these authors wrote under male pseudonyms so that their works, like their male counterparts, would first be published and then recognized for their intellectual and artistic achievements.

During the "feminist" or second phase, female writers helped dramatize the plight of the "slighted" woman, depicting the harsh and often cruel treatment of female characters at the hands of their more powerful male creations. In the third or "female" phase, female writers reject both the feminine social constructs prominent during the "feminine" phase and the secondary or minor position of female characters that dominated the "feminist" phase. Showalter observes that feminist theorists and critics now concerned themselves with developing a peculiarly female understanding of the female experience in art, including a feminine analysis of literary forms and techniques. Such a task necessarily includes the uncovering of **misogyny** in texts, a term Showalter uses to describe the male hatred of women.

Showalter believes that female writers were deliberately excluded from the literary canon by male professors who first established the canon itself. Writers such as Susan Warner (*The Wide, Wide World*, 1851), Emma D.N. Southworth (*The Hidden Hand*, 1888), and Mary E. Wilkins Freeman ("A New England Nun," 1891; *Pembroke*, 1894), by far the most popular authors of the second half of the nineteenth century in American fiction, were not deemed worthy to be included in the canon. Such exclusion, says Showalter, must cease. In her influential essay "Toward a Feminist Poetics" (1997), Showalter asserts that feminist theorists must "construct a female framework for analysis of women's literature to develop new models based on the study of female experience, rather than to adapt to male models and theories," a process she names **gynocriticism**. Through gynocriticism, Showalter exposes the false cultural assumptions and characteristics of women as depicted in canonical literature. By exposing these inaccurate pictures (often caricatures) of women, **gynocritics**—the name Showalter gives to those critics who "construct a female framework for the analysis of women's literature, to develop new models based on the study of female experience, rather than to adapt to male models and theories"—and gynocriticism provide critics with four models that address the nature of women's writing: the biological, the linguistic, the psychoanalytic, and the cultural.

Each of Showalter's models are sequential, subsuming and developing the preceding model or models. The **biological model** emphasizes how the female body marks itself upon a text by providing a host of literary images along with a personal, intimate tone. The **linguistic model** addresses the need for a female discourse, investigating the differences between how women and men use language. This model asserts that women create and write in a language peculiar to their gender and addresses the ways in which this female language can be used in their writings. The **psychoanalytic model** analyzes the female psyche and demonstrates how such an analysis affects the writing process, emphasizing the flux and fluidity of female writing as opposed to male writing's rigidity and structure. The last of Showalter's models, the **cultural model**, investigates how society shapes women's goals, responses, and points of view.

Geographical Strains of Feminism

During the 1960s, 1970s, and 1980s, no one critical theory of writing dominated feminist criticism because feminist theory and criticism highlighted the personal, allowing for diverse theories and approaches to textual analysis. Historically, geography played a significant role in determining the major interests of the various voices of feminist criticisms, with three somewhat distinct, geographical strains of feminism emerging: American, British, and French. These geographical divisions no longer serve as distinct theoretical or practical boundaries, but they remain important historical markers in feminism's development. According to Showalter, American feminism at this time was essentially textual, stressing repression; British feminism was essentially Marxist, stressing oppression; and French feminism was essentially psychoanalytic, stressing repression. The aim of all groups was similar: to rescue women from being considered "the Other."

American For American feminism, Kolodny announced feminism's major concern: the restoration and inclusion of the writings of female writers to the literary canon. Believing that literary history is itself a fiction, Kolodny restores a realistic history of women so that they themselves can tell "herstory." In order to tell and write "herstory," female writers must find a means to gain their voice amid the dominating male voices clamoring for society's attention. In *The Lay of the Land: Metaphor as Experience and History in American Life and Letters* (1975) and *The Land Before Her: Fantasy and Experience of the American Frontiers, 1630–1860* (1984), Kolodny uses feminist-psychoanalytic theories and methodologies to assert that the American colonists attributed to the land feminine characteristics to soften and allay their fears concerning the land's unknown but potential terrors. Whereas some males viewed the American frontier as a new Eden, female colonists often saw it as a home and a "familial human community." In her lastest work, *Failing the Future: A Dean Looks at Higher Education in the Twenty-first Century*, Kolodny provides evidence that women are still "outsiders" of American universities and in colleges campuses and documents the rising anti-feminist and anti-intellectual harassment occuring in higher education.

Similar to Kolodny, Sandra M. Gilbert and Susan Gubar, authors of *The Madwoman in the Attic: The Woman Writer and the Nineteenth-Century Literary Imagination* (1979), assert that the male voice has for too long been dominant. Because men have had the power of the pen and the press, they have been allowed not only to define but also to create images of women as they so chose in their texts. Gilbert and Gubar argue that this male power has caused "anxiety of authorship" in women, causing them to fear the act of literary creation itself along with and the act of writing. Some female writers believe that literary creation will isolate them from society, perhaps destroying them. Gilbert and Gubar's solution is that women develop a "woman's sentence" that can encourage literary autonomy. By inventing such a sentence, a woman can in turn sentence male authors to isolation, fear, and literary banishment from the canon, just as for centuries men have been sentencing women. By formulating a woman's sentence, female writers can and will free themselves from being defined by men.

A woman's sentence, argue Gilbert and Gubar, will also free women from being reduced to the stereotypical images that appear in literature. They identify two such principal stereotypical images: "the angel in the house" and the "madwoman in the attic." When depicted as the angel in the house, a woman supposedly realizes that her physical and material comforts are gifts from her husband. Her goals in life are to please her husband, attend to his every comfort, and obey him. Through these supposedly selfless acts, she finds utmost contentment by serving both him and her children. When a female writer and her characters reject such a role, male critics dub her a "monster," the madwoman in the attic who is also "obviously" sexually fallen.

Gilbert and Gubar assert that both of these images—the angel or the madwoman—are unrealistic representations of women in society. The first image canonizes the woman, placing her simultaneously above and outside her socially constructed world, and the second image denigrates and demonizes the woman, banishing her to the world of myths and the demonic while disavowing her rightful place in both literature and society. The message is clear: If you are not an angel, then you are a monster. These stereotypical, male-created images of women in literature, declare Gilbert and Gubar, must be uncovered, examined, debunked, and transcended if women are to achieve literary autonomy.

British Whereas American feminism emphasized repression, British feminism stressed oppression. Leaning toward Marxist theory, British feminism saw art, literature, and life as inseparable. Some British feminists, although not all, viewed reading, writing, and publishing as facets of material reality. Being part of this material reality, literature, like one's job and one's social activities, is part of a great whole, with each part affecting the other. How a woman is depicted in literature directly affects how women will be treated in real life. Particularly in the West, patriarchal society exploits women not only through literature but also economically and socially. The traditional Western family structure, assert these feminist critics, subordinates women, causing them to be economically dependent. The West's literature reflects such dependency. British feminism of this era challenges the economic and social status of women, both in society and as depicted in the arts, especially in texts. For these critics, the goal of feminist criticism is to change society, not simply critique it.

French French Feminism, the third geographical division of feminism, stressed female oppression both in life and art, highlighting the repression of women. Often, including current feminist criticism, French feminism is closely associated with the theoretical and practical applications of psycho-analysis and the theories of Sigmund Freud and Jacques Lacan. At first, the association with psychoanalysis may be a bit puzzling because Freud and his patriarchal theories seemingly dominate psychoanalysis. Believing that phallus is power, Freud viewed women as incomplete males who possess penis envy, desiring to gain the male phallus and obtain power. In several ways, the French psychoanalytic critic Lacan rescues psychoanalysis from Freud's misogynistic theories. Lacan argues that language ultimately shapes and structures our conscious and unconscious minds, thereby shaping our self-identity. Language as it is structured and understood, he maintains, ulti-mately denies women the power of literature and writing.

Lacan posits that the human psyche consists of three parts, or what he calls orders: the imaginary, the symbolic, and the real. Each of these orders interacts with the others. From birth to age 6 months or so, we primarily function in the **imaginary order**, a preverbal state that contains our wishes, our fantasies, and our physical images. In this state, we are basically gender-less because we are not yet capable of differentiating ourselves from our mothers. As soon as we have successfully navigated the Oedipal crisis, we pass from using a biological language to a socialized language and into the second of the Lacanian orders: the **symbolic order**. In this Lacanian phase, whereas the boy becomes dominate, particularly in the discourse of lan-guage, the girl is socialized into using a subordinated language. On entering this order, the father is the dominant image (the Law), with both the boy and the girl fearing castration by the father. For the boy, this fear of castration means obeying and becoming similar to the father while simultaneously repressing the imaginary order that is most closely associated with the female body. The imaginary order, with its pre-Oedipal boy, becomes a direct threat to the male in the third Lacanian order, **the real order**, or the actual world as perceived by the individual. For the girl, entrance into the symbolic order means submission to law of the father. Such submission brings sub-servience to males. Being socialized through and in the discourse of lan-guage, the girl becomes a second-class citizen. Because language, for Lacan, is a psychological, not a biological construct, he believes that women can learn the dominant discourse of both the symbolic and the real orders and become tools of social, political, and personal change.

French feminists such as Julia Kristeva and Hélène Cixous borrow and amend elements of Freud's and Lacan's theories to develop their own forms of feminist criticism. In works such as *Revolution in Poetic Language* (1974), *Desire in Language* (1980), and *Powers of Horror* (1982), Kristeva posits that the imaginary order is characterized by a continuous flow of fluidity or rhythm, which she calls **chora**. On entering the Lacanian symbolic order, both males and females are separated from chora and repress the feelings of fluidity and rhythm. Similar to a Freudian slip in which an unconscious thought breaks through the conscious mind, the chora can, at times, break through into the real order and disturb the male-dominant discourse. Most recently, in works such as *Tales of Love*, Kristeva's concept of "motherhood" has informed much of her writing because she asks what she believes to be the central though complex question of feminist theory: "How can an enquiry into the nature of motherhood lead to a better understanding of the part played in love by the woman?" Kristeva argues that women must eventually "deal" with men, another woman, or perhaps a child. How does the rejection or acceptance of motherhood shape women?

Cixous explores a different mode of discourse that arises from the Lacan's symbolic, not the imaginary, order. Cixous maintains that words such as "feminine," "masculine," "femininity," and even "man" and "woman" should be exorcised from language. In works such as "Laugh of the Medusa" (1975), Cixous declares that there exists a particular kind of female writing that she calls **l'écriture féminine**, envisioned in terms of bisexuality. L'écriture féminine can best be understood, Cixous asserts, as "the ideal harmony, reached by few, which would be gential, assembling everything and being capable of generosity, of spending." This kind of female writing is the province of metaphor, not limited to written words but also "writing by the voice." Characterized by fluidity, such feminine discourse, when fully explored, says Cixous, will transform the social and cultural structures within literature by freeing both women and men from **phallocentrism**.

PRESENT-DAY FEMINIST CRITICISMS

Because contemporary feminist criticism is not composed of a single ideology, many subcategories or approaches have developed, each creating its own sphere of concern while often intersecting not only with other forms of feminist criticism but also with other schools of literary criticism, such as psychoanalysis, Marxism, and deconstruction. Some scholars categorize feminist criticism into four groups: **Anglo-American feminisms** (e.g., Virginia Woolf, Judith Fetterley, Annette Kolodny, Nina Baym, Elaine Showalter, Sandra Gilbert, Susan Gubar); **poststructuralist feminisms** (e.g., Luce Irigaray, Catherine Clément, Gayatri Chakravorty Spivak, Monique Wittig, Hélène Cixous, Julia Kristeva, Joan Scott, and others); **materialist feminisms** (e.g., Juliet Mitchell, Michèle Barrett, Jacqueline Rose, Rosaling Coward, Toril Moi, Catherine Belsey, Katie King, Donna Haraway); and **postmodern feminisms**, usually dating from 1990 to the present (e.g., Jane Gallop, Judith Butler, Diana Fuss, Chandra Mohanty, Uma Narayan, Mary Daly, Gloria Anzaldúa).

Other critics subdivide feminist criticism into a variety of subcategories, ranging in number from nine to more than 30. Some of these approaches include Amazon feminism, cultural feminism, ecofeminism, material feminism, and separatists, to cite a few. **Amazon feminism** is dedicated to female images—either fictional or real—in literature and art that emphasize the physiques of female athletes and physical equality of both males and females. Opposed to gender roles and discrimination against women based on the false assumptions that females are physically weak and passive, amazon feminism argues that no mention of gender need arise, for example, when discussing such topics as occupations. Whereas some people are not physically capable of being a firefighter, others are likewise not capable of driving a snowplow. Gender is not an issue because there are no characteristics that are peculiarly masculine or feminine.

Sometimes referred to as radical feminism, **cultural feminism** asserts that personality and biological differences exist between men and women. According to cultural feminists such as Elizabeth Gould David (*The First Sex*), the main tenet of cultural feminism states that women are inherently and biologically "kinder and gentler" than men. Such women's ways should be highlighted and celebrated because in the eyes of many cultural feminists, women's ways are better than men's.

Ecofeminism (sometimes spelled eco-feminism) assumes that patriarchal societies are relatively new and that society's original condition (dubbed the feminist Eden) was matriarchal. Patriarchal societies, say ecofeminists, are detrimental to women, children, and nature. Whereas a patriarchal society dominates both women and nature, plundering and destroying our planet, a matriarchal society protects the environment, natural resources, and animal life and especially cares for women and children.

Authored by Charlotte Perkins Gilman, *The Grand Domestic Revolution* highlights the concerns of **material feminism**. Developing in the latter part of the nineteenth century, material feminism aims to improve the material condition of women by unburdening them of the "traditional" female tasks such as housework, cooking, ironing clothes, and other domestic responsibilities. **Separatist feminism**, however, advocates separation from men, either total or partial. Although some separatists may be lesbians, it is inaccurate to assume that all separatists are lesbians. Separatists assume that women must first see themselves in a different context—separating themselves from men, at least for a while—before they can discover who they are as individuals. Such a separation, they maintain, is the necessary first step to achieving personal growth and individuality.

No matter what subcategory and theory they may espouse, feminist critics assert that they are on a journey of self-discovery that will lead them to a better understanding of themselves, their society, and the world at large. Seeking to understand themselves first as individuals, they believe that they will then be equipped to develop their own individual talents and fully participate in all aspects of their culture, including the arts.

ASSUMPTIONS

To onlookers, feminist theory and practice appear to be diffuse, a loosely connected body of criticism that is more divided than unified, more prone to internal disagreements than to unity among its adherents. Feminist criticism cannot claim nor indeed wants to claim any ultimate spokesperson because feminists believe in the personal, advocating for many different voices to be heard and respected. Not to be understood as homogeneous, feminist criticism should actually be dubbed feminist criticisms. Behind all these multivoices, theories, and practices, however, rests a cooperative set of principles.

The core belief of feminist theory and criticism asserts that all people—women and men—are politically, socially, and economically equal. Although diverse in its social theories, values, and politics, feminist criticism chiefly advocates for the rights of women. Its adherents are women (and some men) who are struggling to discover who they are, how they arrived at their present situation, and where they are going. In their search, they value the individual person, validating and giving significance to the individual as opposed to the group. Their search at times is political because their aim is to discover and change both themselves and the world in which they live, a world that must learn to validate all individuals, all cultures, and all subcultures as creative, aesthetic, and rational people who can contribute to their societies and their world. Such a revisionist stance seeks to understand the place of women in society and to analyze every aspect that affects women as citizens and as writers in a male-dominated world. In this patriarchal world, man more frequently than not defines what it means to be human. Woman has become the Other, the "not-male." Man is the subject, the one who defines meaning. Woman is the object, having her existence defined and determined by the male. Whereas the man is the significant (or **privileged**, using Derrida's term) binary in the male/female relationship, the female is subordinate (or **unprivileged**).

By defining the female in relation to the male and simultaneously claiming the superiority of the male, Western society and many other cultures are, for the most part, patriarchal, decreeing that the female, by nature, is inferior. As soon as Western culture both consciously or unconsciously assimilated this belief into its social structures and allowed it to permeate all levels of society, females became an oppressed people, inferiors who must be suppressed least humankind fail to reach its maximum potential.

Feminist theorists and critics want to correct such erroneous ways of thinking. Women, they declare, are individuals, people in their own right; they are not incomplete or inferior men. Despite how frequently literature and society have fictionalized and stereotyped females as angels, bar maids, bitches, whores, brainless housewives, or old maids, women must define themselves and articulate their roles, values, aspirations, and place in society.

To do so, say feminist critics, women must analyze and challenge the established literary canon that has shaped such images of female inferiority and subordination. Women must contest the long-held patriarchal assumptions about their sex and gender, and they must marshall a variety of resources to assert, clarify, and finally implement their beliefs and values. Through a reexamination of the established literature in all disciplines, by defining and validating what it means to be a woman, and by establishing and creating feminist literary theories and criticisms, women can legitimatize their responses to any text; to their own writing; and to their political, economic, and social positions in their culture.

METHODOLOGY

Because feminist theory and criticisms are polyphonic, a variety of feminist approaches to textual analysis exists. Some feminist critics debunk male superiority by exposing stereotypes of women in all literary periods. Women, they assert, cannot be simply depicted and classified as either angels or demons, saints or whores, brainless housewives or eccentric spinsters. Such characterizations must be continually identified and then challenged.

Other feminist critics continue to scrutinize the American, the English, or the non-Western literary canon, rediscovering works written by women. Still other feminist critics reread the canonical works of male authors from a female point of view. Such an analysis develops a uniquely female consciousness based on female experience rather than relying on the traditional male theories of reading, writing, and critiquing. Elaine Showalter's gynocriticism with its multifaceted approach helps feminist critics in such an analysis.

Some feminist critics such as Luce Irigaray use the methodologies of philosophy and psychoanalysis to overturn patriarchy and its accompanying phallogocentrism. These critics' aim is to expose the multiple ways that patriarchal discourses empower males while disenfranchising women. And critics such as Kristeva and Gayatri Chakravorty Spivak employ the methodologies of linguistics, Marxism, deconstruction, and subaltern studies to overturn and provide alternatives to patriarchal discourse.

In similar fashion, critics such as Monique Wittig and Hélène Cixous propose a completely new, nonphallogocentric discourse. Wittig challenges not only patriarchal assumptions in culture but also in the very structure of language itself, experimenting and hoping to eliminate pronouns and nouns, for example, that reflect gender, a process she calls the **lesbianization of language**. Cixous's feminist methodology embraces the creation of a female language, **l' écriture féminine**, to open phallogocentric discourse to both sexes. Providing models to challenge the dominant discourse is also a chief concern for both postcolonial feminism and the women of color feminists.

To use the various approaches to feminist criticisms, an in-depth under-standing of each of the various theoretical positions and methodologies is essential.

QUESTIONS FOR ANALYSIS

Whatever method of feminist criticisms we choose to apply to a text, we can begin such textual analysis by asking some general questions:

- Is the author male or female?
- Is the text narrated by a male or female?
- What types of roles do women have in the text?
- Are the female characters the protagonists or secondary and minor characters?
- Do any stereotypical characterizations of women appear?
- What are the attitudes toward women held by the male characters?
- What is the author's attitude toward women in society?
- How does the author's culture influence her or his attitude?
- Is feminine imagery used? If so, what is the significance of such imagery?
- Do the female characters speak differently than the male characters? In your investigation, compare the frequency of speech for the male characters to the fre-quency of speech for the female characters.

By applying any or all of these questions to a text, we can begin our journey in feminist criticism and simultaneously help ourselves to better understand ourselves as individuals and the world in which we live.

CRITIQUES AND RESPONSES

At the beginning of this chapter are a variety of quotations pronounced by men concerning women; now let us listen to the voices of females:

You have to make more noise than anybody else, you have to make yourself more obstrusive than anybody else, you have to fill all the papers more than anybody else, in fact you have to have to be there all the time and see that they do not snow you under, if you are really going to get your reform realized.

Emmeline Panhurst, British suffragist (1858–1928)

Feminism, like Boston, is a state of mind. It is the state of mind of women who real-ize that their whole position in the social order is antiquated, as a woman cooking over an open fire with heavy iron pots would know that her entire housekeeping was out of date.

Feminism never harmed anybody unless it was some feminists. The danger is that the study and contemplation of "ourselves" may become so absorbing that it builds by slow degress a high wall that shuts out the great world of thought.

Rheta Childe Dorr, journalist (1866–1948)

Feminism is the radical notion that women are people.

Cheris Karamarae and Paula Treichler

The connections between and among women are the most feared, the most problematic, and the most potentially transforming force on the planet.

Adrienne Rich, poet (b. 1929)

Feminism is an entire world view or gestalt, not just a laundry list of women's issues.

Charolotte Bunch, editor, author (1944–)

It is important to remember that feminism is no longer a group of organizations or leaders. It is the expectations that parents have for their daughters, and their sons too. It is the way we talk about and treat one another. It is who makes the money and who makes the compromises and who makes the dinner. It is a state of mind. It is the way of life we live now.

Anna Quindlen, journalist/novelist (1945–)

Feminism is a political term and it must be recognized as such: it is political in women's terms. What are these terms? Essentially it means making connections: between personal power and economic power, between domestic oppression and labor exploitation, between plants and chemicals, feelings and theories; it means making connections between our inside worlds and the outside world.

Anica Vesel Mander (1945–) and Anne K. Rush (1945–)

For many people, Andrienne Rich's quote encapsulates the essence of feminist criticism: it is feared, it is problematic, and it has the ability and the transformative power to reshape our world. A branch of feminist studies grounded in feminist theory and scholarship, feminist criticism is a heterogenous grouping of scholars, writers, linguistics, philosophers, scientists, anthropologists, psychologists, educators, and peoples from all professions and walks of life who believe that women and men are equal. As a social movement, feminist criticism highlights the various ways women, in particular, have been oppressed, suppressed, and repressed. It asks new questions of old texts. It develops and uncovers a female tradition in writing. It analyzes women writers and their works from female perspectives. It attempts to redefine literary concepts and the dominant discourse—language itself—in terms of gender. It disavows the privileged position of males in a predominatedly patriarchal society. It questions basic assumptions about gender, gender difference, and sexuality. And it demands that we become resisting readers to the established male hierarchies upon which our culture and our literature have been shaped.

Critics of feminist criticism often view it as a collection of theorists and critics who cannot decide what they really believe. Its critics assert that one group of feminist criticism defines "female" and "male" one way while another develops conflicting and sometimes contradictory definitions. Even within feminist criticism itself, the various subcategories criticize each other. Postcolonial feminists, for example, harshly critique Western forms of criticism. Psychoanalytic feminist critics often view their cultures and society differently from materialistic or Marxist critics. Because of such differences, critics avow that the multi-voices of feminist criticism(s) cannot sustain a unified ideology.

Feminist criticism's conservative critics advocate that the goal of feminist criticism is to destroy traditional values and gender roles. Males and females, argue these critics, are naturally and biologically different. From these critics' point of view, feminist criticism is rooted in error and has become, for them, the enemy. Some even blame their own lack of success in business or any other area in the public arena on the rise of feminism.

Whether such criticism is real or imagined, present-day feminist critics believe that discrimination against women still exists, not only in America, but worldwide—discrimination in the workplace, in the home, in the church, in government, and in society as a whole. Issues such as the glass ceiling, human trafficking, slavery, and prostitution continue to plague society. Feminist criticisms, maintain its advocates, will continue to add their voices of protest to such injustices.

FURTHER READING

Beauvoir, Simone de. *The Second Sex*. Parshley, H.M. (ed. and trans). New York: Modern Library, 1952.

Butler, Judith. *Undoing Gender*. New York: Taylor & Francis, 2004.

Cohen, Ralph, ed. Feminist directions. *New Literary History: A Journal of Theory and Interpretation* 19 (Autumn 1987):1–208.

Eagleton, Mary, ed. *Feminist Literary Theory: A Reader*, 2nd ed. Oxford: Blackwell, 1996.

Fetterley, Judith. *The Resisting Reader: A Feminist Approach to American Fiction*. Bloomington, IN: Indiana University Press, 1978.

Friedan, Betty. *The Feminine Mystique*. New York: Norton, 2001.

Gates, Henry Louis, Jr., ed. *Reading Black, Reading Feminist: A Critical Anthology*. New York: Plume, 1990.

Gilbert, Sandra M., and Susan Gubar. *The Madwoman in the Attic: The Woman Writer and the Nineteenth-Century Literary Imagination*, 2nd ed. New Haven, CT: Yale UP, 2000.

Humm, Maggie, ed. *Feminism: A Reader*. Hemel Hempstead, UK: Harvester Wheatsheaf, 1992.

Kolodny, Annette. "Dancing through the Minefield: Some Observations on the Theory, Practice, and Politics of a Feminist Literary Criticism." In *The Norton Anthology of Theory and Criticism*. Vincent B. Leitch, ed. New York: Norton, 2001. pp. 2146–65.

———. Some notes on defining a "feminist literary criticism." *Critical Inquiry* 2 (1975):75–92.

Meese, Elizabeth. *Crossing the Double-Cross: The Practice of Feminist Criticism*. Chapel Hill, NC: University of North Carolina Press, 1986.

Millett, Kate. *Sexual Politics*. Bloomingdale, IL: University of Illinois Press, 2000.

Mohanty, Chandra Talpade, Ann Russo, and Lourdes Torres, eds. *Third World Women and the Politics of Feminism*. Bloomington: Indiana UP, 1991.

Moi, Toril. "Feminist Literary Criticism," in *Modern Literary Theory*. Ann Jefferson and Donald Robey, eds. Bastsford, 1982.

———. *Sexual/Textual Politics: Feminist Literary Theory*, 2nd ed. New York: Routledge, 1988.

Nicholson, Linda. *The Second Wave: A Reader in Feminist Theory*. New York: Routledge, 1997.

Oliver, Kelly. *French Feminism Reader*. New York: Rowman & Littlefield, 2000.

Showalter, Elaine. *A Literature of Their Own: British Women Novelists from Brontë to Lessing. Expanded ed*. Princeton: Princeton UP, 1998.

———, ed. *The New Feminist Criticism*. New York: Pantheon Books, 1985.

———. "Toward A Feminist Poetics." In *Twentieth Century Literary Theory: A Reader*. Newton, K.M., ed. New York: St. Martin's, 1997. pp. 216–50.

Todd, Janet. *Feminist Literary History*. New York: Routledge, 1988.

Warhol, Robin, and Diane Price Herndl, eds. *Feminisms: An Anthology of Literary Theory and Criticism. 2nd ed*. New Brunswick: Rutgers University Press, 1997.

Woolf, Virginia. *A Room of One's Own*, reissue ed. New York: Harvest, 1989.

WEB SITES FOR EXPLORATION

www.colostate.edu/Depts/Speech/rccs/theory84.htm
"Different Types of Feminist Theories" provides working definitions for a variety of feminist theories

www.cddc.vt.edu/feminism/lit.html
"Feminist Literary Criticism and Theory" provides information concerning a variety of critics, including Cixous, Irigaray, Kristeva, and others

http://bailiwick.lib.uiowa.edu/wstudies/theory.html
Women's studies resources

http://www.victorianweb.org/gender/femtheory.html
Feminist theory—an overview

http://en.wikipedia.org/wiki/feminist_literary_criticism
"Wikipedia: Feminist Literary Criticism" cites definitions, theories, and additional links

http://en.wikipedia.org/wiki/feminist_theory
"Wikipedia: Feminist Theory" an overview of feminist theory

Sample Essay

In the following student essay, note how the author uses feminist theory to expose the patriarchal society depicted in Washington Irving's "Rip Van Winkle." As you read this essay, ask yourself the following questions:

- What principles of feminist literary theory does the author use in her interpretation?
- What feminist issues does she highlight?
- What feminist issues does she ignore?
- Is the author's use of quotations from the short story accurate and fair—that is, are any quotations taken out of context to help the author prove her point?
- What is the overall tone of the essay? How is this tone established?

Student Essay

Throwing Off the Yoke: "Rip Van Winkle" and Women[1]

As the author of the first American short story and as an intentional creator of an early American archetype, what kind of images of American men and women did Washington Irving develop and perpetuate in the American psyche? As the "first Ambassador whom the New World of Letters sent to the Old," what kind of messages did Irving send across the ocean with his stories? Long ago escorted into the canon of so-called great American literature, and still found in anthologies such as The World's 50 Best Short Stories, Irving's "Rip Van Winkle" blatantly promotes negative stereotypes of women. Revolving around the antics of its male protagonist, Rip, the story uses sexist, demeaning diction to describe women and presents static female characters whose identity is defined in relationship to men. Additionally, as a parable for America's revolt and subsequent freedom from England, Dame Van Winkle represents an overbearing mother country from which Rip, the hero and archetypal American man, is happy to be free.

[1]Reprinted by permission of Lori Huth.

Irving uses blatantly sexist and insulting language to describe Dame Van Winkle. She is a "shrew" and a "termagant"; she is a henpecking wife with "a tart temper [. . .] and a sharp tongue" that only grows sharper with use. Shrew and termagant are words meaning "an ill-tempered or nagging woman," having no equivalent terms for men. By using words that are inherently sexist, Irving singles women out as objects of negative biases. By highlighting Dame Van Winkle's shrill tongue, which is "incessantly going," as her primary characteristic, Irving relegates her and all women to a negative stereotype. With her "shrill voice" she disrupts the "tranquility" of the village's old boys' club. With the comment "what courage can withstand the ever-during and all-besetting terror of a woman's tongue" the narrator extrapolates the Dame's characteristic and applies it to all women. The story implicitly says not only that Rip is afraid of the Dame's tongue but also that everyone is afraid of "a woman's tongue" (all of which can be assumed to be shrill like the Dame's). Irving also stereotypes Dame Van Winkle as a witch, saying she gives Rip's dog the "evil eye."

Rip Van Winkle, on the other hand, is a "simple good-natured fellow." Using positive language and diction to describe Rip, Irving contrasts Rip to the Dame. Although Rip has an "aversion to [. . .] profitable labour," the root causes of this supposed "great error" are positive rather than negative. They are not due to "the want of assiduity or perseverance," but rather to his fear of his witchy, shrewish wife and to his love of activities such as fishing and philosophizing with his buddies.

Always willing to help a neighbor in need or sit patiently for hours waiting for a fish to bite, Rip is obviously favored and forgiven (by Irving and by the narrator) for his minor shortcomings. Despite the Dame's "dinning" and "terror," Rip remains obedient, developing a meek spirit and becoming universally popular in his village. His "great error" is thus nullified and almost made to seem a virtue or, at least, a logical and reasonable reaction to the terrors of his wife. Whereas children shout for joy to see him and dogs refrain from barking at him, not even the other village women support or defend Dame Van Winkle. All the "good wives" favor Rip and take his side in family squabbles. Gossiping among themselves, they place all the blame on Dame Van Winkle and exemplify yet another negative stereotype of women: women as cat-fighters who compete with each other for men's favor and attention.

As this stereotype suggests, the story relegates women to minor, limited roles compared to men and defines women only according to their relationships to men. Significantly, no woman in the story is named besides Rip's daughter, Judith Gardiner, who cares for him in his old age. The only named woman, then, is the "comely and fresh" one who nurtures a man and keeps a "snug, well-furnished house" for him. Because the story names Dame Van Winkle as such, it may seem that she is named, but the essence of this name is that it identifies her as Rip's wife. Like the HandMaid's "Ofrred" and

"Ofwarren" in Margaret Atwood's *The HandMaid's Tale*, she is the dame of Van Winkle, but she has no name or identity of her own.

In contrast to women's namelessness, the story names a great number of men, including minor characters who are mentioned only once. These names include Nicholas Vedder, the village patriarch and innkeeper, Derrick van Bummel, a schoolmaster and a "dapper learned man," Peter Vanderdonk, a "well-versed writer," and Brom Dutcher, an old friend of Rip's. The descriptions of these men and others also reveal the variety and dignity of roles that the men in this story hold. They are philosophers and "sage[s]" who conduct "profound" and "solemn" discussions about politics and news. They are congressmen, soldiers, and generals. They are writers, philosophers, teachers, landlords, leaders, and kings. Women's roles, on the other hand, include "gossipers," housekeepers, "good wives" and termagant wives. They care for babies, old men, and their husbands. Like their names, women's roles are limited to their relationship to men. Dame Van Winkle's one good quality, although the narrator is reluctant to admit even this, is that she always keeps her house in order.

If we view Rip as an early example of the archetypal American who has recently freed himself from England, the story serves as a parable with Dame Van Winkle representing the overbearing British government, and Rip representing the hero who has happily freed himself from that government. Irving found value in the past and the traditions of the Old World and did not share the hopeful vision of America as New Eden. His construction of what it means to be an American, however, as seen in the person of Rip Van Winkle, privileges a man's escape from society and government, both of which Dame Van Winkle embodies. The archetypal American woman, ruling at home through "petticoat government," gossips, cares for babies, fights with other women, and nags her husband incessantly.

Irving's archetypal American would be a bachelor, who, with a dog by his side, escapes the offensive behavior of his wife by sitting around with his buddies by the village tavern, pontificating on his freedom. His overbearing wife drives him to adopt mildly negative qualities as a defense mechanism against domination by an oppressive force. During his twenty years of sleep, Rip threw of the "yoke of matrimony" just as his country "[threw] off the yoke of Old England." Perhaps it is time we throw off the yoke of negative stereotypes and biases against women with which canonical stories such as "Rip Van Winkle" have falsely defined what it means to be a woman.

Lori Huth

8

MARXISM

For Marxism is as inseparable from modern civilization as Darwinism or Freudianism, as much part of our "historical unconscious" as Newton was for the Enlightenment.

Terry Eagleton, *Marxist Literary Theory*

With the collapse of communism and the Soviet Union in the late 1980s, many heard the death knell loudly pronouncing the demise of Marxism and its accompanying political and ideological structures. Down came the Berlin Wall, down came the Iron Curtain, and supposedly, down came Marxism as an alternative form of government to capitalism and as an acceptable worldview. Many capitalists rejoiced because Marxism had fallen. Seemingly, Marxists had only the glorious memories of the earlier decades of the twentieth century in which to rejoice—a time when Stalin ruled Russia, Marxist theory dominated both English and American writings, and college campuses both in the East and the West were led and taught by intellectuals who committed themselves to Marxist ideology. Many now believed that such ideology was finally dead!

Performing only a limited Internet search under the keyword "Marxism" results in a listing of more than 20,000 sites, with titles such as "Marxism and Utopian Vision: El Salvador," "Marxism and the National Question," "Marxism and Problems of Linguistics," "Rethinking Marxism," "Marxism, Psychoanalysis, and Labor Competition," and "Baha's Future and Marxism," proving that Marxist theories and criticism are not only alive but may also even be prospering. Announcements for newly published texts advocating sympathy for and support of Marxist ideology in all academic disciplines appear regularly. College courses in Marxist political theory, sociology, literature, and literary theory abound. Perhaps the death knell for Marxism was struck prematurely.

What is it that fascinates intellectuals, politicians, and others about Marxism? Why did it not disappear with the death of communism in the East? Perhaps the answer lies in some of the core principles of Marxist thought:

* Reality itself can be defined and understood.
* Society shapes our consciousness.

- Social and economic conditions directly influence how and what we believe and value.
- Marxism details a plan for changing the world from a place of bigotry, hatred, and conflict because of class struggle to a classless society in which wealth, opportunity, and education are accessible for everyone.

By articulating a coherent, clear, and comprehensive worldview and plan of action for implementation of its ideas, Marxism asserts that it provides answers to many of the complex questions about how life is and ought to be experienced while simultaneously challenging other ideologies to provide their pragmatic answers for these same concerns.

The self-same problems that gave rise to Marxism exist today. Despite its glory decades of the early 1900s and its present-day seemingly embattled position, Marxism declares that it provides a comprehensive, positive view of human life and history and attempts to show how humanity can save itself from a meaningless life of alienation and despair. A worldview that affords a bright promise for the future and a transformation of society will not vanish with the knocking down of a wall or the collapse of the former USSR. Borrowing Mark Twain's phraseology, "Announcements of Marxism's death have been exaggerated."

HISTORICAL DEVELOPMENT

Karl Marx and Friedrich Engels

Unlike many schools of literary criticism, Marxism did not begin as an alternative, theoretical approach to literary analysis. Before many twentieth-century writers and critics embraced the principles of Marxism and used these ideas in their theory and criticism, Marxism had flourished in the nineteenth century as a pragmatic view of history that offered the working classes an opportunity to change their world and their individual lives. By providing both a philosophical system and a plan of action to initiate change in society, Marxism offered a social, political, economic, and cultural understanding of the nature of reality, society, and the individual, not a literary theory. These and other similar ideas have become the basis of what we know today as socialism and communism.

Marxist literary theory has its roots in the nineteenth-century writings of the German social critic and philosopher Karl Heinrich Marx (1818–1883). Many believe Marx himself said little about the relationship of his ideas to literary theory. Surprisingly, however, in the standard German edition of the collected works of Engels and Marx, these critics/philosophers' comments on literature and art fill almost two volumes. Because neither clearly articulates a literary theory or methodology of criticism, Marxist criticism does not develop until the twentieth century. Using Marx's philosophical assumptions, twentieth-century critics developed a variety of Marxist approaches to textual analysis that focus on the study of the relationship between a text and the society that reads it. At the core of all these diverse approaches are Marx and his philosophical assumptions about the nature of reality itself.

Marx articulates his views on the nature of reality in two works, *The German Ideology* (1845) and *The Communist Manifesto* (1848), a work Marx coauthored with Friedrich Engels (1820–1895). In *The German Ideology*, Marx develops what has become known as **dialectical materialism**, a core belief of Marxism. Originally, the word **dialectic** was used by the Greek philosophers Socrates and Plato to describe a form of logical argumentation involving conflicting ideas, propositions, or both. The German philosopher Georg W.F. Hegel (1770–1831) redefines the term as a process whereby a **thesis** is presented, followed by a counterstatement, the **antithesis**. What develops from the ensuing debate or discussion is a new idea called the **synthesis**. Engels and Marx adapt Hegel's concept of synthesis in formulating dialectical materialism, their understanding of how workers can lead a class war and establish a new social order. Both Engels and Marx assert that "consciousness does not determine life: life determines consciousness." A person's consciousness is not shaped by any spiritual entity; through daily living and interacting with each other, humans define themselves. To Engels and Marx, our ideas and concepts about who we are fashioned in everyday interactions and in the language of real life. They are not derived from some Platonic essence or any other spiritual reality. Marx argues that the economic means of production within a society—what he calls the **base**—both engenders and controls all human institutions and ideologies—the **superstructure**— including all social and legal institutions, all political and educational systems, all religions, and all art. These ideologies and institutions develop as a direct result of the economic means of production, not the other way around.

Marx maintains that all societies are progressing toward communism. Believing progress is reactionary or revolutionary, Marx asserts that as a society progresses in its economic mode of production from a feudal system to a more market-based economy, the actual process for producing, distributing, and consuming goods becomes more complex. Accordingly, people's functions within the economic system become differentiated. This differentiation inevitably divides people into different social classes. Eventually, the desires and expectations of the various social classes clash. Such clashes or class conflicts lead to a radical change in the economic base of society from a feudal system of power based on inherited wealth and status to a capitalist system based on the ownership of private property. This shift entails innumerable changes in a society's laws, customs, and religions. According to Marx, four historical periods developed as a result of these forces: feudalism, capitalism, socialism, and communism. Marx believes that socialism is not a true historical period but a transitional stage between capitalism and society's ultimate goal, communism. When society reaches this goal—what Marx called **the worker's paradise**—then and only then will benevolent self-rule be established.

In their coauthored text *The Communist Manifesto*, Marx and Engels continue to develop their ideas. They maintain that the **capitalists**, or the **bourgeoisie**, have successfully enslaved the working class, or the **proletariat**, through economic policies and production of goods. The proletariat must revolt and strip the bourgeoisie of their economic and political power and place the ownership of all property in the hands of the government, which will then fairly distribute the people's wealth.

In a later work, *Das Kapital* (1867), authored by Marx, Marx enunciates the view of history that has become the basis for twentieth-century Marxism, socialism, and communism. History and a corresponding understanding of people and their actions and beliefs are determined by economic conditions. Marx maintains that an intricate web of social relationships emerges when any group of people engage in the production of goods. A few, for example, will be the employers, but many more will be the employees. The employers (the bourgeoisie) have the economic power and gain social and political control of their society. Eventually, this upper class will control the dominant discourse and formalize and articulate its beliefs, values, and arts to develop its **ideology**. Coined by the French rationalist philosopher Destutt de Tracy in the late eighteenth century, the word *ideology* refers to the "science of ideas" as opposed to metaphysics. Engels and Marx borrow this term and use it pejoratively to refer to the bourgeoisie's ruling ideas, customs, and practices. Consciously and unconsciously, the ruling class forces its ideology on the working class or the **proletariat**, also called the **wage slaves**. In effect, the bourgeoisie develops and controls the superstructure. In such a system, the rich become richer, and the poor become poorer and increasingly more oppressed. The bourgeoisie's ideology effectively works to perpetuate the system upon which it was founded. By controlling material relationships, the bourgeoisie control a society's ideology. The average worker, however, assumes that the material relationships are the expression of the ruling ideas. Engels and Marx call this negative sense of ideology **false consciousness**, which describes the way that the dominant social class shapes and controls each person's self-definition and class consciousness.

Marx believes that in a capitalist society, such an ideology leads to fragmentation and alienation of individuals, particularly those of the proletariat. As a direct result of division of labor within the capitalist society, workers no longer have contact with the entire process of producing, distributing, and consuming material goods. Individuals are cut off from the full value of their work as well as from each other, each performing discrete functional roles assigned to them by the bourgeoisie. To rid society of this situation, Marx believes that the government must own all industries and control the economic production of a country to protect the people from the oppression of the bourgeoisie.

Taken together, *The Communist Manifesto* and *Das Kapital* develop a theory of history, economics, politics, sociology, and metaphysics. In these writings, little or no mention of literature, literary theory, or practical analysis of how to arrive at an interpretation of a text emerges. The link between the Marxism of its founders and literary theory resides in Marx's concept of history and the sociological leanings of Marxism itself. Marx believed that the history of a people is directly based on the production of goods and the social relationships that develop from this situation. He also assumed that the totality of a people's experience—social interactions, employment, and other day-to-day activities—is directly responsible for the shaping and development of an individual's personal consciousness. The idea that our place in society and our social interaction determine our consciousness or who we really are is a theme Marx highlighted throughout his writings.

During Marx's lifetime, the acceptable literary approach to textual analysis was grounded in sociological assumptions similar to those held by Marx. Marx, then, had no difficulty accepting his literary peers' methodology (**hermeneutics**) for interpreting a text. Known today as the **traditional historical approach**, this methodology declares that critics should place works in their historical setting, paying attention to the author's life, the time period in which the work was written, and the cultural milieu of both the text and the author—all of these concerns being related to sociological issues. To these criteria, Marx and Engels add another: the economic means of production. This factor addresses, for example, who decides what texts should be published, when a text should be published, or how a text is to be distributed. Such concerns require an understanding of the social forces at work at the time a text is written or is being interpreted. In addition, these concerns force the critic to investigate the intricate web of social relationships not only within the text itself but also outside the text and within the world of the author. In adding this sociological dimension, Marxism expands the traditional, historical approach to literary analysis by dealing with sociological issues that concern both the characters in a work of fiction as well as the authors and the readers. This added dimension, Marx believed, links literature and society and shows how literature reflects society and how literary texts can reveal truths about our social interactions.

Russia and Marxism

Thanks to Georgi K. Plekhanov's Russian translation of *The Communist Manifesto*, Marx's theories soon gained wide exposure and prominence. Plekhanov (1856–1918), author of such works as *Fundamental Problems of Marxism* (1908) and *Art and Social Life* (1912), is the founder of the Russian

Social Democratic Party and is considered by some scholars to be the founder of Russian Marxism. In his writings, Plekhanov argues that great historical figures like Napoleon Bonaparte appear in history only when an intricate web of social conditions coalesce, directly facilitating their development. Every gifted person that affects society is a product of such social relations. Artists, asserts Plekhanov, best serve society and promote social betterment when their art and societal concerns intersect. For Plekhanov, the then-prospering "art for art's sake" movement signaled a disturbing rift between artists and their social environment. Emphasizing an artist's important role in society, Russian Marxism and the Russian leadership at the beginning of the twentieth century insisted that writers should also play a political role. Embracing Marx's theories, Russia became the first nation to promote Marxist principles as both aesthetic and literary guidelines.

Even before the Russian Revolution of 1917, Communist Party leaders insisted that literature promote the standards set forth by the Party. For example, in 1905, Vladimir Ilyitch Lenin (1870–1924) wrote *Party Organization and Party Literature*, a work in which he directly links good literature with the working-class movement, claiming that literature "must become part of the common cause of the proletariat, a 'cog and screw' of one single great Social-Democratic mechanism." Lenin's works defend all kinds of literature, believing that something can be gleaned from any kind of writing. After the Bolshevik Revolution of 1917, Lenin amends his literary theory and criticism, arguing that the Party could not accept or support literary works that blatantly defied established Party policies.

Soon after the Russian Revolution, the revolutionary Leon Trotsky (1879–1940) authored *Literature and Revolution* (1924), the first of his many pivotal texts. Trotsky is considered the founder of Marxist literary criticism. Advocating a tolerance for open, critical dialogue, Trotsky contends that the content of a literary work need not be revolutionary. To force all poets to write about nothing but factory chimneys or revolts against capitalism, he believed, was absurd. The Party, asserted Trotsky, can offer direct leadership in many areas, but not all. The Party's leadership in art, he claimed, must be indirect, helping to protect, but not dominating it. Furthermore, the Party must give what Trotsky called "its confidence" to those nonparty writers—who he called "literary fellow-travelers"—who are sympathetic to the revolution.

The Soviet Union's next political leader, Joseph Stalin (1879–1953), was not as liberal as Lenin or Trotsky in his aesthetic judgments. In 1927, Stalin established the RAPP (Russian Association of Proletarian Writers) to guard against liberal cultural tendencies. This group proved to be too tolerant for Stalin. In 1932, he abolished all artists' unions and associations and established the Soviet Writers' Union, a group that he also headed. The Union decreed that all literature must glorify Party actions and decisions. In addition, literature should exhibit revolutionary progress and teach the spirit of socialism that revolves around Soviet heroes. Such aesthetic commandments quickly stifled many Russian writers because the Union allowed only "politically correct" works to be published. Not surprisingly, Stalin soon banished Trotsky, with the result that increasingly, most Russian critics and writers succumbed to Stalin's guidelines rather than follow Trotsky's public (and dangerous) example. It was left to critics outside Russia to explore and develop other Marxist approaches to literary criticism.

Georg Lukács

The first major branch of Marxist theory to appear outside Russia was developed by the Hungarian Georg Lukács (1885–1971). Lukács and his followers borrowed and amended the techniques of **Russian Formalism**, believing that a detailed analysis of symbols, images, and other literary devices would reveal class conflict and expose the direct relationship between the economic base and the superstructure reflected in art. Known as **reflection theory**, this approach to literary analysis declares that a text directly reflects a society's consciousness. Reflection theorists such as Lukács are necessarily didactic, emphasizing the negative effects of capitalism such as alienation. Known today as **vulgar Marxism**, reflectionists support a form of Marxism in which a one-way relationship exists between the base and the superstructure. For these theorists, literature is part of the superstructure and directly reflects the economic base. By giving a text a close reading, these critics believe they can reveal the reality of the text and the author's **Weltanschauung**, or worldview. It is the critic's job to show how the characters within the text are typical of their historical, socioeconomic setting and the author's worldview.

The Frankfurt School

Closely allied to Lukács and reflection theory, another group of theorists emerged in Germany, **the Frankfurt school**, a neo-Marxist group devoted to developing Western Marxist principles. Included in this group are Theodor Adorno (1903–1969), Herbert Marcuse (1898–1979), Walter Benjamin (1892–1940), and Max Horkheimer (1895–1973), among others. Agreeing with Lukács that literature reveals a culture's alienation and fragmentation, the Frankfurt school critics such as Benjamin assert that a text is like any other commodity produced by capitalism. The **market**—that is, how well a commodity sells—ultimately determines which texts are published and when. There can exist, then, no purely aesthetic activity that relates directly to human consciousness. That a text reveals a culture's fragmentation, not its wholeness, is for Benjamin a useful bit of knowledge for promoting socialist ideals. Having stripped literature of what Benjamin calls its "quasi-religious aura," a Frankfurt school critic is able to resist the bourgeois ideology embedded within a text and does not mindlessly acquiesce to the inane images, thinking, and desires depicted in some literary works.

Bertolt Brecht (1898–1956), a close friend of Benjamin, applies this new way of thinking directly to the theater. According to Brecht, dramatists use the theater to express their ideas, but the theater actually controls them. Instead of blindly accepting bourgeois conventionality as established through dramatic conventions, dramatists must revolt and seize the modes of production. Applying this principle to what became known as the **epic theater**, Brecht advocated an abandonment of the Aristotelian premise of unity of time, place, and action, including the assumption that the audience should be made to believe that what they are seeing is real. By deliberately seeking to abolish the audience's normal expectations when viewing a drama, Brecht hopes to create the **alienation effect**. For instance, in his dramas, he frequently interrupted the drama with a direct appeal to the audience via a song or speech to keep the audience constantly aware of the moral and social issues to which they were being exposed in the drama. Disavowing Aristotle's concept of **catharsis**, Brecht argued that the audience must be forced into action and be forced to make decisions, not revel in emotions. In the hands of Brecht, the epic theatre became a tool for exposing the bourgeois ideology that had permeated the arts.

Antonio Gramsci

Unlike Georg Lukács and his followers who assert that the superstructure reflects the economic base, the Italian Antonio Gramsci (1891–1937) declares that a complex relationship exists between the base and the superstructure. How, Gramsci asks, is the bourgeoisie able to control and maintain its dominance over the proletariat? His answer: the bourgeoisie establish and maintain what he calls **hegemony**, which is the assumptions, values, and meanings that shape meaning and define reality for the majority of people in a given culture. Because the bourgeoisie actually control the economic base and establish all the elements that comprise the superstructure—music, literature, art, and so forth—they gain the spontaneous accolades of the working class. The working people themselves give their consent to the bourgeoisie and adopt bourgeois values and beliefs. As sustainers of the economic base, the dominant class enjoys the prestige of the masses and controls the ideology— a term often used synonymously with hegemony—that shapes individual consciousness. This shaping of a people's ideologies is, according to Gramsci, a kind of deception whereby the majority of people forget about or abandon their own interests and desires and accept the dominant values and beliefs as their own.

If literature, however, is only a part of the superstructure, then all literature actually concerns itself with the bourgeoisie. In effect, literature becomes a tool of the privileged class, preventing its use in further Marxist revolutions. Why write and study literature if it is only a reflection of the superstructure, which is, in itself, the reflection of bourgeois ideas established in the economic base? Although Gramsci pondered such questions, it is one of his followers who provides the answer.

Louis Althusser

In seeking an answer to the question of why anyone should write and study literature, Louis Althusser (1918–1990) rejects the basic assumption of reflection theory: namely, that the superstructure directly reflects the base. His answer, known today as **production theory**, asserts that literature should not be strictly relegated to the superstructure. In his works, especially *For Marx* (1965) and *Reading "Capital"* (1970), Althusser argues that the superstructure can and does influence the base. Art, then, can and does inspire revolution.

Althusser believes that the dominant hegemony, or prevailing ideology, forms the attitudes of people through a process he calls **interpellation** or **hailing the subject**, which is ideology's power to give individuals identity by the structures and prevailing forces of society. A society's worldview is craftily shaped by a complex network of messages sent to each individual through the elements contained in the superstructure, including the arts. Although the dominant class can use military and police force to repress the working class to maintain its dominance and achieve interpellation, it more frequently than not chooses to use the **Ideological State Apparatus**, or the hegemony. In effect, the dominant class's hegemony prevents the insurrection of the working class.

The dominant class's hegemony is never complete. Such incompleteness suggests that alternative hegemonies exist and are competing with the dominant hegemony for supremacy. If the dominant class's interpellation or hailing the subject fails, then another hegemony can triumph and revolution can occur. Such a revolution can begin if working-class people write their own literature—dramas, poems, and novels—create their own music, and paint their own paintings. If they do so, the working class can establish an alternate hegemony to challenge the bourgeoisie's hegemony. It is not through guns or battles or the shedding of blood, but through artistic expression of their own cultural activities that the working classes can successfully revolt and usurp the hegemony of the dominant class.

After Althusser, a number of post-Althusserian critics, including Pierre Macherey and Raymond Williams, develop various neo-Marxist concepts and theories. A former student of Althusser, Pierre Macherey (1938–) is a pioneer French Marxist critic, developing Marxist theories by using the concepts of poststructuralism. In his most significant work, *A Theory of Literary Production* (1966), Macherey challenges the traditional way readers read texts. Most readers consider a text as an isolated, factual entity that is to be read, described, and critiqued through the methodologies of literary criticism. Macherey declares that reading is actually a form of production and produces many meanings, not simply one. A gap exists, he asserts, between what we as readers and critics say about a text and what the work itself is saying, each being separate discourses. Furthermore, the author's text is not precisely the text being explicated by the critic. What authors mean to say and what they actually write and say are different. The various meanings of their texts continuously escape writers because they themselves do not recognize the multiple ideologies at work in them and in their texts. What Macherey calls an **attentive reading** of texts reveals these ideologies operating in a given text, ideologies that often directly work against what authors assume they are writing.

Another post-Althusserian Marxist critic, Raymond Williams (1921–1988) develops Marxist ideology and theory in **cultural studies**, a late twentieth-century school of criticism whose name was not yet coined nor its tenets codified when Williams began his innotative criticism. In works such as the post World War II journal *Politics and Letters* and his critique of literary traditions and forms commencing with the British Romantics to mid-twentieth century literature in *Culture and Society 1780–1950*, Williams evidences his chief interest: the relationship between ideology and culture. Literature and all cultural forms are intricately intertwined. Authorial ideology, cultural and social institutions, and aesthetic forms as related to the different genres are all manifestly involved in a complex series of relationships that shape and develop each other. Emphasizing the symbolic nature of these relationships, Williams demonstrates how culture and the arts weave their way into the lived experience of a person's everyday life.

MARXIST THEORISTS TODAY

Since the 1960s, the Anglophone Fredric Jameson (1934–) and Terry Eagleton (1943–) in Great Britain dominate Marxist criticism. Jameson develops **dialectical criticism**. In *Marxism and Form* (1971), a text revered by American Marxists, Jameson asserts that all critics must be aware of their own ideology when analyzing a text, possessing what he calls **dialectical self-awareness**. In a later work, *The Political Unconscious* (1981), Jameson merges psychoanalytic and Marxist theories. Borrowing Freud's idea of a repressed unconscious, Jameson discovers a **political unconscious**, the repressed conditions of exploitation and oppression. The function of literary analysis, Jameson believes, is to uncover the political unconscious present in a text.

In 1991, Jameson continues Marxist theory and criticism's evolution with the publication of *Postmoderism, or the Cultural Logic of Late Capitalism*, a work in which he argues that cultural logic itself encodes the classical Marxist dialectic of base and superstructure in every object in society. To read and understand Jameson's text is no easy assignment because his complex and sometimes abstruse sentence structure embodies his postmodern, critical methodology, one that attempts through a Marxist lens to reconfigure present-day political and world systems.

Perhaps the most influential contemporary Marxist critic is the British scholar Terry Eagleton (1943–), author of numerous works, including *Criticism and Ideology* (1976), *Marxism and Literary Crticism* (1976), *Literary Theory: An Introduction* (1983), and *Marx* (1997). Believing that literature is neither a product of pure inspiration nor the product of the author's feelings, Eagleton holds that literature is a product of an ideology that is itself a product of history. This ideology is a result of the actual social interactions that occur between people in definite times and locations. One of the critic's tasks is to reconstruct an author's ideology and the author's ideological milieu.

Throughout his long and prestigious career, Eagleton, like most critics, develops, changes, and redirects his own literary theory. At times, he employs a variety of critical approaches to texts, including the scientific approach of Louis Althusser, the psychoanalytic ideas of Lacan, and the poststructuralism of Jacques Derrida. All of his diverse approaches to textual analysis attack the bourgeois dominance of the hegemony and advocate revolution against such values.

From the mid-1970s to the present, Marxism continues to challenge what it deems the bourgeois concerns of its literary counterparts through the voices of a variety of Marxist critics, including Renée Balibar, Gayatri Chakravorty Spivak, Toril Moi, and Donna Landry. Critical movements and theories such as structuralism, deconstruction, feminism, new historicism, cultural materialism, and postcolonialism have all examined Marxism's basic tenets and share some of its social, political, and revolutionary nature. Like Marxism, these contemporary schools of criticism want to change the way we think about literature and life. Likewise, from these various schools of thought, present-day Marxism borrows many ideas and has now evolved into an array of differing theories, so much so that there no longer exists a single school of Marxist thought but a variety of Marxist critical positions. Common to all these theoretical positions is the assumption that Marx, no matter how he is interpreted, believed that change for the good in society is possible if we will simply stop and examine our culture through the eyes of its methods of economic production.

ASSUMPTIONS

Marxism is not primarily a literary theory that can be used to interpret texts. Unlike other schools of criticism, it is a cultural theory that embodies a set of social, economic, and political ideas that its followers believe will enable them to interpret and, more importantly, change their world. Although a variety of Marxist theories exist, most Marxists posit a few core ideas.

Ultimate reality, declares Marxism, is material, not spiritual. Our existence precedes our consciousness or our essence. What we know is that human beings exist and live in social groups. All our actions and responses to such activities as eating, working, and playing are related in some way to our culture and society. In order to understand ourselves and our world, we must first acknowledge the interrelatedness of all our actions. If, for example, we want to know who we are and how we should live, we must stop trying to find answers by looking solely to religion or philosophy and begin by examining all aspects of our daily activities within our own culture. Upon examining our daily routines, including our beliefs and values, we will discover that our cultural and social circumstances determine who we are. What we believe, what we value, and even what we think are direct results of our culture and society, not our religion, our supposed philosophy of life, or our worldview.

Nothing, Marxists assert, exists in isolation, including our social life. Everything must be understood to exist in a dynamic historical process, what Engels and Marx call **relations** or **Verhältnisse**—that is, nothing exists in isolation or just "is." Everything is interrelated and exists in a dynamic relationship (**Vermittlung**) with a variety of social forces. For example, when we speak about the "worker," we must also speak about the employer, economics, social class, social conflict, morality, values, and a host of other concerns. Everything, claim Marxists, is in a state of becoming, of being transformed. Nothing exists in static isolation.

When we examine our society, declares Marxism, we discover that its structure is built upon a series of ongoing conflicts between social classes. The chief reason for these conflicts is the varying ways the members of society work and use their economic resources. The methods of economic production and the social relationships they engender form the economic structure of society, the base. In the United States, for example, the capitalists exploit the working classes, determining for them their salaries and their working conditions, among a host of other elements of their lives. From this base arises the superstructure, or a multitude of social and legal institutions, political and educational systems, religious beliefs, values, and a body of art and literature that the one dominant social class (e.g., the capitalists in the United States) uses to keep in check members of the working classes.

The exact relationship between the base and the superstructure, however, is not easily defined. Some Marxists believe that the base directly affects the superstructure and determines its existence. Other Marxists assert that the elements in the superstructure have a reality of their own, with each element affecting the other elements of the superstructure while simultaneously affecting the base. Whatever the position held by Marxist theorists, most agree that the relationship between the base and the superstructure is a complex one that will continue to remain a contentious point in Marxist criticism.

The relationship between the base and the superstructure becomes clearer when we consider the capitalistic United States. Marxism declares that in the United States the capitalists hold the economic purse strings, and because they do, they control the base, making the capitalists the center of power. The capitalists decree what beliefs are acceptable, what values are to be held, and what laws are to be formed. In other words, the capitalists, not the working classes, control society's ideology (its hegemony) and its social consciousness. It is they who determine the acceptable standards of behavior and thoughts in their society.

Consciously and unconsciously, this social elite inevitably forces its ideas on the working classes. Almost without their knowing it, the working classes have become trapped in an economic system that decrees how much money they will earn, when they will take vacations, how they will spend their leisure time, what entertainment they will enjoy, and even what they believe concerning the nature of humanity itself.

Marxism addresses its rallying cry to the working classes. All working peoples can free themselves from the chains of social, economic, and political oppression if they will recognize that they are presently not free agents, but individuals controlled by an intricate social web dominated by a self-declared, self-empowered, and self-perpetuating social elite.

Because this social elite shapes a society's superstructure and ideology, the bourgeoisie control its literature, for literature is one of the many elements contained within the superstructure. From this perspective, literature, like any other element of the superstructure, becomes involved in a social process whereby the bourgeoisie indoctrinate the working classes with their self-proclaimed acceptable ideology, as reflected in bourgeois literature. What becomes natural and acceptable behavior in society is now pictured in its literature and, in essence, controlled by the bourgeoisie, who also control the economic means of production.

Because literature is part of a society's superstructure, its relationship to the other elements of the superstructure and the base becomes the central focus in varying Marxist literary theories. If, for example, a Marxist holds to the reflection theory, then such a theorist posits that the economic base directly determines the literature. For this critic, literature will mirror the economic base. On the other hand, if a Marxist theorist believes that elements of the superstructure have realities of their own and affect each other and also affect the base, a text may be responsible for altering not only other elements within the superstructure but also the base. Even the critics who give allegiance to this position hold differing opinions concerning the definition of a text and its relationship to other elements of the superstructure and to the base.

Although Marxists assert that a text must be interpreted in light of its culture, how they define a text and its web-like social relationships provides us with an array of Marxist literary theories and differing methods of analyses. There exists, then, not one Marxist theory of literature, but many, each hoping to change society.

METHODOLOGY

As an approach to literary analysis, Marxism's methodology is a dynamic process that maintains that a proper critique (*proper* defined as that which agrees with socialistic or Marxist beliefs) of a text cannot exist in isolation from the cultural situation in which the text evolved. Necessarily, Marxists argue, the study of literature and the study of society are intricately bound. Such a relationship demands that a Marxist approach to texts must deal with more than the conventional literary themes, matters of style, plot, or characterization and the usual emphasis on figures of speech and other literary devices used by other approaches to literary analysis. Marxist theory moves beyond these literary elements and uncovers the author's world and worldview. By placing the text in its historical context and analyzing the author's view of life, Marxist critics arrive at one of their chief concerns: ideology. The ideology expressed by the author, as evidenced through his or her fictional world, and how this ideology interacts with the reader's personal ideology interests these critics. Studying the literary or aesthetic qualites of a text must include the dynamic relationship of that text to history and the economic means of production and consumption that helped create the text and the ideologies of the author and the readers.

This kind of an ideological and political investigation exposes class conflict, revealing the dominant class and its accompanying ideology being imposed either consciously or unconsciously upon the proletariat. It also reveals the workers' detachment not only from that which they produce but also from society and from each other, a process called **alienation**, revealing what Marxists dub **fragmentation**, a fractured and fragmented society. The task of the critic is to uncover and denounce this antiproletariat ideology and show how such an ideology entraps the working classes and oppresses them in every area of their lives. Most importantly, through such an analysis, Marxist critics wish to reveal to the working classes how they may end their oppression by the bourgeoisie through a commitment to socialism.

A Marxist critic may begin such an analysis by elucidating how an author's text reflects the writer's ideology through an examination of the fictional world's characters, settings, society, or any other aspect of the text. From this starting point, the critic may launch an investigation into that particular author's social class and its effects on the author's society. Or the critic may choose to begin by examining the history and culture of the times reflected in the text and how the author either correctly or incorrectly pictures this historical period.

Whatever method the critic chooses, a Marxist approach exposes the dominant class, demonstrates how the bourgeoisie's ideology controls and oppresses the working class, and highlights elements of society most affected by such oppression. Such an analysis, Marxist critics hope, will lead to action, social change, revolution, and the rise of socialism.

QUESTIONS FOR ANALYSIS

To gain a working understanding of a Marxist approach to literary analysis, we can ask questions of any text that will enable us to see the Marxist concerns that are evidenced or ignored in the text by its author. The following questions provide a working framework for a close analysis of a text through the lens of Marxism and demonstrate Marxism's concern for the interactive relationship between literature and society.

- What class structures are established in the text?
- Which characters or groups control the economic means of production?
- What class conflicts are exhibited?
- Which characters are oppressed, and to what social classes do they belong?
- Which characters are the oppressors?
- What is the hegemony established in the text?
- What social conflicts are ignored?
- Who represents the status quo?
- Does the work suggest a solution to society's class conflicts?
- What is the dominant ideology revealed in the text?
- Did the main character support or defy the dominant ideology?
- Is the narrator a member of the bourgeoisie or the proletariat?
- Whose story gets told in the text? Whose story does not get told?
- When and where was the text published?
- Is the author's stated intention for writing the work known or public?
- What were the economic issues surrounding the publication of the text?
- Who is the audience?
- Who is the ideal reader? Virtual reader? Real reader?

CRITIQUES AND RESPONSES

Like psychoanalytical and feminist criticisms, Marxist criticism concerns itself not only with what a text says but also what it does not say. In the opening chapter of *Criticism and Ideology*, Terry Eagleton, one of Marxism's most prominent contemporary critics, states that the task of Marxist criticism "is to show the text as it cannot know itself, to manifest those conditions of its making about which it is necessarily silent." Texts, like all elements of social life, cannot be analyzed in isolation because they do not exist as isolated entities; rather, they are part of a complex web of social forces and structures. Texts must be understood as part of the dynamic, ever-evolving historical processes of social relations. Included within these social relations are the ongoing, ever-present societal conflicts and clashes, the struggles between the have-nots and the haves. Maintaining their positions of power by controling a society's hegemony and thereby creating false consciousness, capitalists suppress the working classes, coercing them to accept the capitalists' vision of reality. Literary criticism's objective is to reveal the class struggle evidenced in texts, either through what a text says or by its silence, the silence of oppression. From a Marxist perspective, all texts are ideological, and the ideologies contained within them must be exposed to challenge the prevailing social order.

Although Marxism's internal consistency and the sheer breadth of its critique are impressive, critics of Marxist theory abound. Whereas Marx and his adherents call their beliefs a theory and a form of criticism, others dub it a philosophy of life that codifies a quasi-religious worldview. Such a worldview, say some critics, demands a total commitment and devotion, as does any religion. But this religion, they assert, is devoid of God because it is thoroughly atheistic. The god of this religion is found in the mirror and in humankind's imagination. Rejecting spiritual values, the concept of the soul, immortality, and a belief in God, this religion, which goes under the name of theory and criticism, is materialistic. Ultimately, say these critics, an acceptance of Marxist principles denies human worth. Those who stand in the way of Marxism's goal—to change society—will and must be eliminated. Such a worldview, they argue, will lead to a form of totalitarianism that rests upon a subjective understanding of reality, not objective, absolute truths.

Other critics assert that Marxist economic theory is simplistic and cannot provide either the correct lens or the correct solution for contemporary societies' economic ills. Clinging to its basic tenets, orthodox Marxism ignores the multifaceted nature of societies that contain a multiplicity of social groups, each possessing its own understanding of human nature and social institutions. And above all, Marxism either dismisses or simply ignores personal freedom, emphasizing in its place economic concerns.

However an individual critic views Marxism, its theories and criticisms continue to develop and shape our social and cultural institutions.

FURTHER READING

Adorno, Theodor W., Walter Benjamin, Ernst Block, Bertolt Brecht, and Georg Lukács. *Aesthetics and Politics*. London: New Left Books, 1977.

Ahern, Edward J. *Marx and Modern Fiction*. New Haven: Yale University Press, 1989.

Baxandall, Lee, and Stefan Morawski, eds. *Marx and Engels on Literature and Art*. New York: Telos Press, 1973.

Craig, David, ed. *Marxists on Literature*. Harmondsworth: Penguin, 1975.

Eagleton, Terry. *Criticism and Ideology*. New York: Schocken, 1978.

———. *Literary Theory: An Introduction*. Minneapolis, MN: University of Minnesota Press, 1983; 1996.

———. *Marx: The Great Philosophers*. New York: Routledge, 1999.

———. *Marxism and Literary Theory*. Berkeley, CA: University of California Press, 1976.

———. *Marxism and Literary Theory*. London: Methuen, 1976.

Eagleton, Terry, and Drew Milne, eds. *Marxist Literary Theory*. Oxford, England: Blackwell, 1996.

Gottlieb, Roger S., ed. *An Anthology of Western Marxism: From Lukács and Gramsci to Socialist-Feminism*. New York: Oxford University Press, 1989.

Haslett, Mayra. *Marxist Literary and Cultural Theories*. New York: Palgrave, 2000.

Hicks, Granville. *The Great Tradition*, rev. ed. New York: Macmillan, 1935.

Jay, Martin. *Marxism and Totality*. Berkeley, CA: University of California Press, 1990.

Jameson, Fredric. *Marxism and Form: Twentieth-Century Dialectical Theories of Literature*. Princeton, NJ: University Press, 1971.

———. *The Political Unconscious*. Ithaca, NY: Cornell University Press, 1987.

———. *Postmodernism, or the Cultural Logic of Late Capitalism*. Durham, NC: Duke University Press, 1991.

Kadarkay, Arpad, ed. *The Lukács Reader*. London: Blackwell, 1995.

McMurtry, John. *The Structure of Marx's World-View*. Princeton, NJ: Princeton University Press, 1978.

Williams, Raymond. *Marxism and Literature*. Oxford, England: Oxford University Press, 1977.

WEB SITES FOR EXPLORATION

http://social.chass.ncsu.edu/wyrick/DEBCLASS/forg.htm
"Marxist Literary Theories" provides a sound overview of multiple Marxist principles and theories

http://www.answers.com/topic/marxist-literary-criticism
"Introduction to Marxist Literary Criticism" provides a solid overview of Marxist criticism and includes links to various significant Marxist critics

http://www.geocities.com/Athens/Academy/4573/Lectures/marxism.html
"Marxist Literary Theory" provides a philosophical overview of Marxism and applies Marxist theory to Nathaniel Hawthorne's *The Scarlet Letter*

http://www.lawrence.edu/dept/ENGLISH/COURSES/60A/marxist.html
"Marxist Criticism" includes an introduction to Marxist theory, Marxist critics, and additional web links

http://www.sou.edu/english/idtc/timeline/uslit.htm
"Timeline of Major Critical Theories" demonstrates Marxist theories' growth and development in light of other schools of criticism

Sample Essay

The student author of the following essay believes that oftentimes we overlook a Marxist interpretation of the most common and most respected literary works. Such is the case, he believes, with Nathaniel Hawthorne's "Young Goodman Brown." More frequently than not, this short story is read as an initiation story. When the principles of Marxist theory and criticism are applied to this tale, the student author believes that a new perspective on Hawthorne, his works, his society, and ourselves will be revealed. As you read the following student essay, ask yourself the following questions:

- How successful is the author in using Marxist theory and criticism?
- What particular kind of Marxist theory does the author use? That of Georg Lukács? The Frankfort School? That of Antonio Gramsci? That of Louis Althusser? Or that of Fredric Jameson?
- What class structures and conflicts does the author see exhibited in Hawthorne's text?
- What does the author view as the text's dominant ideology?
- Is the narrator of Hawthorne's story supportive of the dominant ideology?
- How does the protagonist of the tale resolve the class conflict?
- Does the text suggest that the protagonist's resolution is a workable or valid one?
- What part does the character of Satan play in this student author's analysis?
- To what social class does Satan belong?
- Does the student author correctly interpret Satan's character in light of the dominant ideology operating in the text?
- Overall, what are this essay's major strengths? Weaknesses?

Student Essay

Heaven's Last Gleaming[1]

In Nathaniel Hawthorne's short story "Young Goodman Brown," we literally and metaphorically follow Young Goodman Brown's journey down a dark forest path that ultimately reveals the true character of the religious people of Puritan New England. Brown has spent his life in service and devotion to these spiritual leaders. But on this journey leading toward Brown's personal illumination, Goodman Brown questions the dominant hegemony of the religious elders—the bourgeoisie—and comes to recognize that he himself is a member of the proletariat. In the tale, Hawthorne juxtaposes the blind subservience of Brown's wife, Faith, to a capitalist system against Satan's holistic understanding of the baseness of humanity amidst

[1]Reprinted by permission of Matthew S. Lasher.

the framework of the established bourgeoisie ideologies. Faith, as her name implies, clings to the idea and the hope of a spiritual heaven in which her life-long devotion to the bourgeois hegemony will be rewarded, enjoying an eternity of equality with all people—a utopia where social class will be forever eradicated. Ironically, it is Satan who brings Goodman Brown and his wife as close to any "heaven" as they will ever experience. Through their forest communion with the religious exemplars, Brown's false consciousness is exposed, and he is ushered into the actual role that religion has played in his life. The bourgeoisie have brilliantly utilized their contrived ideology—their hegemony—to enslave not only Goodman Brown but also all members of the proletariat into a life of ceaseless toil in order to keep the embers of the capitalist fire burning.

At the onset of his journey, Brown is somewhat aware of his entanglements with the dominant ideology. The bourgeois hegemony has declared that the working class must tarry through the day and sleep at night, thereby allowing them, the bourgeoisie, to conduct their ceremonies secure in the sleeping proletariat's ignorance of their dualistic lives. Brown tells his wife that "My journey, as thou callest it, forth and back again, must need be done twixt now and sunrise." The path on which Brown must travel on this journey is fraught with symbolic imagery harkening to an ideology instituted by the wealthy church elders—an ideology that has, up to this point, been unchallenged. Brown, a member of the proletariat, travels down a path that constitutes a "dreary road," one that is "darkened by all the gloomiest trees of the forest, which barely stood aside to let the narrow path creep through." Brown is taking the "narrow path" where no proletariat known to him has seemingly traveled. "It was all as lonely as could be; and there is this peculiarity in such a solitude, that the traveler knows not who may be concealed by the innumerable trunks and thick boughs overhead; so that, with lonely footsteps, he may yet be passing through an unseen multitude." The naturalistic iconography tells the story of the proletariat, disenchanted with the current bourgeois hegemony, daring to rattle the chains which he has up until this point unconsciously allowed to define and to determine his reality.

Brown is not alone in his journey for long. Satan, perhaps the story's ultimate hero, comes to Brown's aid when the Christian dogma accepted by Brown's false consciousness starts to cloud his better judgment. Satan is transcendentally aware of all and more of what Brown merely suspects about class struggle. Satan appears as a man "apparently in the same rank of life as Goodman Brown, and yet though the elder person was as simply clad as the younger, and as simple in manner too, he had an indescribable air of one who knew the world, and would not have felt abashed at the governor's dinner-table or in King William's court, were it possible that his affairs should call him thither." Satan embodies all and is yet transcendent of the traits of all social classes. By his nature and power, he is above the psychological sway of dialectical materialism. He reassures Brown that his (Satan's) company has been kept by many a more "saintly" person than Brown himself: "The deacons of many a church have drunk the communion wine with me; the selectmen, of divers towns, make me their chairman; and a majority of the Great and General Court are firm supporters of my interest." This revelation of bourgeois deceit falls on ears subservient to it: "Howbeit, I have nothing to do with the governor and council; they have their own ways, and are no rule to a simple husbandman like me." Brown's confounded remark shows how the hegemony of the Puritan elect has warped his sense of reality. Working ceaselessly to uphold the base, Goodman Brown believes his cause to be rooted in the prospect of everlasting life, a delusion provided by the dominant hegemony in hopes of controlling people like Brown. In actuality, Brown is working to support the extravagant lifestyles of the governor and the council, those he believes play no hand in the day-to-day affairs of his life.

The communion in the forest, conducted by Satan, is the great leveler of Puritan religious interpellation. With the blindfold of bourgeois hegemony having fallen off, Brown sees all manner of people circled around the communal fire: godly and ungodly, religious Deacon and common lay person, bourgeoisie and proletariat. All are equal in their utter depravity and inherently sinful nature. And yet even here the dominant ideology operates, convincing people that sin actually exists in order to manipulate them.

As Brown stares transfixed, he notices "the lady of the governor," as well as "ancient maidens, all of excellent repute." Brown also recognizes "a score of the church members of Salem village, famous for their especial sanctity." The pinnacle of the religious hierarchy is there as well in the persons of Deacon Gookin and the pastor. But the forest gathering is not only comprised solely of bourgeois society but also of "men of dissolute lives and women of spotted fame, wretches given over to all mean and filthy vice, and suspected even of horrid crimes." Having ascribed to and been duped by bourgeois ideologies all his life, Brown is now confounded by the polarity of the social structure around him. "It was strange to see, that the good shrank not from the wicked, nor were the sinners abashed by the saints." Satan celebrates the link among all humankind, the common stain of humanity's supposed sinfulness. By exposing the lies of the church and the hypocrisy of its leaders, Satan removes the veil from the cleverly disguised bourgeoisie: "There are all whom ye have reverenced from youth. Ye deemed them holier than yourselves, and shrank from your own sin, contrasting it with their lives of righteousness and prayerful aspirations heavenward. Yet, here are they all, in my worshipping assembly!" In one deft swoop, Satan disseminates the hegemony of the religious elders that has kept Brown and his proletariat kinsfolk in a somewhat self-induced bondage. Crowded around the altar of their birthright, "earth's one stain of guilt, one mighty blood-spot," the soul of every person is laid bare. The religious façade is exposed, the hypocrisy of the church's ideology revealed, and the bourgeois hegemony of Puritan New

England fleshed into consciousness. Interestingly, all is accomplished through Satan's use of the bourgeoisie's dominant discourse—the language of the Church and its false definition of humanity's essence, what it dubs evil, sin, or depravity.

Though Brown fails to incite revolution and to gain paradise—a classless society free from the hypocrisy of the Church and bourgeois rule—in one sense the controlling veil of religion that had been placed over a capitalist system by which Brown had been enslaved is now lifted. Through Satan's teaching, Brown realizes that all reality is material. Any hopes, he realizes, of an otherworldly heaven is part of a cleverly devised construct to keep him working for a system that will only serve those richer than he. He knows that those "saintly" people whom he admired and respected his entire life have been successfully enslaving him; their whip, the promise of eternal happiness to be enjoyed in heaven, is just a myth. Brown thus rejects the established dominant ideology formalized by the "upper crust," and chooses to isolate himself rather than to be enslaved by the bourgeoisie's contrived, false, and unjust ideology.

MATTHEW S. LASHER

9

CULTURAL POETICS
OR NEW HISTORICISM

*New Historicism is not a repeatable methodology or a literary critical program. . .
so we sincerely hope you will not be able to say what it all adds up to; if you could,
we would have failed.*

Stephen Greenblatt and Catherine Gallagher, *Practicing New Historicism*

During the 1940s, 1950s, and 1960s, **New Criticism** was the dominant approach to literary analysis. At this time, René Wellek and Austin Warren's text *Theory of Literature* (1942) became the bible of hermeneutics, focusing the interpretive process on the text itself rather than on historical, authorial, or reader concerns.

A NEW-CRITICAL LECTURE

During this high tide of New Criticism, it would have been common to hear a college lecture like the following in a literature classroom:

> Today, class, we will review what we have learned about Elizabethan beliefs from our last lecture so that we can apply this knowledge to our understanding of Act I of Shakespeare's *King Lear*. As you remember, the Elizabethans believed in the interconnectedness of all life. Having created everything, God imposed on creation a cosmic order. At all costs, this cosmic order was not to be upset. Any element of the created universe that portended change, such as a violent storm, eclipses of the sun or moon, or even disobedient children within the family structure, suggested chaos that could lead to anarchy and the destruction of the earth itself. Nothing should break any link in this Great Chain of Being, the name given to this created cosmic order. With God and the angels in their place, the King governing his obedient people in their places, and the animals being subdued and utilized by humankind in theirs, all would be right in the world and operate as ordained by God.

Having gained an understanding of the Elizabethan worldview, let's turn to Act I, Scene ii, lines 101 to 112 of Shakespeare's *King Lear*. You will recall that in this scene, Edmund, the illegitimate son of the Duke of Gloucester, has persuaded the Duke that Edgar, the Duke's legitimate son and heir to the duke-dom, wants his father dead so that he may inherit the Duke's title, lands, and wealth. Believing his natural son has betrayed both Edmund (Edgar's half-brother) and himself, the Duke, says, "These late eclipses in the sun and moon portend no good to us. Though the wisdom of nature can reason it thus and thus, yet nature finds itself scourged by the sequent effects. Love cools, friendship falls off, brothers divide. . . ."

What we see in these lines is the Elizabethan worldview in operation. The Duke believes in the interrelatedness of the created cosmic order and the con-cept of the Great Chain of Being. The significance of the eclipses of the sun and moon rests in their representing change and chaos. Because the Duke believes that the macrocosm (the universe) directly affects the microcosm (the world of humanity on earth), he blames these natural occurrences (the eclipses) for interfering in familial relationships and destroying love between brothers, between father and daughters (King Lear having already banished his most beloved daughter, Cordelia), and between King and servant (Kent, King Lear's loyal courtier also having being expelled from the kingdom). The Duke views his world through the lens of a coherent Renaissance worldview.

OLD HISTORICISM

In such a **Formalist** lecture, the professor's method of literary analysis repre-sents an example of both New Criticism and what is known today as "old historicism." In this methodology, history serves as a background to literature. Of primary importance is the text, the art object itself. The historical back-ground of the text is only secondarily important because it is the aesthetic object, the text, that mirrors the history of its times. The historical context serves only to shed light on the object of primary concern, the text.

Underlying this methodology is a view of history that declares that his-tory, as written, is an accurate view of what really occurred. This view assumes that historians can write objectively about any given historical time period, person, event, or text and are able definitively to state the objective truth about that person, era, occurrence, or text. Through various means of historical analyses, historians discover the mindset, the worldview, or the beliefs of any group of people. For example, when the professor in our hypothetical lecture states the beliefs of the Elizabethans at the beginning of the lecture, he or she is articulating the Elizabethan worldview—the unified set of presuppositions or assumptions that all Elizabethans supposedly held concerning the makeup of their world. By applying these assertions to the Elizabethan text *King Lear*, the professor believes he or she can formulate a more accurate interpretation of the play than if the teacher did not know the play's historical context.

NEW HISTORICISM

That historians can articulate a unified and internally consistent worldview of any given people, country, or era and can reconstruct an accurate and objective picture of any historical event are key assumptions that **Cultural Poetics** or **New Historicism** challenges. Appearing as an alternate approach to textual interpretation in the 1970s and early 1980s, Cultural Poetics—often called New Historicism in America and **Cultural Materialism** in Great Britain—declares that all history is subjective, written by people whose personal biases affect their interpretation of the past. History, asserts Cultural Poetics, can never provide us with *the* objective truth of or give us a totally accurate picture of past events, persons, or eras nor the worldview of a group of people. Disavowing the old historicism's autonomous view of history, Cultural Poetics declares that history is one of many **discourses**, or ways of seeing and thinking about the world. By highlighting and viewing history as one of many equally important discourses such as sociology and politics and by closely examining how all discourses (including that of textual analysis) affect a text's interpretation, Cultural Poetics claims that it provides its adherents with a practice of literary analysis that:

- Highlights the interrelatedness of all human activities.
- Admits its own prejudices.
- Gives a more complete understanding of a text than does the old historicism and other interpretative approaches.

HISTORICAL DEVELOPMENT

New Historicism finds its voice and historical roots in Renaissance scholarship. Such scholarship is especially fertile ground for its development because the Renaissance saw various shifts in Western epistemological assumptions. Marked by historical self-consciousness, this historical era offered New Historicism a repository of cultural dialogue about the relationship between history and literature. The English Renaissance's leading literary spokesperson, Shakespeare, blazed an innovative trail across the disciplines of history, literature, and politics, often blurring the distinctions among them. Perhaps the clearly delineated lines between history and literature are not so distinct after all, decree the New Historicists. In literature can be found history and in history, much literature. Like Shakespeare, the emerging New Historicists seized upon the idea that literature may not be that different from other cultural discourses or "voices," each voice contributing and affecting the other discourses.

Although no one can give a comprehensive, uncontestable history of New Historicism's development, its distinctively American form started to germinate in the late 1970s and early 1980s, especially with the publication of two pivotal works of Renaissance scholarship in 1980: Stephen Greenblatt's *Renaissance Self-Fashioning* and Louis Montrose's essay "Eliza, Queene of Shepheardes." These works begin to clarify the concerns of Cultural Poetics that would develop through the 1980s and 1990s. In 1982, Cultural Poetics coalesced into a critical "site" of literary theory with the publication of a new journal, *Genre*, edited by Greenblatt. In the journal's introduction to a collection of Renaissance essays, Greenblatt announced that a "new historicism" had emerged, thereby proclaiming that New Historicism had become a legitimate and respectable "voice" in the ongoing dialogue of literary theory.

The following year, 1983, Greenblatt and Svetlana Aplers, along with an editorial board based at the University of California at Berkeley, launched another journal, *Representations*, which soon became the chief publication for New Historicist scholars. In the inaugural issue, D.A. Miller, a leading New Historicist, published his essay "Discipline in Different Voices: Bureaucracy, Police, Family and *Bleak House*." In this essay, he declares two of New Historicism's major tenets: Literary texts are embedded in social and political discourses, and all literary texts are vehicles of power. In the next issue of *Representations*, another leading New Historicist, Louis Montrose, published his essay "Shaping Fantasies," reiterating and expanding upon Miller's declaration that literary texts are seats of power. The same year *Representations* was issued, another major New Historical text, *James I and the Politics of Literature*, authored by Jonathan Goldberg, asserted that different historical eras develop different "modes of power," with each epoch viewing reality differently, including conflicting concepts of truth.

Wishing to remain open to differing politics, theories, and ideologies, New Historicists share a similar set of concerns rather than a codified theory or school of criticism. Of key interest is their shared view that from the mid-1800s to the middle of the twentieth century, historical methods of literary analysis were erroneous. During this time, many scholars believed that history served as background information for textual analysis and that historians were objectively able to reproduce any historical period and state "how it really was." New Historicism refutes these assumptions of "old historicism" and formulates its own readings of history and interpretative analysis. Literature, they decree, should be read in relation to culture, history, society, and other factors that help determine a text's meaning. In 1987, Greenblatt published a pivotal essay in the ongoing development of New Historicism titled "Towards a Poetics of Culture." This essay highlights how New Historicists read and view literature in relation to culture and society. Using the ideas of two poststructuralist critics—Jean-Francois Lyotard and Fredric Jameson—Greenblatt asserts that art and society are interrelated, but no scholar can use just one theoretical stance (or school of criticism) to discover this complex web of interrelationships. New Historicism should therefore be viewed as a reading practice, says Greenblatt, not a school of criticism, because when texts and their relationship to society are investigated, an array of often conflicting social and literary patterns evolves that demonstrate how art affects society and how society affects art. In 1988, Greenblatt expands these ideas in his text *Shakespearean Negotiations*, in which he refers to his reading practice as "Cultural Poetics" rather than New Historicism and for all practical purposes renames this site of literary theory. *Cultural Poetics*, he states, is a term that coalesces the concerns of this developing theoretical site better than does the term *New Historicism*.

According to Greenblatt and like-minded scholars, Cultural Poetics was shaped by the institutional character of American literary criticism, culture, and politics of the 1960s, 1970s, and 1980s. In the 1960s, the dominating influence in literary criticism was **New Criticism**, with its accompanying theoretical assumptions and practical methodology. For example, during Greenblatt's graduate studies at Yale—a place he has since called the cathedral of High Church New Criticism—Greenblatt mastered New Critical principles. At Yale, New Critical scholars, writers, and critics such as T.S. Eliot, Allen Tate, John Crowe Ransom, Cleanth Brooks, and Robert Penn Warren were revered, and their methodology was widely practiced.

Aided early in its development by the publication and wide use of Cleanth Brooks and Robert Penn Warren's textbook *Understanding Poetry* (1939), New Criticism presented scholars and teachers with a workable and teachable methodology for interpreting texts. From a theoretical perspective, New Criticism regards a literary text as an artifact with an existence of its own, independent of and not necessarily related to its author, its readers, the historical time it depicts, or the historical period in which it was written. A text's meaning emerges when readers scrutinize the text alone. According to the New Critics, such a close scrutiny results in perceiving a text as an organic whole, wherein all of its parts fit together and support one overarching theme. For the New Critics, a literary text is highly structured and contains its meaning within itself. To a critic–reader who examines the text on its own terms by applying a rigorous and systematic methodology, the text will reveal its meaning. Such an analysis, say the New Critics, is particularly rewarding because literature offers us a unique kind of knowledge and presents us with the deepest truths related to humanity, truths that science is unable to disclose.

What New Criticism did not provide for Greenblatt and other critics was an attempt to understand literature from a historical perspective. In a New Critical analysis, the text was what mattered, not its historical context. Considerations that any given text may be the result of historical phenomena were devalued or silenced. In addition, Greenblatt believed that questions concerning the nature and definition of literature were not encouraged. He and other critics wanted to discuss how literature was formed, whose interest it serves, and what the term *literature* really means. Do contemporary issues and the cultural milieu of the times operate together to create literature, they wondered, or is literature an art form that will always be with us?

Cultural Poetics develops as a result of New Criticism's dominance of literary criticism and its response or lack thereof to questions concerning the nature, the definition, and the function of literature. While Greenblatt was asking a different set of literary questions, a variety of new critical theories and theorists appeared on the literary scene. Deconstruction, Marxism, feminism, and Lacanian psychoanalysis began to challenge the assumptions of New Criticism. Rejecting New Criticism's claim that the meaning of a text can be found mainly in the text, poststructural theorists had been developing a variety of theoretical positions about the nature of the reading process, the part the reader plays in that process, and the definition of a text or the actual work of art. Among this cacophony of voices, Cultural Poetics arose.

After reading sociological and cultural studies authored by Michel Foucault and other poststructuralists, Greenblatt and associates admired and emulated Foucault's tireless questioning of the nature of literature, history, culture, and society. Like Foucault, they refused to accept the traditional, well-worn answers. From the Marxist scholars—Georg Lukács, Walter Benjamin, Raymond Williams, and others—they learned that history is shaped by the people who live it, and they accepted the Marxist idea of the interconnectedness of all life. They also believed that what we do with our hands and how we make our money do affect how and what we think. They also rethought a definition of *culture*, embracing Williams's belief that culture is the combined form of human experience expressed in art, politics, literature, and a host of other elements, each involved in a complex interrelational struggle for power.

But unlike many of the poststructuralist theories—especially deconstruction—Cultural Poetics struggled to find a way out of **undecidability**, or **aporia**, about the nature of reality and the interpretation of a text. Although not denying that many factors affect the writing, the production, and the publication of texts, New Historicists sought to move beyond undecidability rather than simply asserting that a text has many possible meanings. In doing so, they challenged the assumptions of the old historicism, which presupposed historians could actually write an objective history of any situation. In addition, they redefined the meaning of a text and asserted that all critics must acknowledge and openly declare their own biases.

Throughout the 1980s and 1990s, critics such as Catherine Gallagher, Jonathan Dollimore, Jerome McGann, and Greenblatt, to name a few, voiced their concerns that the study of literature and its relationship to history has been too narrow. Viewing a text as culture in action, these critics blur the distinction between an artistic production and any other kind of social production or event. They want us to see that the publication of Swift's "A Modest Proposal" is a political act, while noting that the ceremonies surrounding the inauguration of a U.S. president is an aesthetic event, with all the trappings of symbolism and structure found in any poem. These and similar examples that highlight their critical practices can be found in their chief public voice, the journal *Representations*.

It would be invalid to assume that consensus exists among those who espouse the concerns of Cultural Poetics. Similar to many other approaches to textual analysis, Cultural Poetics is best understood as a practice of literary interpretation that is still in process, one that is continually redefining and fine-tuning its purposes, philosophy, and practices while, at the same time, gaining new followers. Some of these adherents express confidence in Cultural Poetics as being an organized critical school. Others see it as an elusive, abstract method of interpretation. For the sake of clarity, we will somewhat arbitrarily divide Cultural Poetics into two main branches: Cultural Materialism and New Historicism. Members of either group, however, continue to:

- Call for a reawakening of our historical consciousness.
- Declare that history and literature must be seen as disciplines to be analyzed together.
- Place all texts in their appropriate contexts.
- Believe that while we are researching and learning about different societies that provide the historical context for various texts, we are simultaneously learning about ourselves, our own habits, and our own beliefs.

CULTURAL MATERIALISM

Cultural Materialism, the British branch of Cultural Poetics, is Marxist in its theories and political and cultural in its aims. It finds its ideological roots in the writings of Marxist critics such as Louis Althusser and Raymond Williams. Believing that literature can serve as an agent of change, cultural materialists declare that a culture's **hegemony** is unstable. For literature to produce change, a critic must read the works of the established canon "against the grain," becoming "resisting readers." By so doing, critics expose the political unconscious of the text and debunk the social and political myths created by the bourgeoisie.

NEW HISTORICISM

New Historicism is the name given to the American branch of Cultural Poetics. One of its originating voices, Greenblatt, along with a host of other scholars, believes that one's culture permeates both texts and critics. Because all of society is intricately interwoven, so are critics and texts, both to each other and in and to the culture in which they live and in which the texts are produced. Because all critics are influenced by their culture, New Historicists believe that none of us can escape public and private cultural influences. Each critic will formulate a unique interpretation for any given text. Like its British counterpart, New Historicism continues to be refined and redefined by its many practitioners, sometimes providing conflicting and contradictory approaches to textual analysis.

ASSUMPTIONS

Like other poststructuralist practices, Cultural Poetics begins by challenging the long-held belief that a text is an autonomous work of art that contains all elements necessary to arrive at a supposedly correct interpretation. Disavowing the "old historical" assumption that a text simply reflects its historical context—the **mimetic** view of art and history—and that such historical information provides an interesting and sometimes useful backdrop for literary analysis, Cultural Poetics redirects our attention toward a series of philosophical and practical concerns that highlight the complex interconnectedness of all human activities. It redefines both a text and history while simultaneously redefining the relationship between a text and history. Unlike the old historicism, this new historicism, or Cultural Poetics, asserts that an intricate connection exists between an aesthetic object—a text or any work of art—and society, while denying that a text can be evaluated in isolation from its cultural context. We must know, it declares, the societal concerns of the author, of the historical times evidenced in the work, and of other cultural elements exhibited in the text before we can devise a valid interpretation. This approach to textual analysis questions the very act of how we can arrive at a meaning for any human activity, whether it is a text, a social event, a long-held tradition, or a political act.

Michel Foucault

Cultural Poetics critics find the basis for their concerns as well as some of their assumptions in the writings of the twentieth-century French archaeologist, historian, and philosopher Michel Foucault (1926–1984). Foucault begins his rather complex and sometimes paradoxical theoretical structure by redefining the concept of history. Unlike many past historians, Foucault declares that history is not **linear** (i.e., it does not have a definite beginning, a middle, and an end) nor is it necessarily **teleological** (i.e., purposefully going forward toward some known end). Additionally, history cannot be explained as a series of causes and effects controlled by some mysterious destiny or an all-powerful deity. For Foucault, history is the complex interrelationship of a variety of **discourses**, the various ways—artistic, social, political, and so on—that people think and talk about their world. How these discourses interact in any given historical period is not random. Rather, the interaction is dependent on a unifying principle (or pattern) Foucault calls the **episteme**—that is, through language and thought, each period in history develops its own perceptions concerning the nature of reality (or what it defines as truth), sets up its own acceptable and unacceptable standards of behavior; establishes its own criteria for judging what it deems good or bad; and certifies what group of people develop, articulate, protect, and defend the yardstick whereby all established truths, values, and actions will be deemed acceptable.

To unearth the episteme of any given historical period, Foucault borrows techniques and terminology from archaeology. Just as an archaeologist must slowly and meticulously dig through various layers of earth to uncover the symbolic treasures of the past, historians must expose each layer of discourse that comes together to shape a people's episteme. And just as an archaeologist must date each finding and then piece together the artifacts that define and help explain that culture, so must the historian piece together the various discourses and their interconnections among themselves and with nondiscursive practices—any cultural institution such as a form of government, for example—that will assist in articulating the episteme under investigation.

From this point of view, history is a form of power. Because each era or people develop their own episteme, the episteme actually controls how that era or group of people views reality. History, then, becomes the study and unearthing of a vast, complex web of interconnecting forces that ultimately determines what takes place in each culture or society.

Why or how epistemes change from one historical period to another is basically unclear. That they change seemingly without warning is certain. Such a change occurred at the beginning of the nineteenth century—the shift from the Age of Reason to Romanticism, for example—and initiated a new episteme. In this new historical era, different relationships developed among discourses that had not previously evolved or had existed and were deemed unacceptable in the previous historical period. Foucault asserts that the abrupt and often radical changes that cause breaks from one episteme to another are neither good nor bad, valid nor invalid. Similar to the discourses that help produce them, different epistemes exist in their own right; they are neither moral or immoral, but amoral.

According to Foucault, historians must realize that they are influenced and prejudiced by the episteme(s) in which they live. Because their thoughts, customs, habits, and other actions are colored by their epistemes, historians can never be totally objective about their own or any other historical period. To be a historian, Foucault asserts, means one must confront and articulate one's own set of biases before examining the various discourses or the material evidence of past events that comprise an episteme of any given period. Such an archaeological examination of the various discourses, Foucault believes, will not unearth a monological view of an episteme (i.e., one that presupposes a single, overarching, political vision or design); instead, this kind of examination will reveal a set of inconsistent, irregular, and often contradictory discourses that will explain the development of that episteme, including which elements were accepted, changed, or rejected to form the "truth" and to set the acceptable standards for that era.

Clifford Geertz

In addition to borrowing many ideas from Foucault, Cultural Poetics also uses theories and methodologies from the writings of the cultural anthropologist Clifford Geertz. Geertz believes that there exists "no human nature independent of culture," *culture* being defined by Geertz as "a set of control mechanisms—plans, recipes, rules, instructions," for governing behavior. Each person must be viewed as a cultural artifact. How each person views society is always unique because there exists what Geertz calls an "information gap" between what our body tells us and what we have to know in order to function in society. This gap also exists in society because society cannot know everything that happens among all its people. Like individuals, society simply fills in the gaps with what it assumes to have taken place. And it is this information gap, both within people and society, that results in the subjectivity of history.

Cultural Poetics also adapts Geertz's anthropological methodology for describing culture, **thick description**. Coined by Geertz, thick description describes the seemingly insignificant details present in any cultural practice. By focusing on these details, one can then reveal the inherent contradictory forces at work within a culture. Borrowing this idea from Geertz, Cultural Poetics theorists declare that each separate discourse of a culture must be uncovered and analyzed in the hopes of showing how all discourses interact with each other and with institutions, peoples, and other elements of culture. The interaction among the many different discourses shapes a culture and interconnects all human activities, including the writing, reading, and interpretation of a text that the Cultural Poetics critic emphasizes.

Texts, History, and Interpretation

Because texts are simply one of many elements that help shape a culture, Cultural Poetics critics believe that all texts are really social documents that reflect but also, and more importantly, respond to their historical situation.

Since any historical situation is an intricate web of often competing discourses, Cultural Poetics scholars center history, declaring that any interpretation of a text would be incomplete if we do not consider the text's relationship to the discourses that helped fashion it and to which the text is a response. From this point of view, a text becomes a battleground of competing ideas among the author, society, customs, institutions, and social practices that are all eventually negotiated by the author and the reader and influenced by each contributor's episteme. By allowing history a prominent place in the interpretative process and examining the various convoluted webs that interconnect the discourses found within a text and in its historical setting, we can negotiate a text's meaning.

Cultural Poetics holds to the premise of the interconnectedness of all our actions. For a Cultural Poetics critic, everything we do is interrelated to and within a network of practices embedded in our culture. No act is insignificant; everything is important. In our search to attach meaning to our actions, Cultural Poetics critics believe that we can never be fully objective because we are all biased by cultural forces. Only by examining the complex lattice work of these interlocking forces or discourses that empower and shape culture and by realizing that no single discourse reveals the pathway to objective truth about ourselves or our world can we begin to interpret either our world or a text.

In Cultural Poetics theory, the goal of interpretative analysis is the formation and an understanding of a "poetics of culture," a process that sees life and its sundry activities as something more similar to art than we think, certainly a more metaphorical interpretation of reality than an analytic one. Through the practice of their analysis, Cultural Poetics critics maintain that we will discover not only the social world of the text but also the present-day social forces working upon us as we negotiate meaning with printed material. Like history itself, our interaction with a text is a dynamic, ongoing process that will always be somewhat incomplete.

Because Cultural Poetics' history consists of a dynamic relationship between rejecting established norms and concepts while positing and developing new ones, a review of the theoretical assumptions that this site of literary theory rejects and accepts will help us in understanding its multiple methodologies.

WHAT CULTURAL POETICS REJECTS

- Monological interpretations of a given culture, people, or historical era can accurately demonstrate that culture's beliefs and values.
- A historian can establish the "norms" and the "truth" of any social order.
- A writer or a historian can be totally objective.

- Autonomous artifacts, including literary texts, can or do exist.
- Literature is shaped only by historic moments, and that history serves as merely a background for literary study.
- Only one correct interpretation of a text exists.

WHAT CULTURAL POETICS DOES AND ACCEPTS

- It intentionally smudges the line between history and literature, believing that texts (literature) and context (history) are the same and that literature has no history of its own but is ensconced in cultural history.
- It admits that definitive interpretations of a text are unattainable because relevant material is too far spread to gather exhaustively; we can never recover the original meaning of anything because we cannot hear all the voices that contributed to the event.
- It recognizes that power affects literature as deeply as it does history; some narratives are unjustly stifled, being intentionally repressed, subordinated, and forgotten. These seemingly trivial stories or mini-narratives, when uncovered, have a surprisingly large impact, impeding the creation of an overarching historical narrative.
- It believes that texts, like all forms of discourse, help shape and are shaped by social forces.
- It looks to single moments in history that may have influenced or been influenced by a literary text produced at the time, relying heavily on historical documents to discover these significant moments; by so doing, history can no longer be considered simply "background" information for textual analysis but instead is an essential element in the interpretive process.
- It believes that literature is shaped by historical moments while also shaping the individual reader or listener to these texts.
- It believes that one of the most important elements in textual analysis is discovering how a text was formed—that is, investigating the historical and social moments surrounding a text's production, not its supposed interpretation.
- It believes that writers, like texts, are subjected to social biases, cultural influences, and political agendas; hence, no writer or critic can ever be entirely objective.

METHODOLOGY

Like other approaches to literary analysis, Cultural Poetics includes an array of techniques and strategies in its interpretative inquiries, with no one method being dubbed the correct form of investigation. No matter their methodology, Cultural Poetics scholars begin by assuming that language shapes and is shaped by the culture that uses it. By *language*, Cultural Poetics critics mean much more than spoken words. For them, language includes such discourses as literature, social actions, and any social relationship whereby a person or a group imposes their ideas or actions upon another.

Included in this definition of language is history. Like literature, writing, or other relationships that involve either a transfer or a relationship of power, history becomes a narrative discourse. As in literature or any other narrative discourse, history must be viewed as a language that can never be fully articulated or completely explained. From this perspective, history and literature are nearly synonymous, both being narrative discourses that interact with their historical situations, their authors, their readers, and their present-day cultures. Neither can claim a complete or an objective understanding of its content or historical situation because both are ongoing conversations with their creators, readers, and cultures.

Because Cultural Poetics critics view history, literature, and other social activities as forms of discourse, they strongly reject the old historicism, which sees history as necessary background material for the study of literature. They view a work of art, a text, as they would any other social discourse that interacts with its culture to produce meaning. No longer is one discourse superior to another, but all are necessary components that shape and are shaped by society. No longer do clear lines of distinction exist among literature, history, literary criticism, anthropology, art, the sciences, and other disciplines. Blurring the boundaries among disciplines, Cultural Poetics investigates all discourses that affect any social production. Because these practitioners believe that meaning evolves from the interaction of the variously interwoven social discourses, no hierarchy of discourses can exist; all discourses are necessary and must be investigated in the process of textual analysis. The interpretative process must also include questions about the methodological assumptions for discerning meaning for each discourse and for every practitioner because no single discourse, method, or critic can reveal the one single truth about any social production in isolation from other discourses.

Since Cultural Poetics critics view an aesthetic work as a social production, a text's meaning as perceived through the lens of Cultural Poetics resides in the cultural system composed of the interlocking discourses of its author, the text, and its reader. To unlock textual meaning, a Cultural Poetics critic investigates the life of the author, the social rules and dictates found within a text, and all reflections of a work's historical situation. Since an actual person authors a text, his or her actions and beliefs reflect both individual concerns and those of the author's society and are essential elements of the text itself. In addition, the standard of behavior, as reflected in a society's rules of decorum, must also be investigated because these behavioral codes simultaneously helped shape and were shaped by the text. The text must also be viewed as an artistic work that reflects these behavioral social codes. To begin to understand a text's significance and to realize the complex social structure of which it is a part, Cultural Poetics critics declare that all three areas of concern must be investigated. If one area is ignored, the risk of returning to the old historicism, with its lack of understanding about a text as a social production, is great. During the process of textual analysis, Cultural Poetics critics also question their own assumptions and methods because they believe that they, too, are products of and act as shaping influences upon their culture.

To avoid the old historicism's error of thinking that each historical period evidences a single, political worldview, Cultural Poetics avoids sweeping generalizations and seeks out the seemingly insignificant details and manifestations of culture frequently ignored by most historians or literary critics. The anthropologist Geertz describes these seemingly insignificant details as anecdotes that are "quoted raw, a note in a bottle." Anecdotes are well-preserved messages that most often come to us in their original state, unaltered by the ideologies of publishers or other institutions of preservation. As soon as they are gathered together, a collection of anecdotes reveals "counterhistories" or alternative perspectives of an incident or era presented by voices that usually go unheard in a monolithic interpretation of history. Sometimes these stories present a blatantly rebellious attitude toward the powerful history makers, recasting events from the author's perspective of marginalization. At other times, the stories uncovered are simply interested voices recording events that they see. Anecdotes such as personal diaries, for example, can and often do reveal power structures and relationships not found in traditional histories.

Because Cultural Poetics views history and literature as social discourses and therefore battlegrounds for conflicting beliefs, actions, and customs, a text becomes "culture in action." By highlighting seemingly bizarre junctures of anecdotal stories or insignificant happenings, such as a note written by Thomas Jefferson to one of his slaves or a sentence etched on a window pane by Nathaniel Hawthorne, these critics hope to bring to light the competing social codes and forces that mold a given society. Emphasizing a particular moment or incident rather than an overarching vision of society, a Cultural Poetics critic will often point out nonconventional connections, for example, between Sophia Hawthorne's having a headache after reading her husband's first romance, *The Scarlet Letter*, and the ending of Hawthorne's second romance, *The House of the Seven Gables*, or between the climate and environs of Elmira, New York, and some locations, descriptions, and actions in Mark Twain's *Huckleberry Finn*. Cultural Poetics scholars believe that an investigation into these and similar happenings demonstrates the complex relationships that exist among all discourses and shows how narrative discourses such as history, literature, and other social productions interact with, define, and are, in turn, shaped by their culture. What we will learn by applying these principles and methodologies is that there is not one voice but many voices to be heard interpreting texts and our culture: our own, the voices of others, the voices of the past, the voices of the present, and the voices that will be in the future.

QUESTIONS FOR ANALYSIS

When analyzing any text from a Cultural Poetics point of view, Greenblatt and other critics suggest we ask and investigate the following questions:

- What kinds of behavior and models of practice do this work seem to reinforce?
- Why might readers at a particular time and place find this work compelling?
- Are there differences between my values and the values implicit in the work I am reading?
- Upon what social understanding does the work depend?
- Whose freedom of thought or movement might be constrained implicitly or explicitly by this work?
- What are the larger social structures with which these particular acts of praise or blame contained with the text might be connected?
- What authorial biographical facts are relevant to the text?
- What other cultural events occurred surrounding the original production of the text? How may these events be relevant to the text under investigation?

CRITIQUES AND RESPONSES

In the Preface to his 1989 text *The New Historicism*, H. Aram Vesser, the editor, was one of the first scholars to delineate what he perceived as the basic beliefs of Cultural Poetics:

- Every expressive act (including literature) is embedded in a network of material practices.
- Every act of unmasking, critique, and opposition uses the tools it condemns and risks falling prey to the practice it exposes.
- Literary and nonliterary texts circulate inseparably.
- No discourse, imaginative or archival, gives access to unchanging truths nor expresses inalterable human nature.
- A critical method and language adequate to describe culture under capitalism participate in the economy they describe.

Disavowing the tenets of the "old historicism," this New Historicism or Cultural Poetics seeks to uncover the multiple discourses that create a text and are shaped by the text. Believing that art (or literature) and society are interrelated, Cultural Poetics critics embrace the principles of different schools of criticism to unlock a text's power and influence, including the "close reading" principles of the New Criticism and a variety of poststructuralist approaches such as various forms of feminism and Marxism.

Denying a monolithic or monological interpretation of any event, person, or historical era, Cultural Poetics seeks to discover the personal vignettes or "anecdotes" that are ignored, repressed, or suppressed by many critics. Such mini moments in history, they believe, reveal the multiple counterhistories that have been marginalized by previous scholars and writers. These constructed narratives reveal the power structures in both the text and the cultures that produced them, unleashing the silenced voices that can help us reshape our concepts and interpretations of not only texts but also of history, society, and even ourselves.

Similar to other evolving, critical methodologies, Cultural Poetics has faced and continues to face some objections. First, it uses historical methods and artifacts of history; hence, it is working from "inside" the system it is critiquing. Such subjectivity opens Cultural Poetics to being accused of undermining its own arguments. Second, by placing great emphasis on anecdotal evidence, it has been accused of bad historiography. From one single thread of culture—one anecdote—Cultural Poetics critics often create rather significant philosophical, historical, or political theories. Third, although valuing anecdotal evidence or artifacts and other forms of "local knowledge," Cultural Poetics then broadens such knowledge, making claims that reach far into a given culture. Fourth, Cultural Poetics believes that indeterminacy reigns in both literature and history, but it simultaneously holds a strong deterministic attitude toward the effects of these discourses, making pronouncements concerning power in a given culture. And fifth, some critics argue that Cultural Poetics treats all artifacts—texts, social customs, and so on—as literary texts and reduces historical documents and any other cultural form solely to literary terms.

The amount and the various kinds of such criticisms will undoubtedly continue as Cultural Poetics develops in the twenty-first century. Without question, however, Cultural Poetics has impacted every area of literary studies, from Anglo-Saxon to twentieth-century literature, especially influencing both American and British Romanticism. Through its multiple approaches to textual analysis, Cultural Poetics has allowed us to hear many of the silenced voices of the past, speaking once again loud and clear.

FURTHER READING

Brannigan, John. *New Historicism and Cultural Materialism.* New York: St. Martin's, 1998.

Colebrook, Claire. *New Literary Histories: New Historicism and Contemporary Criticism.* Manchester, England: Manchester University Press, 1997.

Collier, Peter, and Helga Geyer-Ryan, eds. *Literary Theory Today.* Ithaca, NY: Cornell University Press, 1990.

Dollimore, Jonathan. *Radical Tragedy: Religion, Ideology, and Power in the Drama of Shakespeare and His Contemporaries*, 2nd ed. Durham, NC: Duke University Press, 1993.

During, Simon. New Historicism. *Text and Performance Quarterly* 11 (July 1991):171–89.

Foucault, Michel. *The Foucault Reader*. Paul Rabinow, ed. New York: Pantheon, 1984.

Gallagher, Catherine, and Stephen Greenblatt. *New Literary Histories*. Chicago: Chicago University Press, 2000.

Geertz, Clifford. *The Interpretation of Cultures: Selected Essays*. New York: Basic, 1973.

———. *Local Knowledge: Further Essays in Interpretive Anthropology*. New York: Routledge, 1991.

Greenblatt, Stephen. Introduction. "The Forms of Power and the Power of Forms in the Renaissance." *Genre* 15 (Summer 1982):3–6.

———. *Renaissance Self-Fashioning: From More to Shakespeare*. Chicago: University of Chicago Press, 1980.

———. *Shakespearean Negotiations: The Circulation of Social Energy in Renaissance England*. Berkeley, CA: University of California Press, 1988.

———. *Will in the World: How Shakespeare Became Shakespeare*. New York: Norton, 2004.

Hamilton, Paul. *Historicism*. New York: Routledge, 1996.

Hens-Piazza, Gena. *The New Historicism*. Minneapolis, MN: Fortress, 2002.

Liu, Alan. The power of formalism. *English Literary History* 56.4 (1989):721–71.

Montrose, Louis. Renaissance literary studies and the subject of history. *English Literary Renaissance* 16 (Winter 1986):5–12.

Sacks, David Harris. Imagination in history. *Shakespeare Studies* 31 (2003):64–86.

Vesser, H. Aram, ed. *The New Historicism*. New York: Routledge, 1989.

———. *The New Historicism Reader*. New York: Routledge, 1994.

WEB SITES FOR EXPLORATION

http://www.sou.edu/English/Hedges/sodashop/RCenter/Theory/Explaind/nhistexp.htm
    Reviews the principles and theories of New Historicism

http://www.cla.purdue.edu/english/theory/newhistoricism
    "Introduction to New Historicism" that includes a good introduction, terms, literary applications, and additional links

http://www-english.tamu.edu/pers/fac/myers/historicism.html
    "The New Criticism in Literary Study" presents a solid critique of New Historicism

http://www.cnr.edu/home/bmcmanus/newhistoricism.htm
    "New Historicism" presents the assumptions of New Historicism and additional links

http://www.arts.gla.ac.uk/SESLL/EngLit/ugrad/hons/theory/CultMaterialism.htm
    A good review of New Historicism's basic premises

Sample Essay

By embracing the principles of Cultural Poetics, this student author seeks to raise the importance of the poem she chose for analysis to that of equal importance to any history text or any other historical document. As you read the following student essay, ask yourself the following questions:

- What principles of Cultural Poetics does the author highlight?
- Does she use any anecdotes in her criticism? If so, what are they, and how does the author incorporate these anecdotes into her interpretation? In addition, do such anecdotes effectively help the author develop her interpretation?
- Does the writer incorporate biographical elements in her analysis? If so, explain how she uses these elements to craft her interpretation of the poem.
- What other artifacts, excluding the text itself, does the author argue should be part of the text's overall interpretation?
- What are the essay's strengths? Weaknesses? How could the essay be improved?

Student Essay

Done Yesterday: A New Historicist Reading of Wilfred Owen's "Dulce et Decorum Est"[1]

Piccadilly is awash with milling civilians, but the stern stare of Kitchener, British Secretary of War, is unyielding. "Join your country's army!" The wind is blowing, and one unfastened edge of the poster slaps the telegraph line with a steady tap, like a muffled version of the rhythmic thud heard when uniformed regiments leave town. A youth, proudly clutching a red toy soldier just bought on Regent, stops to stare back at the brave, noble face. The boy had been taught Horace in grade school, of course: *Dulce et decorum est.* He cannot remember the rest of the maxim. The sign-off at the bottom of the poster stirs his memory—"God save the King." Kitchener salutes, claps his heels together, and turns. Message sent. Message received. The boy smiles with pride at the vision and remembers: *Pro patria mori.*

Wilfred Owen, a British soldier diagnosed with shell shock, lay restlessly in a hospital bed at Craiglockhart, Scotland. The vibrant autumnal colors outside the hospital could not distract him from the hideous images whirling in his mind. He took up a sheet of paper and began writing. On October 16, 1917, Owen posted a letter to his mother, tucking inside the envelope "a gas poem, done yesterday." That poem, "Dulce et Decorum Est," has survived the decades as a revered though emotionally jolting account of the Great War's horrors. From a New Historicist point of view, Owen's "Dulce et Decorum Est"

[1]Reprinted by permission of Anna L. Kruse.

both reveals and shapes its culture and is a no less authoritative account of the War than is a history textbook. All history, like all literature, New Historicists claim, is a narrative; those who translate historical events into text will inevitably add their own ideology to the account. Literature and history are both discourses that influence culture, expose power hierarchies, and express ideology. From a New Historicist perspective, Owen's poems are a valuable avenue to understanding the Great War. "What is history but a fable agreed upon?" Napoleon Bonaparte once asked. Like the New Historicists, Bonaparte recognized that history is a fiction whose appearance of consensus is misleading.

To reach a holistic and New Historicist understanding of Owen's poetry, we need to engage in "thick description," a term borrowed from anthropology that refers to placing an action in its cultural context. In order to be as exhaustive and detailed as possible, New Historicists excavate anecdotal historic sources. Primary texts that were previously ignored as unimportant enjoy newfound credibility; letters, propaganda, and journal entries become relevant. Other communicative media are similarly authoritative. Material culture, encompassing everything from photographic images to the engineering of a kitchen utensil, adds to the historical dialogue. New Historicists place texts in the midst of these contextual elements in an effort to craft a more accurate portrait of the moment than would old historicism with its abortive acceptance of the "fable agreed upon."

Engaging in thick description with various segments of "Dulce et Decorum Est" yields insights into the untold nature of war not expressed in traditional history textbooks. Consider the phrase "In all my dreams, before my helpless sight,/He plunges at me, guttering, choking, drowning," which to Owen warranted its own stanza. The image of a man lunging at him particularly fixates Owen, and he is repeatedly dissatisfied with his capability to coalesce all hideous elements of the vision into words. The original copy of this text, owned by the British Library, indicates Owen's frustration with finding the best word to describe the sound the dying man makes. Owen tries "gargling," "gurgling," and "goggling," finally deciding on "guttering" after striking out the others with a series of lines. No stranger to jarring deaths, Owen served in France during the Great War's most heated years and doubtlessly saw many of his comrades fall. Owen contrasts those vile, undignified deaths with the romanticized version of death those on the home front hold. He especially condemns the lofty phrases that feed what he sees as the naïve notion that war is "sweet" and "decorous." "*Sweet*! and *Decorous*!" Owen wrote in a letter to his mother, implying that those two phrases were perennially misguiding.

Owen's concern for the "children ardent for some desperate glory" was apparently neither protective nor naturally paternal. Little more than a month before he composed "Dulce," he shared with his mother his attitude toward children. "But yesterday [Edinburgh mothers] had to mind their babies, which being self-centred, unmannerly blobs of one to three years bored me utterly," he wrote.[2] His concern for Britain's youth was expansive and principled; despite his personal distaste for children, he saw the pressing importance of debunking the myth that war is glory-filled.

That "old lie" was told through various media, encompassing many cultural discourses. Although cameras were forbidden on the front lines, they were nonetheless present. One military conflict documented in film, "The Battle of the Somme," became a box-office hit on the British home front. The producers, having incomplete information about the battle, presented it as a glorious victory on Britain's part, feeding domestic zeal for the war. Propaganda posters, like the one described in the introductory vignette, exalted the noble burden of joining the fight. "Your King and Country Need You. A Call to Arms," offers one poster, ending with the favorite *pro patria*-inspired salute "God Save the King." Newspapers also expounded the lie. The August 4, 1914 edition of Britain's *The Daily Mirror* recorded that, in response to Germany's attempts to retain Britain's favor, Britain "has preferred the path of honour." The price of that path would be the lives of countless soldiers, but such deaths were deemed honorable—they were sweet and decorous, for, as one Great War poster depicting a Cotswoldian paradise asked, "Isn't this worth fighting for?" One's homeland was overwhelmingly considered a noble cause for self-sacrifice, even to the point of death.

The dying soldier in Owen's "Dulce" is universal. He is *the* everyman, the nameless recruit whose carefully studied face represents the tormented spirits of all those fated to see the hellish affairs of war. The soldier's indistinct identity is especially poignant considering the similar prominence of the *pro patria* mentality in Germany's culture. One early incident in the Great War speaks powerfully of how German youth were indoctrinated with this notion. In 1914 in Belgium, several thousand German students, few older than sixteen, marched into British lines defiantly singing the German anthem "Das Lied der Deutschen": "Germany, Germany above all, above all in the world!" The British hastily decimated the students, leading the incensed Germans to celebrate their brave sacrifice. Lovingly coining that mass fatality the *Kindermord von Ypern*, literally the "Death of the Children in Ypern," the Germans demonstrated their faith in the "old lie." Owen's exhortation at the close of his poem—though the poem was originally addressed to his children's writer "Friend," Jessie Pope—does not indicate national preference. The "old lie" is universally condemnable. Nationality is a superfluous, petty concern when compared to the "thick green light" and "hanging face[s]" of the war front.

Owen's poem stands as an example of a subversive voice that survived the powerful cultural forces that might have silenced its message of resistance.

---

[2]Wilfred Owen, *Selected Letters*, ed. John Bell (Oxford: Oxford University Press, 1985), p. 273.

His message faced overwhelming opposition by the British government, for it was in the interests of those in high governmental positions to recruit all possible military power. Owen shattered the home front's lofty, romanticized visions of war with his jarring descriptions of its horrors. War gores the spirit as well as the body, Owen insisted. The content of "Dulce et Decorum Est" was clearly implicated in its cultural milieu as it responds powerfully to the dominating rhetoric of the time. When Owen's poetry appeared as a post-war compendium in 1920, the British public was war-weary and ready to receive his message. Sadly, Owen did not live to see his poetry affirmed by "the children ardent for some desperate glory," for he was killed in action a few days before the War ended. Though many British children eagerly embraced Owen's poetry, they would, ironically, grow up to become the uniformed regiments of World War II.

Cecil Day Lewis, editor of a collection of Owen's poems decades later, illustrates for us just how engaged we as readers are in our cultural milieu when interpreting Owen's poetry. Lewis notes that Owen's poetry touches "[Lewis's] own generation" so that they "could never again think of war as anything but a vile, *if necessary*, evil" [emphasis added].[3] As a sympathizer with communist ideology, Lewis offers a Marxist interpretation of Owen's poetry. Perhaps you or I, caught in the midst of international uneasiness, would interpret it differently. A satisfying critical analysis of Owen's poetry requires that we engage our own dialogue with his, recognizing our ideological predispositions and doing our best to lay such assumptions aside long enough to immerse ourselves in his world, appreciating the cultural minutiae that joined the force of his episteme in shaping his art.

A young man, proudly clutching a red rose just bought on Regent, stands before a pallid limestone slab that juts skyward from the freshly groomed sod. He lays the rose against his older brother Wilfred's grave. He salutes, claps his heels together, and turns. Message sent. Message received. Owen has changed us—and the world—with his words.

ANNA L. KRUSE

---

[3]Wilfred Owen, *The Collected Poems of Wilfred Owen*, ed. C. Day Lewis (New York: New Directions, 1963), p. 12.

10

CULTURAL STUDIES: POSTCOLONIALISM, AFRICAN-AMERICAN CRITICISM, AND QUEER THEORY

Post-colonial studies are based in the 'historical fact' of European colonialism, and the diverse material effects to which this phenomenon gave rise.

Bill Ashcroft, Gareth Griffiths, and Helen Tiffin,
The Post-Colonial Studies Reader (1995)

The 1960s saw a revolutionary change in literary theory. Until this decade, New Criticism dominated literary theory and criticism, with its insistence that "the" one correct interpretation of a text could be discovered if critical readers follow the prescribed methodology asserted by the New Critics. Positing an autonomous text, New Critics paid little attention to a text's historical context or to the feelings, beliefs, and ideas of a text's readers. For New Critics, a text's meaning is inextricably bound to ambiguity, irony, and paradox found within the structure of the text itself. By analyzing the text alone, New Critics believe that an astute critic can identify a text's central paradox and explain how the text ultimately resolves that paradox while also supporting the text's overarching theme.

Into this seemingly self-assured system of hermeneutics marches Jacques Derrida and other scholar-critics in the late 1960s. Unlike the New Critics, Derrida, the chief spokesperson for deconstruction, disputes a text's objective existence. Denying that a text is an **autotelic artifact**, Derrida and other **postist** (*post*modern, *post*structuralist, *post*colonial) **critics** challenge the accepted definitions and assumptions of both the reading and writing processes. These postist thinkers insist on questioning what part not only the text but also the reader and the author play in the interpretive process.

Joined by a host of critics and scholars—Jonathan Culler, J. Hillis Miller, Barbara Johnson, and Michel Foucault, to name a few—these philosopher-critics also question the language of texts and of literary analysis. Unlike the

New Critics, who believe that the language of literature is somehow different from the language of science and everyday conversation, these postmodernists insist that the language of texts is not distinct from the language used to analyze such writings. For them, language is a **discourse**. In other words, the discourse or culturally bound language of ideas used in literary analysis helps shape and form the text being analyzed. We cannot separate, they maintain, the text and the language used to critique it. For these critics, language helps create and shape what we call "objective reality."

Believing that objective reality can be created by language, many postmodernists posit that all reality is a social construct. From this point of view, no single or primary objective reality exists; instead, many realities exist. In disavowing a universal, objective reality, these critics assert that reality is perspectival, with each individual creating his or her subjective understanding of the nature of reality itself. How, then, do we come to agree upon public and social concerns, such as values, ethics, and the common good, if reality is different for each individual? The answer for many postist thinkers is that each society or culture contains within itself a dominant cultural group which determines that culture's ideology or, using the Marxist term, its **hegemony**—that is, its dominant values, sense of right and wrong, and sense of personal self-worth. All people in a given culture are consciously and unconsciously asked to conform to the prescribed hegemony.

What happens, however, when one's ideas, thinking, or personal background does not conform? What happens, for example, when the dominant culture consists of white, Anglo-Saxon men and you are a black woman? Or how does one respond to a culture dominated by these same white men if you are a Native American? For people of color living in Africa or in the Americas, Native Americans, females, gays and lesbians, and a host of others, the traditional answer has already been articulated by the dominant class and its accompanying hegemony: *silence.* Live quietly, work quietly, think quietly. The message sent to these "Others" by the dominant culture has been clear and consistent—conform and be quiet; deny yourself, and all will be well.

But many have not been quiet. Writers and thinkers, such as Toni Morrison, Alice Walker, Gabriel García Márquez, Carlos Fuentes, Gayatri Spivak, Edward Said, Frantz Fanon, and Judith Butler, to name a few, have dared to speak out and challenge the dominant cultures and the dictates these cultures decree. They continue to refuse silence and choose defiance, if necessary. They believe that an individual's view of life, of values, and of ethics really matters. They assert a different perspective, a vantage point not of the dominant culture but one from which to view the world and its peoples: They speak for not one culture, but many; not one cultural perspective, but a host; not one interpretation of life, but countless.

Joined by postmodern literary theorists and philosophers, these new voices—African, Australian, Native American, women, gays and lesbians, and others—are letting their voices be heard among the cacophony of the insistent, dominant, and generally overpowering cultural voices. Believing that they can effect cultural change, these writers and critics refuse to conform to their culture's hegemony. In their struggle for empowerment, these newly heard but long-existent voices are now articulating their ideas at the contemporary literary table discussions concerning their understanding of reality, society, and personal self-worth.

Accompanied by their various literary theories and criticism, these voices are grouped together under the umbrella of **cultural studies** and include an analysis of gender studies, African-American studies, postcolonial studies, and a host of new voices vying to be heard amid a discussion that has long been dominated by a few voices. In Great Britain, the terms **cultural criticism** and *cultural studies* are often used interchangeably. In North America, whereas cultural criticism primarily focuses on textual analysis or other artistic forms, cultural studies refers to a much broader interdisciplinary study of literary and artistic forms analyzed in their social, economic, or political contexts. This chapter explores three of cultural studies' voices: postcolonialism, African-American criticism, and queer theory. Although each group has its personal concerns, all seek to be heard and understood as valuable and contributing members of their society. Their individual and public histories, they assert, do matter. They believe that their past and their present are intricately interwoven. They declare that by denying and suppressing their past, they would be denying who they are. They desire to articulate their feelings, concerns, and assumptions about the nature of reality in their particular cultures without being treated as marginal, minor, or insignificant voices. Often referred to as **subaltern writers**—a term used by the Marxist critic Antonio Gramsci to refer to those classes who are not in control of a culture's ideology (hegemony)—these theorists/authors/critics provide new ways to see and understand the cultural forces at work in society, literature, and ourselves. Although the literary theory and accompanying criticism of each cultural studies approach is ongoing, an overview of the central tenets of these three approaches will enable us to understand their distinct visions of literature's purposes in today's ever-changing world.

POSTCOLONIALISM: "THE EMPIRE WRITES BACK"

Postcolonialism (or **post-colonialism**—either spelling is acceptable, but each represents slightly different theoretical assumptions) consists of a set of theories in philosophy and various approaches to literary analysis that are concerned with literature written in English in countries that were or still are colonies of other countries. For the most part, postcolonial studies excludes literature that represents either British or American viewpoints and concentrates on writings from colonized or formerly colonized cultures in Australia, New Zealand, Africa, South America, and other places that were once dominated by, but remained outside of, the white, male, European cultural, political, and philosophical tradition. Referred to as "third-world literature" by Marxist critics and "Commonwealth literature" by others—terms many contemporary critics think pejorative—postcolonial literature and its theorists investigate what happens when two cultures clash and when one of them, with its accessory ideology, empowers and deems itself superior to the other.

Historical Development of Postcolonialism

Rooted in colonial power and prejudice, postcolonialism develops from a 4000-year history of strained cultural relations between colonies in Africa and Asia and the Western world. Throughout this long history, the West became the colonizers, and many African and Asian countries and their peoples became the colonized. During the nineteenth century, Great Britain emerged as the largest colonizer and imperial power, quickly gaining control of almost one quarter of the earth's landmass. By the middle of the nineteenth century, terms such as *colonial interests* and the *British Empire* were widely used in the media, government policies, and international politics. Many British people believed that Great Britain was destined to rule the world. Likewise, the assumption that Western Europeans, and, in particular, the British people, were biologically superior to any other **race**—a term for a class of people based on physical, cultural distinctions, or both—remained relatively unquestioned.

Such beliefs directly affected the ways that the colonizers treated the colonized. Using its political and economic muscles, Great Britain, the chief imperialist power of the nineteenth century, dominated her colonies, making them produce and then give up their countries' raw materials in exchange for what material goods the colonized desired or were made to believe they desired by the colonizers. Forced labor of the colonized became the rule of the day, and thus the institution of slavery was commercialized. Often the colonizers justified their cruel treatment of the colonized by invoking European religious beliefs. From the perspective of many white Westerners, the peoples of Africa, the Americas, and Asia were "heathens," possessing ways that must be Christianized. How one treats peoples who are so defined does not really matter, they said, because many Westerners subscribed to the colonialist ideology that all races other than white were inferior or subhuman. These subhumans or "savages" quickly became the inferior and equally "evil" Others, a philosophical concept called **alternity** whereby "the others" are excluded from positions of power and viewed as different and inferior.

By the early twentieth century, England's political, social, economic, and ideological domination of its many colonies began to disappear, a process known as **decolonization**. By mid-century, for example, India had gained its independence. Many scholars believe that this event marks the beginning of postcolonialism or **third-world studies**, a term coined by the French demographer Alfred Sauvy. India's independence ignited the outrage of a vast array of scholars, writers, and critics concerning the social, moral, political, and economic conditions of what were once called third-world countries.

The beginnings of postcolonialism's theoretical and social concerns can be traced to the 1950s. Along with India's independence, this decade witnessed the ending of France's long involvement in Indochina; the parting of the ways between the two leading figures in existential theory, Jean-Paul Sartre and Albert Camus, over their differing views about Algeria; Fidel Castro's now-famous "History Shall Absolve Me" speech; and the publication of Frantz Fanon's *Black Skin, White Masks* (1952) and Chinua Achebe's novel *Things Fall Apart* (1958).

The following decades witnessed the publication of additional key texts that articulated the social, political, and economic conditions of various subaltern groups. In 1960, the Caribbean writer George Lamming published *The Pleasures of Exile*, in which he critiques William Shakespeare's play *The Tempest* from a postcolonial perspective. The next year, Fanon published *The Wretched of the Earth* (1961), a work that highlights the tensions or binary oppositions of white versus black, good versus evil, and rich versus poor, to cite a few. Other writers, philosophers, and critics such as Albert Memmi continued publishing texts that soon became the cornerstone of postcolonial theory and writings. In particular, postcolonialism gained the attention of the West with the publication of Edward Said's *Orientalism* (1978) and Bill Ashcroft, Gareth Griffiths, and Helen Tiffin's monumental text *The Empire Writes Back: Theory and Practice in Post-Colonial Literatures* (1989). With the publication of these two texts, the voices and concerns of many subaltern cultures were heard in both academic and social arenas.

The terms *postcolonial* and *postcolonialism* first appear in scholarly journals in the mid-1980s; as subtitles in texts such as Ashcroft, Griffiths, and Tiffin's book; and in 1990 in Ian Adam and Helen Tiffin's *Past the Last Post: Theorizing Post-Colonialism and Post-Modernism*. By the early and mid-1990s, both terms had become firmly established in academic and popular discourse.

Similar to deconstruction and other postmodern approaches to textual analysis, postcolonialism is a heterogeneous field of study in which even its spelling provides several alternatives. Some argue that it should be spelled *postcolonialism*, with no hyphen between *post* and *colonialism*, and others insist on using the hyphen, as in *post-colonialism*. Many of its adherents suggest there are two branches, one that views postcolonialism as a set of diverse methodologies that possess no unitary quality, as argued by Homi K. Bhabha and Arun P. Mukherjee, and those such as Edward Said, Barbara Harlow, and

Gayatri Chakravorty Spivak, who see postcolonialism as a set of cultural strategies "centered in history." This latter group can also be subdivided into those who believe postcolonialism refers to the period after the colonized societies or countries have become independent as opposed to those who regard postcolonialism as referring to all the characteristics of a society or culture from the time of colonization to the present moment.

Postcolonialism's concerns become evident when we examine the various topics discussed in one of its most prominent texts, Ashcroft, Griffiths, and Tiffin's *The Post-Colonial Studies Reader* (1995). Its subjects include universality, difference, nationalism, postmodernism, representation and resistance, ethnicity, feminism, language, education, history, place, and production. As diverse as these topics appear, they draw attention to postcolonialism's major concern: highlighting the struggle that occurs when one culture is dominated by another. As postcolonial critics point out, to be colonized is "to be removed from history." In its interaction with the conquering culture, the colonized or indigenous culture is forced to go underground or to be obliterated.

Only after colonization occurs and the colonized people have had time to think and then to write about their oppression and loss of cultural identity does postcolonial theory come into existence. Postcolonial theory is born out of the colonized peoples' frustrations; their direct and personal cultural clashes with the conquering culture; and their fears, hopes, and dreams about the future and their own identities. How the colonized respond to changes in language, curricular matters in education, race differences, economic issues, morals, ethics, and a host of other concerns, including the act of writing itself, becomes the context for the evolving theories and practice of postcolonialism.

Assumptions of Postcolonialism

Because different cultures that have been subverted, conquered, and often removed from history respond to the conquering culture in multiple ways, no single approach to postcolonial theory or practice is possible or even preferable. As Nicholas Harrison asserts in *Postcolonial Criticism: History, Theory and the Work of Fiction* (2003), "postcolonial theory is not an identifiable 'type' of theory in the same sense as deconstruction, Marxism, psychoanalysis or feminism." Similar to many critical theorists, Harrison "sees no point in talking as if consensus about what postcolonial studies 'is' might eventually emerge." We can, however, highlight postcolonialism's major concerns. All postcolonialist critics believe:

- European colonialism did occur.
- The British Empire was at the center of this colonialism.
- The conquerors not only dominated the physical land but also the hegemony or ideology of the colonized peoples.

- The social, political, and economic effects of such colonization are still being felt today.

At the center of postcolonial theory exists an inherent tension: Those who develop postcolonial theories and practice its multiple approaches to textual analysis form a heterogeneous group. On the one hand, critics such as Fredric Jameson and Georg Gugelberger come from a European and American cultural, literary, and scholarly background. Another group that includes Spivak, Said, Bhabha, and others were raised in non-Western cultures but have resided or now reside, study, and write in the West. And still another group includes writers such as Aijaz Ahmad, who live and work in subaltern cultures. A theoretical and a practical gap occurs between the theory and practice of those trained and living in the West and subaltern writers living and writing in non-Western cultures. Out of this tension, postcolonial theorists and critics have and will continue to discover problematic topics for exploration and debate.

A number of postcolonial theorists and critics provide postcolonial theory with pivotal texts, concepts, and assumptions that continue to be used, adopted, and amended by contemporary postcolonialists. One of the earliest postcolonial theorists was Frantz Fanon. Born in the French colony of Martinique, Fanon fought with the French in World War II, remaining in France after the war to study medicine and psychiatry. Throughout his rather short career and life, Fanon provides postcolonialism with two influential texts: *Black Skin, White Masks* (1952) and *The Wretched of the Earth* (1961). In *Black Skin, White Masks*, Fanon uses psychoanalytic theory to examine the condition of blacks under French colonial rule. As a result of colonialism, Fanon asserts that both the colonized (the **other**—that is, any person defined as "different from") and the colonizer suffer "psychic warping," often causing what Fanon describes as "a collapse of the ego." Fanon believes that as soon as the colonized (the blacks living in Martinique) were forced to speak the language of the colonizer (the French), the colonized either accepted or were coerced into accepting the collective consciousness of the French, thereby identifying blackness with evil and sin and whiteness with purity and righteousness.

In *The Wretched of the Earth*, Fanon argues that an entirely new world must come into being to overcome the binary system in which black is evil and white is good. In this work, Fanon elaborates a Marxist-influenced postcolonial theory in which he calls for violent revolution, a type of revolution in which Fanon himself was involved when he became a participant and a spokesperson for the Algerian revolutionaries against France. He also develops in this work one of his major concerns, the problem of the "native bourgeoisie" who assume power after the colonial powers have either departed or been driven out. When this situation occurs, the native proletariat, "the wretched of the earth," are left on their own, often in a worse situation than before the conquerors arrived. Throughout his writings, Fanon develops key postcolonial concerns such as the "otherness," subject formation, and an emphasis on linguistic and psychoanalytic frameworks on which postcolonialism developed in the decades to follow.

Perhaps the key text in the establishment of postcolonial theory is Edward Wadie Said's *Orientalism* (1978). A Palestinian–American theorist and critic, Said was born in Jerusalem, where he lived with his family until the 1948 Arab–Israeli War, at which time his family became refugees in Egypt and then Lebanon. Educated at Princeton and Harvard Universities, Said taught at Johns Hopkins University, where, as a professor he authored many papers and texts, *Orientalism* being his most influential. In this work, Said chastises the literary world for not investigating and taking seriously the study of colonization or imperialism. He then develops several concepts that are central to postcolonial theory. According to Said, nineteenth-century Europeans tried to justify their territorial conquests by propagating a manufactured belief called **Orientalism**: the creation of non-European stereotypes that suggested so-called Orientals were indolent, thoughtless, sexually immoral, unreliable, and demented. The European conquerors, Said notes, believed that they were accurately describing the inhabitants of their newly acquired lands in "the East." What they failed to realize, maintains Said, is that all human knowledge can be viewed only through one's political, cultural, and ideological framework. No theory, either political or literary, an be totally objective. In effect, the colonizers were revealing their unconscious desires for power, wealth, and domination, not the nature of the colonized subjects.

In *Culture and Imperialism* (1994), a work in which Said continues to develop his ideas, Said captures the basic thought behind colonization and imperialism: "'They're not like us,' and for that reason deserve to be ruled." The colonized became **the Other**, the "not me." Said argues that the established binary opposition of "the West"/"the Other" must be abolished along with its intricate web of racial and religious prejudices. What must be rejected, Said maintains, is the "vision" mentality of writers who want to describe the Orient from a panoramic view. This erroneous view of humanity creates a simplistic interpretation of human experience. It must be replaced by one based on "narrative," a historical view that emphasizes the variety of human experiences in all cultures. The narrative view does not deny differences but presents them in an objective way. Scholarship, asserts Said, must be derived from first-hand experience of a particular region, giving voice to the critics who live and write in these regions, not scholarship from "afar" or second-hand representation. Although such ideas helped shape the central issues of postcolonial theory, Said's use of French "high theory" and Marxist ideology as a methodology to deconstruct and examine historically the roots of Orientalism attracted the attention of the academic world and helped inspire a new direction in postcolonial thought.

Homi K. Bhabha, one of the leading contemporary voices in postcolonial studies, builds on Said's concept of the other and Orientalism. Born into a Parsi family in Mumbai, India, Bhabha received his undergraduate degree in

India and his master's and doctoral degrees from Oxford University. Having taught at several prestigious universities, including Princeton, Dartmouth, and the University of Chicago, Bhabha is currently a professor at Harvard University. In works such as *The Location of Culture* (1994), Bhabha emphasizes the concerns of the colonized. What of the individual who has been colonized? On the one hand, the colonized observes two somewhat distinct views of the world: that of the colonizer (the conqueror) and that of himself or herself (the colonized, the one who has been conquered). To what culture does this person belong? Seemingly, neither culture feels like home. Bhabha calls this feeling of homelessness, of being caught between two clashing cultures, **unhomeliness**, a concept referred to as **double consciousness** by some postcolonial theorists. This feeling or perception of abandonment by both cultures causes the colonial subject (the colonized person) to become a psychological refugee. Because each psychological refugee uniquely blends his or her two cultures, no two writers who have been colonial subjects will interpret their culture(s) exactly alike. Hence, Bhabha argues against the tendency to essentialize third-world countries into a homogenous identity. One of Bhabha's major contributions to postcolonial studies is his belief that there is always ambivalence at the site of colonial dominance.

Bhabha proposes an answer to the colonial subject's sense of unhomeliness. The colonized writer must create a new **discourse** by rejecting all the established **transcendental signifieds** created by the colonizers. Such a writer must also embrace pluralism, believing that no single truth or metatheory of history exists. To accomplish such goals, Bhabha consistently uses the tools of deconstruction theory to expose cultural metaphors and discourse.

Although Fanon, Said, and Bhabha lay much of the theoretical framework of postcolonialism, many other voices have joined them in continuing the dialogue between what Bhabha calls "the Occident" and "the Orient." Concentrating on what some critics call the "flows of culture," postcolonialism divides into smaller theoretical schools identified by their choice of theoretical background and methodology. Marxism, poststructuralism, feminism, African-American cultural studies, and psychoanalytic criticism (usually of the Lacanian variety) are all identifiable influences on postcolonial theory. For example, Gayatri Spivak, the publisher of the English translation of Jacques Derrida's *Of Grammatology* (1974), is a feminist, postcolonial critic who applies deconstructive interpretations of imperialism while simultaneously questioning the premises of the Marxism, feminism, and Derridean deconstruction that she espouses.

Although postcolonialism is undoubtedly heterogeneous, such a varied approach to textual analysis assumes that literature, culture, and history all affect each other in significant ways. Postcolonial critics also believe in the unavoidability of subjective and political interpretations in literary studies, arguing that criticism and theory must be revelant to society as it really is. As such, these critics assert that colonialism was and is a cause of suffering and oppression, a cause that is inherently unjust. Colonialism is not a thing of the past but continues today—albeit in subtler and less open ways—as a form of oppression, so it must be opposed. As the contemporary critic Sam Durrant writes in *Postcolonial Narrative and the Work of Mourning* (2004), "Post-colonialism as a praxis is grounded in an appeal to an ethical universal entailing a simple respect for human suffering and a fundamental revolt against it." Suffering and enslavement, maintain postcolonialists, are elements of oppression and are "simply wrong."

Methodology

Similar to many schools of criticism, postcolonialism uses a variety of approaches to textual analysis. Deconstruction, feminism, Marxism, reader-oriented criticism, and African-American cultural studies use postcolonial theories in their critical methodologies. Some critics, however, identify two major approaches or "strains" of postcolonial criticism: postcolonial criticism and postcolonial theory. Those who engage in **postcolonial criticism** investigate ways that texts bear the traces of colonialism's ideology and interpret such texts as challenging or promoting the colonizer's purposes and hegemony. More frequently than not, those who engage in this type of criticism analyze canonical texts from colonizing countries. **Postcolonial theory**, on the other hand, moves beyond the bounds of literary studies and investigates social, political, and economic concerns of the colonized and the colonizer. No matter which methodology a postcolonial critic may choose, it matters greatly whether or not the critic has been a colonial subject. Those who have been the subjects of colonization ask themselves a somewhat different set of questions than postcolonialists who have not.

The person living and writing in a colonized culture asks three significant questions:

- Who am I?
- How did I develop into the person I am?
- To what country or countries or to what cultures am I forever linked?

In asking and answering the first question, the colonized author is connecting himself or herself to historical roots. By asking and answering the second question, the writer is admitting a tension between these historical roots and the new culture or hegemony imposed on him or her by the conquerors. By asking and answering the third question, the writer confronts the fact that he or she is both an individual and a social construct created and shaped primarily by the dominant culture. The written works penned by these authors will be personal and always political and ideological. Furthermore, both the creation of a text and its reading may be painful and disturbing but also enlightening. Whatever the result, the story will certainly be a message sent back to the Empire, telling the imperialists the efforts of their colonization and how their Western hegemony has damaged and suppressed the ideologies of those who were conquered.

Postcolonialists are quick to point out that they do not claim that they make no value judgments. They ask us, their readers and critics, to examine carefully the standards against which we are making our value judgments. Said cautions us that "it is not necessary to regard every reading or interpretation of a text as the moral equivalent of war, but whatever else they are, works of literature are not merely texts." A postcolonial aim is to read a text in its fullest context, not to remain solely in academia and academic discourse. This diverse and often psychologically laden and complex theory centers around the "writing back" of those who have experienced colonial oppression in a variety of circumstances. Postcolonial critics give such texts a close reading, particularly noting the language of the text. Such analysis questions the taken-for-granted positions usually held by the Western mindset. How truth is constructed must be examined rather than exposing errors of the colonizers. Because a variety of prejudices and attitudes may be present from text to text, postcolonial critics vary their approach for each text, letting the text itself establish its critical agenda. Postcolonial critics also guard against ascribing their own cultural ideas onto postcolonial works, realizing that any attempt to understand completely a subaltern group will be impossible and can lead to another form of repression. How postcolonial criticism is actually put into practice depends strongly on the critic's individual theoretical commitments. All postcolonial criticism, however, is united in its opposition to colonial and neocolonial hegemonies and its concern with the best way or ways to create a just and true decolonized culture and literature.

Questions for Analysis

When applying postcolonialist theory to a text, consider the following questions:

- What happens in the text when the two cultures clash, when one sees itself as superior to another?
- Describe the two or more cultures exhibited in the text. What does each value? What does each reject?
- Who in the text is "the Other"?
- Describe the worldviews of each of the cultures.
- What are the forms of resistance against colonial control?
- Demonstrate how the superior or privileged culture's hegemony affects the colonized culture.
- How do the colonized people view themselves? Is there any change in this view by the end of the text?

- Describe the language of the two cultures. How are they alike? Different?
- Is the language of the dominant culture used as a form of oppression? Suppression?
- Cite the various ways that the colonized culture is silenced.
- Are there any emergent forms of postcolonial identity after the departure of the colonizers?
- How do gender, race, or social class function in the colonial and postcolonial elements of the text?

AFRICAN-AMERICAN CRITICISM

The growing interest in postcolonialism in American literary theory during the late 1970s to the present propelled a renewed interest in the works of African-American writers and African-American literary theory and criticism. But to say that postcolonialism or other postist theories initiated African-American theory and criticism would be inaccurate. Similar to all schools of criticism, this body of theory and criticism has been evolving over time since the publication of the earliest African-American literature, poems written by the African-American authors Jupiter Hammon (1711–1806) and Phillis Wheatley (1753–1784). Since the publication of these poets' works to the writings of contemporary African-Americans, present-day African-American criticism challenges established ideologies, racial boundaries, and racial prejudice. It also acknowledges and incorporates the writings of past African-American literature, the major historical movements that have influenced African-American writings, and both historical and current attitudes toward African-Americans. Since the emergence of Derridean deconstruction and other postist theories, African-American criticism frequently uses binary oppositions, viewing white Americans as the oppressors of black art and black people. Its strong historical sense, understanding of racial issues, and concept of what being black means combine to create a school of criticism that is unique and multifaceted.

Historical Development, Assumptions, and Methodology

Without question, the twentieth century gave rise to a dramatic increase in African-American literature and literary criticism. The increased presence of African-American works directly influences American culture while the culture is also influencing the literature. The writings, concerns, and critiques of the earliest African-American writers foreshadow the body of criticism that developed in the past three centuries in the United States.

Since its beginning, African-American literature has been shaped by the enslavement of blacks in colonial America by white Western Europeans and the suppression of the black race that follows. The personal story of Phillis Wheatley, one of the first prominent African-American poets in early America, embodies the concerns and effects of slavery in American litera-ture, American culture, and the personal life of one of America's earliest poets.

On August 3, 1761, the following advertisement appeared in the Boston *Evening Post*:

> To Be Sold
> A parcel of likely Negroes, imported from Africa, cheap for cash, or short credit. Enquire near the South Market; Also, if any Persons have any Negro Men, they may have an exchange for small Negroes.

Among this group of small Negroes stood a frail, 7-year-old child who would soon be given the name Phillis Wheatley by her new owners, the Wheatleys. Recognizing Phillis's innate intelligence, Susannah Wheatley, the wife of a prosperous Boston tailor and Phillis's "owner," encouraged Phillis's intellectual endeavors, and in a little more than 16 months after her "adoption" by the Wheatleys, Phillis had mastered English, memorized many passages from the Bible, and was well on her way to fluency in several classical languages. Because she was a brillliant conversationalist, Phillis frequently accompanied her owners on the circuit of Boston social events. By her own choice, she never sat at the same dining tables as her owners and their peers but requested a side table, where she would eat alone. She similarly spent the most significant part of her life in isolation from both whites and blacks, her most frequent company being the works of the eighteenth-century British writers.

By age 13, Phillis published her first poem, with many more to follow. In 1770, the publication of her poem written in memory of "the late Reverend, and Pious George Whitefield" propelled her to fame throughout Boston and the colonies. At age 23, she traveled to London and was greeted as the "Sable Muse," finding herself in the company of Benjamin Franklin, counts and countesses, and even the Lord Mayor of London. While in London, the collected edition of her poems, *Poems on Various Subjects, Religious and Moral*, was published, the first published volume of poems by a black American. Because both her British and American audience would find it startling and unbelievable that a black woman could write such ele-gant poetry, the preface to her collected poems contained the testimony of no less than 18 distinguished Bostonians, including John Hancock, attesting to the authenticity of her work.

Upon her return to America, Wheatley continued to publish her poems, and her work was praised by such prominent Americans as George Washington. Many people, however, questioned how a black woman could be so intelligent as to write such "good" poetry and took her to court so that she would be forced to recant her ownership of her poems. Wheatley won her case and continued to publish poems in such prestigious publications as the *Pennsylvania Magazine.*

Upon the death of her owners, Phillis was awarded her freedom and married a free black man, John Peters. Ignored by white society, Phillis and John faced numerous struggles in their marriage, including the deaths of all three of their children in childhood. In frail health and unable to publish any poems, Phillis took employment as a cleaner for "a common negro boarding-house." In 1774, soon after the death of her husband, Phillis Wheatley died in poverty and obscurity.

An examination of Wheatley's life highlights the multiple concerns of contemporary African-American criticism:

- Marginalization of blacks
- Social, political, economic, ideological, and literary oppression
- The historical and cultural significance of the black experience that has ties to African-language and culture
- Celebrating that which is black in black art
- The significance of slavery as a past historical event and its present-day racial implications
- Reading race into all American literature because whiteness is "the Other" of blackness

Wheatley and the many other black Americans who penned words during the next three centuries grappled with their "blackness" in a dominant white culture.

Although Wheatley's black contemporary writers were indeed few—Jupiter Hammon, author of the first poem published by a black American, "An Evening Thought: Salvation by Christ with Penitential Cries," (1761), and the first African-American critic, Ignatius Sancho, who praised Wheatley's poetry (1778)—by the mid-1800s, another form of black literature developed that influenced American culture: slave narratives. Written by former slaves, the autobiographical slave narrative recounts an individual's personal life as a slave and that individual's escape to freedom. The slave narrative was used by the antislavery movement preceding the Civil War to convince readers of the evils of slavery and to argue for its abolishment. The best known slave narratives include Harriet Jacobs's *Incidents in the Life of a Slave Girl* (1861) and Frederick Douglass's *Narrative of the Life of Frederick Douglass* (1845). Like Wheatley, Douglass was accused of not being the author of his work because many white Americans could not believe that a black man was capable of such distinguished and "eloquent" prose.

During the post–Civil War era (1865–1920), African-American authors continued to write nonfiction works concerning the condition of African-Americans in America. One of the prominent writers was W.E.B. DuBois, author of a collection of essays titled *The Souls of Black Folk* (1903), and a founding member of the National Association for the Advancement of Colored People (NAACP). "The problem of the twentieth century," says DuBois, "is the problem of the color-line." Only by working together, argues DuBois, can African-Americans fight for equality and justice. Another prominent African-American writer and educator during this era was Booker T. Washington, founder of Tuskegee Institute in Alabama and author of *Up From Slavery* (1901) and *My Larger Education* (1911), to name a few of his works. Unlike DuBois, Washington believes that African-Americans must work within the social, political, and educational systems already established by the dominant white culture. Borrowing the words of Benjamin Franklin, Washington maintains that African-Americans should "pick themselves up by their own bootstraps" before they ask for social or political justice.

African-American literature and criticism continued to develop throughout the 1920s and 1930s largely because of a "rebirth" of black literature and art, what became known as the Harlem Renaissance. After World War I, New York City, particularly Harlem, saw a huge influx of African-Americans from the South. Black artists, poets, dancers, dramatists, and musicians gathered together in Harlem and celebrated African-American culture, giving the African-Americans a sense of pride in being black. Harlem became, if only for a short time, the idealized center of hope for African-Americans: One day they, like their white counterparts, would receive equal rights under the law. Under the editorship of DuBois, the *Crisis*, the journal of the NAACP, echoes this cry for equality, insisting that art should become a tool in the struggle for social justice. "All art is propaganda and ever must be" argued the writers of the *Crisis*, stating that "the great mission of the Negro to America and to the modern world is the development of Art and the appreciation of Beauty." This development of African-American art and culture was best articulated in the Harlem Renaissance by Alain Locke's anthology of African-American writers, *New Negro* (1925). In the opening essay of this work, "The New Negro," Locke presents his understanding of modern black culture and agrues that the united African-Americans of the North, especially Harlem, are becoming a "progressive force" in society, leading toward black equality with whites.

The two leading literary figures of the Harlem Renaissance are Langston Hughes and Zora Neale Hurston. Novelist, dramatist, short story writer, translator, children's author, and poet Langston Hughes became famous with the publication of his poem "The Negro Speaks of Rivers" in 1921. Unlike Alain Locke and other African-Americans arguing for social equality by embracing the qualities of what Hughes dubbed "whiteness," Hughes asserts that African-Americans should embrace their blackness and their cultural integrity, qualities Hughes sees in lower-class black life, not the middle or upper classes. In this process, says Hughes, African-Americans must recognize the importance of their music, especially jazz. For Hughes, jazz "is one of the inherent expressions of Negro life in America: the eternal tom-tom beating in the Negro soul—the tom-tom of revolt against weariness in a white world, the tom-tom of joy and laughter, and pain swallowed in a smile." The other leading figure of the Harlem Renaissance, Zora Neale Hurston, agrees with Hughes. Author of more than 14 books, Hurston wrote the now American classic *Their Eyes Were Watching God* (1937). Like Hughes, Hurston usually avoids fiction of protest, choosing to write literature that affirms the black consciousness. Because she did not author protest fiction and because of her gender, her works received little attention until the 1970s, when her body of fiction was "rediscovered" by Alice Walker, author of *The Color Purple*.

With the coming of the Great Depression in the late 1920s and early 1930s and World War II in the 1940s, the ideals that sparked the Harlem Renaissance were quieted, but not before the writings and music of African-Americans were embraced by mainstream American culture.

After fighting for their country, as did white men and women, black men and women returned home from the war to face mounting racism in the South. Leaving the Southern states, blacks migrated to the northern cities, seeking equality and economic opportunity. Once again, African-American artists and poets called for social justice.

In what eventually became known as the Civil Rights Era of the 1950s and 1960s, three new African-Ameican voices took center stage: James Baldwin, Richard Wright, and Ralph Ellison. Author of the novel *Go Tell It on the Mountain* (1953), James Baldwin addresses in his fiction the concerns of the Civil Rights movement. Avoiding the typical protest fiction, Baldwin captures in his prose what it is like to be black in an intensively personal way. Baldwin believed that America was in a process of being, not an arrived-at entity. In his vision or aesthetics, he addresses the problems of race and social justice in American democracy but attempts to create a world that transcends such inequity. For Baldwin, like Wheatley and other artists before him, alienation from both white and black society was the norm. At a time when being black and homosexual were suspect identities, Baldwin was both. Authoring more than 18 works, Baldwin found no home in American society of the 1950s.

Unlike Baldwin, Richard Wright, another literary voice for African-Americans, embraces Marxist principles and opts to change the society in which he lives. Author of *Native Son* (1940), *The Outsider* (1953), and *White Man, Listen!* (1957), Richard Wright was a novelist, essayist, and activist who believed that "Negro writers must accept the nationalist implications of their lives, not in order to encourage them, but to change and transcend them." In his works, Wright asserts that the African-American writers should concentrate their talents on describing the material conditions of black, not white, life in American society. The ideology of the black working classes, not the white upper classes, must be embraced. What this means for the writer, says

Wright, is an interaction with, not an isolation from, society. The act of writing is a social act that should bring about change for the better in the lives of blacks. For Wright, writing highlights the oppression of blacks and must become a radical agent of social change.

Perhaps the greatest literary work of this time is Ralph Ellison's only novel, *Invisible Man* (1953). In this work and in his collection of essays, *Shadow and Act* (1966) and *Going to the Territory* (1986), Ellison asserts that in America race is the central and most profound issue. Unlike Wright, Ellison argues that literature, especially the novel, should be a place of experimentation and speculation, where various ideas could be examined and pondered. For Ellison, literature is not politics or a bully pulpit to advocate social change. Texts must engage their culture but not be primarily agents of change. African-American art, Ellison declares, must be written and analyzed with the same literary and cultural sophistication as any other kind of art.

In the ongoing development of African-American literature and criticism, the Black Arts movement provides a radical change in direction from its immediate past, the 1940s and 1950s. The African-American scholar–critic Henry Louis Gates, Jr. calls this movement the "shortest and least successful" in African-American cultural history. This Black Arts movement spans the decade from 1965 to 1975, its beginning dated with the assassination of Malcolm X in February 1965. Radically breaking with the philosophy of the Civil Rights era, this movement advocates Black Power—that is, militant advocacy of armed self defense—while inspiring a renewal and pride in African heritage and asserting the goodness and beauty of all things black. Its foremost spokesperson is Amiri Baraka, a Greenwich village beat poet who became the Black Arts Movements' voice through its literary magazine, *Cricket*. The movement's chief concern was the establishment of a black nation, and its literary goal was to describe and develop black men in a racist white society in order to change the African-American consciousness from one based on shame because of its blackness to one based on being proud of everything black, especially skin color. Although the Black Arts movement produced a variety of literary works by writers such as Nikki Giovanni, Sonia Sanchez, and Mae Jackson, to name a few, its existence was short lived. Perhaps its major strength, its visionary gleam, was also its major weakness, alienating African-Americans from other segments of society by attempting to establish its own black nation and making blacks a group of people seemingly standing apart from history.

African-American literature and criticism needed a theory on which to base its criticism. Throughout the first seven decades of the twentieth century, African-American writers wrote texts depicting African-Americans interacting with their culture. In this body of literature, these American subaltern writers concerned themselves mainly with issues of nationalism and the exposure of the unjust treatment of African-Americans—a suppressed, repressed, and colonized subculture—at the hands of their white conquerors.

Presenting a variety of themes in their fiction, essays, and autobiographical writings—the African-American's search for personal identity; the bitterness of the struggle of black men and women in America to achieve political, economic, and social success; and both mild and militant pictures of racial protest and hatred—these authors gave America the personal portraits of what it meant to be a black writer struggling with personal, cultural, and national identity.

While literature authored by black writers was gaining in popularity, it was also being interpreted through the lens of the dominant culture, a lens that was focused on one color—white, the dominant element in the binary opposition white/black, as Derrida would soon explain. Black aesthetics had not yet been established, and critics and theorists alike applied the principles of Western metaphysics and Western hermeneutics to this ever-evolving and steadily increasing body of literature. Although theoretical and critical essays authored by DuBois, Hughes, Wright, and Ellison announced to the literary world that black literature was a distinctive literary practice with its own aesthetics and should not be dubbed a subcategory or a footnote of American literature, it was not until the late 1970s and the 1980s that black theorists began to articulate the distinctive characteristics of African-American literature. In this increasingly important group of literary critics, two stand out: Abdul R. JanMohamed and Henry Louis Gates, Jr.

The founding editor of *Cultural Critique*, Abdul JanMohamed is one of the most influential postcolonial theorists. A professor of English at the University of California at Berkeley, JanMohamed has authored a variety of scholarly articles and texts highlighting the interdisciplinary nature of literary criticism. Raised in Kenya (and therefore not considered by some to be an African-American), JanMohamed witnessed firsthand British imperialism and colonial methods that attempt to dominate, quell, and otherwise eliminate the vital elements of the colonized culture. He has spent his life studying the effects of colonization and the intertwined economic and social dynamics of both the conqueror and the conquered. Of particular importance is his text *Manichean Aesthetics: The Politics of Literature in Colonial Africa* (1983), in which JanMohamed argues that literature authored by the colonized (e.g., Africans in Kenya and African-Americans in America) is more interesting for its **noematic** value—the complexities of the world it reveals—than for its **noetic** or subjective qualities concerning what it perceives. JanMohamed delineates the antagonistic relationship that develops between a hegemonic and a nonhegemonic literature. In African-American literature, for example, he notes that black writers such as Richard Wright and Frederick Douglass were shaped by their personal socioeconomic conditions. At some point in their development as writers and as persons who were on the archetypal journey of self-realization, these writers became "agents of resistance" and were no longer willing to "consent" to the hegemonic culture. According to JanMohamed, at some point, subaltern writers will resist being shaped by their oppressors and become literary agents of change. This process of change from passive observers to resistors forms the basis of JanMohamed's aesthetics.

Perhaps the most important and leading contemporary African-American theorist is Henry Louis Gates, Jr. Unlike many African-American writers and critics, Gates directs much of his attention to other African-American critics, declaring that they and he "must redefine 'theory' itself from within [their] own black cultures, refusing to grant the premise that theory is something that white people do. We are all heirs to critical theory, but we Black critics are heir to the black vernacular as well." In his critical theory, Gates provides a theoretical framework for developing a peculiarly African-American literary canon. In this framework, he insists that African-American literature be viewed as a form of language, not a representation of social practices or culture. For black literary criticism to develop, its principles must be derived from the black tradition itself and include what he calls "the language of blackness, the signifying difference which makes the Black tradition our very own." In his texts *The Signifying Monkey* (1988) and *Figures in Black: Words, Signs, and the "Radical" Self* (1989), Gates develops these ideas and announces the **double-voicedness** of African-American literature—that is, African-American literature draws upon two voices and cultures, the white and the black. The joining of these two discourses, Gates declares, produces the uniqueness of African-American literature.

Along with other theorists such as Houston Baker, Deborah McDowell, Hazel Carby, bell hooks, Gloria Hull, Toni Morrison, Claudia Tate, Maya Angelou, Rita Dove, Ntozake Shange, and a host of African-American feminist, Marxist, psychoanalytic, and gay and lesbian critics, present-day African-American theorists and critics are developing a body of culture-specific theory and criticism of African-American literature. Theirs, they believe, is a significant discourse that has for too long been neglected. The study of this body of literature, they insist, needs to be reformed. The beginning of this reformation, reclamation, and ongoing development of peculiarly African-American literary theories and criticism have helped other marginalized groups such as gays and lesbians to develop their own critical theories and practical criticism.

Questions for Analysis

When reading a text through the lens of African-American theory and criticism, consider the following questions:

- Is race evident?
- Who are the marginalized characters? What color is their skin?
- Who are the oppressors?
- What are the means of oppression?

- What does it mean to be black in this text?
- What is the dominant hegemony?
- Are the marginalized characters aware of their oppression?
- What are the ties of the black characters to African language and cultural practices?
- Who speaks for blacks?
- Are any characters marginalized through silence?

QUEER THEORY

Brokeback Mountain, the most discussed and controversial Hollywood movie of 2005, is based on a short story by E. Annie Proulx. Proulx writes that one day she saw an old cowboy in a bar with a certain look in his eye, a look of dissatisfaction with his life, as he observed the younger cowboys. Deciding that the older cowboy was gay, Proulx began to write her short story, one that would simmer in her mind for a protracted time. Years after the story was published, Larry McMurty and Diana Ossana wrote the screenplay for what would become Hollywood's love story for 2005.

Brokeback Mountain tells the story of two 19-year-old Wyoming cowboys, Ennis Del Mar and Jack Twist. In the summer of 1963, the cowboys are employed by a sheep farmer to guard his flock while the sheep graze on Brokeback Mountain. After a few days of work and drinking, one night, without warning and seemingly any premeditation, the two cowboys have a sexual encounter. After the night's event, Ennis says to Jack, "You know I ain't queer," and Jack responds, "Me, neither." Then Ennis remarks, "This is a one-shot thing we got going on here." But it wasn't.

When the summer ends, Ennis and Jack part ways, assuming they will work at the same job the following summer. But when Jack returns the following year and applies for work, his former boss tells him that he and his kind are not wanted there.

Years pass, during which time Ennis and Jack each fall in love with beautiful women and marry. One day, Jack surprises Ennis with a visit. Upon meeting, both cowboys embrace and passionately kiss, shocking both of them, a scene that is viewed through an upstairs window by Ennis's wife, Alma. Periodically, Ennis and Jack decide to go on "fishing" trips to Brokeback Mountain. As Alma soon discovers, no fish are ever caught on these many outings.

Both men struggle with their feelings for each other. Ennis's father had taught him to hate homosexuals, telling Ennis the story of two old men who lived together and who were both killed by the townspeople, probably Ennis's dad being one of the murderers. Jack, on the other hand, finds an outlet for his feelings by traveling to Mexico to seek a male prostitute. Toward the end of the movie, Ennis has divorced his wife, and Jack's marriage is in trouble. Ennis is now living in a rundown trailer and continues to struggle with his feelings for Jack, saying, "Why don't you let me be? It's because of you, Jack, that I'm like this—nothing, and nobody." The movie's ending portrays a lonely, confused, and heartbroken Ennis struggling with his passion for Jack, who has been murdered by men who despise Jack's love for Ennis.

The critical reviews of *Brokeback Mountain* are as varied as the personal responses to the movie:

"Brokeback Mountain," if you are willing to give it a chance, is an emotional, heartbreaking movie.

Willie Waffle, Wafflemovies.com

This ostensible gay Western is marked by a heightened degree of sensitivity and tact, as well as an outstanding performance.

Todd McCarthy, Variety. com

Some American audiences may reject out of hand a gay-themed tale set in the macho sanctity of the West. But they'd be missing great performances.

James Verniere, *Boston Herald*

While the message at the core is that love is love, the way the initial sexual encounter is shown will only reinforce the negative views that bigots have of gay culture.

John Venable, Supercala.com

Ang Lee (the director) conveys maddening delirium rendered in the way one man's eyes gaze at another's, and then look away, and the looking-away amounts to the murder of two souls as surely as if they'd drawn guns and hit each other in the heart.

Ken Tucker, *New York Magazine*

Any of us can imagine a forbidden passion so sweeping that it carries us off at flood tide, never allowing us to question it. Whether the object of our affection would carry a purse, a lariat or both is beside the point.

Lawrence Toppman, *Charlotte Observer*

A beautiful tragedy about the anguish of unfulfilled love. It's an absolute triumph, in every way.

Dawn Taylor, *Portland Tribune*

This story of suppressed passion is, irrespective of gender considerations, a deeply moving, indeed lacerating film.

Frank Swietek, *One Guy's Opinion*

Lee strips away all the pizzazz for something that is much more pure—a rough and tough emotional journey.

Mark Sells, *Oregon Herald*

Eloquently sums up and universalizes the hopelessness of Jack and Ennis' situation while showing the staggering cost of hyprocrisy and deceit.

James Sanford, *Kalamazoo Gazette*

It is up to date in its version of forbidden love because its conflict is based on one of the last socially-sanctioned forms of discrimination.

Robert Roten, *Laramie Movie Scope*

One of the all-time greatest love stories, its potent poignancy comes from universally relatable ideas like nagging love, lost dreams, a half-lived life and comfort in knowing incomplete joy is better than none at all.

Nick Rogers, *State Journal-Register* (Springfield, IL)

Michelle Williams nearly steals the film as Ennis's wife in a quiet, complex, heartbreaking performance.

Jon Popick, *Planet Sickboy*

Explores repressed feelings, loneliness, suffering, and alienation as adroitly as any film in recent memory.

John A. Nesbit, Toxicuniverse.com

You can't take the "gay" out of the "gay cowboy" move. What gives "Brokeback Mountain" its punch is the (no pun intended) straight way in which its romance is told.

Eric Melin, Scenestealers.com

I never became emotionally involved in their story.

Sean McBride, *Sean the Movie Guy*

Change the names and genders as you wish. This is the sort of adult drama that people can relate to if they have any sort of romantic regrets.

Daniel M. Kimmel, *Worcester Telegram & Gazette*

Lee's film says unequivocally that it's in everyone's best interest for gay couples to live openly and safely.

Ken Fox, *TV Guide's Movie Guide*

Foremost about a love that can never break out of its societal prison.

Jeffrey Chen, *Window to the Movies*

The hubbub seems more politically driven in the wake of the gay marriage debate. And an Oscar win will be pandering to that.

Kevin Carr, *7M Pictures*

The film's edge is its same-sex controversy.

Kevin A. Ransom, Moviecrypt.com

What these reviews of *Brokeback Mountain* successfully capture is the central concerns and questions of **queer theory**, the most recent school of literary criticism to appear in academia. Influenced by deconstruction, feminism, gay and lesbian studies, psychoanalysis, postcolonialism, and other postist theories, queer theory questions the very terms we use to describe ourselves. Terms such as *heterosexual* and *homosexual*, queer theorists argue, are socially constructed concepts that do not define who we really are. As demonstrated in the movie reviews, queer theory challenges the assumption that human nature is unchangeable and can be defined by a finite list of characteristics. In queer theory's ongoing development, it asks questions such as:

- What is a man?
- What is a woman?
- What is gender?
- What does it mean to be a heterosexual? Homosexual? Gay? Lesbian? Bisexual? Queer?
- What does it mean to be masculine? Feminine?
- What does it mean to be human?
- What is normal? Abnormal?
- What is a "macho" man?
- What is love?
- What is "forbidden" passion? Forbidden by whom?
- What is "unfulfilled" love? What are its causes?
- Why do hypocrisy and deceit operate in a so-called forbidden love relationship?
- Who or what in society sanctions or does not sanction the various kinds of love? Heterosexuality? Homosexuality? Bisexuality?

- How and why do some elements of society form a "societal prison" out of some love relationships?
- What does it mean to be homophobic?

These questions and their multiple answers provide the basis for queer theory and its continuing development that challenges traditional ways of viewing our sexuality and our identities.

Historical Development and Assumptions

Throughout much of the twentieth century, the word *queer* was a pejorative term used to describe homosexuals, particularly males. Using a Marxist technique called **hailing the subject** or **interpellation**, queer theorists embraced the word and turned it on its head, making it a respectable critical term in academic studies. The term was first coined by the gender theorist Teresa de Lauretis in a special edition of the feminist journal *differences* entitled *Queer Theory: Lesbian and Gay Sexualities*, published in 1991. Since its inception, queer theory has tried to debunk the idea that a person's identity is stable or fixed at birth. Similar to all schools of criticism, queer theory borrows, adopts, and adapts concepts, terms, theories, and methodologies from previously developed critical schools and finds its multipronged, historical roots in feminism, deconstruction theory, gender studies, and gay and lesbian studies.

Beginning with Mary Wollstonecraft's *A Vindication of the Rights of Women* (1792), feminist theory and criticism demands that women define for themselves what it means to be a woman. Following Wollstonecraft, Virginia Woolf asserts in *A Room of One's Own* (1929) that women must reject the social construct of femaleness and establish and define their own identify. A decade later, Simone de Beauvoir declares in *The Second Sex* (1949) that women must reject that they are the **Other**, an object defined and interpreted by men. Two decades later, Kate Millett writes in *Sexual Politics* (1969) that a female is born, but a woman is created. One's sex, Millet asserts, is biologically determined, but one's gender is a social construct created by society. Many feminist theorists and critics of the last three decades of the twentieth century have embraced Millet's assertion that gender is not innate or biological but socially constructed and perpetuated by social institutions and power structures. Our sex, which is biologically determined, fixed, and stable, is *different* from our gender, which is mutable and attributive. Because gender is a product of social ideas, feminists declare that gender should not and must not shape the identity of what it means to be a woman.

By asserting that gender must not shape a woman's identity, feminist theorists attack the long-held classical humanist belief called **essentialism**, which asserts that the true essence or identity of a human being is composed of finite and fixed properties that are the essential components of what it means to be human. Essentialism posits that to be human means that we have an unchangeable human nature, a true invariable essence. Essentialists believe that our sexuality and our gender are determined by our essential features, our true selves that give us our core sense of who we are, our identity, and our selfhood. Nothing—not society, education, or spiritual beliefs—can change this unchangeable core, our essence.

Many feminist theorists and critics of the latter part of the twentieth century reject essentialism with its assumption of an unchangeable human essence and accept what is known as **social constructivism**. Social constructivists reject essentialism's belief in an unalterable human essence but assert that gender is a socially constructed term and concept. Words such as *homosexual*, *heterosexual*, *male*, and *female* are likewise constructed and shaped distinctions that are subject to constant change. All such terms are laden with ideological suppositions and must be deconstructed and eventually reconstructed. Unlike essentialists who believe that knowledge is discovered, forgotten, and repressed and must then be rediscovered through history and experimentation, social constructivists agree with the poststructuralist assumptions of Jacques Derrida's deconstruction.

For Derrida and many other postist critics, Western metaphysics assumes **logocentrism**, which is a belief in an ultimate reality or center of truth that serves as the basis for all thoughts and actions. Various centers of truth can exist: the self, a spiritual being, reason, and so forth. According to Derrida, logocentric thinking has its origin in Aristotle's principle of noncontradiction: A thing cannot both have and not have a property. Hence, Western metaphysics has developed an "either/or" mentality that leads to dualistic thinking and to the constant centering and decentering of stated truths. Once a center is established, it can be quickly decentered. Such reasoning leads Derrida to conclude that Western metaphysics is based on a system of **binary operations** or conceptual oppositions: good/bad, honesty/falsehood, up/down, right/wrong, God/humanity, and so forth. In each of these binary operations, one concept (the numerator) is superior or privileged, and the second (the denominator) is inferior or unprivileged. Both the privileged and the unprivileged parts of a binary opposition relate directly to a concept of truth Derrida calls the **transcendental signified**. What we privilege in binary oppositions thus supports our concept of truth.

Social constructivist feminists agree with Derrida that we think logocentrically. But what happens if truth is not absolute, but relative? If no absolute truth exists, then truth becomes socially constructed. If there is no transcendental signified that gives meaning to the concept of selfhood, then selfhood is not an absolute, not a quality that is an "essential," objective part of our human nature acquired at birth. The core argument of essentialism is thus turned on its head. Selfhood—our identity—is not prescribed or predetermined but is subjective. No transcendental signified exists that determines who or what we are; rather, human language itself shapes us. Our identities are subjective, not objective, and are constantly in the process of change. Any binary opposition we create to define ourselves is simply a social construct that must undergo constant revision. In particular, the male/female, man/woman, and masculine/feminine binaries do not represent stable concepts; rather, these binaries are unstable and are products of culture and institutions of power. There exists no stable concept of the self or selfhood because both terms are subjective and unstable. Similarly, one's sexuality is unstable, as are the concepts of maleness and femaleness. These concepts become what Derrida calls free-floating signifieds—that is, concepts whose meanings are not fixed but are instead ever shifting. The meaning of these signifieds resides in how language is used or constructed.

Throughout the last three decades of the twentieth century, feminist and gender critics highlight the unstable relationship expressed in the man/woman, male/female, and masculine/feminine binary oppositions. Because these critics believe that no transcendental signified exists to stabilize language with its accompanying binary oppositions, the term *gender* becomes for them a free-floating signified that shifts on a daily basis. For example, the "male" head of the home in 1960 probably did not wash dishes, make the bed, or clean the house. Nor did he pierce his ears or other body parts. The male of 2006, however, often performs household tasks and may wear pierced earrings.

In the mid-1980s, another school of criticism borrows and develops the gender concerns of the feminists and gender critics: **gay and lesbian studies**. Whereas feminist and gender critics debate and redefine the man/woman binary and emphasize gender differences, gay and lesbian studies target the heterosexual/homosexual binary, emphasizing sexual differences. Gay studies examine sexual differences applicable to males, and lesbian studies examine sexual differences that are applicable to females. Both groups analyze the social structures that have defined gays and lesbians as deviant or abnormal, questioning how such definitions developed throughout history and why heterosexuality has been so positively defined. Similar to feminist studies, gay and lesbian studies are studies of recovery, seeking to rediscover gay and lesbian writers who, throughout the centuries, have been silenced, masked, or erased, not only from the literary canon but also from history.

In the early 1990s, another group of literary theorists and critics developed from gay and lesbian studies: queer theory. Unlike gay and lesbian studies, which emphasize the male and female gender, queer theory abandons the discussion of gender while enlarging the discussion of sexual differences. Although not abandoning an analysis of homosexuality, queer studies is more inclusive than gay and lesbian studies, analyzing, discussing, and debating sexual topics that are considered queer—that is, odd, abnormal, or peculiar. Similar to the feminist social constructivists, queer theorists posit that our identities and our sexuality are not fixed; rather, they are unstable. No set of prerequisites exists that defines our human nature or our sexuality. From queer theory's point of view, it is pointless to discuss what it means to be male or female because our sexual identities are all different, each being socially constructed. Queer theory also challenges the compartmentalization of any person into a socially assigned group based on some shared lifestyle or habit. No identity or group can be defined as abnormal, lacking, complete, or incomplete. Our identities, including our sexuality, are shaped and developed by social codes, our individual actions, power structures within society, and a host of complex forces that are in continuous flux.

Queer Critical Theorists

Eve Kosofsky Sedgwick is queer theory's leading theorist and critic. Earning her undergraduate degree at Cornell University and her PhD from Yale University, Sedgwick has taught at Hamilton, Dartmouth, and Amherst Colleges and is presently a professor of English at Duke University. Her groundbreaking texts include *Between Men: English Literature and Male Homosocial Desire* (1985); *Epistemology of the Closet* (1990); *Tendencies* (1993), *A Dialogue of Love* (1999); and *Touching Feeling: Affect, Pegagogy, Performativity* (2003). In *Epistemology*, Sedgwick affirms the necessity of studying gay and lesbian and queer theories, asserting:

> An understanding of virtually any aspect of modern Western culture must be, not merely incomplete, but damaged in its central substance to the degree that it does not incorporate a critical analysis of modern homo/heterosexual defini- tion, especially form the relatively de-centered perspective of modern gay and anti-homophobic theory. (1)

Sedgwick's working thesis is simple yet profound: "People are different from each other." These differences should not be exploited but accepted. In *Tendencies*, she "attempts to find new ways to think about lesbian, gay, and other sexually dissident loves and identities in a complex social ecology in which the presence of different genders, identities, and identifications will be taken as a given." For Sedgwick, the word *queer*, when directed toward or about a person, hinges upon performative acts—that is, only people who use the word *queer* in the first person about themselves are queer.

Another leading queer theorist is Judith Butler. Author of *Gender Trouble* (1990), *Bodies that Matter* (1993), *Excitable Speech: A Politics of the Performative* (1997), *Giving an Account of Oneself* (2005), and many others, Butler is a pro- fessor of comparative literature and rhetoric at the University of California,

Berkeley. Her most influential work, *Gender Trouble*, asserts that feminism made a mistake when it declared that women were a special group with common interests. By so doing, feminists, maintains Butler, reinforced the patriarchal culture that assumed the masculine/feminine and male/female binary oppositions. For Butler, gender is not stable, but fluid, so it changes from person to person and from context to context. Like gender, self-identity is performative—that is, what one does at a particular time, place, and context determines one's gender and identity, not a universal concept of who we are. Our identities are not connected to our supposed essence (essentialism) but to what we do and are. Our identities are the *effect*, not the cause, of our performances. For Butler, the performative nature of our identities is queer theory's key concept.

Other queer theorists such as Jonathan Goldberg, Michael Warner, Sandy Stone, and Joseph Litvak use postist theories to investigate such diverse topics as cross-dressing, bisexuality, public sex, gay marriage, and gay media, to name a few. Unlike other schools of criticism, queer studies desires to be open ended, refusing at times to define itself by using any binary oppositions. If such binaries were established, queer theorists believe, queer theory would become too exclusionary, and its development would be hindered. Queer theorists believe that queer theory does not enable them to define their identity but is a critique of it. For queer theorists, their theory and criticism are "always under construction," and always performative.

Questions for Analysis

When analyzing a text through the lens of queer theory, ask yourself the following questions:

- How are the binaries male/female and masculine/feminine being defined?
- Who attributes masculine or feminine qualities to whom?
- How is gender being ascribed?
- Are the critical assumptions of essentialism or social constructivism established? By what character(s)?
- How are the characters' sexual identities shaped and formed?
- Is gender performative?
- What prejudices exist about any character's supposed sexuality?
- What social forces or constructs determine sexual identity?
- What is queer about the text?
- Is any character in crisis concerning his or her sexual identity?

CRITIQUES AND RESPONSES

Postcolonialism

Similar to other approaches to textual analysis, postcolonialism is not a homogenous school of literary theory but a loosely defined set of theories and methodologies that seeks to uncover and discover what happens to the colonized after they have been conquered by the colonizers. Postcolonialism chiefly deals with literature that has been written by the colonized in colonized countries. What happens, it asks, when two cultures clash and then combine? According to many postcolonialists, a process known as **hybridity** or **hybridization** occurs, wih each culture changing the other. Through the interaction of these clashing cultures, new cultural forms emerge. Postcolonialism's aim is to examine what has been missing from literary analyses by highlighting the interests of the colonized and the destructive forces of the colonizer's hegemony as forced on the colonized. As such, postcolonialism becomes, like deconstruction, more of a reading strategy than a codified school of literary criticism. In its methdology, it gives voice to "the Other," the people who have become the separate ones and who stand apart from the dominant, colonizing culture. And its goal is to win back a place in history for the colonized, enabling all readers to value the many different kinds of cultures and peoples who inhabit the earth. Whether the postcolonial critic embraces the tenets of feminism, psychoanalysis, Marxism, or any theoretical framework, such a critic emphasizes each person's humanity and right to personal freedom.

Some critics of postcolonialism point out that many of its most influential spokespersons have been and continue to be educated in the West and are products of the Western mindset, not subaltern cultures. How can such "Western"-minded individuals speak for subaltern cultures? Other critics observe that postcolonial studies remain situated in academia, in the "upper classes" of society, having little or no effect on real people in real places. Can academic discussions, assert these critics, bring any change in the lives of subaltern cultures? If postcolonialism seeks to help and change the lives of colonized peoples, some of its critics argue that its reading strategies and methodologies must be performed by those who have been colonized, not by academics living in the West. Postcolonialism must seek to empower those who have been stripped of power, dignity, and self-worth, maintain some critics, rather than continually marginalizing the colonized through discourse that can be understood only by the cultually elite. Perhaps, say critics, postcolonialism is only radical in its words, not in life-changing power.

Similar to cultural studies, postcolonial studies is becoming more and more diverse, including Carribean, Latin American, and Pacific geographical regions, although some traditional postcolonial sites such as India remain important. By embracing a variety of theories and approaches to textual analysis, postcolonialism has ensured its place in literary theory and practice for decades to come.

African-American Criticism

Recent demographics from the U.S. Census Bureau estimate that 40 million African-Americans live in the United States, comprising about 13% of the total population. Most live in the South, followed by the Northeast and the Midwest, with 88% living in metropolitan areas. In comparison to whites and other minorities, as a group, African-Americans remain economically, educationally, and socially disadvantaged. Earning about 55% of the median income of European Americans, African-Americans face discrimination in housing, employment, and accessible health care. These statistics lend support to the central concerns of African-American literature: oppression, suppression, and enslavement of blacks as depicted in black literature. And such are the major issues of African-American literary theory and criticism: marginalization of blacks; economic, social, political, and literary oppression; the historical significance of slavery and its present-day racial ramifications; and the celebration of all things black in the arts.

According to Henry Louis Gates, Jr., the task of African-American theory and criticism is not to cry "special"—that is, demand a unique approach to theory and criticism unlike any other past or contemporary school of criticism. Gates argues that instead, black theorists and critics must use the most sophisticated contemporary theories and practices to redefine the language of critical theory and to allow black language to enter academic discourse and help disclose prejudice and ethnic differences in literature. Accordingly, critics such as Toni Morrison, Farh Jasmine Griffin, Claudia Tate, and Deborah G. Chay use the theories and methodologies of cultural studies, feminism, psychoanalysis, and gay and lesbian studies not only to highlight the concerns of African-Americans in their own literature but also to develop new critical theories that will reveal the as yet unspoken and silenced concerns of the past and the present in black literature.

Some critics of African-American theory and criticism, both black and white, ask questions that are debated by African-American theorists themselves: Who really can speak—conceive, develop, and write both theory and criticism—for African-Americans? Only blacks? Whites? Other minorities? Is African-American literature an integral part of American literature or unique unto itself? Is present-day interest in African-American literature a reflection of America's contemporary concern for minorities that will wane, or is it an interest that is reshaping the fabric of American literature? And are African-American writers themselves depicting blacks unduly negatively? Such complex questions and their multifaceted answers will continue to shape contemporary African-American criticism for the next several decades.

Queer Theory

Queer theory assumes that our personal identities are unstable and in constant flux. An anti-essentialist theory, queer studies decrees that we have no essential core to our humanness that defines us as human. As Sedgwick maintains, all people are different. We must not allow society to shape our identities; instead, we ourselves must declare by our acts who we are. No predetermined societal binary oppositions with their accompanying prejudices should determine our identity. We must challenge the concepts of sexual identity, gender, and sexual differences. What it means to be a male or a female is always in flux, always a process of becoming. Seeing all life as becoming, queer theorists challenge all notions of a fixed self-identity and examine areas of human activity, such as bisexuality, cross-dressing, and gay marriage, which often cause emotional debate, especially among queer theory's dissenters.

Similar to all schools of criticism, queer theory has its critics. Some believe it is deviant or weird and should not be studied at all. Others are ignorant of its content but somewhat fearful to read its theories. Many disagree with its social constructivist position and believe that a person's sexual identity is not fluid or unstable. Still others decree that queer theory is too theoretical and unlike real life. And many claim that gay and lesbian studies and queer theory (these two schools of criticism are often viewed as one) empower gay and lesbian politics, making them more important than they actually are while at the same time celebrating sexual desires.

Queer theorists themselves affirm that they do not know where their theories may take them because, as Butler notes, there are many queer theories, not one. Queer theory is, from Butler's perspective, unlimited in it possibilities because it refuses to define itself, seeing itself, like the concept of self-identity, always in flux.

FURTHER READING

Ashcroft, Bill, Gareth Griffiths, and Helen Tiffin. *The Empire Writes Back: Theory and Practice in Post-Colonial Literatures*. London: Routledge, 1994.

———, eds. *The Post-Colonial Studies Reader*. New York: Routledge, 1995.

Bhabha, Homi K., ed. *The Location of Culture*. New York: Routledge, 1994.

———. *Nation and Narration*. New York: Routledge and Kegan Paul, 1990.

Boehmer, Elleke. *Colonial and Postcolonial Literature: Migrant Metaphors*. New York: Oxford University Press, 1995.

Butler, Judith. *Gender Trouble: Feminism and the Subversion of Identity*. New York: Routledge, 1990.

———. *Giving an Account of Oneself*. New York: Fordham University Press, 2005.

———. *Subjects of Desire*. New York: Columbia University Press, 1999.

———. *Undoing Gender*. New York: Taylor and Francis, 2004.

Durrant, Sam. *Postcolonial Narrative and the Work of Mourning*. Albany, NY: State University of New York Press, 2004.

Fanon, Frantz. *Black Skin, White Masks*. New York: Grove Press, 1967.

———. *The Wretched of the Earth*. Constance Farrington (trans). New York: Grove, 1968.

Gates, Henry Louis, Jr. *Figures in Black: Words, Signs, and the Racial Self*. New York: Oxford University Press, 1989.

———. *Loose Canons: Notes on the Culture Wars*. New York: Oxford University Press, 1992.

———. *The Signifying Monkey: A Theory of African-American Literary Criticism*. New York: Oxford University Press, 1988.

Harrison, Nicholas. *Postcolonial Criticism: History, Theory and the Work of Fiction*. Cambridge, England: Polity Press, 2003.

Hazel, Ervin, ed. *African American Literary Criticism*. New York: Twayne, 1999.

JanMohamed, Abdul R. *Manichean Aesthetics: The Politics of Literature in Colonial Africa*. Cambridge: University of Massachusetts Press, reprint, 1988.

Kennedy, Valerie. *Edward Said: A Critical Introduction*. Cambridge, England: Polity Press, 2000.

Lacapra, Dominick, ed. *The Bounds of Race: Perspectives on Hegemony and Resistance*. Ithaca, NY: Cornell University Press, 1991.

Mohanty, Chandra Talpade, Anne Russo, and Lourdes Torres, eds. *Third World Women and the Politics of Feminism*. Bloomington, IN: Indiana University Press, 1991.

Niranjana, Tejaswine. *Sitting Translation: History, Post-Structuralism, and the Colonial Context*. Berkeley, CA: University of California Press, 1990.

Rushdie, Salman. *Imaginary Homelands: Essays and Criticism, 1981–91*. London: Penguin, 1991.

Said, Edward W. *Culture and Imperialism*. New York: Knopf, 1994.

———. Figures, configurations, transfigurations. *Race & Class* 32.1 (July–September 1990):1–16.

———. *Orientalism*. New York: Vintage, 1979.

Sedgwick, Eve Korofsky. *Between Men*. New York: Columbia University Press, 1985.

———. *A Dialogue on Love*. New York: Beacon, 2000.

———. *Epistemology of the Closet*. Berkeley, CA: University of California Press, 1992.

———. *Tendencies*. Durham, NC: Duke University Press, 1993.

Spivak, Gayatri Chakavorty. The making of Americans, the teaching of English, and the future of culture studies. *New Literary History* 21 (1990):781–98.

———. *In Other Worlds: Essays in Cultural Politics*. New York: Routledge, 1987.

Suleri, Sara. Woman skin deep: Feminism and the postcolonial condition. *Critical Inquiry*, 18 (Summer, 1992):756–69.

———. *The Rhetoric of English India*. Chicago: University of Chicago Press, 1992.

Thomas, Lorenzo. *Extraordinary Measures: Afrocentric Modernism and Twentieth Century American Poetry*. Tuscaloosa, AL: The University of Alabama Press, 2000.

Tiffin, Helen. Post-colonial literatures and counter-discourse. *Kunapipi* 9.3 (1987):17–34.

Williams, Patrick, and Laura Chrisman, eds. *Colonial Discourse and Post-Colonial Theory: A Reader*. New York: Columbia University Press, 1994.

Winston, Napier, ed. *African American Literary Theory*. New York: New York University Press, 2000.

WEB SITES FOR EXPLORATION

www.brocku.ca/english/courses/4F70/postcol.html
    Some issues in postcolonial theory

www.english.emory.edu/Bahri/Intro.html
    Introduction to postcolonial studies

www.thecore.nus.edu.sg/post/poldiscourse/bibl.html
    A bibliography: postcolonialism

www.photoinsight.org.uk/theory/theory.pdf
    Postcolonialism explained

www.accd.edu/sac/english/bailey/aframlit.htm
    A brief chronology of African-American literature

www.public.iastate.edu/~savega/afr_amer.htm
    Recommended African-American web sites on diversity and ethnic studies

www.scils.rutgers.edu/~cybers/critical.html
    Women of color women of words

www.mtsu.edu/~vvesper/afam.html
    African-American writers: A celebration

www.csustan.edu/english/reuben/pal/chap9/chap9.html
    The Harlem Renaissance

www.queertheory.com
    Queer theory: academics, arts, bodies, theories

www.theory.org.uk/ctr-quee.htm
    Queer theory—links, theorists, philosophers

www.lib.latrobe.edu.au/AHR/archive/Issue-Dec-1996/jagose.html
    Queer theory explained

www.sou.edu/English/IDTC/Issues/Gender/queer2.htm
    Queer theory—theorists, terms, links

www.erraticimpact.com/~lgbt
    Queer theory studies, history, terms, and links

Sample Essay

As you read the following student essay, ask yourself these questions:
    In the following student essay, the student author applies the assumptions and methodology of postcolonialism to Rudyard Kipling's short story "At the End of the Passage." Because Kipling is known as the spokesperson for British

imperialism, the student author specifically chose a Kipling short story to highlight the concerns of postcolonial theory. As you read this essay, ask your-self who is "the Other" in the story? What cultures and their values clash? How is the privileged cultural hegemony affecting the colonized? Be able to explain how hybridity functions in the story. Also note the languages of the clashing cultures and be able to explain how the language of the dominant culture acts as a form of oppression and suppression.

Student Essay

The Empire Fights Back: Spectral Persecution and the Nightmare of Decolonization in Kipling's "At the End of the Passage"[1]

Some critics dub Rudyard Kipling literature's foremost spokesperson and propagandist for British imperialism. His novel *Kim*, for example, is analyzed in depth in Edward Said's *Culture and Imperialism* as a prime example of colo-nialist discourse. Kipling's Orientalist attitudes toward "the native" are read-ily apparent in his short story "At the End of the Passage." This Victorian ghost story bears intriguing similarities to Coleridge's "Rime of the Ancient Mariner." Both are about "spectral persecution" which, in Kipling as in Coleridge, is a manifestation of guilt. The difference is that the guilt of the Mariner is acknowledged and eventually expiated while in "At the End of the Passage" the guilt of colonization's inherent violence is repressed into the authorial subconscious. While the Ancient Mariner experiences moral redemption, Kipling's character Hummil does not escape his haunting but is killed by it. In "At the End of the Passage," colonial uprising, repressed into the symbolic form of the ghost story, is an object of horror and destruction, and its victory (an act of decolonization) is represented as the victory of irra-tional supernatural evil over the vanguard of rational civilization.

"At the End of the Passage" is set in a fictional state in northern India at the site of a railway line under construction. All identified by their last names, the main characters are young Englishmen working in the service of Empire: Mottram "of the Indian Survey"; the civil servant Lowndes; Spurstow, the railway line's doctor; and Hummil, assistant engineer for the railway line. The story takes place at Hummil's camp-tent on the railway site, where the four have gathered for their weekly game of whist. The nar-rator's description of Lowndes's political post is revealing in its diction: "Lowndes of the Civil Service, on special duty in the political department, had come as far to escape for an instant the miserable intrigues of an impov-erished native State whose kind alternately fawned and blustered for more

[1]Reprinted by permission of Benjamin K. Walker.

money from the pitiful revenues contributed by hard-wrung peasants and despairing camel-breeder." The king is the first native Indian described in the story, and hardly in complimentary terms. He is portrayed as a petty, deceitful despot, servile to the English and tyrannical to his people. A few paragraphs later, Hummil reads a news clipping from England in which a populist politician accuses the Civil Service of acting as the "pet preserve" of the English aristocracy and living lavishly on the riches of India. Though he asserts that India has been "step by step fraudulently annexed," the problem upon which the politician focuses is that "the people" of England are getting no return from their Indian "investment." What seems to be a voice raised in defense of the silent Other turns out simply to reinforce the dominant imperialist discourse. The right of England to the wealth of the world is never seriously questioned. It is simply a matter of how the English divide that wealth among themselves.

Lowndes's response—that he would "give three months' pay to have that gentleman spend one month with me and see how the free and independent native prince works things"—then seems slightly off-topic. After all, the main accusation, that the Civil Service gets rich on the wealth of India, is answered sufficiently by the men's rather shabby circumstances. Lowndes slips into defending not the distribution of wealth among the Civil Service, but the necessity of the British presence in India. Through Lowndes, Kipling misspeaks, unconsciously acknowledging the injustice of British colonialism by reprising the Orientalist truism that "the native" is naturally prone to mismanagement and fit only to be governed.

The story's entire first scene, in fact, is an attempt to demonstrate the great sacrifice which "the white man's burden" requires. Kipling uses obvious situational irony in juxtaposing the newspaper accusation that colonial service is a life of luxury with the harsh realities of these men's harsh lives. At their remote posts in the scorching desert they are shown facing Herculean tasks of engineering, diplomacy, cartography, or medicine, giving the best years of their lives to build up India, bring it to "progress," and "save" it from the mismanagement of its own rulers. To underscore the message, Kipling soon reveals that another Englishman, Hummil's subcontractor, Jevins, has already succumbed to the despair of his thankless post and committed suicide. Kipling portrays these young men as imperfect yet heroic, foot soldiers of "Civilization" destroyed by the ignorant brutality of the inscrutable East.

Though the first scene demonstrates Kipling's defense of the necessity of colonialism, it may be argued that the story as a whole is hardly political. Is it not, after all, in terms of genre a Victorian ghost story? The bulk of the story reveals the horrors experienced by Hummil, who is convinced that when he sleeps, there is some force pursuing him, trying to capture his soul. The story climaxes with his eventual death, which seems to be caused by some supernatural agency. The first scene's defense of imperialism, though apparently serving only a scene setting or window-dressing, is essentially connected to the ghost story form of the tale. The anonymous force that haunts Hummil is the imperialist's fear of native uprising, transmuted and disguised in classic Freudian displacement into the world of dreams, a place in which the otherwise supposedly passive native acts violently. This spectral force represents the literally "unspeakable" neuroses, ambivalences, and fears within colonialist discourse. These fears are displaced and neutralized by their containment in the tight literary framework of the ghost story, which deals with fear within a setting controlled and restricted within certain preset safe conventions.

The story construes "the East" and its ways as inscrutable, irrational, and frightening, starting from the epigraph at the beginning of the story, a poem with the attribution "Himalayan." It begins: "The sky is lead and ours faces are red,/And the gates of Hell are opened and riven/And the winds of Hell are loosened and driven," a subtle, indirectly discursive method (by using "the orient's" supposed "own words" against it) of investing the story's geographical setting with malevolent supernatural force. Linking "the East" with the supernatural is significant because Hummil's death at the story's end is attributed to something that the doctor Spurstow admits—"[Isn't] in medical science"— something outside the rational limits of his knowledge, totally incommensurable with his ruling discourse. From the very beginning, Kipling prepares the way for Hummil's death at the hands of the irrational, vindictive, mystical powers of "the Orient." When Hummil tells the others of Jevins, the subcontractor's death, he refuses to label it a suicide, despite his knowledge to the contrary, with the excuses, "I judge no man *in this weather*" (which Mottram later repeats to Hummil), and "A man hasn't many privileges *in this country*, but he might at least be allowed to mishandle his own rifle" (italics added). In all of these statements "the East" has some quality that makes it so different, so inscrutable, that even moral law cannot circumscribe its Otherness. The narrator's later comment that "the Great Indian Empire. . . turns herself for six months into a house of torment," essentially personifying "the East" as a stern, capricious (and, of course, female) deity, reinforces that idea.

The final connection forged between Hummil's madness and the Orient is the native manservant Chuma's recognition and diagnosis of the cause of Hummil's death, while the "knowledgeable" English doctor Spurstow is stumped. "East is East and West is West and ne'er the twain shall meet," wrote Kipling in "The Ballad of the East and West." While Kipling may have supposed this saying to be constative, within the confines of imperialist discourse, it functions almost as a performative prescription, as seen in the segregation of "appropriate" knowledge between the Westerner Spurstow and the "Oriental" Chuma. Chuma is portrayed as incapable of understanding Western medical science and Western technology, but having privileged knowledge about things in the irrational, supernatural realm, a stereotypically "Eastern" kind of knowledge. Only through this strict separation is the hierarchical imperialist hegemony possible.

Though "the East" is construed throughout the story as a unified, monolithic essence which is incomprehensibly, irrationally, and fully Other,

Hummil's madness becomes the point at which the binary opposition between West and East can no longer be maintained, and resistance has destroyed imperialism's artificially imposed barriers. The specter that pursues Hummil is described as "A blind face that cries and can't wipe its eyes, a blind face that chases him down corridors." It is almost as if the objectified East has come to life. It appears exactly as constructed in the colonialist mind: silent and seemingly passive (as suggested by its blindness and inability to wipe its eyes), yet even when imaged as passive and blind, it is able to inspire terror actively pursuing and frightening the colonizer. Hummil's silent persecutor represents the colonial bogeyman of a successful "native revolt": successful because it eventually "catches up" with Hummil and kills him (despite the personal intervention and best efforts of Spurstow). Kipling's discourse requires that Hummil die when confronted by an independent "native" culture. It simply does not conceive of or permit anything like Said's "hybridization" in which cultures and cultural forms are mixed and radically impure. From within the colonialist framework, destruction, anarchy, and the loss of civilization must result when the counter-discourse gains it own voice.

It is crucial that the story's last sentence is exactly as it is: "Neither Mottram nor Lowndes had any answer to the question." At the end of this colonialist fable, the two Englishmen are left in the position of lacking both knowledge (which in Foucaltian terms *is* power) and the voice to answer. In the first scene, Kipling asserts England's right and responsibility to rule India. By the story's end, however, power relations have been turned on their heads. Chuma, the native, is elevated to the position of knowledge, while Spurstow the doctor is confounded, and Mottram and Lowndes are voiceless, unable to answer or even comprehend the questions posed by a supernatural event. Kipling's choice of the vehicle of the ghost story is suddenly clear. The ghost story provides a permissible cultural structure for the narration of a traumatic, incommensurable event. Bill Ashcroft, Gareth Griffiths, and Helen Tiffin make the claim that historically European modes of dealing with alterity have depicted it as either "*terror* or *lack*" (italics theirs). This story utilizes both techniques as the plot progresses. The first scene depicts India as *lacking* and incomplete, unable to govern itself, but by the story's conclusion, the East becomes a source of powerful, infernal *terror*, completely overpowering any response of the colonizers. "At the End of the Passage" reveals Kipling's own highly symbolized allegory of decolonization, one declawed, articulated, and projected onto the safe structure of the Victorian ghost story.

BENJAMIN K. WALKER

LITERARY SELECTIONS

On First Looking into Chapman's Homer (1816)

by John Keats

Much have I travell'd in the realms of gold,
   And many goodly states and kingdoms seen:
   Round many western islands have I been
Which bards in fealty to Apollo hold.
Oft of one wide expanse had I been told   5
   That deep-brow'd Homer ruled as his demesne
   Yet did I never breathe its pure serene;
Till I heard Chapman speak out loud and bold:
Then felt I like some watcher of the skies
   When a new planet swims into his ken   10
Or like stout Cortez when with eagle eyes
   He star'd at the Pacific—and all his men
Look'd at each other with a wild surmise—
   Silent, upon a peak in Darien.

Rappaccini's Daughter (From the Writings of Aubépine; 1844)

by Nathaniel Hawthorne

We do not remember to have seen any translated specimens of the productions of M. de l'Aubépine—a fact the less to be wondered at, as his very name is unknown to many of his own countrymen as well as to the student of foreign literature. As a writer, he seems to occupy an unfortunate position between the Transcendentalists (who, under one name or another, have their share in all the current literature of the world) and the great body of pen-and-ink men who address the intellect and sympathies of the multitude. If not too refined, at all events too remote, too shadowy, and unsubstantial in his modes of development to suit the taste of the latter class, and yet too popular to satisfy the spiritual or metaphysical requisitions of the former, he must necessarily find himself without an audience, except here and there an individual or possibly an isolated clique. His writings, to do them justice, are not altogether destitute of fancy and originality; they might have won him greater reputation but for an inveterate love of allegory, which is apt to invest his plots and characters with the aspect of scenery and people in the clouds, and to steal away the human warmth out of his conceptions. His fictions are sometimes historical, sometimes of the present day, and sometimes, so far as can be discovered, have little or no reference either to time or space. In any case, he generally contents himself with a very slight embroidery of outward manners—the faintest possible counterfeit of real life—and endeavors to create an interest by some less obvious peculiarity of the subject. Occasionally a breath of Nature, a raindrop of pathos and tenderness, or a gleam of humor, will find its way into the midst of his fantastic imagery, and make us feel as if, after all, we were yet within the limits of our native earth. We will only add to this very cursory notice that M. de l'Aubépine's productions, if the reader chance to take them in precisely the proper point of view, may amuse a leisure hour as well as those of a brighter man; if otherwise, they can hardly fail to look excessively like nonsense.

Our author is voluminous; he continues to write and publish with as much praiseworthy and indefatigable prolixity as if his efforts were crowned with the brilliant success that so justly attends those of Eugene Sue. His first appearance was by a collection of stories in a long series of volumes entitled "Contes deux fois racontees." The titles of some of his more recent works (we quote from memory) are as follows: "Le Voyage Celeste a Chemin de Fer," 3 tom., 1838; "Le nouveau Pere Adam et la nouvelle Mere Eve," 2 tom., 1839; "Roderic; ou le Serpent a l'estomac," 2 tom., 1840; "Le Culte du Feu," a folio volume of ponderous research into the religion and ritual of the old Persian Ghebers, published in 1841; "La Soiree du Chateau en Espagne,"

1 tom., 8vo, 1842; and "L'Artiste du Beau; ou le Papillon Mecanique," 5 tom., 4to, 1843. Our somewhat wearisome perusal of this startling catalogue of volumes has left behind it a certain personal affection and sympathy, though by no means admiration, for M. de l'Aubépine; and we would fain do the little in our power towards introducing him favorably to the American public. The ensuing tale is a translation of his "Beatrice; ou la Belle Empoisonneuse," recently published in *La Revue Anti-Aristocratique*. This journal, edited by the Comte de Bearhaven, has for some years past led the defense of liberal principles and popular rights with a faithfulness and ability worthy of all praise.

A young man, named Giovanni Guasconti, came, very long ago, from the more southern region of Italy, to pursue his studies at the University of Padua. Giovanni, who had but a scanty supply of gold ducats in his pocket, took lodgings in a high and gloomy chamber of an old edifice which looked not unworthy to have been the palace of a Paduan noble, and which, in fact, exhibited over its entrance the armorial bearings of a family long since extinct. The young stranger, who was not unstudied in the great poem of his country, recollected that one of the ancestors of this family, and perhaps an occupant of this very mansion, had been pictured by Dante as a partaker of the immortal agonies of his Inferno. These reminiscences and associations, together with the tendency to heartbreak natural to a young man for the first time out of his native sphere, caused Giovanni to sigh heavily as he looked around the desolate and ill-furnished apartment.

"Holy Virgin, signor!" cried old Dame Lisabetta, who, won by the youth's remarkable beauty of person, was kindly endeavoring to give the chamber a habitable air, "what a sigh was that to come out of a young man's heart! Do you find this old mansion gloomy? For the love of Heaven, then, put your head out of the window, and you will see as bright sunshine as you have left in Naples."

Guasconti mechanically did as the old woman advised, but could not quite agree with her that the Paduan sunshine was as cheerful as that of southern Italy. Such as it was, however, it fell upon a garden beneath the window and expended its fostering influences on a variety of plants, which seemed to have been cultivated with exceeding care.

"Does this garden belong to the house?" asked Giovanni.

"Heaven forbid, signor, unless it were fruitful of better pot herbs than any that grow there now," answered old Lisabetta. "No; that garden is cultivated by the own hands of Signor Giacomo Rappaccini, the famous doctor, who, I warrant him, has been heard of as far as Naples. It is said that he distils these plants into medicines that are as potent as a charm. Oftentimes you may see the signor doctor at work, and perchance the signora, his daughter, too, gathering the strange flowers that grow in the garden."

The old woman had now done what she could for the aspect of the chamber; and, commending the young man to the protection of the saints, took her departure.

Giovanni still found no better occupation than to look down into the garden beneath his window. From its appearance, he judged it to be one of those botanic gardens which were of earlier date in Padua than elsewhere in Italy or in the world. Or, not improbably, it might once have been the pleasure-place of an opulent family; for there was the ruin of a marble fountain in the centre, sculptured with rare art, but so woefully shattered that it was impossible to trace the original design from the chaos of remaining fragments. The water, however, continued to gush and sparkle into the sunbeams as cheerfully as ever. A little gurgling sound ascended to the young man's window, and made him feel as if the fountain were an immortal spirit that sung its song unceasingly and without heeding the vicissitudes around it, while one century embodied it in marble and another scattered the perishable garniture on the soil. All about the pool into which the water subsided grew various plants, that seemed to require a plentiful supply of moisture for the nourishment of gigantic leaves, and in some instances, flowers gorgeously magnificent. There was one shrub in particular, set in a marble vase in the midst of the pool, that bore a profusion of purple blossoms, each of which had the luster and richness of a gem; and the whole together made a show so resplendent that it seemed enough to illuminate the garden, even had there been no sunshine. Every portion of the soil was peopled with plants and herbs, which, if less beautiful, still bore tokens of assiduous care, as if all had their individual virtues, known to the scientific mind that fostered them. Some were placed in urns, rich with old carving, and others in common garden pots; some crept serpent-like along the ground or climbed on high, using whatever means of ascent was offered them. One plant had wreathed itself round a statue of Vertumnus, which was thus quite veiled and shrouded in a drapery of hanging foliage, so happily arranged that it might have served a sculptor for a study.

While Giovanni stood at the window he heard a rustling behind a screen of leaves, and became aware that a person was at work in the garden. His figure soon emerged into view, and showed itself to be that of no common laborer, but a tall, emaciated, sallow, and sickly-looking man, dressed in a scholar's garb of black. He was beyond the middle term of life, with gray hair, a thin, gray beard, and a face singularly marked with intellect and cultivation, but which could never, even in his more youthful days, have expressed much warmth of heart.

Nothing could exceed the intentness with which this scientific gardener examined every shrub which grew in his path: it seemed as if he was looking into their inmost nature, making observations in regard to their creative essence, and discovering why one leaf grew in this shape and another in that, and wherefore such and such flowers differed among themselves in hue and perfume. Nevertheless, in spite of this deep intelligence on his part, there was no approach to intimacy between himself and these vegetable existences. On the contrary, he avoided their actual touch or the direct inhaling of their odors with a caution that impressed Giovanni most disagreeably; for the man's demeanor was that of one walking among malignant influences, such as savage beasts, or deadly snakes, or evil spirits, which, should he allow them one moment of license, would wreak upon him some terrible fatality. It was strangely frightful to the young man's imagination to see this air of insecurity in a person cultivating a garden, that most simple and innocent of human toils, and which had been alike the joy and labor of the unfallen parents of the race. Was this garden, then, the Eden of the present world? And this man, with such a perception of harm in what his own hands caused to grow—was he the Adam?

The distrustful gardener, while plucking away the dead leaves or pruning the too luxuriant growth of the shrubs, defended his hands with a pair of thick gloves. Nor were these his only armor. When, in his walk through the garden, he came to the magnificent plant that hung its purple gems beside the marble fountain, he placed a kind of mask over his mouth and nostrils, as if all this beauty did but conceal a deadlier malice; but, finding his task still too dangerous, he drew back, removed the mask, and called loudly, but in the infirm voice of a person affected with inward disease, "Beatrice! Beatrice!"

"Here am I, my father. What would you?" cried a rich and youthful voice from the window of the opposite house—a voice as rich as a tropical sunset, and which made Giovanni, though he knew not why, think of deep hues of purple or crimson and of perfumes heavily delectable. "Are you in the garden?"

"Yes, Beatrice," answered the gardener, "and I need your help."

Soon there emerged from under a sculptured portal the figure of a young girl, arrayed with as much richness of taste as the most splendid of the flowers, beautiful as the day, and with a bloom so deep and vivid that one shade more would have been too much. She looked redundant with life, health, and energy; all of which attributes were bound down and compressed, as it and girdled tensely, in their luxuriance, by her virgin zone. Yet Giovanni's fancy must have grown morbid while he looked down into the garden; for the impression which the fair stranger made upon him was as if here were another flower, the human sister of those vegetable ones, as beautiful as they, more beautiful than the richest of them, but still to be touched only with a glove, nor to be approached without a mask. As Beatrice came down the garden path, it was observable that she handled and inhaled the odor of several of the plants which her father had most sedulously avoided.

"Here, Beatrice," said the latter, "see how many needful offices require to be done to our chief treasure. Yet, shattered as I am, my life might pay the penalty of approaching it so closely as circumstances demand. Henceforth, I fear, this plant must be consigned to your sole charge."

"And gladly will I undertake it," cried again the rich tones of the young lady, as she bent towards the magnificent plant and opened her arms as if to embrace it. "Yes, my sister, my splendor, it shall be Beatrice's task to nurse and serve thee; and thou shalt reward her with thy kisses and perfumed breath, which to her is as the breath of life."

Then, with all the tenderness in her manner that was so strikingly expressed in her words, she busied herself with such attentions as the plant seemed to require; and Giovanni, at his lofty window, rubbed his eyes and almost doubted whether it were a girl tending her favorite flower, or one sister performing the duties of affection to another. The scene soon terminated. Whether Dr. Rappaccini had finished his labors in the garden, or that his watchful eye had caught the stranger's face, he now took his daughter's arm and retired. Night was already closing in; oppressive exhalations seemed to proceed from the plants and steal upward past the open window; and Giovanni, closing the lattice, went to his couch and dreamed of a rich flower and beautiful girl. Flower and maiden were different, and yet the same, and fraught with some strange peril in either shape.

But there is an influence in the light of morning that tends to rectify whatever errors of fancy, or even of judgment, we may have incurred during the sun's decline, or among the shadows of the night, or in the less wholesome glow of moonshine. Giovanni's first movement, on starting from sleep, was to throw open the window and gaze down into the garden which his dreams had made so fertile of mysteries. He was surprised and a little ashamed to find how real and matter-of-fact an affair it proved to be, in the first rays of the sun which gilded the dew-drops that hung upon leaf and blossom, and, while giving a brighter beauty to each rare flower, brought everything within the limits of ordinary experience. The young man rejoiced that, in the heart of the barren city, he had the privilege of overlooking this spot of lovely and luxuriant vegetation. It would serve, he said to himself, as a symbolic language to keep him in communion with Nature. Neither the sickly and thoughtworn Dr. Giacomo Rappaccini, it is true, nor his brilliant daughter, were now visible; so that Giovanni could not determine how much of the singularity which he attributed to both was due to their own qualities and how much to his wonder-working fancy; but he was inclined to take a most rational view of the whole matter.

In the course of the day he paid his respects to Signor Pietro Baglioni, professor of medicine in the university, a physician of eminent repute to whom Giovanni had brought a letter of introduction. The professor was an elderly personage, apparently of genial nature, and habits that might almost be called jovial. He kept the young man to dinner, and made himself very agreeable by the freedom and liveliness of his conversation, especially when warmed by a flask or two of Tuscan wine. Giovanni, conceiving that men of science, inhabitants of the same city, must needs be on familiar terms with one another, took an opportunity to mention the name of Dr. Rappaccini. But the professor did not respond with so much cordiality as he had anticipated.

"Ill would it become a teacher of the divine art of medicine," said Professor Pietro Baglioni, in answer to a question of Giovanni, "to withhold due and well-considered praise of a physician so eminently skilled as Rappaccini; but, on the other hand, I should answer it but scantily to my conscience were I to permit a worthy youth like yourself, Signor Giovanni, the son of an ancient friend, to imbibe erroneous ideas respecting a man who might hereafter chance to hold your life and death in his hands. The truth is, our worshipful Dr. Rappaccini has as much science as any member of the faculty—with perhaps one single exception—in Padua, or all Italy; but there are certain grave objections to his professional character."

"And what are they?" asked the young man.

"Has my friend Giovanni any disease of body or heart, that he is so inquisitive about physicians?" said the professor, with a smile. "But as for Rappaccini, it is said of him—and I, who know the man well, can answer for its truth—that he cares infinitely more for science than for mankind. His patients are interesting to him only as subjects for some new experiment. He would sacrifice human life, his own among the rest, or whatever else was dearest to him, for the sake of adding so much as a grain of mustard seed to the great heap of his accumulated knowledge."

"Methinks he is an awful man indeed," remarked Guasconti, mentally recalling the cold and purely intellectual aspect of Rappaccini. "And yet, worshipful professor, is it not a noble spirit? Are there many men capable of so spiritual a love of science?"

"God forbid," answered the professor, somewhat testily; "at least, unless they take sounder views of the healing art than those adopted by Rappaccini. It is his theory that all medicinal virtues are comprised within those substances which we term vegetable poisons. These he cultivates with his own hands, and is said even to have produced new varieties of poison, more horribly deleterious than Nature, without the assistance of this learned person, would ever have plagued the world withal. That the signor doctor does less mischief than might be expected with such dangerous substances is undeniable. Now and then, it must be owned, he has effected, or seemed to effect, a marvelous cure; but, to tell you my private mind, Signor Giovanni, he should receive little credit for such instances of success—they being probably the work of chance—but should be held strictly accountable for his failures, which may justly be considered his own work."

The youth might have taken Baglioni's opinions with many grains of allowance had he known that there was a professional warfare of long continuance between him and Dr. Rappaccini, in which the latter was generally thought to have gained the advantage. If the reader be inclined to judge for himself, we refer him to certain black-letter tracts on both sides, preserved in the medical department of the University of Padua.

"I know not, most learned professor," returned Giovanni, after musing on what had been said of Rappaccini's exclusive zeal for science, "I know not how dearly this physician may love his art; but surely there is one object more dear to him. He has a daughter."

"Aha!" cried the professor, with a laugh. "So now our friend Giovanni's secret is out. You have heard of this daughter, whom all the young men in Padua are wild about, though not half a dozen have ever had the good hap to see her face. I know little of the Signora Beatrice save that Rappaccini is said to have instructed her deeply in his science, and that, young and beautiful as fame reports her, she is already qualified to fill a professor's chair. Perchance her father destines her for mine! Other absurd rumors there be, not worth talking about or listening to. So now, Signor Giovanni, drink off your glass of lachryma."

Guasconti returned to his lodgings somewhat heated with the wine he had quaffed, and which caused his brain to swim with strange fantasies in reference to Dr. Rappaccini and the beautiful Beatrice. On his way, happening to pass by a florist's, he bought a fresh bouquet of flowers.

Ascending to his chamber, he seated himself near the window, but within the shadow thrown by the depth of the wall, so that he could look down into the garden with little risk of being discovered. All beneath his eye was a solitude. The strange plants were basking in the sunshine, and now and then nodding gently to one another, as if in acknowledgment of sympathy and kindred. In the midst, by the shattered fountain, grew the magnificent shrub, with its purple gems clustering all over it; they glowed in the air, and gleamed back again out of the depths of the pool, which thus seemed to overflow with colored radiance from the rich reflection that was steeped in it. At first, as we have said, the garden was a solitude. Soon, however—as Giovanni had half hoped, half feared, would be the case—a figure appeared beneath the antique sculptured portal, and came down between the rows of plants, inhaling their various perfumes as if she were one of those beings of old classic fable that lived upon sweet odors. On again beholding Beatrice, the young man was even startled to perceive how much her beauty exceeded his recollection of it; so brilliant, so vivid, was its character, that she glowed amid the sunlight, and, as Giovanni whispered to himself, positively illuminated the more shadowy intervals of the garden path. Her face being now more revealed than on the former occasion, he was struck by its expression of simplicity and sweetness—qualities that had not entered into his idea of her character, and which made him ask anew what manner of mortal she might be. Nor did he fail again to observe, or imagine, an analogy between the beautiful girl and the gorgeous shrub that hung its gemlike flowers over the fountain—a resemblance which Beatrice seemed to have indulged a fantastic humor in heightening, both by the arrangement of her dress and the selection of its hues.

Approaching the shrub, she threw open her arms, as with a passionate ardor, and drew its branches into an intimate embrace—so intimate that her features were hidden in its leafy bosom and her glistening ringlets all intermingled with the flowers.

"Give me thy breath, my sister," exclaimed Beatrice; "for I am faint with common air. And give me this flower of thine, which I separate with gentlest fingers from the stem and place it close beside my heart."

With these words the beautiful daughter of Rappaccini plucked one of the richest blossoms of the shrub, and was about to fasten it in her bosom. But now, unless Giovanni's draughts of wine had bewildered his senses, a singular incident occurred. A small orange-colored reptile, of the lizard or chameleon species, chanced to be creeping along the path, just at the feet of Beatrice. It appeared to Giovanni—but, at the distance from which he gazed, he could scarcely have seen anything so minute—it appeared to him, however, that a drop or two of moisture from the broken stem of the flower descended upon the lizard's head. For an instant the reptile contorted itself violently, and then lay motionless in the sunshine. Beatrice observed this remarkable phenomenon and crossed herself, sadly, but without surprise; nor did she therefore hesitate to arrange the fatal flower in her bosom. There it blushed, and almost glimmered with the dazzling effect of a precious stone, adding to her dress and aspect the one appropriate charm which nothing else in the world could have supplied. But Giovanni, out of the shadow of his window, bent forward and shrank back, and murmured and trembled.

"Am I awake? Have I my senses?" said he to himself. "What is this being? Beautiful shall I call her, or inexpressibly terrible?"

Beatrice now strayed carelessly through the garden, approaching closer beneath Giovanni's window, so that he was compelled to thrust his head quite out of its concealment in order to gratify the intense and painful curiosity which she excited. At this moment there came a beautiful insect over the garden wall; it had, perhaps, wandered through the city, and found no flowers or verdure among those antique haunts of men until the heavy perfumes of Dr. Rappaccini's shrubs had lured it from afar. Without alighting on the flowers, this winged brightness seemed to be attracted by Beatrice, and lingered in the air and fluttered about her head. Now, here it could not be but that Giovanni Guasconti's eyes deceived him. Be that as it might, he fancied that, while Beatrice was gazing at the insect with childish delight, it grew faint and fell at her feet; its bright wings shivered; it was dead—from no cause that he could discern, unless it were the atmosphere of her breath. Again Beatrice crossed herself and sighed heavily as she bent over the dead insect.

An impulsive movement of Giovanni drew her eyes to the window. There she beheld the beautiful head of the young man—rather a Grecian than an Italian head, with fair, regular features, and a glistening of gold among his ringlets—gazing down upon her like a being that hovered in mid air. Scarcely knowing what he did, Giovanni threw down the bouquet which he had hitherto held in his hand.

"Signora," said he, "there are pure and healthful flowers. Wear them for the sake of Giovanni Guasconti."

"Thanks, signor," replied Beatrice, with her rich voice, that came forth as it were like a gush of music, and with a mirthful expression half childish and half woman-like. "I accept your gift, and would fain recompense it with this precious purple flower; but if I toss it into the air it will not reach you. So Signor Guasconti must even content himself with my thanks."

She lifted the bouquet from the ground, and then, as if inwardly ashamed at having stepped aside from her maidenly reserve to respond to a stranger's greeting, passed swiftly homeward through the garden. But few as the moments were, it seemed to Giovanni, when she was on the point of vanishing beneath the sculptured portal, that his beautiful bouquet was already beginning to wither in her grasp. It was an idle thought; there could be no possibility of distinguishing a faded flower from a fresh one at so great a distance.

For many days after this incident the young man avoided the window that looked into Dr. Rappaccini's garden, as if something ugly and monstrous would have blasted his eyesight had he been betrayed into a glance. He felt conscious of having put himself, to a certain extent, within the influence of an unintelligible power by the communication which he had opened with Beatrice. The wisest course would have been, if his heart were in any real danger, to quit his lodgings and Padua itself at once; the next wiser, to have accustomed himself, as far as possible, to the familiar and daylight view of Beatrice—thus bringing her rigidly and systematically within the limits of ordinary experience. Least of all, while avoiding her sight, ought Giovanni to have remained so near this extraordinary being that the proximity and possibility even of intercourse should give a kind of substance and reality to the wild vagaries which his imagination ran riot continually in producing. Guasconti had not a deep heart—or, at all events, its depths were not sounded now; but he had a quick fancy, and an ardent southern temperament, which rose every instant to a higher fever pitch. Whether or no Beatrice possessed those terrible attributes, that fatal breath, the affinity with those so beautiful and deadly flowers which were indicated by what Giovanni had witnessed, she had at least instilled a fierce and subtle poison into his system. It was not love, although her rich beauty was a madness to him; nor horror, even while he fancied her spirit to be imbued with the same baneful essence that seemed to pervade her physical frame; but a wild offspring of both love and horror that had each parent in it, and burned like one and shivered like the other. Giovanni knew not what to dread; still less did he know what to hope; yet hope and dread kept a continual warfare in his breast, alternately vanquishing one another and starting up afresh to renew the contest. Blessed are all simple emotions, be they dark or bright! It is the lurid intermixture of the two that produces the illuminating blaze of the infernal regions.

Sometimes he endeavored to assuage the fever of his spirit by a rapid walk through the streets of Padua or beyond its gates: his footsteps kept time with the throbbings of his brain, so that the walk was apt to accelerate itself to a race. One day he found himself arrested; his arm was seized by a portly personage, who had turned back on recognizing the young man and expended much breath in overtaking him.

"Signor Giovanni! Stay, my young friend!" cried he. "Have you forgotten me? That might well be the case if I were as much altered as yourself."

It was Baglioni, whom Giovanni had avoided ever since their first meeting, from a doubt that the professor's sagacity would look too deeply into his secrets. Endeavoring to recover himself, he stared forth wildly from his inner world into the outer one and spoke like a man in a dream.

"Yes; I am Giovanni Guasconti. You are Professor Pietro Baglioni. Now let me pass!"

"Not yet, not yet, Signor Giovanni Guasconti," said the professor, smiling, but at the same time scrutinizing the youth with an earnest glance. "What! did I grow up side by side with your father? and shall his son pass me like a stranger in these old streets of Padua? Stand still, Signor Giovanni; for we must have a word or two before we part."

"Speedily, then, most worshipful professor, speedily," said Giovanni, with feverish impatience. "Does not your worship see that I am in haste?"

Now, while he was speaking there came a man in black along the street, stooping and moving feebly like a person in inferior health. His face was all overspread with a most sickly and sallow hue, but yet so pervaded with an expression of piercing and active intellect that an observer might easily have overlooked the merely physical attributes and have seen only this wonderful energy. As he passed, this person exchanged a cold and distant salutation with Baglioni, but fixed his eyes upon Giovanni with an intentness that seemed to bring out whatever was within him worthy of notice. Nevertheless, there was a peculiar quietness in the look, as if taking merely a speculative, not a human interest, in the young man.

"It is Dr. Rappaccini!" whispered the professor when the stranger had passed. "Has he ever seen your face before?"

"Not that I know," answered Giovanni, starting at the name.

"He HAS seen you! he must have seen you!" said Baglioni, hastily. "For some purpose or other, this man of science is making a study of you. I know that look of his! It is the same that coldly illuminates his face as he bends over a bird, a mouse, or a butterfly, which, in pursuance of some experiment, he has killed by the perfume of a flower; a look as deep as Nature itself, but without Nature's warmth of love. Signor Giovanni, I will stake my life upon it, you are the subject of one of Rappaccini's experiments!"

"Will you make a fool of me?" cried Giovanni, passionately. "THAT, signor professor, were an untoward experiment."

"Patience! patience!" replied the imperturbable professor. "I tell thee, my poor Giovanni, that Rappaccini has a scientific interest in thee. Thou hast fallen into fearful hands! And the Signora Beatrice—what part does she act in this mystery?"

But Guasconti, finding Baglioni's pertinacity intolerable, here broke away, and was gone before the professor could again seize his arm. He looked after the young man intently and shook his head.

"This must not be," said Baglioni to himself. "The youth is the son of my old friend, and shall not come to any harm from which the arcana of medical science can preserve him. Besides, it is too insufferable an impertinence in Rappaccini, thus to snatch the lad out of my own hands, as I may say, and make use of him for his infernal experiments. This daughter of his! It shall be looked to. Perchance, most learned Rappaccini, I may foil you where you little dream of it!"

Meanwhile Giovanni had pursued a circuitous route, and at length found himself at the door of his lodgings. As he crossed the threshold he was met by old Lisabetta, who smirked and smiled, and was evidently desirous to attract his attention; vainly, however, as the ebullition of his feelings had momentarily subsided into a cold and dull vacuity. He turned his eyes full upon the withered face that was puckering itself into a smile, but seemed to behold it not. The old dame, therefore, laid her grasp upon his cloak.

"Signor! Signor!" whispered she, still with a smile over the whole breadth of her visage, so that it looked not unlike a grotesque carving in wood, darkened by centuries. "Listen, signor! There is a private entrance into the garden!"

"What do you say?" exclaimed Giovanni, turning quickly about, as if an inanimate thing should start into feverish life. "A private entrance into Dr. Rappaccini's garden?"

"Hush! hush! not so loud!" whispered Lisabetta, putting her hand over his mouth. "Yes; into the worshipful doctor's garden, where you may see all his fine shrubbery. Many a young man in Padua would give gold to be admitted among those flowers."

Giovanni put a piece of gold into her hand.

"Show me the way," said he.

A surmise, probably excited by his conversation with Baglioni, crossed his mind, that this interposition of old Lisabetta might perchance be connected with the intrigue, whatever were its nature, in which the professor seemed to suppose that Dr. Rappaccini was involving him. But such a suspicion, though it disturbed Giovanni, was inadequate to restrain him. The instant that he was aware of the possibility of approaching Beatrice, it seemed an absolute necessity of his existence to do so. It mattered not whether she were angel or demon; he was irrevocably within her sphere, and must obey the law that whirled him onward, in ever-lessening circles, towards a result which he did not attempt to foreshadow; and yet, strange to say, there came across him a sudden doubt whether this intense interest on his part were not delusory; whether it were really of so deep and positive a nature as to justify him in now thrusting himself into an incalculable position; whether it were not merely the fantasy of a young man's brain, only slightly or not at all connected with his heart.

He paused, hesitated, turned half about, but again went on. His withered guide led him along several obscure passages, and finally undid a door, through which, as it was opened, there came the sight and sound of rustling leaves, with the broken sunshine glimmering among them. Giovanni stepped forth, and, forcing himself through the entanglement of a shrub that wreathed its tendrils over the hidden entrance, stood beneath his own window in the open area of Dr. Rappaccini's garden.

How often is it the case that, when impossibilities have come to pass and dreams have condensed their misty substance into tangible realities, we find ourselves calm, and even coldly self-possessed, amid circumstances which it would have been a delirium of joy or agony to anticipate! Fate delights to thwart us thus. Passion will choose his own time to rush upon the scene, and lingers sluggishly behind when an appropriate adjustment of events would seem to summon his appearance. So was it now with Giovanni. Day after day his pulses had throbbed with feverish blood at the improbable idea of an interview with Beatrice, and of standing with her, face to face, in this very garden, basking in the Oriental sunshine of her beauty, and snatching from her full gaze the mystery which he deemed the riddle of his own existence. But now there was a singular and untimely equanimity within his breast. He threw a glance around the garden to discover if Beatrice or her father were present, and, perceiving that he was alone, began a critical observation of the plants.

The aspect of one and all of them dissatisfied him; their gorgeousness seemed fierce, passionate, and even unnatural. There was hardly an individual shrub which a wanderer, straying by himself through a forest, would not have been startled to find growing wild, as if an unearthly face had glared at him out of the thicket. Several also would have shocked a delicate instinct by an appearance of artificialness indicating that there had been such commixture, and, as it were, adultery, of various vegetable species, that the production was no longer of God's making, but the monstrous offspring of man's depraved fancy, glowing with only an evil mockery of beauty. They were probably the result of experiment, which in one or two cases had succeeded in mingling plants individually lovely into a compound possessing the questionable and ominous character that distinguished the whole growth of the garden. In fine, Giovanni recognized but two or three plants in the collection, and those of a kind that he well knew to be poisonous. While busy with these contemplations he heard the rustling of a silken garment, and, turning, beheld Beatrice emerging from beneath the sculptured portal. Giovanni had not considered with himself what should be his deportment; whether he should apologize for his intrusion into the garden, or assume that he was there with the privity at least, if not by the desire, of Dr. Rappaccini or his daughter; but Beatrice's manner placed him at his ease, though leaving him still in doubt by what agency he had gained admittance. She came lightly along the path and met him near the broken fountain. There was surprise in her face, but brightened by a simple and kind expression of pleasure.

"You are a connoisseur in flowers, signor," said Beatrice, with a smile, alluding to the bouquet which he had flung her from the window. "It is no marvel, therefore, if the sight of my father's rare collection has tempted you to take a nearer view. If he were here, he could tell you many strange and interesting facts as to the nature and habits of these shrubs; for he has spent a lifetime in such studies, and this garden is his world."

"And yourself, lady," observed Giovanni, "if fame says true—you likewise are deeply skilled in the virtues indicated by these rich blossoms and these spicy perfumes. Would you deign to be my instructress, I should prove an apter scholar than if taught by Signor Rappaccini himself."

"Are there such idle rumors?" asked Beatrice, with the music of a pleasant laugh. "Do people say that I am skilled in my father's science of plants? What a jest is there! No; though I have grown up among these flowers, I know no more of them than their hues and perfume; and sometimes methinks I would fain rid myself of even that small knowledge. There are many flowers here, and those not the least brilliant, that shock and offend me when they meet my eye. But pray, signor, do not believe these stories about my science. Believe nothing of me save what you see with your own eyes."

"And must I believe all that I have seen with my own eyes?" asked Giovanni, pointedly, while the recollection of former scenes made him shrink. "No, signora; you demand too little of me. Bid me believe nothing save what comes from your own lips."

It would appear that Beatrice understood him. There came a deep flush to her cheek; but she looked full into Giovanni's eyes, and responded to his gaze of uneasy suspicion with a queenlike haughtiness.

"I do so bid you, signor," she replied. "Forget whatever you may have fancied in regard to me. If true to the outward senses, still it may be false in its essence; but the words of Beatrice Rappaccini's lips are true from the depths of the heart outward. Those you may believe."

A fervor glowed in her whole aspect and beamed upon Giovanni's consciousness like the light of truth itself; but while she spoke there was a fragrance in the atmosphere around her, rich and delightful, though evanescent, yet which the young man, from an indefinable reluctance, scarcely dared to draw into his lungs. It might be the odor of the flowers. Could it be Beatrice's breath which thus embalmed her words with a strange richness, as if by steeping them in her heart? A faintness passed like a shadow over Giovanni and flitted away; he seemed to gaze through the beautiful girl's eyes into her transparent soul, and felt no more doubt or fear.

The tinge of passion that had colored Beatrice's manner vanished; she became gay, and appeared to derive a pure delight from her communion with the youth not unlike what the maiden of a lonely island might have felt conversing with a voyager from the civilized world. Evidently her experience of life had been confined within the limits of that garden. She talked now about matters as simple as the daylight or summer clouds, and now asked questions in reference to the city, or Giovanni's distant home, his friends, his mother, and his sisters—questions indicating such seclusion, and such lack of familiarity with modes and forms, that Giovanni responded as if to an infant. Her spirit gushed out before him like a fresh rill that was just catching its first glimpse of the sunlight and wondering at the reflections of earth and sky which were flung into its bosom. There came thoughts, too, from a deep source, and fantasies of a gemlike brilliancy, as if diamonds and rubies sparkled upward among the bubbles of the fountain. Ever and anon there gleamed across the young man's mind a sense of wonder that he should be walking side by side with the being who had so wrought upon his imagination, whom he had idealized in such hues of terror, in whom he had positively witnessed such manifestations of dreadful attributes—that he should be conversing with Beatrice like a brother, and should find her so human and so maidenlike. But such reflections were only momentary; the effect of her character was too real not to make itself familiar at once.

In this free intercourse they had strayed through the garden, and now, after many turns among its avenues, were come to the shattered fountain, beside which grew the magnificent shrub, with its treasury of glowing blossoms. A fragrance was diffused from it which Giovanni recognized as identical with that which he had attributed to Beatrice's breath, but incomparably more powerful. As her eyes fell upon it, Giovanni beheld her press her hand to her bosom as if her heart were throbbing suddenly and painfully.

"For the first time in my life," murmured she, addressing the shrub, "I had forgotten thee."

"I remember, signora," said Giovanni, "that you once promised to reward me with one of these living gems for the bouquet which I had the happy boldness to fling to your feet. Permit me now to pluck it as a memorial of this interview."

He made a step towards the shrub with extended hand; but Beatrice darted forward, uttering a shriek that went through his heart like a dagger. She caught his hand and drew it back with the whole force of her slender figure. Giovanni felt her touch thrilling through his fibers.

"Touch it not!" exclaimed she, in a voice of agony. "Not for thy life! It is fatal!"

Then, hiding her face, she fled from him and vanished beneath the sculptured portal. As Giovanni followed her with his eyes, he beheld the emaciated figure and pale intelligence of Dr. Rappaccini, who had been watching the scene, he knew not how long, within the shadow of the entrance.

No sooner was Guasconti alone in his chamber than the image of Beatrice came back to his passionate musings, invested with all the witchery that had been gathering around it ever since his first glimpse of her, and now likewise imbued with a tender warmth of girlish womanhood. She was human; her nature was endowed with all gentle and feminine qualities; she was worthiest to be worshipped; she was capable, surely, on her part, of the height and heroism of love. Those tokens which he had hitherto considered as proofs of a frightful peculiarity in her physical and moral system were now either forgotten, or, by the subtle sophistry of passion transmitted into a golden crown of enchantment, rendering Beatrice the more admirable by so much as she was the more unique. Whatever had looked ugly was now beautiful; or, if incapable of such a change, it stole away and hid itself among those shapeless half ideas which throng the dim region beyond the daylight of our perfect consciousness. Thus did he spend the night, nor fell asleep until the dawn had begun to awake the slumbering flowers in Dr. Rappaccini's garden, whither Giovanni's dreams doubtless led him. Up rose the sun in his due season, and, flinging his beams upon the young man's eyelids, awoke him to a sense of pain. When thoroughly aroused, he became sensible of a burning and tingling agony in his hand—in his right hand—the very hand which Beatrice had grasped in her own when he was on the point of plucking one of the gemlike flowers. On the back of that hand there was now a purple print like that of four small fingers, and the likeness of a slender thumb upon his wrist.

Oh, how stubbornly does love—or even that cunning semblance of love which flourishes in the imagination, but strikes no depth of root into the heart—how stubbornly does it hold its faith until the moment comes when it is doomed to vanish into thin mist! Giovanni wrapped a handkerchief about his hand and wondered what evil thing had stung him, and soon forgot his pain in a reverie of Beatrice.

After the first interview, a second was in the inevitable course of what we call fate. A third; a fourth; and a meeting with Beatrice in the garden was no longer an incident in Giovanni's daily life, but the whole space in which he might be said to live; for the anticipation and memory of that ecstatic hour made up the remainder. Nor was it otherwise with the daughter of Rappaccini. She watched for the youth's appearance, and flew to his side with confidence as unreserved as if they had been playmates from early infancy—as if they were such playmates still. If, by any unwonted chance, he failed to come at the appointed moment, she stood beneath the window and sent up the rich sweetness of her tones to float around him in his chamber and echo and reverberate throughout his heart: "Giovanni! Giovanni! Why tarriest thou? Come down!" And down he hastened into that Eden of poisonous flowers.

But, with all this intimate familiarity, there was still a reserve in Beatrice's demeanor, so rigidly and invariably sustained that the idea of infringing it scarcely occurred to his imagination. By all appreciable signs, they loved; they had looked love with eyes that conveyed the holy secret from the depths of one soul into the depths of the other, as if it were too sacred to be whispered by the way; they had even spoken love in those gushes of passion when their spirits darted forth in articulated breath like tongues of long-hidden flame; and yet there had been no seal of lips, no clasp of hands, nor any slightest caress such as love claims and hallows. He had never touched one of the gleaming ringlets of her hair; her garment—so marked was the physical barrier between them—had never been waved against him by a breeze. On the few occasions when Giovanni had seemed tempted to overstep the limit, Beatrice grew so sad, so stern, and withal wore such a look of desolate separation, shuddering at itself, that not a spoken word was requisite to repel him. At such times he was startled at the horrible suspicions that rose, monster-like, out of the caverns of his heart and stared him in the face; his love grew thin and faint as the morning mist, his doubts alone had substance. But, when Beatrice's face brightened again after the momentary shadow, she was transformed at once from the mysterious, questionable being whom he had watched with so much awe and horror; she was now the beautiful and unsophisticated girl whom he felt that his spirit knew with a certainty beyond all other knowledge.

A considerable time had now passed since Giovanni's last meeting with Baglioni. One morning, however, he was disagreeably surprised by a visit from the professor, whom he had scarcely thought of for whole weeks, and would willingly have forgotten still longer. Given up as he had long been to a pervading excitement, he could tolerate no companions except upon condition of their perfect sympathy with his present state of feeling. Such sympathy was not to be expected from Professor Baglioni.

The visitor chatted carelessly for a few moments about the gossip of the city and the university, and then took up another topic.

"I have been reading an old classic author lately," said he, "and met with a story that strangely interested me. Possibly you may remember it. It is of an Indian prince, who sent a beautiful woman as a present to Alexander the Great. She was as lovely as the dawn and gorgeous as the sunset; but what especially distinguished her was a certain rich perfume in her breath—richer than a garden of Persian roses. Alexander, as was natural to a youthful conqueror, fell in love at first sight with this magnificent stranger; but a certain sage physician, happening to be present, discovered a terrible secret in regard to her."

"And what was that?" asked Giovanni, turning his eyes downward to avoid those of the professor.

"That this lovely woman," continued Baglioni, with emphasis, "had been nourished with poisons from her birth upward, until her whole nature was so imbued with them that she herself had become the deadliest poison in existence. Poison was her element of life. With that rich perfume of her breath she blasted the very air. Her love would have been poison—her embrace death. Is not this a marvelous tale?"

"A childish fable," answered Giovanni, nervously starting from his chair. "I marvel how your worship finds time to read such nonsense among your graver studies."

"By the by," said the professor, looking uneasily about him, "what singular fragrance is this in your apartment? Is it the perfume of your gloves?

It is faint, but delicious; and yet, after all, by no means agreeable. Were I to breathe it long, methinks it would make me ill. It is like the breath of a flower; but I see no flowers in the chamber."

"Nor are there any," replied Giovanni, who had turned pale as the professor spoke; "nor, I think, is there any fragrance except in your worship's imagination. Odors, being a sort of element combined of the sensual and the spiritual, are apt to deceive us in this manner. The recollection of a perfume, the bare idea of it, may easily be mistaken for a present reality."

"Ay; but my sober imagination does not often play such tricks," said Baglioni; "and, were I to fancy any kind of odor, it would be that of some vile apothecary drug, wherewith my fingers are likely enough to be imbued. Our worshipful friend Rappaccini, as I have heard, tinctures his medicaments with odors richer than those of Araby. Doubtless, likewise, the fair and learned Signora Beatrice would minister to her patients with draughts as sweet as a maiden's breath; but woe to him that sips them!"

Giovanni's face evinced many contending emotions. The tone in which the professor alluded to the pure and lovely daughter of Rappaccini was a torture to his soul; and yet the intimation of a view of her character opposite to his own, gave instantaneous distinctness to a thousand dim suspicions, which now grinned at him like so many demons. But he strove hard to quell them and to respond to Baglioni with a true lover's perfect faith.

"Signor professor," said he, "you were my father's friend; perchance, too, it is your purpose to act a friendly part towards his son. I would fain feel nothing towards you save respect and deference; but I pray you to observe, signor, that there is one subject on which we must not speak. You know not the Signora Beatrice. You cannot, therefore, estimate the wrong— the blasphemy, I may even say—that is offered to her character by a light or injurious word."

"Giovanni! my poor Giovanni!" answered the professor, with a calm expression of pity, "I know this wretched girl far better than yourself. You shall hear the truth in respect to the poisoner Rappaccini and his poisonous daughter; yes, poisonous as she is beautiful. Listen; for, even should you do violence to my gray hairs, it shall not silence me. That old fable of the Indian woman has become a truth by the deep and deadly science of Rappaccini and in the person of the lovely Beatrice."

Giovanni groaned and hid his face

"Her father," continued Baglioni, "was not restrained by natural affection from offering up his child in this horrible manner as the victim of his insane zeal for science; for, let us do him justice, he is as true a man of science as ever distilled his own heart in an alembic. What, then, will be your fate? Beyond a doubt you are selected as the material of some new experiment. Perhaps the result is to be death; perhaps a fate more awful still. Rappaccini, with what he calls the interest of science before his eyes, will hesitate at nothing."

"It is a dream," muttered Giovanni to himself; "surely it is a dream."

"But," resumed the professor, "be of good cheer, son of my friend. It is not yet too late for the rescue. Possibly we may even succeed in bringing back this miserable child within the limits of ordinary nature, from which her father's madness has estranged her. Behold this little silver vase! It was wrought by the hands of the renowned Benvenuto Cellini, and is well worthy to be a love gift to the fairest dame in Italy. But its contents are invaluable. One little sip of this antidote would have rendered the most virulent poisons of the Borgias innocuous. Doubt not that it will be as efficacious against those of Rappaccini. Bestow the vase, and the precious liquid within it, on your Beatrice, and hopefully await the result."

Baglioni laid a small, exquisitely wrought silver vial on the table and withdrew, leaving what he had said to produce its effect upon the young man's mind.

"We will thwart Rappaccini yet," thought he, chuckling to himself, as he descended the stairs; "but, let us confess the truth of him, he is a wonderful man—a wonderful man indeed; a vile empiric, however, in his practice, and therefore not to be tolerated by those who respect the good old rules of the medical profession."

Throughout Giovanni's whole acquaintance with Beatrice, he had occasionally, as we have said, been haunted by dark surmises as to her character; yet so thoroughly had she made herself felt by him as a simple, natural, most affectionate, and guileless creature, that the image now held up by Professor Baglioni looked as strange and incredible as if it were not in accordance with his own original conception. True, there were ugly recollections connected with his first glimpses of the beautiful girl; he could not quite forget the bouquet that withered in her grasp, and the insect that perished amid the sunny air, by no ostensible agency save the fragrance of her breath. These incidents, however, dissolving in the pure light of her character, had no longer the efficacy of facts, but were acknowledged as mistaken fantasies, by whatever testimony of the senses they might appear to be substantiated. There is something truer and more real than what we can see with the eyes and touch with the finger. On such better evidence had Giovanni founded his confidence in Beatrice, though rather by the necessary force of her high attributes than by any deep and generous faith on his part. But now his spirit was incapable of sustaining itself at the height to which the early enthusiasm of passion had exalted it; he fell down, groveling among earthly doubts, and defiled therewith the pure whiteness of Beatrice's image. Not that he gave her up; he did but distrust. He resolved to institute some decisive test that should satisfy him, once for all, whether there were those dreadful peculiarities in her physical nature which could not be supposed to exist without some corresponding monstrosity of soul. His eyes, gazing down afar, might have deceived him as to the lizard, the insect, and the flowers; but if he could witness, at the distance of a few paces, the sudden blight of one fresh and healthful flower in Beatrice's hand, there would be room for no further question. With this idea he hastened to the florist's and purchased a bouquet that was still gemmed with the morning dew-drops.

It was now the customary hour of his daily interview with Beatrice. Before descending into the garden, Giovanni failed not to look at his figure in the mirror—a vanity to be expected in a beautiful young man, yet, as displaying itself at that troubled and feverish moment, the token of a certain shallowness of feeling and insincerity of character. He did gaze, however, and said to himself that his features had never before possessed so rich a grace, nor his eyes such vivacity, nor his cheeks so warm a hue of super-abundant life.

"At least," thought he, "her poison has not yet insinuated itself into my system. I am no flower to perish in her grasp."

With that thought he turned his eyes on the bouquet, which he had never once laid aside from his hand. A thrill of indefinable horror shot through his frame on perceiving that those dewy flowers were already beginning to droop; they wore the aspect of things that had been fresh and lovely yesterday. Giovanni grew white as marble, and stood motionless before the mirror, staring at his own reflection there as at the likeness of something frightful. He remembered Baglioni's remark about the fragrance that seemed to pervade the chamber. It must have been the poison in his breath! Then he shuddered—shuddered at himself. Recovering from his stupor, he began to watch with curious eye a spider that was busily at work hanging its web from the antique cornice of the apartment, crossing and recrossing the artful system of interwoven lines—as vigorous and active a spider as ever dangled from an old ceiling. Giovanni bent towards the insect, and emitted a deep, long breath. The spider suddenly ceased its toil; the web vibrated with a tremor originating in the body of the small artisan. Again Giovanni sent forth a breath, deeper, longer, and imbued with a venomous feeling out of his heart: he knew not whether he were wicked, or only desperate. The spider made a convulsive gripe with his limbs and hung dead across the window.

"Accursed! Accursed!" muttered Giovanni, addressing himself. "Hast thou grown so poisonous that this deadly insect perishes by thy breath?"

At that moment a rich, sweet voice came floating up from the garden

"Giovanni! Giovanni! It is past the hour! Why tarriest thou? Come down!"

"Yes," muttered Giovanni again. "She is the only being whom my breath may not slay! Would that it might!"

He rushed down, and in an instant was standing before the bright and loving eyes of Beatrice. A moment ago his wrath and despair had been so fierce that he could have desired nothing so much as to wither her by a glance; but with her actual presence there came influences which had too real an existence to be at once shaken off: recollections of the delicate and benign power of her feminine nature, which had so often enveloped him in a religious calm; recollections of many a holy and passionate outgush of her heart, when the pure fountain had been unsealed from its depths and made visible in its transparency to his mental eye; recollections which, had Giovanni known how to estimate them, would have assured him that all this ugly mystery was but an earthly illusion, and that, whatever mist of evil might seem to have gathered over her, the real Beatrice was a heavenly angel. Incapable as he was of such high faith, still her presence had not utterly lost its magic. Giovanni's rage was quelled into an aspect of sullen insensibility. Beatrice, with a quick spiritual sense, immediately felt that there was a gulf of blackness between them which neither he nor she could pass. They walked on together, sad and silent, and came thus to the marble fountain and to its pool of water on the ground, in the midst of which grew the shrub that bore gem-like blossoms. Giovanni was affrighted at the eager enjoyment—the appetite, as it were—with which he found himself inhaling the fragrance of the flowers.

"Beatrice," asked he, abruptly, "whence came this shrub?"

"My father created it," answered she, with simplicity.

"Created it! Created it!" repeated Giovanni. "What mean you, Beatrice?"

"He is a man fearfully acquainted with the secrets of Nature," replied Beatrice; "and, at the hour when I first drew breath, this plant sprang from the soil, the offspring of his science, of his intellect, while I was but his earthly child. Approach it not!" continued she, observing with terror that Giovanni was drawing nearer to the shrub. "It has qualities that you little dream of. But I, dearest Giovanni—I grew up and blossomed with the plant and was nourished with its breath. It was my sister, and I loved it with a human affection; for, alas!—hast thou not suspected it?—there was an awful doom."

Here Giovanni frowned so darkly upon her that Beatrice paused and trembled. But her faith in his tenderness reassured her, and made her blush that she had doubted for an instant.

"There was an awful doom," she continued, "the effect of my father's fatal love of science, which estranged me from all society of my kind. Until Heaven sent thee, dearest Giovanni, oh, how lonely was thy poor Beatrice!"

"Was it a hard doom?" asked Giovanni, fixing his eyes upon her.

"Only of late have I known how hard it was," answered she, tenderly. "Oh, yes; but my heart was torpid, and therefore quiet."

Giovanni's rage broke forth from his sullen gloom like a lightning flash out of a dark cloud.

"Accursed one!" cried he, with venomous scorn and anger. "And, finding thy solitude wearisome, thou hast severed me likewise from all the warmth of life and enticed me into thy region of unspeakable horror!"

"Giovanni!" exclaimed Beatrice, turning her large bright eyes upon his face. The force of his words had not found its way into her mind; she was merely thunderstruck.

"Yes, poisonous thing!" repeated Giovanni, beside himself with passion. "Thou hast done it! Thou hast blasted me! Thou hast filled my veins with poison! Thou hast made me as hateful, as ugly, as loathsome and deadly a creature as thyself—a world's wonder of hideous monstrosity! Now, if our breath be happily as fatal to ourselves as to all others, let us join our lips in one kiss of unutterable hatred, and so die!"

"What has befallen me?" murmured Beatrice, with a low moan out of her heart. "Holy Virgin, pity me, a poor heart-broken child!"

"Thou—dost thou pray?" cried Giovanni, still with the same fiendish scorn. "Thy very prayers, as they come from thy lips, taint the atmosphere with death. Yes, yes; let us pray! Let us to church and dip our fingers in the holy water at the portal! They that come after us will perish as by a pestilence! Let us sign crosses in the air! It will be scattering curses abroad in the likeness of holy symbols!"

"Giovanni," said Beatrice, calmly, for her grief was beyond passion, "why dost thou join thyself with me thus in those terrible words? I, it is true, am the horrible thing thou namest me. But thou—what hast thou to do, save with one other shudder at my hideous misery to go forth out of the garden and mingle with thy race, and forget there ever crawled on earth such a monster as poor Beatrice?"

"Dost thou pretend ignorance?" asked Giovanni, scowling upon her. "Behold! this power have I gained from the pure daughter of Rappaccini."

There was a swarm of summer insects flitting through the air in search of the food promised by the flower odors of the fatal garden. They circled round Giovanni's head, and were evidently attracted towards him by the same influence which had drawn them for an instant within the sphere of several of the shrubs. He sent forth a breath among them, and smiled bitterly at Beatrice as at least a score of the insects fell dead upon the ground.

"I see it! I see it!" shrieked Beatrice. "It is my father's fatal science! No, no, Giovanni; it was not I! Never! never! I dreamed only to love thee and be with thee a little time, and so to let thee pass away, leaving but thine image in mine heart; for, Giovanni, believe it, though my body be nourished with poison, my spirit is God's creature, and craves love as its daily food. But my father—he has united us in this fearful sympathy. Yes; spurn me, tread upon me, kill me! Oh, what is death after such words as thine? But it was not I. Not for a world of bliss would I have done it."

Giovanni's passion had exhausted itself in its outburst from his lips. There now came across him a sense, mournful, and not without tenderness, of the intimate and peculiar relationship between Beatrice and himself. They stood, as it were, in an utter solitude, which would be made none the less solitary by the densest throng of human life. Ought not, then, the desert of humanity around them to press this insulated pair closer together? If they should be cruel to one another, who was there to be kind to them? Besides, thought Giovanni, might there not still be a hope of his returning within the limits of ordinary nature, and leading Beatrice, the redeemed Beatrice, by the hand? O, weak, and selfish, and unworthy spirit, that could dream of an earthly union and earthly happiness as possible, after such deep love had been so bitterly wronged as was Beatrice's love by Giovanni's blighting words! No, no; there could be no such hope. She must pass heavily, with that broken heart, across the borders of Time—she must bathe her hurts in some fount of paradise, and forget her grief in the light of immortality, and THERE be well.

But Giovanni did not know it.

"Dear Beatrice," said he, approaching her, while she shrank away as always at his approach, but now with a different impulse, "dearest Beatrice, our fate is not yet so desperate. Behold! There is a medicine, potent, as a wise physician has assured me, and almost divine in its efficacy. It is composed of ingredients the most opposite to those by which thy awful father has brought this calamity upon thee and me. It is distilled of blessed herbs. Shall we not quaff it together, and thus be purified from evil?"

"Give it me!" said Beatrice, extending her hand to receive the little silver vial which Giovanni took from his bosom. She added, with a peculiar emphasis, "I will drink; but do thou await the result."

She put Baglioni's antidote to her lips; and, at the same moment, the figure of Rappaccini emerged from the portal and came slowly towards the marble fountain. As he drew near, the pale man of science seemed to gaze with a triumphant expression at the beautiful youth and maiden, as might an artist who should spend his life in achieving a picture or a group of statuary and finally be satisfied with his success. He paused; his bent form grew erect with conscious power; he spread out his hands over them in the attitude of a father imploring a blessing upon his children; but those were the same hands that had thrown poison into the stream of their lives. Giovanni trembled. Beatrice shuddered nervously, and pressed her hand upon her heart.

"My daughter," said Rappaccini, "thou art no longer lonely in the world. Pluck one of those precious gems from thy sister shrub and bid thy bridegroom wear it in his bosom. It will not harm him now. My science and the sympathy between thee and him have so wrought within his system that he now stands apart from common men, as thou dost, daughter of my pride and triumph, from ordinary women. Pass on, then, through the world, most dear to one another and dreadful to all besides!"

"My father," said Beatrice, feebly—and still as she spoke she kept her hand upon her heart—"wherefore didst thou inflict this miserable doom upon thy child?"

"Miserable!" exclaimed Rappaccini. "What mean you, foolish girl? Dost thou deem it misery to be endowed with marvelous gifts against which no power nor strength could avail an enemy—misery, to be able to quell the mightiest with a breath—misery, to be as terrible as thou art beautiful? Wouldst thou, then, have preferred the condition of a weak woman, exposed to all evil and capable of none?"

"I would fain have been loved, not feared," murmured Beatrice, sinking down upon the ground. "But now it matters not. I am going, father, where the evil which thou hast striven to mingle with my being will pass away like a dream—like the fragrance of these poisonous flowers, which will no longer taint my breath among the flowers of Eden. Farewell, Giovanni! Thy words of hatred are like lead within my heart; but they, too, will fall away as I ascend. Oh, was there not, from the first, more poison in thy nature than in mine?"

To Beatrice—so radically had her earthly part been wrought upon by Rappaccini's skill—as poison had been life, so the powerful antidote was death; and thus the poor victim of man's ingenuity and of thwarted nature, and of the fatality that attends all such efforts of perverted wisdom, perished there, at the feet of her father and Giovanni. Just at that moment Professor Pietro Baglioni looked forth from the window, and called loudly, in a tone of triumph mixed with horror, to the thunderstricken man of science, "Rappaccini! Rappaccini! And is THIS the upshot of your experiment!"

Young Goodman Brown (1835)

by Nathaniel Hawthorne

Young Goodman Brown came forth at sunset into the street of Salem village; but put his head back, after crossing the threshold, to exchange a parting kiss with his young wife. And Faith, as the wife was aptly named, thrust her own pretty head into the street, letting the wind play with the pink ribbons of her cap, while she called to Goodman Brown.

"Dearest heart," whispered she, softly and rather sadly, when her lips were close to his ear, "prithee put off your journey until sunrise and sleep in your own bed to-night. A lone woman is troubled with such dreams and such thoughts, that she's afeard of herself sometimes. Pray tarry with me this night, dear husband, of all nights in the year!"

"My love and my Faith," replied young Goodman Brown, "of all nights in the year, this one night must I tarry away from thee. My journey, as thou callest it, forth and back again, must needs be done 'twixt now and sunrise. What, my sweet, pretty wife, dost thou doubt me already, and we but three months married!"

"Then God bless you!" said Faith with the pink ribbons, "and may you find all well, when you come back."

"Amen!" cried Goodman Brown. "Say thy prayers, dear Faith, and go to bed at dusk, and no harm will come to thee."

So they parted; and the young man pursued his way until, being about to turn the corner by the meeting-house, he looked back and saw the head of Faith still peeping after him, with a melancholy air, in spite of her pink ribbons.

"Poor little Faith!" thought he, for his heart smote him. "What a wretch am I, to leave her on such an errand! She talks of dreams, too. Methought, as she spoke, there was trouble in her face, as if a dream had warned her what work is to be done tonight. But no, no! 'twould kill her to think it. Well, she's a blessed angel on earth; and after this one night, I'll cling to her skirts and follow her to Heaven."

With this excellent resolve for the future, Goodman Brown felt himself justified in making more haste on his present evil purpose. He had taken a dreary road, darkened by all the gloomiest trees of the forest, which barely stood aside to let the narrow path creep through, and closed immediately behind. It was all as lonely as could be; and there is this peculiarity in such a solitude, that the traveller knows not who may be concealed by the innumerable trunks and the thick boughs overhead; so that with lonely footsteps he may yet be passing through an unseen multitude.

"There may be a devilish Indian behind every tree," said Goodman Brown to himself; and he glanced fearfully behind him, as he added, "What if the devil himself should be at my very elbow!"

His head being turned back, he passed a crook of the road, and, looking forward again, beheld the figure of a man, in grave and decent attire, seated at the foot of an old tree. He arose at Goodman Brown's approach, and walked onward, side by side with him.

"You are late, Goodman Brown," said he. "The clock of the Old South was striking as I came through Boston; and that is full fifteen minutes agone."

"Faith kept me back awhile," replied the young man, with a tremor in his voice, caused by the sudden appearance of his companion, though not wholly unexpected.

It was now deep dusk in the forest, and deepest in that part of it where these two were journeying. As nearly as could be discerned, the second traveller was about fifty years old, apparently in the same rank of life as Goodman Brown, and bearing a considerable resemblance to him, though perhaps more in expression than features. Still they might have been taken for father and son. And yet, though the elder person was as simply clad as the younger and as simple in manner too, he had an indescribable air of one who knew the world, and would not have felt abashed at the governor's dinner-table, or in King William's court, were it possible that his affairs should call him thither. But the only thing about him that could be fixed upon as remarkable was his staff, which bore the likeness of a great black snake, so curiously wrought, that it might almost be seen to twist and wriggle itself like a living serpent. This, of course, must have been an ocular deception, assisted by the uncertain light.

"Come, Goodman Brown," cried his fellow-traveller, "this is a dull pace for the beginning of a journey. Take my staff, if you are so soon weary."

"Friend," said the other, exchanging his slow pace for a full stop, "having kept covenant by meeting thee here, it is my purpose now to return whence I came. I have scruples, touching the matter thou wot'st of."

"Sayest thou so?" replied he of the serpent, smiling apart. "Let us walk on, nevertheless, reasoning as we go, and if I convince thee not, thou shalt turn back. We are but a little way in the forest yet."

"Too far, too far!" exclaimed the goodman, unconsciously resuming his walk. "My father never went into the woods on such an errand, nor his father before him. We have been a race of honest men and good Christians, since the days of the martyrs; and shall I be the first of the name of Brown that ever took this path and kept—"

"Such company, thou wouldst say," observed the elder person, interrupting his pause. "Well said, Goodman Brown! I have been as well acquainted with your family as ever a one among the Puritans; and that's no trifle to say. I helped your grandfather, the constable, when he lashed the Quaker woman so smartly through the streets of Salem. And it was I that brought your father a pitch-pine knot, kindled at my own hearth, to set fire to an Indian village, in King Philip's war. They were my good friends, both; and many a pleasant walk have we had along this path, and returned merrily after midnight. I would fain be friends with you, for their sake."

"If it be as thou sayest," replied Goodman Brown, "I marvel they never spoke of these matters; or, verily, I marvel not, seeing that the least rumor of the sort would have driven them from New England. We are a people of prayer, and good works to boot, and abide no such wickedness."

"Wickedness or not," said the traveller with twisted staff, "I have a very general acquaintance here in New England. The deacons of many a church have drunk the communion wine with me; the selectmen of divers towns make me their chairman; and a majority of the Great and General Court are firm supporters of my interest. The governor and I, too—But these are state secrets."

"Can this be so!" cried Goodman Brown, with a stare of amazement at his undisturbed companion. "Howbeit, I have nothing to do with the governor and council; they have their own ways, and are no rule for a simple husbandman like me. But, were I to go on with thee, how should I meet the eye of that good old man, our minister, at Salem village? Oh, his voice would make me tremble, both Sabbath-day and lecture-day!"

Thus far, the elder traveller had listened with due gravity, but now burst into a fit of irrepressible mirth, shaking himself so violently that his snake-like staff actually seemed to wriggle in sympathy.

"Ha! ha! ha!" shouted he again and again; then composing himself, "Well, go on, Goodman Brown, go on; but, prithee, don't kill me with laughing!"

"Well, then, to end the matter at once," said Goodman Brown, considerably nettled, "there is my wife, Faith. It would break her dear little heart; and I'd rather break my own!"

"Nay, if that be the case," answered the other, "e'en go thy ways, Goodman Brown. I would not, for twenty old women like the one hobbling before us, that Faith should come to any harm."

As he spoke, he pointed his staff at a female figure on the path, in whom Goodman Brown recognized a very pious and exemplary dame, who had taught him his catechism in youth, and was still his moral and spiritual adviser, jointly with the minister and Deacon Gookin.

"A marvel, truly, that Goody Cloyse should be so far in the wilderness, at nightfall," said he. "But, with your leave, friend, I shall take a cut through the woods, until we have left this Christian woman behind. Being a stranger to you, she might ask whom I was consorting with, and whither I was going."

"Be it so," said his fellow-traveller. "Betake you to the woods, and let me keep the path."

Accordingly the young man turned aside, but took care to watch his companion, who advanced softly along the road until he had come within a staff's length of the old dame. She, meanwhile, was making the best of her way, with singular speed for so aged a woman, and mumbling some indistinct words— a prayer, doubtless—as she went. The traveller put forth his staff and touched her withered neck with what seemed the serpent's tail.

"The devil!" screamed the pious old lady.

"Then Goody Cloyse knows her old friend?" observed the traveller, confronting her, and leaning on his writhing stick.

"Ah, forsooth, and is it your worship, indeed?" cried the good dame. "Yea, truly is it, and in the very image of my old gossip, Goodman Brown, the grandfather of the silly fellow that now is. But, would your worship believe it?—my broomstick hath strangely disappeared, stolen, as I suspect, by that unhanged witch, Goody Cory, and that, too, when I was all anointed with the juice of smallage and cinquefoil and wolf's-bane—"

"Mingled with fine wheat and the fat of a new-born babe," said the shape of old Goodman Brown.

"Ah, your worship knows the recipe," cried the old lady, cackling aloud. "So, as I was saying, being all ready for the meeting, and no horse to ride on, I made up my mind to foot it; for they tell me there is a nice young man to be taken into communion tonight. But now your good worship will lend me your arm, and we shall be there in a twinkling."

"That can hardly be," answered her friend. "I will not spare you my arm, Goody Cloyse, but here is my staff, if you will."

So saying, he threw it down at her feet, where, perhaps, it assumed life, being one of the rods which its owner had formerly lent to the Egyptian magi. Of this fact, however, Goodman Brown could not take cognizance. He had cast up his eyes in astonishment, and looking down again, beheld neither Goody Cloyse nor the serpentine staff, but his fellow-traveller alone, who waited for him as calmly as if nothing had happened.

"That old woman taught me my catechism!" said the young man; and there was a world of meaning in this simple comment.

They continued to walk onward, while the elder traveller exhorted his companion to make good speed and persevere in the path, discoursing so aptly that his arguments seemed rather to spring up in the bosom of his auditor, than to be suggested by himself.

As they went, he plucked a branch of maple to serve for a walking-stick, and began to strip it of the twigs and little boughs, which were wet with evening dew. The moment his fingers touched them they became strangely withered and dried up as with a week's sunshine.

Thus the pair proceeded, at a good free pace, until suddenly, in a gloomy hollow of the road, Goodman Brown sat himself down on the stump of a tree and refused to go any farther.

"Friend," said he, stubbornly, "my mind is made up. Not another step will I budge on this errand. What if a wretched old woman do choose to go to the devil, when I thought she was going to heaven; is that any reason why I should quit my dear Faith and go after her?"

"You will think better of this by and by," said his acquaintance, composedly. "Sit here and rest yourself a while; and when you feel like moving again, there is my staff to help you along."

Without more words, he threw his companion the maple stick, and was as speedily out of sight as if he had vanished into the deepening gloom. The young man sat a few moments by the roadside, applauding himself greatly, and thinking with how clear a conscience he should meet the minister in his morning walk, nor shrink from the eye of good old Deacon Gookin. And what calm sleep would be his that very night, which was to have been spent so wickedly, but purely and sweetly now, in the arms of Faith! Amidst these pleasant and praiseworthy meditations, Goodman Brown heard the tramp of horses along the road, and deemed it advisable to conceal himself within the verge of the forest, conscious of the guilty purpose that had brought him thither, though now so happily turned from it.

On came the hoof-tramps and the voices of the riders, two grave old voices, conversing soberly as they drew near. These mingled sounds appeared to pass along the road, within a few yards of the young man's hiding-place; but owing doubtless to the depth of the gloom at that particular spot, neither the travellers nor their steeds were visible. Though their figures brushed the small boughs by the wayside, it could not be seen that they intercepted, even for a moment, the faint gleam from the strip of bright sky athwart which they must have passed. Goodman Brown alternately crouched and stood on tiptoe, pulling aside the branches and thrusting forth his head as far as he durst without discerning so much as a shadow. It vexed him the more, because he could have sworn, were such a thing possible, that he recognized the voices of the minister and Deacon Gookin, jogging along quietly, as they were wont to do, when bound to some ordination or ecclesiastical council. While yet within hearing, one of the riders stopped to pluck a switch.

"Of the two, reverend sir," said the voice like the deacon's, "I had rather miss an ordination dinner than to-night's meeting. They tell me that some of our community are to be here from Falmouth and beyond, and others from Connecticut and Rhode Island, besides several of the Indian powwows, who, after their fashion, know almost as much deviltry as the best of us. Moreover, there is a goodly young woman to be taken into communion."

"Mighty well, Deacon Gookin!" replied the solemn old tones of the minister. "Spur up, or we shall be late. Nothing can be done, you know, until I get on the ground."

The hoofs clattered again; and the voices, talking so strangely in the empty air, passed on through the forest, where no church had ever been gathered, or solitary Christian prayed. Whither, then, could these holy men be journeying, so deep into the heathen wilderness? Young Goodman Brown caught hold of a tree for support, being ready to sink down on the ground, faint and over-burthened with the heavy sickness of his heart. He looked up to the sky, doubting whether there really was a heaven above him. Yet there was the blue arch, and the stars brightening in it.

"With Heaven above and Faith below, I will yet stand firm against the devil!" cried Goodman Brown.

While he still gazed upward, into the deep arch of the firmament and had lifted his hands to pray, a cloud, though no wind was stirring, hurried across the zenith and hid the brightening stars. The blue sky was still visible except directly overhead, where this black mass of cloud was sweeping swiftly northward. Aloft in the air, as if from the depths of the cloud, came a confused and doubtful sound of voices. Once the listener fancied that he could distinguish the accents of town's people of his own, men and women, both pious and ungodly, many of whom he had met at the communion table, and had seen others rioting at the tavern. The next moment, so indistinct were the sounds, he doubted whether he had heard aught but the murmur of the old forest, whispering without a wind. Then came a stronger swell of those familiar tones, heard daily in the sunshine at Salem village, but never, until now, from a cloud at night. There was one voice, of a young woman, uttering lamentations, yet with an uncertain sorrow, and entreating for some favor, which, perhaps, it would grieve her to obtain; and all the unseen multitude, both saints and sinners, seemed to encourage her onward.

"Faith!" shouted Goodman Brown, in a voice of agony and desperation; and the echoes of the forest mocked him, crying, "Faith! Faith!" as if bewildered wretches were seeking her all through the wilderness.

The cry of grief, rage, and terror was yet piercing the night, when the unhappy husband held his breath for a response. There was a scream, drowned immediately in a louder murmur of voices fading into far-off laughter, as the dark cloud swept away, leaving the clear and silent sky above Goodman Brown. But something fluttered lightly down through the air and caught on the branch of a tree. The young man seized it, and beheld a pink ribbon.

"My Faith is gone!" cried he, after one stupefied moment. "There is no good on earth; and sin is but a name. Come, devil; for to thee is this world given."

And, maddened with despair, so that he laughed loud and long, did Goodman Brown grasp his staff and set forth again, at such a rate that he seemed to fly along the forest path, rather than to walk or run. The road grew wilder and drearier and more faintly traced, and vanished at length, leaving him in the heart of the dark wilderness, still rushing onward with the instinct that guides mortal man to evil. The whole forest was peopled with frightful sounds—the creaking of the trees, the howling of wild beasts, and the yell of Indians; while sometimes the wind tolled like a distant church bell, and sometimes gave a broad roar around the traveller, as if all Nature were laughing him to scorn. But he was himself the chief horror of the scene, and shrank not from its other horrors.

"Ha! ha! ha!" roared Goodman Brown, when the wind laughed at him. "Let us hear which will laugh loudest! Think not to frighten me with your deviltry. Come witch, come wizard, come Indian powwow, come devil himself, and here comes Goodman Brown. You may as well fear him as he fear you!"

In truth, all through the haunted forest there could be nothing more frightful than the figure of Goodman Brown. On he flew among the black pines, brandishing his staff with frenzied gestures, now giving vent to an inspiration of horrid blasphemy, and now shouting forth such laughter as set all the echoes of the forest laughing like demons around him. The fiend in his own shape is less hideous than when he rages in the breast of man. Thus sped the demoniac on his course, until, quivering among the trees, he saw a red light before him, as when the felled trunks and branches of a clearing have been set on fire, and throw up their lurid blaze against the sky, at the hour of midnight. He paused, in a lull of the tempest that had driven him onward, and heard the swell of what seemed a hymn, rolling solemnly from a distance with the weight of many voices. He knew the tune; it was a familiar one in the choir of the village meeting-house. The verse died heavily away, and was lengthened by a chorus, not of human voices, but of all the sounds of the benighted wilderness pealing in awful harmony together. Goodman Brown cried out; and his cry was lost to his own ear, by its unison with the cry of the desert.

In the interval of silence he stole forward until the light glared full upon his eyes. At one extremity of an open space, hemmed in by the dark wall of the forest, arose a rock, bearing some rude, natural resemblance either to an altar or a pulpit, and surrounded by four blazing pines, their tops aflame, their stems untouched, like candles at an evening meeting. The mass of foliage that had overgrown the summit of the rock, was all on fire, blazing high into the night and fitfully illuminating the whole field. Each pendent twig and leafy festoon was in a blaze. As the red light arose and fell, a numerous congregation alternately shone forth, then disappeared in shadow, and again grew, as it were, out of the darkness, peopling the heart of the solitary woods at once.

"A grave and dark-clad company!" quoth Goodman Brown.

In truth, they were such. Among them, quivering to-and-fro between gloom and splendor, appeared faces that would be seen next day at the council-board of the province, and others which, Sabbath after Sabbath, looked devoutly heavenward, and benignantly over the crowded pews, from the holiest pulpits in the land. Some affirm that the lady of the governor was there. At least there were high dames well known to her, and wives of honored husbands, and widows, a great multitude, and ancient maidens, all of excellent repute, and fair young girls, who trembled lest their mothers should espy them. Either the sudden gleams of light flashing over the obscure field bedazzled Goodman Brown, or he recognized a score of the church members of Salem village famous for their especial sanctity. Good old Deacon Gookin had arrived, and waited at the skirts of that venerable saint, his reverend pastor. But, irreverently consorting with these grave, reputable, and pious people, these elders of the church, these chaste dames and dewy virgins, there were men of dissolute lives and women of spotted fame, wretches given over to all mean and filthy vice, and suspected even of horrid crimes. It was strange to see that the good shrank not from the wicked, nor were the sinners abashed by the saints. Scattered also among their pale-faced enemies were the Indian priests, or pow-wows, who had often scared their native forest with more hideous incantations than any known to English witchcraft.

"But, where is Faith?" thought Goodman Brown, and, as hope came into his heart, he trembled.

Another verse of the hymn arose, a slow and mournful strain, such as the pious love, but joined to words which expressed all that our nature can conceive of sin, and darkly hinted at far more. Unfathomable to mere mortals is the lore of fiends. Verse after verse was sung; and still the chorus of the desert swelled between like the deepest tone of a mighty organ; and, with the final peal of that dreadful anthem there came a sound, as if the roaring wind, the rushing streams, the howling beasts, and every other voice of the unconverted wilderness were mingling and according with the voice of guilty man in homage to the prince of all. The four blazing pines threw up a loftier flame, and obscurely discovered shapes and visages of horror on the smoke wreaths above the impious assembly. At the same moment the fire on the rock shot redly forth and formed a glowing arch above its base, where now appeared a figure. With reverence be it spoken, the figure bore no slight similitude, both in garb and manner, to some grave divine of the New England churches.

"Bring forth the converts!" cried a voice, that echoed through the field and rolled into the forest.

At the word, Goodman Brown stepped forth from the shadow of the trees and approached the congregation, with whom he felt a loathful brotherhood by the sympathy of all that was wicked in his heart. He could have well nigh sworn that the shape of his own dead father beckoned him to advance, looking downward from a smoke wreath, while a woman, with dim features of despair, threw out her hand to warn him back. Was it his mother? But he had no power to retreat one step, nor to resist, even in thought, when the minister and good old Deacon Gookin seized his arms and led him to the blazing rock. Thither came also the slender form of a veiled female, led between Goody Cloyse, that pious teacher of the catechism, and Martha Carrier, who had received the devil's promise to be queen of hell. A rampant hag was she. And there stood the proselytes beneath the canopy of fire.

"Welcome, my children," said the dark figure, "to the communion of your race! Ye have found, thus young, your nature and your destiny. My children, look behind you!"

They turned; and flashing forth, as it were, in a sheet of flame, the fiend-worshippers were seen; the smile of welcome gleamed darkly on every visage.

"There," resumed the sable form, "are all whom ye have reverenced from youth. Ye deemed them holier than yourselves, and shrank from your own sin, contrasting it with their lives of righteousness and prayerful aspirations heavenward. Yet, here are they all, in my worshipping assembly. This night it shall be granted you to know their secret deeds; how hoary-bearded elders of the church have whispered wanton words to the young maids of their households; how many a woman, eager for widow's weeds, has given her husband a drink at bedtime and let him sleep his last sleep in her bosom; how beardless youths have made haste to inherit their father's wealth; and how fair damsels—blush not, sweet ones—have dug little graves in the garden, and bidden me, the sole guest, to an infant's funeral.

By the sympathy of your human hearts for sin, ye shall scent out all the places—whether in church, bed-chamber, street, field, or forest—where crime has been committed, and shall exult to behold the whole earth one stain of guilt, one mighty blood-spot. Far more than this. It shall be yours to penetrate, in every bosom, the deep mystery of sin, the fountain of all wicked arts, and which inexhaustibly supplies more evil impulses than human power—than my power at its utmost—can make manifest in deeds. And now, my children, look upon each other."

They did so; and, by the blaze of the hell-kindled torches, the wretched man beheld his Faith, and the wife her husband, trembling before that unhallowed altar.

"Lo! there ye stand, my children," said the figure, in a deep and solemn tone, almost sad, with its despairing awfulness, as if his once angelic nature could yet mourn for our miserable race. "Depending upon one another's hearts, ye had still hoped that virtue were not all a dream. Now are ye undeceived. Evil is the nature of mankind. Evil must be your only happiness. Welcome, again, my children, to the communion of your race!"

"Welcome!" repeated the fiend-worshippers, in one cry of despair and triumph.

And there they stood, the only pair, as it seemed, who were yet hesitating on the verge of wickedness in this dark world. A basin was hollowed, naturally, in the rock. Did it contain water, reddened by the lurid light? or was it blood? or, perchance, a liquid flame? Herein did the shape of evil dip his hand, and prepare to lay the mark of baptism upon their foreheads, that they might be partakers of the mystery of sin, more conscious of the secret guilt of others, both in deed and thought, than they could now be of their own. The husband cast one look at his pale wife, and Faith at him. What polluted wretches would the next glance show them to each other, shuddering alike at what they disclosed and what they saw!

"Faith! Faith!" cried the husband. "Look up to Heaven, and resist the Wicked One!"

Whether Faith obeyed, he knew not. Hardly had he spoken, when he found himself amid calm night and solitude, listening to a roar of the wind which died heavily away through the forest. He staggered against the rock, and felt it chill and damp; while a hanging twig, that had been all on fire, besprinkled his cheek with the coldest dew.

The next morning young Goodman Brown came slowly into the street of Salem village, staring around him like a bewildered man. The good old minister was taking a walk along the grave-yard to get an appetite for breakfast and meditate his sermon, and bestowed a blessing, as he passed, on Goodman Brown. He shrank from the venerable saint as if to avoid an anathema. Old Deacon Gookin was at domestic worship, and the holy words of his prayer were heard through the open window. "What God doth the wizard pray to?" quoth Goodman Brown. Goody Cloyse, that excellent old Christian, stood in the early sunshine at her own lattice, catechising a little girl who had brought her a pint of morning's milk. Goodman Brown snatched away the child as from the grasp of the fiend himself. Turning the corner by the meeting house, he spied the head of Faith, with the pink ribbons, gazing anxiously forth, and bursting into such joy at the sight of him that she skipped along the street and almost kissed her husband before the whole village. But Goodman Brown looked sternly and sadly into her face, and passed on without a greeting.

Had Goodman Brown fallen asleep in the forest, and only dreamed a wild dream of a witch-meeting?

Be it so, if you will; but, alas! it was a dream of evil omen for young Goodman Brown. A stern, a sad, a darkly meditative, a distrustful, if not a desperate, man did he become, from the night of that fearful dream. On the Sabbath day, when the congregation were singing a holy psalm, he could not listen, because an anthem of sin rushed loudly upon his ear and drowned all the blessed strain. When the minister spoke from the pulpit, with power and fervid eloquence and with his hand on the open Bible, of the sacred truths of our religion, and of saint-like lives and triumphant deaths, and of future bliss or misery unutterable, then did Goodman Brown turn pale, dreading lest the roof should thunder down upon the gray blasphemer and his hearers. Often, awaking suddenly at midnight, he shrank from the bosom of Faith, and at morning or eventide, when the family knelt down in prayer, he scowled, and muttered to himself, and gazed sternly at his wife, and turned away. And when he had lived long, and was borne to his grave, a hoary corpse, followed by Faith, an aged woman, and children and grandchildren, a goodly procession, besides neighbors not a few, they carved no hopeful verse upon his tombstone; for his dying hour was gloom.

The Road Not Taken (1915)

by Robert Frost

Two roads diverged in a yellow wood,
And sorry I could not travel both
And be one traveler, long I stood
And looked down one as far as I could
To where it bent in the undergrowth;   5

Then took the other, as just as fair,
And having perhaps the better claim,
Because it was grassy and wanted wear;
Though as for that the passing there
Had worn them really about the same,   10

And both that morning equally lay
In leaves no step had trodden black.
Oh, I kept the first for another day!
Yet knowing how way leads on to way,
I doubted if I should ever come back.   15

I shall be telling this with a sigh
Somewhere ages and ages hence:
Two roads diverged in a wood, and I—
I took the one less traveled by,
And that has made all the difference.   20

Ligeia

by Edgar Allan Poe

And the will therein lieth, which dieth not. Who knoweth the mysteries of the will, with its vigor? For God is but a great will pervading all things by nature of its intentness. Man doth not yield himself to the angels, nor unto death utterly, save only through the weakness of his feeble will.

Joseph Glanvill

I cannot, for my soul, remember how, when, or even precisely where, I first became acquainted with the lady Ligeia. Long years have since elapsed, and my memory is feeble through much suffering. Or, perhaps, I cannot *now* bring these points to mind, because, in truth, the character of my beloved, her rare learning, her singular yet placid cast of beauty, and the thrilling and enthralling eloquence of her low musical language, made their way into my heart by paces so steadily and stealthily progressive that they have been unnoticed and unknown. Yet I believe that I met her first and most frequently in some large, old, decaying city near the Rhine. Of her family—I have surely heard her speak. That it is of a remotely ancient date cannot be doubted. Ligeia! Ligeia! Buried in studies of a nature more than all else adapted to deaden impressions of the outward world, it is by that sweet word alone—by Ligeia—that I bring before mine eyes in fancy the image of her who is no more. And now, while I write, a recollection flashes upon me that I have *never known* the paternal name of her who was my friend and my betrothed, and who became the partner of my studies, and finally the wife of my bosom. Was it a playful charge on the part of my Ligeia? or was it a test of my strength of affection, that I should institute no inquiries upon this point? or was it rather a caprice of my own—a wildly romantic offering on the shrine of the most passionate devotion? I but indistinctly recall the fact itself—what wonder that I have utterly forgotten the circumstances which originated or attended it? And, indeed, if ever that spirit which is entitled *Romance*—if ever she, the wan and the misty-winged *Ashtophet* of idolatrous Egypt, presided, as they tell, over marriages ill-omened, then most surely she presided over mine.

There is one dear topic, however, on which my memory fails me not. It is the *person* of Ligeia. In stature she was tall, somewhat slender, and, in her latter days, even emaciated. I would in vain attempt to portray the majesty, the quiet ease of her demeanor, or the incomprehensible lightness and elasticity of her footfall. She came and departed as a shadow. I was never made aware of her entrance into my closed study save by the dear music of her low sweet voice, as she placed her marble hand upon my shoulder. In beauty of face no maiden ever equalled her. It was the radiance of an opium-dream—an airy and spirit-lifting vision more wildly divine than the fantasies which hovered about the slumbering souls of the daughters of Delos. Yet her features were not of that regular mould which we have been falsely taught to worship in the classical labors of the heathen. "There is no exquisite beauty," says Bacon, Lord Verulam, speaking truly of all the forms and *genera* of beauty, "without some *strangeness* in the proportion." Yet, although I saw that the features of Ligeia were not of a classic regularity—although I perceived that her loveliness was indeed "exquisite," and felt that there was much of "strangeness" pervading it, yet I have tried in vain to detect the irregularity and to trace home my own perception of "the strange." I examined the contour of the lofty and pale forehead—it was faultless—how cold indeed that word when applied to a majesty so divine!—the skin rivalling the purest ivory, the commanding extent and repose, the gentle prominence of the regions above the temples; and then the raven-black, the glossy, the luxuriant and naturally curling tresses, setting forth the full force of the Homeric epithet, "hyacinthine!"

I looked at the delicate outlines of the nose—and nowhere but in the graceful medallions of the Hebrews had I beheld a similar perfection.

There were the same luxurious smoothness of surface, the same scarcely perceptible tendency to the aquiline, the same harmoniously curved nostrils speaking the free spirit. I regarded the sweet mouth. Here was indeed the triumph of all things heavenly—the magnificent turn of the short upper lip—the soft, voluptuous slumber of the under—the dimples which sported, and the color which spoke—the teeth glancing back, with a brilliancy almost startling, every ray of the holy light which fell upon them in her serene and placid, yet most exultingly radiant of all smiles. I scrutinized the formation of the chin—and here, too, I found the gentleness of breadth, the softness and the majesty, the fullness and the spirituality, of the Greek—the contour which the god Apollo revealed but in a dream, to Cleomenes, the son of the Athenian. And then I peered into the large eyes of Ligeia. For eyes we have no models in the remotely antique. It might have been, too, that in these eyes of my beloved lay the secret to which Lord Verulam alludes. They were, I must believe, far larger than the ordinary eyes of our own race. They were even fuller than the fullest of the gazelle eyes of the tribe of the valley of Nourjahad. Yet it was only at intervals—in moments of intense excitement—that this peculiarity became more than slightly noticeable in Ligeia. And at such moments was her beauty—in my heated fancy thus it appeared perhaps—the beauty of beings either above or apart from the earth—the beauty of the fabulous Houri of the Turk. The hue of the orbs was the most brilliant of black, and, far over them, hung jetty lashes of great length. The brows, slightly irregular in outline, had the same tint. The "strangeness," however, which I found in the eyes, was of a nature distinct from the formation, or the color, or the brilliancy of the features, and must, after all, be referred to the *expression*. Ah, word of no meaning! behind whose vast latitude of mere sound we intrench our ignorance of so much of the spiritual. The expression of the eyes of Ligeia! How for long hours have I pondered upon it! How have I, through the whole of a midsummer night, struggled to fathom it! What was it—that something more profound than the well of Democritus—which lay far within the pupils of my beloved?

What *was* it? I was possessed with a passion to discover. Those eyes! those large, those shining, those divine orbs! they became to me twin stars of Leda, and I to them devoutest of astrologers.

There is no point, among the many incomprehensible anomalies of the science of mind, more thrillingly exciting than the fact—never, I believe, noticed in the schools—that, in our endeavors to recall to memory something long forgotten, we often find ourselves *upon the very verge* of remembrance, without being able, in the end, to remember. And thus how frequently, in my intense scrutiny of Ligeia's eyes, have I felt approaching the full knowledge of their expression—felt it approaching—yet not quite be mine—and so at length entirely depart! And (strange, oh strangest mystery of all!) I found, in the commonest objects of the universe, a circle of analogies to that expression. I mean to say that, subsequently to the period when Ligeia's beauty passed into my spirit, there dwelling as in a shrine, I derived, from many existences in the material world, a sentiment such as I felt always aroused within me by her large and luminous orbs. Yet not the more could I define that sentiment, or analyze, or even steadily view it. I recognized it, let me repeat, sometimes in the survey of a rapidly-growing vine—in the contemplation of a moth, a butterfly, a chrysalis, a stream of running water. I have felt it in the ocean; in the falling of a meteor. I have felt it in the glances of unusually aged people. And there are one or two stars in heaven—(one especially, a star of the sixth magnitude, double and changeable, to be found near the large star in Lyra) in a telescopic scrutiny of which I have been made aware of the feeling. I have been filled with it by certain sounds from stringed instruments, and not unfrequently by passages from books. Among innumerable other instances, I well remember something in a volume of Joseph Glanvill, which (perhaps merely from its quaintness—who shall say?) never failed to inspire me with the sentiment;—"And the will therein lieth, which dieth not. Who knoweth the mysteries of the will, with its vigor? For God is but a great will pervading all things by nature of its intentness. Man doth not yield him to the angels, nor unto death utterly, save only through the weakness of his feeble will."

Length of years, and subsequent reflections, have enabled me to trace, indeed, some remote connection between this passage in the English moralist and a portion of the character of Ligeia. An *intensity* in thought, action, or speech, was possibly, in her, a result, or at least an index, of that gigantic volition which, during our long intercourse, failed to give other and more immediate evidence of its existence. Of all the women whom I have ever known, she, the outwardly calm, the ever-placid Ligeia, was the most violently a prey to the tumultuous vultures of stern passion. And of such passion I could form no estimate, save by the miraculous expansion of those eyes which at once so delighted and appalled me—by the almost magical melody, modulation, distinctness, and placidity of her very low voice—and by the fierce energy (rendered doubly effective by contrast with her manner of utterance) of the wild words which she habitually uttered.

I have spoken of the learning of Ligeia; it was immense—such as I have never known in woman. In the classical tongues was she deeply proficient, and as far as my own acquaintance extended in regard to the modern dialects of Europe, I have never known her at fault. Indeed upon any theme of the most admired, because simply the most abstruse of the boasted erudition of the academy, have I *ever* found Ligeia at fault? How singularly—how thrillingly, this one point in the nature of my wife has forced itself, at this late period only, upon my attention! I said her knowledge was such as I have never known in woman—but where breathes the man who has traversed, and successfully, *all* the wide areas of moral, physical, and mathematical science? I saw not then what I now clearly perceive, that the acquisitions of Ligeia were gigantic, were astounding; yet I was sufficiently aware of her infinite supremacy to resign myself, with a childlike confidence, to her guidance through the chaotic world of metaphysical investigation at which I was most busily occupied during the earlier years of our marriage. With how vast a triumph—with how vivid a delight—with how much of all that is ethereal in hope—did I *feel*, as she bent over me in studies but little sought—but less known—that delicious vista by slow degrees expanding before me, down whose long, gorgeous, and all untrodden path, I might at length pass onward to the goal of a wisdom too divinely precious not to be forbidden!

How poignant, then, must have been the grief with which, after some years, I beheld my well-grounded expectations take wings to themselves and fly away! Without Ligeia I was but as a child groping benighted. Her presence, her readings alone, rendered vividly luminous the many mysteries of the transcendentalism in which we were immersed. Wanting the radiant lustre of her eyes, letters, lambent and golden, grew duller than Saturnian lead. And now those eyes shone less and less frequently upon the pages over which I pored. Ligeia grew ill. The wild eyes blazed with a too— too glorious effulgence; the pale fingers became of the transparent waxen hue of the grave, and the blue veins upon the lofty forehead swelled and sank impetuously with the tides of the most gentle emotion. I saw that she must die—and I struggled desperately in spirit with the grim Azrael. And the struggles of the passionate wife were, to my astonishment, even more energetic than my own. There had been much in her stern nature to impress me with the belief that, to her, death would have come without its terrors;—but not so. Words are impotent to convey any just idea of the fierceness of resistance with which she wrestled with the Shadow. I groaned in anguish at the pitiable spectacle. I would have soothed—I would have reasoned; but, in the intensity of her wild desire for life,—for life—*but* for life—solace and reason were alike the uttermost of folly. Yet not until the last instance, amid the most convulsive writhings of her fierce spirit, was shaken the external placidity of her demeanor. Her voice grew more gentle—grew more low—yet I would not wish to dwell upon the wild meaning of the quietly uttered words. My brain reeled as I harkened entranced, to a melody more than mortal—to assumptions and aspirations which mortality had never before known.

That she loved me I should not have doubted; and I might have been easily aware that, in a bosom such as hers, love would have reigned no ordinary passion. But in death only, was I fully impressed with the strength of her affection. For long hours, detaining my hand, would she pour out before me the overflowing of a heart whose more than passionate devotion amounted to idolatry. How had I deserved to be so blessed by such confessions?—how had I deserved to be so cursed with the removal of my beloved in the hour of her making them? But upon this subject I cannot bear to dilate. Let me say only, that in Ligeia's more than womanly abandonment to a love, alas! all unmerited, all unworthily bestowed, I at length recognized the principle of her longing with so wildly earnest a desire for the life which was now fleeing so rapidly away. It is this wild longing—it is this eager vehemence of desire for life—*but for life*—that I have no power to portray—no utterance capable of expressing.

At high noon of the night in which she departed, beckoning me, peremptorily, to her side, she bade me repeat certain verses composed by herself not many days before. I obeyed her.—They were these:

Lo! 'tis a gala night
Within the lonesome latter years!
An angel throng, bewinged, bedight
In veils, and drowned in tears,
Sit in a theatre, to see   5
A play of hopes and fears,
While the orchestra breathes fitfully
The music of the spheres.

Mimes, in the form of God on high,
Mutter and mumble low,   10
And hither and thither fly—
Mere puppets they, who come and go
At bidding of vast formless things
That shift the scenery to and fro,
Flapping from out their Condor wings   15
Invisible Wo!

That motley drama!—oh, be sure
It shall not be forgot!
With its Phantom chased forever more,
By a crowd that seize it not,   20
Through a circle that ever returneth in
To the self-same spot,
And much of Madness and more of Sin

And Horror the soul of the plot.
But see, amid the mimic rout,   25
A crawling shape intrude!
A blood-red thing that writhes from out
The scenic solitude!
It writhes!—it writhes!—with mortal pangs
The mimes become its food,   30
And the seraphs sob at vermin fangs
In human gore imbued.

Out—out are the lights—out all!
And over each quivering form,
The curtain, a funeral pall,   35
Comes down with the rush of a storm,
And the angels, all pallid and wan,
Uprising, unveiling, affirm
That the play is the tragedy, "Man,"
And its hero the Conqueror Worm.   40

"O God!" half shrieked Ligeia, leaping to her feet and extending
her arms aloft with a spasmodic movement, as I made an end of those
lines—"O God! O Divine Father!—shall these things be undeviatingly
so?—shall this Conqueror be not once conquered? Are we not part and par-
cel in Thee? Who—who knoweth the mysteries of the will with its vigor?
Man doth not yield him to the angels, *nor unto death utterly*, save only
through the weakness of his feeble will."

And now, as if exhausted with emotion, she suffered her white arms
to fall, and returned solemnly to her bed of death. And as she breathed
her last sighs, there came mingled with them a low murmur from her lips.
I bent to them my ear and distinguished, again, the concluding words of the
passage in Glanvill—*"Man doth not yield him to the angels, nor unto death
utterly, save only through the weakness of his feeble will."*

She died;—and I, crushed into the very dust with sorrow, could no
longer endure the lonely desolation of my dwelling in the dim and decaying
city by the Rhine. I had no lack of what the world calls wealth. Ligeia
had brought me far more, very far more than ordinarily falls to the lot of
mortals. After a few months, therefore, of weary and aimless wandering,
I purchased, and put in some repair, an abbey, which I shall not name, in one
of the wildest and least frequented portions of fair England. The gloomy
and dreary grandeur of the building, the almost savage aspect of the
domain, the many melancholy and time-honored memories connected with
both, had much in unison with the feelings of utter abandonment which
had driven me into that remote and unsocial region of the country. Yet
although the external abbey, with its verdant decay hanging about it, suffered but little alteration, I gave way, with a child-like perversity, and
perchance with a faint hope of alleviating my sorrows, to a display of more
than regal magnificence within.—For such follies, even in childhood, I had
imbibed a taste, and now they came back to me as if in the dotage of grief.
Alas, I feel how much even of incipient madness might have been discovered in the gorgeous and fantastic draperies, in the solemn carvings
of Egypt, in the wild cornices and furniture, in the Bedlam patterns of the
carpets of tufted gold! I had become a bounden slave in the trammels of
opium, and my labors and my orders had taken a coloring from my dreams.
But these absurdities I must not pause to detail. Let me speak only of that
one chamber, ever accursed, whither in a moment of mental alienation, I led

from the altar as my bride—as the successor of the unforgotten Ligeia—the fair-haired and blue-eyed Lady Rowena Trevanion, of Tremaine.

There is no individual portion of the architecture and decoration of that bridal chamber which is not now visibly before me. Where were the souls of the haughty family of the bride, when, through thirst of gold, they permitted to pass the threshold of an apartment *so* bedecked, a maiden and a daughter so beloved? I have said that I minutely remember the details of the chamber—yet I am sadly forgetful on topics of deep moment—and here there was no system, no keeping, in the fantastic display, to take hold upon the memory. The room lay in a high turret of the castellated abbey, was pentagonal in shape, and of capacious size. Occupying the whole southern face of the pentagon was the sole window—an immense sheet of unbroken glass from Venice—a single pane, and tinted of a leaden hue, so that the rays of either the sun or moon, passing through it fell with a ghastly lustre on the objects within. Over the upper portion of this huge window, extended the trellice-work of an aged vine, which clambered up the massy walls of the turret. The ceiling, of gloomy-looking oak, was excessively lofty, vaulted, and elaborately fretted with the wildest and most grotesque specimens of a semi-Gothic, semi-Druidical device. From out the most central recess of this melancholy vaulting, depended, by a single chain of gold with a long link, a huge censer of the same metal, Saracenic in pattern, and with many perforations so contrived that there writhed in and out of them, as if endued with a serpent vitality, a continual succession of parti-colored fires. Some few ottomans and golden candelabra, of Eastern figure, were in various stations about—and there was the couch, too—the bridal couch—of an Indian model, and low, and sculptured of solid ebony, with a pall-like canopy above. In each of the angles of the chamber stood on end a gigantic sarcophagus of black granite, from the tombs of the kings over against Luxor, with their aged lids full of immemorial sculpture. But in the draping of the apartment lay, alas! the chief phantasy of all. The lofty walls, gigantic in height—even unproportionably so—were hung from summit to foot, in vast folds, with a heavy and massive-looking tapestry—tapestry of a material which was found alike as a carpet on the floor, as a covering for the ottomans and the ebony bed, as a canopy for the bed, and as the gorgeous volutes of the curtains which partially shaded the window. The material was the richest cloth of gold. It was spotted all over, at irregular intervals, with arabesque figures, about a foot in diameter, and wrought upon the cloth in patterns of the most jetty black. But these figures partook of the true character of the arabesque only when regarded from a single point of view. By a contrivance now common, and indeed traceable to a very remote period of antiquity, they were made changeable in aspect. To one entering the room, they bore the appearance of simple monstrosities; but upon further advance, this appearance gradually departed; and step by step, as the visitor moved his station in the chamber, he saw himself surrounded by an endless succession of the ghastly forms which belong to the superstition of the Norman, or arise in the guilty slumbers of the monk. The phantasmagoric effect was vastly heightened by the artificial introduction of a strong continual current of wind behind the draperies—giving a hideous and uneasy animation to the whole.

In halls such as these—in a bridal chamber such as this—I passed, with the Lady of Tremaine, the unhallowed hours of the first month of our marriage— passed them with but little disquietude. That my wife dreaded the fierce moodiness of my temper—that she shunned me and loved me but little— I could not help perceiving; but it gave me rather pleasure than otherwise. I loathed her with a hatred belonging more to demon than to man. My memory flew back, (oh, with what intensity of regret!) to Ligeia, the beloved, the august, the beautiful, the entombed. I revelled in recollections of her purity, of her wisdom, of her lofty, her ethereal nature, of her passionate, her idolatrous love. Now, then, did my spirit fully and freely burn with more than all the fires of her own. In the excitement of my opium dreams (for I was habitually fettered in the shackles of the drug) I would call aloud upon her name, during the silence of the night, or among the sheltered recesses of the glens by day, as if, through the wild eagerness, the solemn passion, the consuming ardor of my longing for the departed, I could restore her to the pathway she had abandoned—ah, *could* it be forever?—upon the earth.

About the commencement of the second month of the marriage, the Lady Rowena was attacked with sudden illness, from which her recovery was slow. The fever which consumed her rendered her nights uneasy; and in her perturbed state of half-slumber, she spoke of sounds, and of motions, in and about the chamber of the turret, which I concluded had no origin save in the distemper of her fancy, or perhaps in the phantasmagoric influences of the chamber itself. She became at length convalescent—finally well. Yet but a brief period elapsed, ere a second more violent disorder again threw her upon a bed of suffering; and from this attack her frame, at all times feeble, never altogether recovered. Her illnesses were, after this epoch, of alarming character, and of more alarming recurrence, defying alike the knowledge and the great exertions of her physicians. With the increase of the chronic disease which had thus, apparently, taken too sure hold upon her constitution to be eradicated by human means, I could not fail to observe a similar increase in the nervous irritation of her temperament, and in her excitability by trivial causes of fear. She spoke again, and now more frequently and pertinaciously, of the sounds—of the slight sounds—and of the unusual motions among the tapestries, to which she had formerly alluded.

One night, near the closing in of September, she pressed this distressing subject with more than usual emphasis upon my attention. She had just awakened from an unquiet slumber, and I had been watching, with feelings half of anxiety, half of vague terror, the workings of her emaciated countenance. I sat by the side of her ebony bed, upon one of the ottomans of India. She partly arose, and spoke, in an earnest low whisper, of sounds which she *then* heard, but which I could not hear—of motions which she *then* saw, but which I could not perceive. The wind was rushing hurriedly behind the tapestries, and I wished to show her (what, let me confess, I could not *all* believe) that those almost inarticulate breathings, and those very gentle variations of the figures upon the wall, were but the natural effects of that customary rushing of the wind. But a deadly pallor, overspreading her face, had proved to me that my exertions to reassure her would be fruitless. She appeared to be fainting, and no attendants were within call. I remembered where was deposited a decanter of light wine which had been ordered by her physicians, and hastened across the chamber to procure it. But, as I stepped beneath the light of the censer, two circumstances of a startling nature attracted my attention. I had felt that some palpable although invisible object had passed lightly by my person; and I saw that there lay upon the golden carpet, in the very middle of the rich lustre thrown from the censer, a shadow—a faint, indefinite shadow of angelic aspect—such as might be fancied for the shadow of a shade. But I was wild with the excitement of an immoderate dose of opium, and heeded these things but little, nor spoke of them to Rowena. Having found the wine, I recrossed the chamber, and poured out a goblet-ful, which I held to the lips of the fainting lady. She had now partially recovered, however, and took the vessel herself, while I sank upon an ottoman near me, with my eyes fastened upon her person. It was then that I became distinctly aware of a gentle foot-fall upon the carpet, and near the couch; and in a second thereafter, as Rowena was in the act of raising the wine to her lips, I saw, or may have dreamed that I saw, fall within the goblet, as if from some invisible spring in the atmosphere of the room, three or four large drops of a brilliant and ruby colored fluid. If this I saw— not so Rowena. She swallowed the wine unhesitatingly, and I forbore to speak to her of a circumstance which must, after all, I considered, have been but the suggestion of a vivid imagination, rendered morbidly active by the terror of the lady, by the opium, and by the hour.

Yet I cannot conceal it from my own perception that, immediately subsequent to the fall of the ruby-drops, a rapid change for the worse took place in the disorder of my wife; so that, on the third subsequent night, the hands of her menials prepared her for the tomb, and on the fourth, I sat alone, with her shrouded body, in that fantastic chamber which had received her as my bride.—Wild visions, opium-engendered, flitted, shadow-like, before me. I gazed with unquiet eye upon the sarcophagi in the angles of the room, upon the varying figures of the drapery, and upon the writhing of the parti-colored fires in the censer overhead. My eyes then fell, as I called to mind the circumstances of a former night, to the spot beneath the glare of the censer where I had seen the faint traces of the shadow. It was there, however, no longer; and breathing with greater freedom, I turned my glances to the pallid and rigid figure upon the bed. Then rushed upon me a thousand memories of Ligeia—and then came back upon my heart, with the turbulent violence of a flood, the whole of that unutterable woe with which I had regarded *her* thus enshrouded. The night waned; and still, with a bosom full of bitter thoughts of the one only and supremely beloved, I remained gazing upon the body of Rowena.

It might have been midnight, or perhaps earlier, or later, for I had taken no note of time, when a sob, low, gentle, but very distinct, startled me from my revery.—I *felt* that it came from the bed of ebony—the bed of death. I listened in an agony of superstitious terror—but there was no repetition of the sound. I strained my vision to detect any motion in the corpse—but there was not the slightest perceptible. Yet I could not have been deceived. I *had* heard the noise, however faint, and my soul was awakened within me. I resolutely and perseveringly kept my attention riveted upon the body. Many minutes elapsed before any circumstances occurred tending to throw light upon the mystery. At length it became evident that a slight, a very feeble, and barely noticeable tinge of color had flushed up within the cheeks, and along the sunken small veins of the eyelids. Through a species of unutterable horror and awe, for which the language of mortality has no sufficiently energetic expression, I felt my heart cease to beat, my limbs grow rigid where I sat. Yet a sense of duty finally operated to restore my self-possession. I could no longer doubt that we had been precipitate in our preparations—that Rowena still lived. It was necessary that some immediate exertion be made; yet the turret was altogether apart from the portion of the abbey tenanted by the servants—there were none within call—I had no means of summoning them to my aid without leaving the room for many minutes—and this I could not venture to do. I therefore struggled alone in my endeavors to call back the spirit still hovering. In a short period it was certain, however, that a relapse had taken place; the color disappeared from both eyelid and cheek, leaving a wanness even more than that of marble; the lips became doubly shrivelled and pinched up in the ghastly expression of death; a repulsive clamminess and coldness overspread rapidly the surface of the body; and all the usual rigorous stiffness immediately supervened. I fell back with a shudder upon the couch from which I had been so startlingly aroused, and again gave myself up to passionate waking visions of Ligeia.

An hour thus elapsed when (could it be possible?) I was a second time aware of some vague sound issuing from the region of the bed. I listened—in extremity of horror. The sound came again—it was a sigh. Rushing to the corpse, I saw—distinctly saw—a tremor upon the lips. In a minute afterward they relaxed, disclosing a bright line of the pearly teeth. Amazement now struggled in my bosom with the profound awe which had hitherto reigned there alone. I felt that my vision grew dim, that my reason wandered; and it was only by a violent effort that I at length succeeded in nerving myself to the task which duty thus once more had pointed out. There was now a partial glow upon the forehead and upon the cheek and throat; a perceptible warmth pervaded the whole frame; there was even a slight pulsation at the heart. The lady *lived*; and with redoubled ardor I betook myself to the task of restoration. I chafed and bathed the temples and the hands, and used every exertion which experience, and no little medical reading, could suggest. But in vain. Suddenly, the color fled, the pulsation ceased, the lips resumed the expression of the dead, and, in an instant afterward, the whole body took upon itself the icy chilliness, the livid hue, the intense rigidity, the sunken outline, and all the loathsome peculiarities of that which has been, for many days, a tenant of the tomb.

And again I sunk into visions of Ligeia—and again, (what marvel that I shudder while I write?) *again* there reached my ears a low sob from the region of the ebony bed. But why shall I minutely detail the unspeakable horrors of that night? Why shall I pause to relate how, time after time, until near the period of the gray dawn, this hideous drama of revivification was repeated; how each terrific relapse was only into a sterner and apparently more irredeemable death; how each agony wore the aspect of a struggle with some invisible foe; and how each struggle was succeeded by I know not what of wild change in the personal appearance of the corpse? Let me hurry to a conclusion.

The greater part of the fearful night had worn away, and she who had been dead, once again stirred—and now more vigorously than hitherto, although arousing from a dissolution more appalling in its utter hopelessness than any. I had long ceased to struggle or to move, and remained sitting rigidly upon the ottoman, a helpless prey to a whirl of violent emotions, of which extreme awe was perhaps the least terrible, the least consuming. The corpse, I repeat, stirred, and now more vigorously than before. The hues of life flushed up with unwonted energy into the countenance—the limbs relaxed—and, save that the eyelids were yet pressed heavily together, and that the bandages and draperies of the grave still imparted their charnel character to the figure, I might have dreamed that Rowena had indeed shaken off, utterly, the fetters of Death. But if this idea was not, even then, altogether adopted, I could at least doubt no longer, when, arising from the bed, tottering, with feeble steps, with closed eyes, and with the manner of one bewildered in a dream, the thing that was enshrouded advanced boldly and palpably into the middle of the apartment.

I trembled not—I stirred not—for a crowd of unutterable fancies connected with the air, the stature, the demeanor of the figure, rushing hurriedly through my brain, had paralyzed—had chilled me into stone. I stirred not—but gazed upon the apparition. There was a mad disorder in my thoughts—a tumult unappeasable. Could it, indeed, be the *living* Rowena who confronted me? Could it indeed be Rowena *at all*—the fair-haired, the blue-eyed Lady Rowena Trevanion of Tremaine? Why, *why* should I doubt it? The bandage lay heavily about the mouth—but then might it not be the mouth of the breathing Lady of Tremaine? And the cheeks—there were the roses as in her noon of life—yes, these might indeed be the fair cheeks of the living Lady of Tremaine. And the chin, with its dimples, as in health, might it not be hers?—but *had she then grown taller since her malady?* What inexpressible madness seized me with that thought? One bound, and I had reached her feet! Shrinking from my touch, she let fall from her head, unloosened, the ghastly cerements which had confined it, and there streamed forth, into the rushing atmosphere of the chamber, huge masses of long and dishevelled hair; *it was blacker than the raven wings of the midnight!* And now slowly opened *the eyes* of the figure which stood before me. "Here then, at least," I shrieked aloud, "can I never—can I never be mistaken—these are the full, and the black, and the wild eyes—of my lost love—of the lady—of the LADY LIGEIA." 1838

Dulce et Decorum Est (1920)

by Wilfred Owen

Bent double, like old beggars under sacks,
Knock-kneed, coughing like hags, we cursed through sludge,
Till on the haunting flares we turned our backs
And towards our distant rest began to trudge.
Men marched asleep. Many had lost their boots   5
But limped on, blood-shod. All went lame; all blind;
Drunk with fatigue; deaf even to the hoots
Of disappointed shells that dropped behind.

GAS! Gas! Quick, boys!— An ecstasy of fumbling,
Fitting the clumsy helmets just in time;   10
But someone still was yelling out and stumbling
And floundering like a man in fire or lime.—
Dim, through the misty panes and thick green light
As under a green sea, I saw him drowning.

In all my dreams, before my helpless sight,   15
He plunges at me, guttering, choking, drowning.

If in some smothering dreams you too could pace
Behind the wagon that we flung him in,
And watch the white eyes writhing in his face,
His hanging face, like a devil's sick of sin;   20
If you could hear, at every jolt, the blood
Come gargling from the froth-corrupted lungs,
Obscene as cancer, bitter as the cud
Of vile, incurable sores on innocent tongues,—
My friend, you would not tell with such high zest   25
To children ardent for some desperate glory,
The old Lie: Dulce et decorum est
Pro patria mori.

At the End of the Passage

by Rudyard Kipling

The sky is lead and our faces are red,
And the gates of Hell are opened and riven,
And the winds of Hell are loosened and driven, And the dust flies up in the
    face of Heaven, And the clouds come down in a fiery sheet,
Heavy to raise and hard to be borne.   5
And the soul of man is turned from his meat,
Turned from the trifles for which he has striven
Sick in his body, and heavy hearted,
And his soul flies up like the dust in the sheet
Breaks from his flesh and is gone and departed,   10
As the blasts they blow on the cholera-horn.

Himalayan

Four men, each entitled to 'life, liberty, and the pursuit of happiness', sat at a table playing whist. The thermometer marked—for them—one hundred and one degrees of heat. The room was darkened till it was only just possible to distinguish the pips of the cards and the very white faces of the players. A tattered, rotten punkah of whitewashed calico was puddling the hot air and whining dolefully at each stroke. Outside lay gloom of a November day in London. There was neither sky, sun, nor horizon—nothing but a brown purple haze of heat. It was as though the earth were dying of apoplexy.

From time to time clouds of tawny dust rose from the ground without wind or warning, flung themselves tablecloth-wise among the tops of the parched trees, and came down again. Then a-whirling dust-devil would scutter across the plain for a couple of miles, break, and fall outward, though there was nothing to check its flight save a long low line of piled railway-sleepers white with the dust, a cluster of huts made of mud, condemned rails, and canvas, and the one squat four-roomed bungalow that belonged to the assistant engineer in charge of a section of the Gaudhari State line then under construction.

The four, stripped to the thinnest of sleeping-suits, played whist crossly, with wranglings as to leads and returns. It was not the best kind of whist, but they had taken some trouble to arrive at it. Mottram of the Indian Survey had ridden thirty and railed one hundred miles from his lonely post in the desert since the night before; Lowndes of the Civil Service, on special duty in the political department, had come as far to escape for an instant the miserable intrigues of an impoverished native State whose king alternately fawned and blustered for more money from the pitiful revenues contributed by hard-wrung peasants and despairing camel-breeders; Spurstow, the doctor of the line, had left a cholera-stricken camp of coolies to look after itself for forty-eight hours while he associated with white men once more. Hummil, the assistant engineer, was the host. He stood fast and received his friends thus every Sunday if they could come in. When one of them failed to appear, he would send a telegram to his last address, in order that he might know whether the defaulter were dead or alive. There are very many places in the East where it is not good or kind to let your acquaintances drop out of sight even for one short week.

The players were not conscious of any special regard for each other. They squabbled whenever they met; but they ardently desired to meet, as men without water desire to drink. They were lonely folk who understood the dread meaning of loneliness. They were all under thirty years of age—which is too soon for any man to possess that knowledge.

'Pilsener?' said Spurstow, after the second rubber, mopping his forehead.

'Beer's out, I'm sorry to say, and there's hardly enough soda-water for tonight,' said Hummil.

'What filthy bad management!' Spurstow snarled.

'Can't help it. I've written and wired; but the trains don't come through regularly yet. Last week the ice ran out—as Lowndes knows.'

'Glad I didn't come. I could ha' sent you some if I had known, though. Phew! it's too hot to go on playing bumblepuppy.' This with a savage scowl at Lowndes, who only laughed. He was a hardened offender.

Mottram rose from the table and looked out of a chink in the shutters.

'What a sweet day!' said he.

The company yawned all together and betook themselves to an aimless investigation of all Hummil's possessions—guns, tattered novels, saddlery, spurs, and the like. They had fingered them a score of times before, but there was really nothing else to do.

'Got anything fresh?' said Lowndes.

'Last week's *Gazette of India*, and a cutting from a home paper. My father sent it out. It's rather amusing.'

'One of those vestrymen that call 'emselves M.P.s again, is it?' said Spurstow, who read his newspapers when he could get them.

'Yes. Listen to this. It's to your address, Lowndes. The man was making a speech to his constituents, and he piled it on. Here's a sample, "And I assert unhesitatingly that the Civil Service in India is the preserve—the pet preserve—of the aristocracy of England. What does the democracy—what do the masses—get from that country, which we have step by step fraudulently annexed? I answer, nothing whatever. It is farmed with a single eye to their own interests by the scions of the aristocracy. They take good care to maintain their lavish scale of incomes, to avoid or stifle any inquiries into the nature and conduct of their administration, while they themselves force the unhappy peasant to pay with the sweat of his brow for all the luxuries in which they are lapped." Hummil waved the cutting above his head.' Ear! 'ear!' said his audience.

Then Lowndes, meditatively, 'I'd give—I'd give three months' pay to have that gentleman spend one month with me and see how the free and independent native prince works things. Old Timbersides'—this was his flippant title for an honoured and decorated feudatory prince—'has been wearing my life out this week past for money. By Jove, his latest performance was to send me one of his women as a bribe!'

'Good for you! Did you accept it?' said Mottram.

'No. I rather wish I had, now. She was a pretty little person, and she yarned away to me about the horrible destitution among the king's women-folk. The darlings haven't had any new clothes for nearly a month, and the old man wants to buy a new drag from Calcutta—solid silver railings and silver lamps, and trifles of that kind. I've tried to make him understand that he has played the deuce with the revenues for the last twenty years and must go slow. He can't see it.'

'But he has the ancestral treasure-vaults to draw on. There must be three millions at least in jewels and coin under his palace,' said Hummil.

'Catch a native king disturbing the family treasure! The priests forbid it except as the last resort. Old Timbersides has added something like a quarter of a million to the deposit in his reign.'

'Where the mischief does it all come from?' said Mottram.

'The country. The state of the people is enough to make you sick. I've known the taxmen wait by a milch-camel till the foal was born and then hurry off the mother for arrears. And what can I do? I can't get the court clerks to give me any accounts; I can't raise anything more than a fat smile from the commander-in-chief when I find out the troops are three months in arrears; and old Timbersides begins to weep when I speak to him. He has taken to the King's Peg heavily, liqueur brandy for whisky, and Heidsieck for soda-water.'

'That's what the Rao of Jubela took to. Even a native can't last long at that,' said Spurstow. 'He'll go out.'

'And a good thing, too. Then I suppose we'll have a council of regency, and a tutor for the young prince, and hand him back his kingdom with ten years' accumulations.'

'Whereupon that young prince, having been taught all the vices of the English, will play ducks and drakes with the money and undo ten years' work in eighteen months. I've seen that business before,' said Spurstow. 'I should tackle the king with a light hand if I were you, Lowndes. They'll hate you quite enough under any circumstances.

'That's all very well. The man who looks on can talk about the light hand; but you can't clean a pig-sty with a pen dipped in rose-water. I know my risks; but nothing has happened yet. My servant's an old Pathan, and he cooks for me. They are hardly likely to bribe him, and I don't accept food from my true friends, as they call themselves. Oh, but it's weary work! I'd sooner be with you, Spurstow. There's shooting near your camp.'

'Would you? I don't think it. About fifteen deaths a day don't incite a man to shoot anything but himself. And the worst of it is that the poor devils look at you as though you ought to save them. Lord knows, I've tried everything. My last attempt was empirical, but it pulled an old man through. He was brought to me apparently past hope, and I gave him gin and Worcester sauce with cayenne. It cured him; but I don't recommend it.'

'How do the cases run generally?' said Hummil.

'Very simply indeed. Chlorodyne, opium pill, chlorodyne, collapse, nitre, bricks to the feet, and then—the burning-ghaut. The last seems to be the only thing that stops the trouble. It's black cholera, you know. Poor devils! But, I will say, little Bunsee Lal, my apothecary, works like a demon. I've recommended him for promotion if he comes through it all alive.'

'And what are your chances, old man?' said Mottram.

Don't know; don't care much; but I've sent the letter in. What are you doing with yourself generally?

'Sitting under a table in the tent and spitting on the sextant to keep it cool,' said the man of the survey. 'Washing my eyes to avoid ophthalmia, which I shall certainly get, and trying to make a sub-surveyor understand that an error of five degrees in an angle isn't quite so small as it looks. I'm altogether alone, y' know, and shall be till the end of the hot weather.'

'Hummil's the lucky man,' said Lowndes, flinging himself into a long chair. 'He has an actual roof-torn as to the ceiling-cloth, but still a roof-over his head. He sees one train daily. He can get beer and soda-water and ice 'em when God is good. He has books, pictures—they were torn from the *Graphic*—and the society of the excellent sub-contractor Jevins, besides the pleasure of receiving us weekly.'

Hummil smiled grimly. 'Yes, I'm the lucky man, I suppose. Jevins is luckier.'

'How? Not——'

'Yes. Went out. Last Monday.'

'By his own hand?' said Spurstow quickly, hinting the suspicion that was in everybody's mind. There was no cholera near Hummil's section. Even fever gives a man at least a week's grace, and sudden death generally implied self-slaughter.

'I judge no man this weather,' said Hummil. 'He had a touch of the sun, I fancy; for last week, after you fellows had left, he came into the verandah and told me that he was going home to see his wife, in Market Street, Liverpool, that evening.

'I got the apothecary in to look at him, and we tried to make him lie down. After an hour or two he rubbed his eyes and said he believed he had had a fit, hoped he hadn't said anything rude. Jevins had a great idea of bettering himself socially. He was very like Chucks in his language.'

'Well?'

'Then he went to his own bungalow and began cleaning a rifle. He told the servant that he was going to shoot buck in the morning. Naturally he fumbled with the trigger, and shot himself through the head—accidentally. The apothecary sent in a report to my chief; and Jevins is buried somewhere out there. I'd have wired to you, Spurstow, if you could have done anything.'

'You're a queer chap,' said Mottram. 'If you'd killed the man yourself you couldn't have been more quiet about the business.'

'Good Lord! what does it matter?' said Hummil calmly. 'I've got to do a lot of his overseeing work in addition to my own. I'm the only person that suffers. Jevins is out of it, by pure accident, of course, but out of it. The apothecary was going to write a long screed on suicide. Trust a babu to drivel when he gets the chance.'

'Why didn't you let it go in as suicide?' said Lowndes.

'No direct proof. A man hasn't many privileges in his country, but he might at least be allowed to mishandle his own rifle. Besides, some day I may need a man to smother up an accident to myself. Live and let live. Die and let die.'

'You take a pill,' said Spurstow, who had been watching Hummil's white face narrowly. 'Take a pill, and don't be an ass. That sort of talk is skittles. Anyhow, suicide is shirking your work. If I were Job ten times over, I should be so interested in what was going to happen next that I'd stay on and watch.'

'Ah! I've lost that curiosity,' said Hummil.

'Liver out of order?' said Lowndes feelingly.

'No. Can't sleep. That's worse.'

'By Jove, it is!' said Mottram. 'I'm that way every now and then, and the fit has to wear itself out. What do you take for it?'

'Nothing. What's the use? I haven't had ten minutes' sleep since Friday morning.'

'Poor chap! Spurstow, you ought to attend to this,' said Mottram. 'Now you mention it, your eyes are rather gummy and swollen.'

Spurstow, still watching Hummil, laughed lightly. 'I'll patch him up, later on. Is it too hot, do you think, to go for a ride?'

'Where to?' said Lowndes wearily. 'We shall have to go away at eight, and there'll be riding enough for us then. I hate a horse when I have to use him as a necessity. Oh, heavens! what is there to do?'

'Begin whist again, at chick points ['a chick' is supposed to be eight shillings] and a gold mohur on the rub,' said Spurstow promptly.

'Poker. A month's pay all round for the pool—no limit—and fifty-rupee raises. Somebody would be broken before we got up,' said Lowndes.

'Can't say that it would give me any pleasure to break any man in this company,' said Mottram. 'There isn't enough excitement in it, and it's foolish.' He crossed over to the worn and battered little camp-piano—wreckage of a married household that had once held the bungalow—and opened the case.

'It's used up long ago,' said Hummil. 'The servants have picked it to pieces.'

The piano was indeed hopelessly out of order, but Mottram managed to bring the rebellious notes into a sort of agreement, and there rose from the ragged keyboard something that might once have been the ghost of a popular music-hall song. The men in the long chairs turned with evident interest as Mottram banged the more lustily.

'That's good!' said Lowndes. 'By Jove! the last time I heard that song was in '79, or thereabouts, just before I came out.'

'Ah!' said Spurstow with pride, 'I was home in '80.' And he mentioned a song of the streets popular at that date.

Mottram executed it roughly. Lowndes criticized and volunteered emendations. Mottram dashed into another ditty, not of the music-hall character, and made as if to rise.

'Sit down,' said Hummil. 'I didn't know that you had any music in your composition. Go on playing until you can't think of anything more. I'll have that piano tuned up before you come again. Play something festive.'

Very simple indeed were the tunes to which Mottram's art and the limitations of the piano could give effect, but the men listened with pleasure, and in the pauses talked all together of what they had seen or heard when they were last at home. A dense dust-storm sprung up outside, and swept roaring over the house, enveloping it in the choking darkness of midnight, but Mottram continued unheeding, and the crazy tinkle reached the ears of the listeners above the flapping of the tattered ceiling-cloth.

In the silence after the storm he glided from the more directly personal songs of Scotland, half humming them as he played, into the Evening Hymn.

'Sunday,' said he, nodding his head.

'Go on. Don't apologize for it,' said Spurstow.

Hummil laughed long and riotously. 'Play it, by all means. You're full of surprises today. I didn't know you had such a gift of finished sarcasm. How does that thing go?'

Mottram took up the tune.

'Too slow by half. You miss the note of gratitude,' said Hummil. 'It ought to go to the "Grasshopper's Polka"—this way.' And he chanted, prestissimo,

'Glory to thee, my God, this night,
For all the blessings of the light.
That shows we really feel our blessings. How does it go on?—
If in the night I sleepless lie,
My soul with sacred thoughts supply;
May no ill dreams disturb my rest,—
Quicker, Mottram!—
Or powers of darkness me molest!'

'Bah! what an old hypocrite you are!'

'Don't be an ass,' said Lowndes. 'You are at full liberty to make fun of anything else you like, but leave that hymn alone. It's associated in my mind with the most sacred recollections——'

'Summer evenings in the country, stained-glass window, light going out, and you and she jamming your heads together over one hymnbook,' said Mottram.

'Yes, and a fat old cockchafer hitting you in the eye when you walked home. Smell of hay, and a moon as big as a bandbox sitting on the top of a haycock; bats, roses, milk and midges,' said Lowndes.

'Also mothers. I can just recollect my mother singing me to sleep with that when I was a little chap,' said Spurstow.

The darkness had fallen on the room. They could hear Hummil squirming in his chair.

'Consequently,' said he testily, 'you sing it when you are seven fathom deep in Hell! It's an insult to the intelligence of the Deity to pretend we're anything but tortured rebels.'

'Take *two* pills,' said Spurstow; 'that's tortured liver.'

'The usually placid Hummil is in a vile bad temper. I'm sorry for his coolies tomorrow,' said Lowndes, as the servants brought in the lights and prepared the table for dinner.

As they were settling into their places about the miserable goat-chops, and the smoked tapioca pudding, Spurstow took occasion to whisper to Mottram, 'Well done, David!'

'Look after Saul, then,' was the reply.

'What are you two whispering about?' said Hummil suspiciously.

'Only saying that you are a damned poor host. This fowl can't be cut,' returned Spurstow with a sweet smile. 'Call this a dinner?'

'I can't help it. You don't expect a banquet, do you?'

Throughout that meal Hummil contrived laboriously to insult directly and pointedly all his guests in succession, and at each insult Spurstow kicked the aggrieved persons under the table; but he dared not exchange a glance of intelligence with either of them. Hummil's face was white and pinched, while his eyes were unnaturally large. No man dreamed for a moment of resenting his savage personalities, but as soon as the meal was over they made haste to get away.

'Don't go. You're just getting amusing, you fellows. I hope I haven't said anything that annoyed you. You're such touchy devils.' Then, changing the note into one of almost abject entreaty, Hummil added, 'I say, you surely aren't going?'

'In the language of the blessed Jorrocks, where I dines I sleeps,' said Spurstow. 'I want to have a look at your coolies tomorrow, if you don't mind. You can give me a place to lie down in, I suppose?'

The others pleaded the urgency of their several duties next day, and, saddling up, departed together, Hummil begging them to come next Sunday. As they jogged off, Lowndes unbosomed himself to Mottram—

'. . . And I never felt so like kicking a man at his own table in my life. He said I cheated at whist, and reminded me I was in debt! 'Told you you were as good as a liar to your face! You aren't half indignant enough over it.'

'Not I,' said Mottram. 'Poor devil! Did you ever know old Hummy behave like that before or within a hundred miles of it?'

'That's no excuse. Spurstow was hacking my shin all the time, so I kept a hand on myself. Else I should have—'

'No, you wouldn't. You'd have done as Hummy did about Jevins; judge no man this weather. By Jove! the buckle of my bridle is hot in my hand! Trot out a bit, and 'ware rat-holes.' Ten minutes' trotting jerked out of Lowndes one very sage remark when he pulled up, sweating from every pore—

'Good thing Spurstow's with him tonight.'

'Ye-es. Good man, Spurstow. Our roads turn here. See you again next Sunday, if the sun doesn't bowl me over.'

'S'pose so, unless old Timbersides' finance minister manages to dress some of my food. Goodnight, and—God bless you!'

'What's wrong now?'

'Oh, nothing.' Lowndes gathered up his whip, and, as he flicked Mottram's mare on the flank, added, 'You're not a bad little chap, that's all.' And the mare bolted half a mile across the sand, on the word.

In the assistant engineer's bungalow Spurstow and Hummil smoked the pipe of silence together, each narrowly watching the other. The capacity of a bachelor's establishment is as elastic as its arrangements are simple. A servant cleared away the dining-room table, brought in a couple of rude native bedsteads made of tape strung on a light wood frame, flung a square of cool Calcutta matting over each, set them side by side, pinned two towels to the punkah so that their fringes should just sweep clear of the sleeper's nose and mouth, and announced that the couches were ready.

The men flung themselves down, ordering the punkah-coolies by all the powers of Hell to pull. Every door and window was shut, for the outside air was that of an oven. The atmosphere within was only 104 degrees, as the thermometer bore witness, and heavy with the foul smell of badly-trimmed kerosene lamps; and this stench, combined with that of native tobacco, baked brick, and dried earth, sends the heart of many a strong man down to his boots, for it is the smell of the Great Indian Empire when she turns herself for six months into a house of torment. Spurstow packed his pillows craftily so that he reclined rather than lay, his head at a safe elevation above his feet. It is not good to sleep on a low pillow in the hot weather if you happen to be of thick-necked build, for you may pass with lively snores and gugglings from natural sleep into the deep slumber of heat-apoplexy.

'Pack your pillows,' said the doctor sharply, as he saw Hummil preparing to lie down at full length.

The night-light was trimmed; the shadow of the punkah wavered across the room, and the *'flick'* of the punkah-towel and the soft whine of the rope through the wall-hole followed it. Then the punkah flagged, almost ceased. The sweat poured from Spurstow's brow. Should he go out and harangue the coolie? It started forward again with a savage jerk, and a pin came out of the towels. When this was replaced, a tomtom in the coolie-lines began to beat with the steady throb of a swollen artery inside some brain-fevered skull. Spurstow turned on his side and swore gently. There was no movement on Hummil's part. The man had composed himself as rigidly as a corpse, his hands clinched at his sides. The respiration was too hurried for any suspicion of sleep. Spurstow looked at the set face. The jaws were clinched, and there was a pucker round the quivering eyelids.

'He's holding himself as tightly as ever he can,' thought Spurstow. 'What in the world is the matter with him?—Hummil!'

'Yes,' in a thick constrained voice.

'Can't you get to sleep?'

'No.'

'Head hot? Throat feeling bulgy? or how?'

'Neither, thanks. I don't sleep much, you know.'

"Feel pretty bad?'

'Pretty bad, thanks. There is a tomtom outside, isn't there? I thought it was my head at first. . . . Oh, Spurstow, for pity's sake give me something that will put me asleep, sound asleep, if it's only for six hours!' He sprang up, trembling from head to foot. 'I haven't been able to sleep naturally for days, and I can't stand it! I can't stand it!'

'Poor old chap!'

'That's no use. Give me something to make me sleep. I tell you I'm nearly mad. I don't know what I say half my time. For three weeks I've had to think and spell out every word that has come through my lips before I dared say it. Isn't that enough to drive a man mad? I can't see things correctly now, and I've lost my sense of touch. My skin aches—my skin aches! Make me sleep. Oh, Spurstow, for the love of God make me sleep sound. It isn't enough merely to let me dream. Let me sleep!'

'All right, old man, all right. Go slow; you aren't half as bad as you think.'

The flood-gates of reserve once broken, Hummil was clinging to him like a frightened child. 'You're pinching my arm to pieces.'

'I'll break your neck if you don't do something for me. No, I didn't mean that. Don't be angry, old fellow.' He wiped the sweat off himself as he fought to regain composure. 'I'm a bit restless and off my oats, and perhaps you could recommend some sort of sleeping mixture—bromide of potassium.'

'Bromide of skittles! Why didn't you tell me this before? Let go of my arm, and I'll see if there's anything in my cigarette-case to suit your complaint.' Spurstow hunted among his day-clothes, turned up the lamp, opened a little silver cigarette-case, and advanced on the expectant Hummil with the daintiest of fairy squirts.

'The last appeal of civilization,' said he, 'and a thing I hate to use. Hold out your arm. Well, your sleeplessness hasn't ruined your muscle; and what a thick hide it is! Might as well inject a buffalo subcutaneously. Now in a few minutes the morphia will begin working. Lie down and wait.'

A smile of unalloyed and idiotic delight began to creep over Hummil's face. 'I think,' he whispered,—'I think I'm going off now. Gad! it's positively heavenly! Spurstow, you must give me that case to keep; you——' The voice ceased as the head fell back.

'Not for a good deal,' said Spurstow to the unconscious form. 'And now, my friend, sleeplessness of your kind being very apt to relax the moral fibre in little matters of life and death, I'll just take the liberty of spiking your guns.'

He paddled into Hummil's saddle-room in his bare feet and uncased a twelve-bore rifle, an express, and a revolver. Of the first he unscrewed the nipples and hid them in the bottom of a saddlery-case; of the second he abstracted the lever, kicking it behind a big wardrobe. The third he merely opened, and knocked the doll-head bolt of the grip up with the heel of a riding-boot.

'That's settled,' he said, as he shook the sweat off his hands. 'These little precautions will at least give you time to turn. You have too much sympathy with gun-room accidents.'

And as he rose from his knees, the thick muffled voice of Hummil cried in the doorway, 'You fool!'

Such tones they use who speak in the lucid intervals of delirium to their friends a little before they die.

Spurstow started, dropping the pistol. Hummil stood in the doorway, rocking with helpless laughter.

'That was awf'ly good of you, I'm sure,' he said, very slowly, feeling for his words. 'I don't intend to go out by my own hand at present. I say, Spurstow, that stuff won't work. What shall I do? What shall I do?' And panic terror stood in his eyes.

'Lie down and give it a chance. Lie down at once.'

'I daren't. It will only take me half-way again, and I shan't be able to get away this time. Do you know it was all I could do to come out just now? Generally I am as quick as lightning; but you had clogged my feet. I was nearly caught.'

'Oh yes, I understand. Go and lie down.'

'No, it isn't delirium; but it was an awfully mean trick to play on me. Do you know I might have died?'

As a sponge rubs a slate clean, so some power unknown to Spurstow had wiped out of Hummil's face all that stamped it for the face of a man, and he stood at the doorway in the expression of his lost innocence. He had slept back into terrified childhood.

'Is he going to die on the spot?' thought Spurstow. Then, aloud, 'All right, my son. Come back to bed, and tell me all about it. You couldn't sleep; but what was all the rest of the nonsense?'

'A place, a place down there,' said Hummil, with simple sincerity. The drug was acting on him by waves, and he was flung from the fear of a strong man to the fright of a child as his nerves gathered sense or were dulled.

'Good God! I've been afraid of it for months past, Spurstow. It has made every night hell to me; and yet I'm not conscious of having done anything wrong.'

'Be still, and I'll give you another-dose. We'll stop your nightmares, you unutterable idiot!'

'Yes, but you must give me so much that I can't get away. You must make me quite sleepy, not just a little sleepy. It's so hard to run then.'

'I know it; I know it. I've felt it myself. The symptoms are exactly as you describe.'

'Oh, don't laugh at me, confound you! Before this awful sleeplessness came to me I've tried to rest on my elbow and put a spur in the bed to sting me when I fell back. Look!'

'By Jove! the man has been rowelled like a horse! Ridden by the night-mare with a vengeance! And we all thought him sensible enough. Heaven send us understanding! You like to talk, don't you?'

'Yes, sometimes. Not when I'm frightened. *Then* I want to run. Don't you?'

'Always. Before I give you your second dose try to tell me exactly what your trouble is.'

Hummil spoke in broken whispers for nearly ten minutes, whilst Spurstow looked into the pupils of his eyes and passed his hand before them once or twice.

At the end of the narrative the silver cigarette-case was produced, and the last words that Hummil said as he fell back for the second time were, 'Put me quite to sleep; for if I'm caught I die, I die!'

'Yes, yes; we all do that sooner or later, thank Heaven who has set a term to our miseries,' said Spurstow, settling the cushions under the head. 'It occurs to me that unless I drink something I shall go out before my time. I've stopped sweating, and—I wear a seventeen-inch collar.' He brewed himself scalding hot tea, which is an excellent remedy against heat-apoplexy if you take three or four cups of it in time. Then he watched the sleeper.

'A blind face that cries and can't wipe its eyes, a blind face that chases him down corridors! H'm! Decidedly, Hummil ought to go on leave as soon as possible; and, sane or otherwise, he undoubtedly did rowel himself most cruelly. Well, Heaven send us understanding!'

At mid-day Hummil rose, with an evil taste in his mouth, but an unclouded eye and a joyful heart.

'I was pretty bad last night, wasn't I?' said he.

'I have seen healthier men. You must have had a touch of the sun. Look here: if I write you a swinging medical certificate, will you apply for leave on the spot?'

'No.'

'Why not? You want it.'

'Yes, but I can hold on till the weather's a little cooler.'

'Why should you, if you can get relieved on the spot?'

'Burkett is the only man who could be sent; and he's a born fool.'

'Oh, never mind about the line. You aren't so important as all that. Wire for leave, if necessary.'

Hummil looked very uncomfortable.

'I can hold on till the Rains,' he said evasively.

'You can't. Wire to headquarters for Burkett.'

'I won't. If you want to know why, particularly, Burkett is married, and his wife's just had a kid, and she's up at Simla, in the cool, and Burkett has a very nice billet that takes him into Simla from Saturday to Monday. That little woman isn't at all well. If Burkett was transferred she'd try to follow him. If she left the baby behind she'd fret herself to death. If she came—and Burkett's one of those selfish little beasts who are always talking about a wife's place being with her husband—she'd die. It's murder to bring a woman here just now. Burkett hasn't the physique of a rat. If he came here he'd go out; and I know she hasn't any money, and I'm pretty sure she'd go out too. I'm salted in a sort of way, and I'm not married. Wait till the Rains, and then Burkett can get thin down here. It'll do him heaps of good.'

'Do you mean to say that you intend to face—what you have faced, till the Rains break?'

'Oh, it won't be so bad, now you've shown me a way out of it. I can always wire to you. Besides, now I've once got into the way of sleeping, it'll be all right. Anyhow, I shan't put in for leave. That's the long and the short of it.'

'My great Scott! I thought all that sort of thing was dead and done with.'

'Bosh! You'd do the same yourself. I feel a new man, thanks to that cigarette-case. You're going over to camp now, aren't you?'

'Yes; but I'll try to look you up every other day, if I can.'

'I'm not bad enough for that. I don't want you to bother. Give the coolies gin and ketchup.'

'Then you feel all right?'

'Fit to fight for my life, but not to stand out in the sun talking to you. Go along, old man, and bless you!'

Hummil turned on his heel to face the echoing desolation of his bungalow, and the first thing he saw standing in the verandah was the figure of himself. He had met a similar apparition once before, when he was suffering from overwork and the strain of the hot weather.

'This is bad—already,' he said, rubbing his eyes. 'If the thing slides away from me all in one piece, like a ghost, I shall know it is only my eyes and stomach that are out of order. If it walks—my head is going.'

He approached the figure, which naturally kept at an unvarying distance from him, as is the use of all spectres that are born of overwork. It slid through the house and dissolved into swimming specks within the eyeball as soon as it reached the burning light of the garden. Hummil went about his business till even. When he came in to dinner he found himself sitting at the table. The vision rose and walked out hastily. Except that it cast no shadow it was in all respects real.

No living man knows what that week held for Hummil. An increase of the epidemic kept Spurstow in camp among the coolies, and all he could do was to telegraph to Mottram, bidding him go to the bungalow and sleep there. But Mottram was forty miles away from the nearest telegraph, and knew nothing of anything save the needs of the survey till he met, early on Sunday morning, Lowndes and Spurstow heading towards Hummil's for the weekly gathering.

'Hope the poor chap's in a better temper,' said the former, swinging himself off his horse at the door. 'I suppose he isn't up yet.'

'I'll just have a look at him,' said the doctor. 'If he's asleep there's no need to wake him.'

And an instant later, by the tone of Spurstow's voice calling upon them to enter, the men knew what had happened. There was no need to wake him.

The punkah was still being pulled over the bed, but Hummil had departed this life at least three hours.

The body lay on its back, hands clinched by the side, as Spurstow had seen it lying seven nights previously. In the staring eyes was written terror beyond the expression of any pen.

Mottram, who had entered behind Lowndes, bent over the dead and touched the forehead lightly with his lips. 'Oh, you lucky, lucky devil!' he whispered.

But Lowndes had seen the eyes, and withdrew shuddering to the other side of the room.

'Poor chap! poor old chap! Arid the last time I met him I was angry. Spurstow, we should have watched him. Has he——?'

Deftly Spurstow continued his investigations, ending by a search round the room.

'No, he hasn't,' he snapped. 'There's no trace of anything. Call the servants.'

They came, eight or ten of them, whispering and peering over each other's shoulders.

'When did your Sahib go to bed?' said Spurstow.

'At eleven or ten, we think,' said Hummil's personal servant.

'He was well then? But how should you know?'

'He was not ill, as far as our comprehension extended. But he had slept very little for three nights. This I know, because I saw him walking much, and specially in the heart of the night.'

As Spurstow was arranging the sheet, a big straight-necked hunting-spur tumbled on the ground. The doctor groaned. The personal servant peeped at the body.

'What do you think, Chuma?' said Spurstow, catching the look on the dark face.

'Heaven-born, in my poor opinion, this that was my master has descended into the Dark Places, and there has been caught because he was not able to escape with sufficient speed. We have the spur for evidence that he fought with Fear. Thus have I seen men of my race do with thorns when a spell was laid upon them to overtake them in their sleeping hours and they dared not sleep.'

'Chuma, you're a mud-head. Go out and prepare seals to be set on the Sahib's property.'

'God has made the Heaven-born. God has made me. Who are we, to enquire into the dispensations of God? I will bid the other servants hold aloof while you are reckoning the tale of the Sahib's property. They are all thieves, and would steal.'

'As far as I can make out, he died from—oh, anything; stoppage of the heart's action, heat-apoplexy, or some other visitation,' said Spurstow to his companions. 'We must make an inventory of his effects, and so on.'

'He was scared to death,' insisted Lowndes. 'Look at those eyes! For pity's sake don't let him be buried with them open!'

'Whatever it was, he's clear of all the trouble now,' said Mottram softly.

Spurstow was peering into the open eyes.

'Come here,' said he. 'Can you see anything there?'

'I can't face it!' whimpered Lowndes. 'Cover up the face! Is there any fear on earth that can turn a man into that likeness? It's ghastly. Oh, Spurstow, cover it up!'

'No fear—on earth,' said Spurstow. Mottram leaned over his shoulder and looked intently.

'I see nothing except some grey blurs in the pupil. There can be nothing there, you know.'

'Even so. Well, let's think. It'll take half a day to knock up any sort of coffin; and he must have died at midnight. Lowndes, old man, go out and tell the coolies to break ground next to Jevins's grave. Mottram, go round the house with Chuma and see that the seals are put on things. Send a couple of men to me here, and I'll arrange.'

The strong-armed servants when they returned to their own kind told a strange story of the doctor Sahib vainly trying to call their master back to life by magic arts—to wit, the holding of a little green box that clicked to each of the dead man's eyes, and of a bewildered muttering on the part of the doctor Sahib, who took the little green box away with him.

The resonant hammering of a coffin-lid is no pleasant thing to hear, but those who have experience maintain that much more terrible is the soft swish of the bed-linen, the reeving and unreeving of the bed-tapes, when he who has fallen by the roadside is apparelled for burial, sinking gradually as the tapes are tied over, till the swaddled shape touches the floor and there is no protest against the indignity of hasty disposal.

At the last moment Lowndes was seized with scruples of conscience. 'Ought you to read the service, from beginning to end?' said he to Spurstow.

'I intend to. You're my senior as a civilian. You can take it if you like.'

'I didn't mean that for a moment. I only thought if we could get a chaplain from somewhere, I'm willing to ride anywhere, and give poor Hummil a better chance. That's all.'

'Bosh!' said Spurstow, as he framed his lips to the tremendous words that stand at the head of the burial service.

After breakfast they smoked a pipe in silence to the memory of the dead. Then Spurstow said absently—

' 'Tisn't medical science.'

'What?'

'Things in a dead man's eye.'

'For goodness' sake leave that horror alone!' said Lowndes. 'I've seen a native die of pure fright when a tiger chivied him. I know what killed Hummil.'

'The deuce you do! I'm going to try to see.' Arid the doctor retreated into the bathroom with a Kodak camera. After a few minutes there was the sound of something being hammered to pieces, and he emerged, very white indeed.

'Have you got a picture?' said Mottram. 'What does the thing look like?'

'It was impossible, of course. You needn't look, Mottram. I've torn up the films. There was nothing there. It was impossible.'

'That,' said Lowndes, very distinctly, watching the shaking hand striving to relight the pipe, 'is a damned lie.'

Mottram laughed uneasily. 'Spurstow's right,' he said. 'We're all in such a state now that we'd believe anything. For pity's sake let's try to be rational.'

There was no further speech for a long time. The hot wind whistled without, and the dry trees sobbed. Presently the daily train, winking brass, burnished steel, and spouting steam, pulled up panting in the intense glare. 'We'd better go on that,' said Spurstow. 'Go back to work. I've written my certificate. We can't do any more good here, and work'll keep our wits together. Come on.'

No one moved. It is not pleasant to face railway journeys at mid-day in June. Spurstow gathered up his hat and whip, and, turning in the doorway, said—

'There may be Heaven—there must be Hell.
Meantime, there is our life here. We-ell?'

Neither Mottram nor Lowndes had any answer to the question.

GLOSSARY

absolutist critic One who believes that there is one and only one theory or set of principles a reader may use when interpreting a text.

actual reader A term devised by Wolfgang Iser to distinguish between two kinds of readers: the implied and the actual reader. The actual reader is the person who physically picks up the text and reads it. According to Iser, the actual reader comes to the text shaped by cultural and personal norms and prejudices. See **implied reader**.

aesthetic experience The effects produced in and upon an individual when contemplating a work of art. See **aesthetic reading**.

aesthetic reading A term used by Louise M. Rosenblatt in *The Reader, the Text, the Poem: The Transactional Theory of the Literary Work* (1978) to describe the act of reading or the process whereby a reader transacts with a text. During this event, the "object of aesthetic contemplation is what perceivers or readers make of their responses to the artistic stimulus, no matter whether this be a physical object, such as a statue, or a set of verbal symbols. Readers contemplate their own shaping of their responses to the text." The term refers to each reader's personal response to a text and how individual readers find and create meaning when transacting with printed material. Such a process assumes an active role on the part of the reader to create meaning or individual interpretations with and from a text.

aesthetics The branch of philosophy that deals with the concept of the beautiful and strives to determine the criteria for beauty in any work of art. It asks such questions as: Where is the source of beauty? In the object? In the perceiver? What is beauty? and How is beauty recognized?

aesthetic theory A systematic, philosophical body of beliefs concerning how meaning occurs and functions in texts, especially the element of beauty or pleasure.

affective fallacy A term used by New Critics to explain that a reader's emotional response to a text is neither important nor equivalent to its interpretation. Believing those who evaluate a work of art on the basis of its emotional effect on its perceiver to be incorrect, New Critics assert that the affective fallacy confuses what a poem is (its meaning) and what it does. The term was first introduced by W.K. Wimsatt, Jr. and M.C. Beardsley, who believed that a poem's meaning was determined solely from a **close reading** of a text.

affective stylistics A term coined by the reader-oriented critic Stanley Fish to describe his reading strategy (also referred to as *reception aesthetics*). Fish believes that the meaning of any text resides in the reading community to which the reader belongs, what Fish calls the interpretive community. The interpretation of a text therefore depends on a reader's subjective experience in one or more of these interpretive communities. See **interpretive community** and **reception aesthetics**.

African American criticism An approach to literary analysis that develops a black aesthetics to be applied when interpreting African American writings. One of its leading advocates, Henry Louis Gates, Jr., believes such an aesthetics provides a new theoretical framework for developing and analyzing the ever-growing and popular African American canon. In this new framework, Gates insists that African American literature be viewed as a form of language, not as a representation of social practices or culture. According to Gates, a black aesthetics must be derived from the black tradition itself and must include what he calls "the language of blackness, the signifying difference which makes the black tradition our very own." Gates asserts the "double-voicedness" of African American literature, declaring that this literature draws upon two voices and cultures, the white and the black. It is the joining of these two discourses, Gates declares, that produces the uniqueness of this literature. Also see **cultural studies, double consciousness,** and **postcolonialism.**

aggressive instinct   According to Freud, one of two instincts housed in the unconscious, the other being the sexual instinct or libido. Although these two instincts can work harmoniously, often they act as enemies. See **destructive instinct**.

alienation effect   A term coined by the Marxist theater critic Bertolt Brecht to describe his technique to abolish the theater audience's normal expectations when viewing a drama. For example, in the middle of a drama, Brecht may have one of the actors directly appeal to the audience via song or speech to keep the audience constantly aware of the moral and social issues to which they are being exposed in the drama.

allegoric reading   A reading in which one character, place, or idea represents another. The characters, events, or places within a text represent meanings independent of the action in the surface story. These interpretations are most often religious, but may also be moral, political, personal, or satiric.

allophone   The family of nearly identical speech sounds that comprise a phoneme (see **phoneme**). For example, the sound of the *p* in *pit* and the *p* in *spit* are allophones of the phoneme /p/.

alterity   Differentness: to become the **Other**. Postcolonial theory asserts that the colonized quickly become excluded from positions of power in their "conquered" society and viewed as different and inferior by the colonizers.

Amazon feminism   A contemporary approach to feminist criticism that is dedicated to female images, either fictional or real, in literature and art that emphasize the physiques of female athletes and physical equality of both males and females. It argues that no mention of gender need arise when discussing such topics as occupations. No characteristics exist that are peculiarly masculine or feminine.

ambiguity   Commonly defined as a stylistic error in everyday speech in which a word or expression has multiple meanings. Since the publication of William Empson's *Seven Types of Ambiguity* (1930) and the specialized use of this term adopted by New Criticism, ambiguity is now synonymous with *plurisignation*, both terms implying the complexity and richness of poetic language that allows for a word or expression to simultaneously have two or more distinct meanings. New Critics believe that ambiguity becomes one of the chief tools that good poets use intentionally and effectively to demonstrate the valid meanings contained in a word or expression. See **connotation** and **denotation**.

anal stage   The second stage of child development, as articulated by Sigmund Freud. In this stage, the anus becomes the object of pleasure when the child learns the delights of defecation.

analytical psychology Founded and developed by Carl Gustav Jung, this system of psychology is akin to psychoanalysis, with its emphasis on the functions that the conscious and the unconscious play in influencing human behavior. In this branch of psychology, Jung emphasizes humankind's racial origins and adapts the use of the free association technique in studying an individual's problems.

Anglo-American feminisms A type of contemporary feminist theory and criticism authored by British and American feminist critics, notably Virginia Woolf, Judith Fetterley, Annette Kolodny, Nina Baym, Elaine Showalter, Sandra Gilbert, Susan Gubar, and others.

anima A term used by Carl Jung in mythic criticism to describe the archetype of the feminine in the male.

animus A term used by Carl Jung in mythic criticism to describe the archetype of the masculine in the female.

anti-cathexes A term used by Freud in his economic model of the unconscious. In this model, the pleasure principle is held in check by the anti-cathexes, an anti-charge of energy governed by the reality principle that inhibits free reign of the pleasure principle in an individual's psyche.

anti-romance phase One of four phrases that comprise Northrop Frye's concept of the monomyth or what Frye calls the complete story of literature. This phrase or season in literary works tells the story of bondage, imprisonment, frustration, and fear.

antithesis According to the German philosopher Georg Hegel, for every thesis presented, there exists a counterstatement or antithesis. Out of debate and discussion of the thesis and antithesis, a new idea develops called the synthesis.

aporia Postmodernism's undecidability about the nature of reality and the interpretation of texts. This term is also used in deconstruction theory denoting paradoxes, contradictions, and other puzzling statements that cannot be resolved—apparent contradictions.

appetencies A term brought into literary criticism via the writings of the formalist critic I.A. Richards. According to Richards, human beings are basically bundles of desires called *appetencies*. Richards believes that to achieve psychic health, every person must balance these desires by creating a personally acceptable vision of the world. Whereas religion once provided this vision, Richards declares that poetry can now best harmonize and satisfy humankind's appetencies and thereby create a fulfilling and intellectually acceptable worldview. See **formalism**.

applied criticism Applies the theories and tenets of theoretical criticism to a particular work of art. Also known as *practical criticism*. In applied criticism, the critic defines the standards of taste and explains, evaluates, or justifies a particular text.

archetypal criticism An approach to literary analysis that applies the theories of Carl Jung, Northrop Frye, and other critics to literary analysis. An archetypal critic studies images or patterns of repeated human experiences (archetypes) found within a specific text and common to other works of art. See **archetype**.

archetype A recurrent plot pattern, image, descriptive detail, or character that evokes from the reader strong but illogical responses. This term was brought into literary criticism via the psychological writings of Carl Jung. Jung believed that the mind was composed of three parts: the *personal conscious*, the *personal unconscious*, and the *collective unconscious*. Lying deep within the mind in the collective unconscious is the collective knowledge of humanity, the memories of humanity's past. Formed through the repeated experiences of humankind, this knowledge can be tapped through images of birth, death, rebirth, the seasons, and so forth, within a text and can cause profound emotions to surface within a reader. See **collective unconscious**.

arche-writing (archi-écriture)   A term used by the deconstructionist Jacques Derrida in *Of Grammatology* (1974) to assert that language is a kind of writing. Derrida, however, redefines the term *writing*. Derrida asserts that writing cannot be reduced to letters or other symbols inscribed on a page. Rather, writing is directly related to what Saussure believed to be the basic element of language: difference. We can know a word because it differs from another word. The word *tall* could just as easily have become *sall* in American English. This free play or element of undecidability in any system of communication Derrida calls writing.

Aristotelian poetics   The name given to the underlying principles of interpretation found in Aristotle's *Poetics*. In this work, Aristotle states the first definition of tragedy. The *Poetics* has now become the cornerstone of Western literary criticism.

artifacts   Any product of artistic endeavor, such as a poem, a novel, a painting, a short story, and so on. The word implies that the artistic endeavor can be analyzed or studied to help ascertain its meaning because its general meaning is "something created by humans," which implies an analyzable entity or object.

aspirated   A linguistic term designating a sound such as the *p* in *pat*, in which a brief delay occurs before pronouncing the vowel sound with an accompanying release of air.

attentive reading   Coined by the post-Althusserian Marxist critic Pierre Macherey to describe a type of reading that reveals the multiple ideologies operating in any given text, ideologies that often directly work against what the writer assumes he or she is saying or writing.

autotelic artifact   A term used most often by New Critics that refers to the existence of a text. For the New Critics, a text exists in its own right as an autonomous object that can be analyzed.

bad critic   A term used by New Criticism for the kind of critic who insists on imposing extrinsic evidence such as historical or biographical information upon a text to discover its meaning.

Bakhtin Circle   A group of Russian scholars and critics, including Mikhail Bakhtin, who addressed the social and cultural influences of the Russian revolution and its rule under Joseph Stalin. The group met from 1913 until 1929, first at Vitebsk and then Leningrad and included Bakhtin, P.N. Medvede, V.N. Voloshinov, and others.

base   A term used by Karl Marx to designate the economic structure of society. According to Marx, the various methods of economic production and the social relationships they engender form the base. In the United States, for example, Marxism asserts that the capitalists exploit the working classes, determining for them their salaries and their working conditions; their salaries and working conditions are the base.

binary operations (binary oppositions)   A term introduced into literary theory by Jacques Derrida to represent the conceptual oppositions on which he believes Western metaphysics is based, such as light/dark, good/bad, and big/small. See **metaphysics**.

biological model   A term coined by the feminist critic Elaine Showalter to describe one of four models or ways to construct a female framework for analyzing women's literature. This model emphasizes how the female body marks itself upon a text by providing a host of literary images along with a personal, intimate tone.

Black Arts movement Spans the decade from 1965 to 1975, beginning with the assassination of Malcolm X in 1965 and advocates Black Power or militant advocacy of armed self-defense while inspiring a renewal and pride in African heritage and asserting the goodness and beauty of all things black. Its chief spokesperson was the Greenwich Village beat poet Amiri Baraka and its literary magazine, *Cricket*.

bourgeoisie According to Karl Marx and Fredrich Engels in *The Communist Manifesto* (1848), this term refers to the social elite, or members of the upper class, who control and define the economic base of society through economic policies and the production of goods. The bourgeoisie also defines a society's superstructure and its hegemony. See **hegemony**.

canon The collected works of an author or of a tradition.

capitalist Another name given to the bourgeoisie by Marx and Engels. The capitalists in society enslave the working class (the **proletariat**) through economic policies and the production of goods.

carnival Coined by the Russian Formalist critic Mikhail Bakhtin to describe some novels' polyphonic style—that is, some novels have a carnival sense of the world, a sense of joyful abandonment in which many different voices are simultaneously heard and directly influence their hearers (and readers). Each participant in the novel tests both the ideas and the lives of other participants, creating a somewhat serio-comic environment. This notation of carnival is one of Bakhtin's most significant contributions to literary theory.

carnivalistic Coined by the Russian Formalist critic Mikhail Bakhtin to describe a sense of joyful relativity in a polyphonic novel caused by the readers' watching multiple characters influence each other with their particular understanding of truth. See **carnival** and **polyphonic**.

castration complex According to Sigmund Freud, if a child's sexual development is to proceed normally, each much pass through the castration complex. Boys, for example, know they have a penis like their fathers, but their mother and sisters do not. What stops the male child from having incestuous desires for his mother is fear of castration by his father. The child therefore represses his sexual desire, identifies with his father, hopes to possess a woman as his father now possesses his mother, and unconsciously makes a successful transition to manhood. The female child realizes that, like her mother, she is already castrated. Knowing that her father possesses what she desires (a penis), she turns her attention away from her mother and toward her father. After unsuccessfully attempting to seduce her father, she turns back toward her mother, identifies with her, and successfully makes her transition to womanhood.

catalyst An agent or element that causes but is not affected by a reaction.

catharsis A term used by Aristotle in the *Poetics* in discussing the nature and function of tragedy. Although its meaning is highly controversial and by no means clear, *catharsis* had both a medical and a religious meaning in Aristotle's day. Medically, the word referred to a body's discharge of excess elements during sickness and its subsequent return to health. In a religious sense, the word referred to the soul's method of purification, freeing itself from the body and becoming unfettered. As to its use in tragedy, Aristotle writes, "Through tragedy, then, the audience's emotions would somehow be purified." How this process actually occurs is open to debate.

cathexes   Coined by Freud to describe an individual's instinctual and psychic energy, its chief aim being to maximize the pleasure sensed and desired by the **pleasure principle** in the human psyche.

chora   A term used by the feminist critic Julia Kristeva to refer to the continuous flow of fluidity or rhythm that characterizes the imaginary order of psychic development. See **imaginary order**.

close reader   A term used by the New Critics for the kind of reader or critic who applies the principles of New Criticism to a text to arrive at an interpretation. Implied in the term is a close and detailed analysis of the text itself to derive its meaning without historical, authorial, or cultural input. See **New Criticism**.

close reading   A term used by the New Critics for the kind of reading or analysis of a text that applies the principles of New Criticism. Implied in the term is a close and detailed analysis of the text itself (its verbal qualities) to arrive at an interpretation without referring to historical, authorial, or cultural concerns. A close reading of a text became the hallmark of the New Critics' methodology. Sometimes referred to as *explication de texte* in French literary studies. See **New Criticism**.

collective meaning   A term used by the reader-oriented, subjective critic David Bleich as a substitute for the word *interpretation*. According to Bleich, a text's meaning is developed when a reader works in cooperation with other readers to achieve the text's collective meaning or its interpretation. Bleich argues that only when each reader is able to articulate his or her individual responses within a group about the text, then and only then can the group, working together, negotiate meaning and arrive at the text's collective meaning.

collective unconscious   A term brought into literary criticism via the psychology of Carl Jung. The collective unconscious is the part of the psyche that contains the cumulative knowledge, experiences, and images of the human race. This knowledge evidences itself as "primordial images" in humankind's religions, myths, dreams, and literature and can be tapped by writers through the use of archetypes. See **archetype**.

concretized   A term used by reader-oriented critics to mean the phenomenological process whereby the text registers upon the reader's consciousness. See **phenomenology**.

condensation   A term used by Sigmund Freud in psychoanalysis and dream interpretation to designate the process whereby one compacts a feeling or emotion toward a person or group and objectifies it into a simple sentence, phrase, or symbol.

connotation   The implied meaning of a word, as opposed to its dictionary definition. See **denotation**.

conscious   A term brought into literary criticism via the psychoanalysis of Carl Jung that refers to one of the three parts of the human psyche, a person's waking state. The term was also used by Sigmund Freud to define the rational and waking part of the human psyche. See **personal unconscious** and **collective unconscious**.

cultural criticism   A term used interchangeably with **cultural studies** in Great Britain. See **cultural studies**.

cultural feminism   Also known as radical feminism. This kind of feminist criticism asserts that personality and biological differences exist between men and women. Its main tenet is that women are inherently and biologically kinder and gentler than men. According to cultural feminists, women's gentler and kinder ways should be highlighted and celebrated because women's ways are better than men's.

cultural materialism   The British branch of cultural poetics. Compared with New Historicism or the American branch of cultural poetics, cultural materialism is overtly political and cultural in its aims. Accordingly, adherents to this critical methodology (mainly Marxists) believe we should read the works of the established canon "against the grain." By doing so, critics can expose the political unconscious of the text and debunk the social and political myths created by the bourgeoisie.

cultural model   One of four models developed by the feminist critic Elaine Showalter to construct a female framework for analyzing women's literature known as **gynocriticism**. The cultural model investigates how society shapes women's goals, responses, and points of view.

cultural poetics   According to Stephen Greenblatt, one of its founders, cultural poetics is now the preferred name for New Historicism. See **New Historicism** and **cultural materialism**.

cultural studies   The body of literary theorists, philosophers, and critics that study the works of subaltern writers, those such as Africans, Australians, Native Americans, women, and a host of others who are suppressed and repressed by their dominant cultures. These newly heard but long existent voices are now taking their place at the literary table, where they can present their understanding of reality, of society, and of personal self-worth. Some scholars divide this broad group into three categories: postcolonialism, African American criticism, and gender studies. See **subaltern writers, postcolonialism, African American criticism**, and **gender studies**.

decolonization   A term used in postcolonialism to describe Great Britain's slowly disappearing political, social, economic, and ideological domination of its many former colonies at the beginning of the twentieth century.

deconstruction   Introduced in America in 1966 by Jacques Derrida's speech at Johns Hopkins University, this poststructural approach to literary analysis is best considered a strategic device for interpreting a text rather than a critical theory, school of criticism, or philosophy. Such theories, schools of criticism, and philosophies, Derrida asserts, must identify with a body of knowledge that they decree to be true or, at least, to contain truth. The idea that truth or a core of metaphysical ideals can be definitely believed, articulated, and supported is exactly what Derrida and **deconstructists** wish to "deconstruct."

Considered to be the most intellectually formidable approach to literary analysis, deconstruction bases its ideas on the linguistics of Ferdinand de Saussure and his assertion that language is a system based on differences; for example, we know the difference between the sounds /b/ and /p/ because we have heard both and can note the difference. Derrida enlarges this concept of difference by declaring that how we come to know concepts is also a matter of difference.

Denying any center of truth, such as God, humanity, or the self, deconstruction maintains that we can never be certain about our values, beliefs, and assumptions. If this is the case, then we can never be certain about a text's meaning, and we can therefore never declare a text to have but one meaning. The "undecidability" of a text's meaning is the cardinal rule of deconstruction.

deconstruction theory   An approach or strategy for reading devised by the French literary critic Jacques Derrida to discover "how" a text means by asking a different set of questions than structuralist critics. Its aim is to show that what a text claims it says and what it actually says are discernibly different. See **deconstruction**.

defamiliarization   A termed coined by the Russian Formalist Victor Shklovsky. It is the process of making strange (see **ostranenie**) the familiar or putting the old in new light or in a new sphere of perception. Through poetic diction or word choice, a poet "makes strange" the poetic line or word, slowing down the act of perception, thereby forcing readers to reexamine the word, line, image, or any other poetic device. In so doing, readers experience a small part of their world in a new way by intensifying the act of perception.

denotation   The dictionary definition of a word, as distinct from its *connotation* or its suggestive or emotional meaning. See **connotation**.

destructive instinct   Also known as the **aggressive instinct**, this word was coined by Freud to describe the two basic instincts housed in a human's unconscious. More frequently than not, the destructive instinct attacks the **eros** or **sexual instinct** (later called the **libido** by Freud). According to Freud, the unconscious houses our biographical memories along with suppressed and unresolved conflicts.

devices   A word used by the Russian Formalists to denote the internal mechanics of a work of literature, especially its poetic language. These devices are an integral part of the work's form. See **form**.

diachronic   A term used in linguistics to designate a process of language study in which language change is traced over long expanses of time. Such study can discover, for example, how a particular phenomenon in one language has changed through several centuries and whether a similar change could be noted in other languages. (The term is also used in other fields in which cultural phenomena are studied as they occur or change over time.)

dialectial criticism   A term coined by the Marxist postcolonialist critic Fredric Jameson that refers to his belief that all critics must be consciously aware of their own ideology when analyzing a text, what Jameson calls "dialectial self-awareness." See **dialectial self-awareness**.

dialectical materialism   A term used to refer to the core beliefs of Marxism as defined by Marx and Engels in *The Communist Manifesto* (1848) and by Marx in *The German Ideology* (1846). For Marx and Engels, "Consciousness does not determine life: life determines consciousness." In other words, our ideas and concepts about ourselves are fashioned in everyday discourse in the language of real life and are not derived from any spiritual reality. The basis of reality is material; no spiritual reality exists. In addition, the economic means of production within a society—its *base*—engenders and controls all human institutions and ideologies—the *superstructure*. See **Marxism**.

dialectial self-awareness   Brought into Marxist criticism by the American critic Fredric Jameson, this term posits that all readers or critics must be consciously aware of their own ideology when analyzing a text.

dialectic   First used by the Greek philosophers Socrates and Plato to describe a form of logical argumentation involving conflicting ideas and propositions. The German philosopher Georg Hegel borrows its form to establish his **thesis–antithesis–synthesis** dynamic.

dialogic   A concept developed by the Russian Formalist critic Mikhail Bakhtin that asserts that all language is a dialogue in which a speaker and a listener form a relationship. All language, argues Bakhtin, is the product of at least two people.

dialogic heteroglossia   Coined by the Russian Formalist critic Mikhail Bakhtin, this concept literally means "many voices in multiple conversations" and explains Bakhtin's idea that multiple conversations occur in all texts. No text is a monologue. See **dialogic**.

dialogic utterance   Coined by the Russian Formalist critic Mikhail Bakhtin, this term asserts that each individual speech act is oriented toward a particular listener or audience and demonstrates the relationship that exists between the speaker and listener.

dialogized heteroglossia   A term coined by the Russian Formalist critic Mikhail Bakhtin that for Bakhtin characterizes the novel. Within the novel, multiple worldviews and a variety of experiences are continually dialoguing with each other, resulting in multiple interactions, some of which are real and others of which are imagined.

diction   A term used by all schools of literary criticism referring to an author or speaker's word choice.

différance   Introduced by the French deconstructionist Jacques Derrida. Différance is derived from the French word *différer*, meaning (1) to defer, postpone, or delay and (2) to differ, to be different from. Derrida deliberately coined this word to be ambiguous, taking on both meanings simultaneously. One of the keys to understanding deconstruction, différance is Derrida's "What if?" question. What if there is no ultimate truth? What if there is no essence, being, or inherently unifying element in the universe? What then? Derrida's answer is that all meaning or interpretations of a text are undecidable because a text can have innumerable meanings and interpretations.

discourse   A way of seeing and thinking about the world. Bounded by ideology, culture, education, politics, and a variety of other influences, discourse refers not only to speech patterns but also to a particular mindset secured by philosophical assumptions that predispose a person to interpret the world in a particular fashion.

displacement   A term used by Sigmund Freud in psychoanalysis to designate the process whereby we suppress wishes and desires that are too difficult for our psyches to handle by concealing them in symbols that take the place of the original desire. Our unconscious mind may switch, for example, a person's hatred of another onto a rotting apple in a dream.

double consciousness   A postcolonial term used synonymously with unhomeliness. See **unhomeliness**.

double-voicedness   A term coined by the African American literary critic Henry Louis Gates, Jr. to assert that African American literature draws upon two voices and cultures, the white and the black. According to Gates, this joining of the two distinct discourses produces the uniqueness of African American literature.

dynamic model   The earliest of Sigmund Freud's models of the human psyche; with it, Freud declared that our minds are based in a dichotomy consisting of the **conscious** (the rational) and the **unconscious** (the irrational).

economic model   Sigmund Freud's later or revised model of the human psyche, which he developed after the dynamic model. In the economic model, Freud introduces two new concepts: the pleasure principle and the reality principle. See **pleasure principle** and **reality principle**.

ecofeminism   (or eco-feminism) A contemporary approach in feminist studies that assumes that patriarchal societies are relatively new and that society's original condition, known as Feminist Eden, was matriarchal. Whereas patriarchal societies, say ecofeminists, are detrimental to women, children, and nature, matriarchal societies protect the environment, natural resources, and animal life while caring for women and children.

écriture féminine   A term used in feminist criticism to refer specifically to "women's writing." Modern feminist critics speculate that a style of writing peculiar to women exists and that this écriture féminine is fundamentally different from the way men write and obtain meaning through the writing process.

efferent reading   A term used by Louise M. Rosenblatt in *The Reader, the Text, the Poem* (1978) to refer to that type of reading "in which the primary concern of the reader is with what he or she will carry away from the reading." We read efferently, for example, when we read solely for information, as we do when we read the directions on heating a can of soup. During this process, we are interested only in newly gained information. This is different from aesthetic reading, in which the reader "lives through" and experiences the reading process. See **aesthetic reading**.

ego   A term used by Sigmund Freud to designate the rational, logical, waking part of the psyche as differentiated from the id and the superego.

Electra complex   The female version of the Oedipus complex as defined by Sigmund Freud. Freud borrows the name from Greek mythology: Electra, the sister of Orestes, aids him in killing their mother, Clytemnestra, to avenge their father, Agamemnon, who Clytemnestra murdered. According to Freud, all girls must successfully negotiate the Electra complex in order to make the transition from girlhood to being a normal, mature woman. Similar to a boy, a young girl is erotically attracted to her mother and recognizes that her father is a rival for her mother's affection. Unconsciously, however, the girl realizes she is already castrated, as is her mother. Because she knows her father possesses that which she desires, a penis, she turns her desires to him and away from her mother. After the seduction of her father fails, she turns back toward her mother and identifies with her, thus successfully negotiating the Electra complex. See **Oedipus complex**.

eme   A linguistic term used by Ferdinand de Saussure to designate the basic units or building blocks of language, such as phonemes, morphemes, words, and so on.

epic theater   Developed by the playwright and Marxist critic Bertolt Brecht, the kind of theatrical theory and production that advocates an abandonment of the Aristotelian premise of unity of time, place, and action, including the assumption that the audience should be made to believe that what they are seeing is real. Epic theater seeks to create alienation effects such as interrupting the drama by a direct appeal to the audience via a song or speech to keep the audience constantly aware of the moral and social issues to which they are being exposed in the drama. Brecht believed that dramatists should not blindly accept bourgeois conventionality within the drama and thus should revolt and seize the modes of production within this genre.

epiphany   A sudden understanding or insight, especially concerning a divine being or the essential nature of truth. The term is often used in its Christian sense, the first Epiphany having taken place on January 6 with the manifestation of Christ to the Gentiles in the form of the Magi, and thereafter observed as a Holy Day in the

Christian Church. James Joyce is responsible for bringing this term into literary critical usage to mean a sudden, intuitive understanding of a person, situation, or object.

episteme   A term borrowed from the French writer, philosopher, and critic Michel Foucault and used by New Historicists to define the unifying principle or pattern that develops in each historical epoch. Through language and thought, each period in history develops its own perceptions about the nature of reality (or what it defines as truth) and sets up its own standards of behavior.

epistemological   Of or relating to the branch of philosophy called epistemology, which studies the nature of knowledge, especially its limits and validity.

erasure   Coined by the French deconstrutionist critic Jacques Derrida to describe the process of believing, if only temporarily and for the sake of investigation, that values and beliefs are stable and are objectively true. By positing the objective existence of such values and beliefs, Derrida declares that he can show through a deconstructive reading the absence of any definitive meaning for these values or beliefs.

eros   Another name for the **sexual instinct**, one of two basic human instincts that, according to Freud, are housed in the unconscious.

esoteric work   A text meant for private as opposed to public circulation.

essentialism   The classical humanist belief that the true essence or identity of a person is composed of finite and fixed properties that make up the essential component of what it means to be human. Essentialists believe that to be human means having an unchangeable human nature, a true and invariable essence.

estrangement   A term used by Russian Formalists to show poetic language's ability to make strange the familiar, thereby causing the readers of a text to reexamine the word or image and to experience it anew. See **defamiliarization** and **ostranenie**.

etymologically   The adverbial form of etymology, or the process of tracing the historical development of a word, including its various meanings and forms, from the word's earliest recorded occurrence in a language to the present.

exoteric treatise   A text meant for general publication.

expressive school   Emphasizing the individuality of the artist and the reader's privilege to share in this individuality. Disavowing rhetorical or objective theories of art, expressive critics emphasize the subjective experience of sharing emotions. Wordsworth and other nineteenth-century Romantics are prime examples of this school of thought.

extrinsic analysis   The process of examining elements outside the text (e.g., historical events and biographies) to uncover the text's meaning.

fabula   A term coined by the Russian Formalist Victor Shklovsky. According to Shklovsky, all prose narrative is composed of either fabula or syuzhet. Fabula (or translated story) is the raw material of the story and can be considered somewhat akin to the author's working outline that contains the chronological series of events of the story. See **syuzhet**.

fall phase   According to the mythic critic Northrop Fyre, all literature comprise one complete story called the **monomyth**, which is composed of four phases. One of these phases is the fall phase, which recognizes humanity's tendency to "fall" from happiness and freedom to disaster and bondage.

false consciousness   A term used by Karl Marx to describe how the consciousness of the working class is shaped and controlled by the bourgeoisie. By defining what it means to be an individual and thereby prescribing its class consciousness, the bourgeoisie creates a false consciousness for the proletariat and perpetuates the dominant class's social structure.

female phase   The name given by the feminist critic Elaine Showalter to the present state, direction, and concerns of contemporary feminist criticism, usually dated from 1970 to the present.

feminine phase   The name given by the feminist critic Elaine Showalter to the first historical period of feminist theory and criticism, dating from 1840 to 1880.

feminism   An approach to textual analysis having its roots in the Progressive Era in the early decades of the twentieth century. Some of its earliest and major philosophical tenets are articulated by the British feminist Virginia Woolf (*A Room of One's Own*, published in 1919) and the French feminist Simone de Beauvoir (*The Second Sex*, published in 1949). Feminists assert that Western societies are patriarchal, or controlled by men. Either consciously or unconsciously, men have oppressed women, allowing them little or no voice in the political, social, or economic issues of their society. By not giving voice, and therefore value, to women's opinions, responses, and writings, men have suppressed the female, defined what it means to be feminine, and thereby devoiced, devalued, and trivialized what it means to be a woman. Men have made women the "nonsignificant Other."

   A goal of feminism is to change this view of women so that each woman will realize that she is a valuable person possessing the same privileges and rights as every man. Women must define themselves and assert their own voices in politics, education, the arts, and all other areas of society. By debunking stereotypical images of women found throughout the literary canon, rediscovering and publishing texts written by females but suppressed by men, rereading the canonized works of male authors from a woman's point of view, and engaging in the discussion of literary theory and criticism, women can challenge the concept of male superiority and work toward creating equality between the sexes.

   Because feminism is more an approach or mindset than a school of criticism, feminist theory and criticism have been embraced by scholars belonging to a variety of critical schools, such as Marxism, deconstruction, psychoanalysis, and New Historicism. Some of the leading twentieth-century feminists are Virginia Woolf, Simone de Beauvoir, Elaine Showalter, Hélène Cixous, Sandra Gilbert, and Gayatri Chakravorty Spivak.

feminist phase   The name given by the feminist critic Elaine Showalter to the second historical period of feminist theory and criticism, dating from 1880 to 1920.

foregrounding   A term used by the Russian formalists that refers to the language of a work of art. Literary language is different from everyday language. Unlike every day conversation or language, literary language shouts, "Look at me; I am special." For example, when a poet writes, "The cow jumped over the moon," such language stands out and demands contemplation and analysis.

foregrounds   The verb form of **foregrounding**.

forestructure   The fund of past experiences (memories) that readers bring to the reading process.

form   A term used by the Russian Formalists to denote the constituent parts—both linguistic and structural features—of a poem. Such features include the internal mechanics of the work itself, specially its poetic language (see **devices**). Also, form is a term used by the New Critics—adherents of New Criticism—to mean the overall effect a text creates. From this perspective, a text's form encompasses the actual structure of the text along with the text's overall effect on the reader. In New Critical theory, all the elements of a text work together to form a single, unified effect known as the text's form.

formalism   A term used to designate critics (**formalists**) who rely on a work's form or structure to determine its meaning. The term is often applied to the Russian Formalists and New Critics who insist that the interpretation of a work of art must evolve from the work's structure, not from extrinsic elements such as the author's life or historical context. For such critics, a work of art is an object in its own right that can be analyzed without referring to any extratextual evidence or sources such as history, politics, or sociology.

formalists   Literary theorists and critics who adhere to the principles of formalism. See **formalism**.

fragmentation   A term developed by Marxist critics to describe the fractured and fragmented nature of society caused by the workers' detachment from what they produce and from each other. See **alienation**.

Frankfurt school   Neo-Marxist critics devoted to developing Western Marxist principles. These critics assert that the superstructure reflects the economic base. They also believe that a text reveals a culture's fragmentation, not its wholeness. See **superstructure** and **base**.

Freudian slips   A term used in psychoanalysis to describe accidental slips of the tongue. According to Freud, these "disguised truths" are stored in a person's unconscious until, inadvertently, they slip into our conscious minds and pop out in statements in one's speech.

gay and lesbian studies   Beginning in the mid-1980s, this school of criticism borrows and develops the gender concerns of the feminist and gender critics and targets the heterosexual/homosexual binary, emphasizing sexual differences. Gay studies examines sexual differences applicable to the male and lesbian studies to the female. Both groups analyze the social structures that have defined gays and lesbians as deviant or abnormal, questioning how such definitions developed throughout history and seeking to know the reasons why heterosexuality has been so positively defined but homosexuality has not.

gender studies   A term sometimes used synonymously with **feminism**; however, the field broadens traditional feminist criticism to include an investigation of not only femaleness but also maleness. To the multivoiced feminist theories, gender studies adds the ever-growing and increasingly diverse voices of black feminists, the ongoing concerns of French feminism, and the impact of poststructural theories on customary feminist issues.

good critic   A term used by New Criticism to characterize the kind of critic who examines a poem's (or any text's) structure by scrutinizing its poetic elements, rooting out and showing its inner tensions, and demonstrating how the poem supports its overall meaning as the writer reconciles these tensions into a unified whole.

grammar   The system of rules that governs the production and interpretation of language. **Prescriptive grammar** refers to matters of "correctness," such as not using the word *ain't* or saying "It is I" rather than "It is me." **Descriptive grammar** is the process of describing how actual speakers use their language for communication.

grammatical Of or referring to the rules of grammar that establish relationships between words or groups of words.

grammatical sentence See **sentence**.

grammatology The French deconstructionist Jacque Derrida's name for the science of writing and the investigation of the origin of language. Derrida argues for a redefining of writing, asserting that writing is a precondition for speech and occurs prior to it.

grapheme The symbols of a writing system (e.g., the letters of the alphabet) that represent a phoneme. See **phoneme**.

gynocriticism A term coined by the feminist scholar–critic Elaine Showalter that has become synonymous with the study of women as writers. It provides critics with four models about the nature of women's writing that help answer some of the chief concerns of feminist criticism. Each of Showalter's models are sequential, subsuming and developing the preceding model(s), to encompass the full analytical scope: **biological, linguistic, psychoanalytic,** and **cultural**.

gynocritics A term coined by the feminist scholar–critic Elaine Showalter to define the process of constructing "a female framework for analysis of women's literature [in order] to develop new models [of interpretation] based on the study of female experience, rather than to adapt to male models and theories." See **gynocriticism**.

hailing the subject Coined by the Marxist critic Louis Althusser to describe the process whereby the dominant ideology forms the attitudes of people. See **interpellation**.

hamartia A term used by Aristotle in the *Poetics* to refer to the tragic hero's mistake or error that leads to a downfall. Literally, the word means "missing the mark" (from the Greek *hamartanein*, "to err"). Aristotle explains that the hero of a tragedy will commit an action or exhibit a frailty (*hamartia*) that will lead to a reversal of fortune.

hegemony A term used in Marxist criticism to refer to the system of beliefs, values, and meanings to which most people in a given society subscribe. Marxist critics assert that the dominant culture in a given society is under the control of the bourgeoisie. It is the bourgeoisie who controls and dictates the hegemony of a culture. According to the Italian Marxist Antonio Gramsci, a given society's hegemony may be successful but never complete. Rather than one all-encompassing ruling class, there usually exist several, interconnected yet somewhat divergent classes, each influencing the super-structure at different times and in different ways. Marxist revolutions, then, can begin within alternative hegemonies rather than direct political action.

heresy of paraphrase A term used by New Critics to suggest that a work of art is not equal to its paraphrase. A poem, for example, is not the same as its paraphrased version because the paraphrased version will miss the poem's uniqueness, with its many connotations and various complexities of thought.

hermeneutical principles The rules governing the interpretation of a text. See hermeneutics.

hermeneutics First defined by religious scholars as the art and science of biblical interpretation, this term now refers to any theory and practice of interpretation. (From the Greek *hermeneutike*, meaning the "act of interpretation.")

hermeneutics of recovery The process of investigating how a text was received and evaluated by its contemporary readers.

hermeneutics of suspicion The process of investigating the implied assumptions—political, sexual, religious, linguistic, and so forth—of a text and its author.

heteroglossia Literally interpreted "other or different tongues" from the Russian word *raznorecie*, this term was coined by the Russian Formalist critic Mikhail Bakhtin to demonstrate the multiple languages that operate in any given culture. For Bakhtin, all forms of social speech that people use in their daily activities constitute heteroglossia.

holistic approach An approach to literary study that investigates, analyzes, and interprets all elements of the artistic situation—text, author, historical context, and so on—instead of concentrating on one or more specific aspects.

horizons of expectation A term used by reader-oriented critics to refer to all of a historical period's critical vocabulary and assessments of a particular text. Used especially by those who adhere to reception theory. See **reception theory**.

hybridity A disputed term used by postcolonial theorists that refers to a mix or blending of two cultures. When two cultures commingle, the nature and characteristics of the newly created culture changes each of the commingled cultures. The philosophical and practical nature of these changes varies greatly depending on the theorist discussions then.

hybridization A term used by the Russian Formalist critic Mikhail Bakhtin for the clashing of two different languages in a single utterance. See **heteroglossia**. In postcolonial theory, the process whereby hybridity occurs.

hyperprotected cooperative principle The belief that published works are worthy to be called literature because they have been evaluated and declared literary texts by a group of well-informed people such as scholars, critics, and publishers.

id A term used by Sigmund Freud to designate the irrational, instinctual, unknown, and unconscious part of the psyche as differentiated from the **ego** and **superego**.

ideal reader A term devised by the narratologist Gerard Prince to differentiate among the real, virtual, and ideal reader. According to Prince, the ideal reader is one who explicitly and implicitly understands all the nuances, terminology, and structure of a text. See **virtual reader** and **real reader**.

identity theme A term devised by the Freudian psychoanalyst Norman Holland, who argues that, at birth, all of us receive from our mothers a primary identity. Through each of our life's experiences, we personalize this identity, transforming it into our own individualized identity theme, which becomes the lens through which we see the world.

ideological state apparatus A term used by the Marxist critic Louis Althusser as a synonym for **hegemony**, the dominant class's ideology.

ideology A much-debated term in Marxist criticism, ideology often refers to a culture's collective or social consciousness (as opposed to the material reality on which experience is based)—that is, to the culture's internal awareness of a body of laws or codes governing its politics, law, religion, philosophy, and art to which that culture's bourgeoisie and its superstructure subscribe. For Marx and Engels, a culture's ideology is more frequently than not synonymous with "false consciousness" because it has been defined and established by the bourgeoisie and represents a set of false assumptions or illusions used by the elite to dominate the working classes and to maintain stability. An ideology, then, may be conscious or explicit (in precepts that state and shape a society's philosophy, laws, or acceptable customs), or it may be a somewhat vaguer and implicit understanding of its controlling beliefs (e.g., as in ceremony).

imaginary order   According to psychoanalyst Jacques Lacan, one of three parts of the human psyche; it contains our wishes, fantasies, and images. In this preverbal state (from birth to age 6 months), Lacan believes humans are joyfully united with their mothers, receiving food, care, and all comforts from them and relying on images as a means of perceiving and interpreting the world. In this psychic stage of development, our image of ourselves is always in flux because we are not able to differentiate where one image stops and another begins.

implied reader   A term devised by the German phenomenologist Wolfgang Iser to differentiate between two kinds of readers: the implied reader and the **actual reader**. According to Iser, the implied reader is the reader who "embodies all those predispositions laid down, not by an empirical outside reality, but by the text itself. Hence, the implied reader has his or her roots firmly planted in the structure of the text." See **actual reader**.

impressionistic critics   Critics who believe that how we feel and what we personally see in a work of art are what really matter. Capturing what we see from a particular point of view and at a specific moment in time is what is important, not an objective, lengthy investigation of text or an aesthetic object. The term *impressionism* was first used by nineteenth-century French painters such as Claude Monet and Pierre-August Renoir and referred to the impressions an object makes upon the artist rather than the actual representation of an objective picture of that object.

inflection   Used in linguistics to describe the various forms a word undergoes to mark changes in elements such as tense, number, gender, and mood. For example, the *-ed* in the word *worked* signals the past tense, and the *-s* in the word *dogs* signals the plural form of that word.

in medias res   From the Latin, meaning "in the middle of things." This term refers to a story or narrative such as *The Iliad* that begins in the middle rather than at its chronological starting point in time.

intentional fallacy   A term used by New Critics to refer to what they believe is the erroneous assumption that the interpretation of a literary work can be equated to the author's stated or implied intentions or private meanings. Claiming such external information to be irrelevant in ascertaining a text's meaning, New Critics base interpretation on the text itself. The term was first used by W.K. Wimsatt and Monroe C. Beardsley in "The Intentional Fallacy" (1946).

interpellation   Also known as "hailing the subject," this term was coined by the Marxist critic Louis Althusser to refer to the process whereby the dominant hegemony or prevailing ideology forms the attitudes of people in society. See **hegemony**.

interpretive community   A term coined by the reader-oriented critic Stanley Fish to designate a group of readers who share the same interpretive strategies.

intertexuality   A term denoting that any given text's meaning or interpretation is related or interrelated to the meaning of all other texts. Hence, no text can be interpreted in isolation, and all texts are **intertexual**.

irony   The use of words whereby a writer or speaker suggests the opposite of what is actually stated. According to New Critics such as Cleanth Brooks, John Crowe Ransom, and I.A. Richards, irony is the key to the "dramatic structure" of poetry and unlocks the door to show how meaning is contained in and evolves from a poem's structure. New Critics believe a poem's meaning is structurally determined, created by the tension between the denotative meaning of a poem's words and their connotations, which are, in turn, determined by the context of that particular poem. Irony, then, is "an equilibrium of [these] opposing attitudes and evaluations," which ultimately determines the poem's meaning and is the master trope in New Criticism.

jouissance   A term used by the psychoanalytic critic Jacques Lacan to refer to a brief moment of joy, terror, or desire that somehow arises from deep within the unconscious psyche and reminds us of a time of perfect wholeness when we were incapable of differentiating among images from the real order. See **real order, imaginary order**, and **symbolic order**.

language   Defined by the linguist Thomas Pyles as "a systematized combination of sounds that have meaning for all people in a given cultural community." Broadly speaking, language may be considered any system of signs or codes that convey meaning, such as road signs, the language of fashion (wearing different clothes in different social settings), or even the language of eating.

langue   The linguistic term used by Ferdinand de Saussure to refer to the rules that comprise a language or the structure of the language that is mastered and shared by all its speakers. By the age of 5 or 6, children have mastered their language's langue, although they have not mastered the language's prescriptive grammar. For example, a 6-year-old may say, "I drinked a glass of milk" and "I climbed a tree." Having mastered his or her langue, the child has learned that most English verbs form their past tense by adding -d or -ed. What the child has not mastered is the many exceptions to this rule, in this case, the past tense of the irregular verb *to drink*.

latent content   A term used by Sigmund Freud in psychoanalytic dream interpretation. It is Freud's view that the ego (the rational part of the psyche) hides the true wish or latent content of our dreams, thereby allowing the dreamer to remember a somewhat changed and often radically different dream than the one that actually occurred.

l'écriture féminine   See écriture féminine.

lexical   Used in linguistics to refer to the base or root meaning of a word. For example, the word *love* is the base word in the following word model: *loves, loved, loving*.

lesbianization of language   A term coined by the contemporary feminist critic Monique Wittig to challenge patriarchal assumptions embedded in the structure of language itself by experimenting with and hoping to eliminate pronouns and nouns that reflect gender.

lexicon   The word stock or the entire vocabulary of a language.

libido   A term used by Sigmund Freud in psychoanalysis that has become synonymous with sexual drive. Freud used this designation to refer to the emotional energy that springs from primitive biological urges and is usually directed toward some goal.

linear   A term used to refer to something that has a definite beginning, middle, and end. A philosophy of life or one's worldview, for example, may be considered linear.

linguistics   The science of language and human speech, including the study of sounds, inflections, structure, and modification of language.

linguistic model   A term coined by the feminist critic Elaine Showalter to describe one of the four ways for constructing a female framework for analyzing literature. Showalter's overall model is known as **gynocriticism**. The linguistic model particularly addresses the need for a female discourse, investigating the differences between how men and women use language. According to Showalter, women create and write in a language peculiar to their gender.

linguistic sign   A term used in linguistics in reference to words. As used by Ferdinand de Saussure, a sign is composed of two parts: the signifier (a written or spoken mark) and the signified (the concept it represents). See **sign**.

literacy experience   A term used by the reader-oriented critic Louise Rosenblatt to explain what happens when a reader interacts with print. According to Rosenblatt, a literacy experience or event occurs; the reader and the text transact, effectively shaping each other.

literariness   A term used by the Russian Formalists to refer to the language used in a work of art. Such language calls attention to itself as language, thus foregrounding itself. See **foregrounding**.

literary competence   An internalized set of rules that govern a reader's interpretation of a text. The critic Jonathan Culler states that all readers possess literary competence or the ability to make sense of a text.

literary critic   One who interprets literature. This term often implies one who is an expert at interpreting a text. Anyone, however, who reads and offers an interpretation of a text is a practicing literary critic.

literary criticism   According to the nineteenth-century English critic and writer Matthew Arnold, literary criticism is "a disinterested endeavor to learn and propagate the best that is known and thought in the world." Literary criticism is therefore a disciplined activity that attempts to study, analyze, interpret, and evaluate works of art.

literary theory   A set of principles or assumptions on which our interpretation of a text is based. Our personal literary theory is our conscious or unconscious development of a mindset—including values, aesthetics sense, morals, and so on—concerning our expectations when reading any type of literature. By articulating this framework and piecing together the various elements of our practical criticism into a coherent, unified body of knowledge, we create a literary theory.

literature   Derived from the Latin word *littera*, meaning "letter," the word *literature* refers primarily to the written word, especially prose or verse.

logocentrism   A term used by the French deconstructionist Jacques Derrida that refers to Western culture's proclivity for desiring absolute truths, or what Derrida calls "centers." Logocentrism is the belief that an ultimate reality or center of truth can serve as the basis for all our thoughts and actions.

manifest content   A term used by Sigmund Freud in psychoanalytic dream interpretation. Freud argues that the ego or the rational part of the psyche hides the true wish or **latent content** of our dreams and allows the dreamer to remember a somewhat changed and often radically different dream than what actually occurred. This changed dream is the manifest content that the dreamer remembers and tells his or her dream analyst.

market   A term used by Marxist critics to define how successfully a commodity sells.

Marxism   An approach to literary analysis founded on principles articulated by Friedrich Engels and Karl Marx. Unlike other schools of criticism, Marxism is not primarily a literary theory that can be used to interpret a text because it is first a set of social, economic, and political ideas that its followers believe will enable them to interpret and change their world. Ultimate reality, they declare, is material, not spiritual. What we know beyond any doubt is that human beings exist and live in social groups. To understand ourselves and our world, we must first acknowledge the interrelatedness of all our actions within society. Once understood properly, we will note that our cultural and our social circumstances determine who we are. What we believe, what we value, and how we think are a direct result of our society, and that society, says Marxism, is built upon a series of ongoing conflicts between the "haves" and the "have nots."

In *The Communist Manifesto* (1848), Engels and Marx declare that the "haves" (the capitalists or the **bourgeoisie**) have successfully enslaved the "have nots" (the working class or the **proletariat**) through economic policies and control of the production of goods. In addition, the bourgeoisie has established society's beliefs, values, and even art. Now the proletariat must revolt and strip the bourgeoisie of its economic and political power and place the ownership of all property in the hands of the government, which will fairly distribute the people's wealth.

Because the bourgeoisie controls a society's art and therefore its literature, **Marxist critics** believe they must move beyond the usual analysis of literary devices, themes, and style and concentrate on determining an author's worldview, the historical context of the work, and the sociological concerns of the text to see if such an analysis of the author's ideology advances either the bourgeoisie's or the proletariat's concerns.

Some of the leading Marxist critics of the twentieth century are Georg Lukács, Raymond Williams, Walter Benjamin, Fredric Jameson, and Terry Eagleton.

materialist feminisms   One of four major categories of contemporary feminism that emphasizes goods and material reality. Includes critics such as Juliet Mitchell, Jacqueline Rose, and Catherine Belsey.

metalanguage   A language (words) used to describe or talk about language.

metaphor   A figure of speech that directly compares two unlike objects (without using *like* or *as*), in which the qualities of one object are ascribed to the other. For example, in the sentence, "My love is a rose," the qualities of the rose are directly ascribed to "my love."

metaphysics   A term derived from Aristotle's treatise *Metaphysica*, denoting a division of philosophy that studies the nature of Being. The term implies a reality beyond what we can see and experience with our five senses.

metaphysics of presence   A term coined by the French deconstructionist Jacques Derrida to encompass ideas such as **logocentrism, phonocentrism**, the operation of **binary oppositions**, and other notions held in Western thought and culture about the nature of language and metaphysics. Derrida's objectives are to demonstrate the shaky foundations on which such beliefs have been established and thereby "deconstruct" or take apart what Western culture values and show how such a deconstructive process will lead to new and exciting interpretations of a text.

metatheory   An overarching or all-inclusive literary theory—that is, a theory of all theories—that encompasses all possible interpretations of a text suggested by its readers.

mimesis   From the Greek, meaning "imitation." Often refers to Aristotle's theory of imitation.

mimetic   Adjectival form for **mimetic theory**.

mimetic theory   A term used in literary criticism to refer to art as an imitation or copy of various elements of the universe. In linguistics, the mimetic theory of language asserts that words are symbols for things in the world—that is, each word has its own referent, or the object, concept, or idea that is represented or symbolized by that word. Accordingly, a word equals its **referent**.

minimal pair Two words that differ by one significant phonological sound. For example, *pit* and *bit* differ only in their first phonemes or significant first sounds.

mirror stage A term coined by the psychoanalyst Jacques Lacan to describe what happens during the development of the human psyche sometime between 6 to 18 months of age. According to Lacan, the human psyche consists of three parts or orders: the **imaginary**, the **symbolic**, and the **Real**. During the latter part of development in the first order, the imaginary, Lacan asserts that we literally see ourselves in a mirror, or we may metaphorically see ourselves in our mothers' image. Seeing this mirror image permits us to perceive images that have discrete boundaries, thereby allowing us to become aware of ourselves as independent beings who are separate from our mothers.

misogyny A term used in feminist criticism to refer to a hatred or distrust of women.

misspeaks According to the deconstructionist critic Jacques Derrida, at some point in all texts, the author loses control of language and says what was supposedly not meant to be said and thus "misspeaks." Such slips of tongue usually occur in questions, figurative language, and strong declarations. By examining these slips and the binary operations that govern them, Derrida believes he is able to demonstrate the undecidability of a text's meaning. See **binary operations** and **undecidability**.

modernism A literary movement in both England and the United States considered by some to have begun with the influence of the French symbolist poetry of Charles Baudelaire and Paul Valéry at the beginning of the twentieth century. Some assert that this period begins in 1914, with the start of World War I and ends right after World War II; still others mark its ending around 1965.

However its span is dated, modernism is marked, as T.S. Eliot notes, by an impersonal view of humanity and produced a literature that is distinctly anti-romantic and anti-expressionistic. In its ardent search for meaning through form, modernism typically uses hard, dry language that asserts that feelings and emotions are elicited by the text itself through the textual arrangement of its images. By rejecting a merely personal reading of a work, modernism declares that a text's meaning can be found by examining its structure, a technique that is especially true for poetry. The modernist period provides literary criticism with a formal explanation for how a poem or any other work of literature achieves or produces meaning through its form.

modernity A term used synonymously with the Enlightenment or Age of Reason (18th century) by many critics. Modernity holds to two basic premises: a belief that reason is humankind's best guide to life and that science can lead humanity to a new "promised land."

monomyth A term used in the archetypal criticism of Northrop Frye, who states that all literature comprises one complete and whole story called the monomyth. This monomyth can best be diagrammed as a circle containing four separate phases, with each phase corresponding to a season of the year and to peculiar cycles of human experiences. The phases are **romance** (the summer story of total happiness and wish fulfillment), **anti-romance** (the winter story of bondage, imprisonment, frustration, and fear), **comedy** (the spring story that tells of our rise from frustration to freedom and happiness), and **tragedy** (the fall story, narrating our fall from happiness to disaster). According to Frye, all stories fall somewhere within these categories.

morpheme Used in linguistics to describe the smallest part of a word that has lexical or grammatical significance. For example, whereas the word *dog* contains one morpheme, {*dog*}, the word *dogs* contains two morphemes, {*dog*} and {-*s*.}

morphology Used in linguistics to describe the process of word formation, such as compound words and inflections.

mythemes A term coined by the structuralist critic Claude Lévi-Strauss that refers to the many recurrent themes running through humankind's countless myths. These basic structures, he maintains, are similar to the individual sounds of language, the primary building blocks of language itself. Like these sounds, mythemes find meaning in and through their relationships within the mythic structure, not in their own individuality. The meaning of any individual myth depends on the interaction and order of the mythemes found within the story.

mythic criticism Criticism that examines **archetypes** and archetypal patterns to explain the structure and significance of texts. This type of criticism was especially emphasized by Carl Jung and Northrop Frye. See **archetypal criticism**.

narratee A term used by the structuralist and narratologist Gerard Prince to refer to the person to whom the narrator of a text is speaking. It is Prince's view that the narratee is not the actual person reading the text but, in fact, is produced by the narrative itself.

narrative functions According to the Russian narratologist Vladimir Propp, all folk or fairy tales are composed of a sequence of 31 fixed elements or narrative functions that occur in the same order in all fairy tales. Each function identifies predictable patterns that central characters will enact to further the plot of the story.

narratologists A particular kind of structuralist who uses the principles of narratology to interpret texts. See **narratology**.

narratology   A form of structuralism espoused by Vladimir Propp, Tzvetan Todorov, Roland Barthes, and Gerard Genette that illustrates how a story's meaning develops from its overall structure (its **langue**) rather than from each individual story's isolated theme. To ascertain a text's meaning, narratologists emphasize grammatical elements such as verb tenses and the relationships and configurations of figures of speech within the story.

naturalism A term that refers to the late nineteenth and early twentieth-century view of life that emphasizes the importance of scientific thought and determinism in literary study. A naturalistic critic views humans as animals who respond in deterministic ways to their environment and internal drives.

neo-Platonic A term used to describe any philosophical system that closely resembles that established by Plato, thus the prefix *neo*, meaning "new." The term originated in the third century in Alexandria in a philosophical system that mixed Asian, Platonic, and Christian beliefs.

neurosis A nervous disorder that has no known bodily or physical cause that can lead to a variety of physical and psychological abnormalities.

New Criticism A loosely structured school of criticism that dominated American literary criticism from the early 1930s to the 1960s. Named after John Crowe Ransom's 1941 book *The New Criticism*, the theory is based on the view that a work of art or a text is a concrete object that can, like any other concrete object, be analyzed to discover its meaning independent of its author's intention or the emotional state or values of either its author or reader. For **New Critics**, a poem's meaning must reside within its own structure. (In New Criticism, the word *poem* refers to any text, not only a poem.) By giving a poem a close reading, the New Critics believe they can ascertain the text's correct meaning. See **close reading**.

Often referred to as "the text and text alone" approach to literary analysis, New Criticism has found many practitioners, such as John Crowe Ransom, René Wellek, W.K. Wimsatt, R.P. Blackmur, I.A. Richards, Cleanth Brooks, and Robert Penn Warren. With the publication of Brooks and Warren's 1938 college text *Understanding Poetry*, New Criticism became the dominant approach to textual analysis until the 1960s.

New Critics   Critics who use the doctrines, assumptions, and methodology of New Criticism in their literary analysis. See **New Criticism**.

New Historicism   The American branch of cultural poetics. Appearing in the late 1970s and early 1980s, New Historicism is one of the most recent approaches to textual analysis. Led by such scholars as Stephen Greenblatt and Louis Montrose, New Historicism challenges the "old historicism" founded in nineteenth-century thought, which declares that history serves as a background to literature; history, as written, is an accurate view of what really occurred; and historians can articulate a unified and internally consistent worldview of any people, country, or era.

New Historicism declares that all history is subjective; historians can never provide us with the truth or give us a totally accurate picture of past events or the worldview of a people. Similar to language, history is but one of many discourses or ways of viewing the world. By viewing history as one of several important discourses that directly affect the interpretation of a text, **New Historicists** assert that their approach provides its followers with a practice of literary analysis that highlights the interrelatedness of all human activities, admits its own prejudices, and gives a more complete understanding of a text than do the old historicism and other interpretative approaches.

Adherents to the multiple approaches to textual analysis inherent in New Historicism now prefer to call this approach **cultural poetics**, emphasizing and noting the multiple factors that help determine a text's meaning. Its British counterpart is known as cultural materialism. See **cultural materialism**.

New Humanists   A school of twentieth-century American literary critics who value the moral qualities of art. Declaring that human experience is basically ethical, these critics demand that literary analysis should be based on the moral values exhibited in a text.

noematic   The complexities of the objective world—its cultural, social, religious, and political realities—as detailed by an individual or class of writers.

noetic   A term that refers to the subjective qualities of authors as exhibited in their writings.

objective correlative   A term coined by T.S. Eliot that refers to a set of objects, a situation, a chain of events, or reactions that can serve to awaken in the reader the emotional response that the author desires without being a direct statement of that emotion.

objective theory of art   A term introduced by M.H. Abrams that declares that the literary work itself is an object. Every work of art is a public text that can be understood by applying the standards of public discourse, not the private experience, intentions, and vocabulary of its author or a particular audience.

objet petit a A term used by Jacques Lacan to refer to those images that we discover in our mirror stage of psychic development. These images are separate from ourselves, such as bodily wastes, our mothers' voice and breasts, and our own speech sounds, and according to Lacan, they become for us symbols of lack that will plague us our entire lives. See **mirror stage**.

Oedipus complex According to Sigmund Freud's theory of child development, all children between the ages of 3 and 6 develop sexual or libidinal feelings toward the parent of the opposite sex and hostile feelings toward the parent of the same sex. In boys, this is known as the Oedipus complex, named after the legendary Theban Oedipus, who murdered his father and married his mother. In girls, this period is called the **Electra complex**, named after the legendary Electra, who avenged her father's death by killing her mother and her mother's lover.

The One The term used by Plato to describe his concept of spiritual reality. Plato says The One possesses ontological status, existing whether any mind posits its existence or reflects its attributes. It is composed of three elements: absolute beauty, truth, and goodness. The term was more clearly defined several hundred years later by Plotinus.

ontological Relating to or based on being or existence. The term is used by New Critics in recognition of their belief that a work of art is a concrete entity (one that really exists) and can be analyzed and dissected like any other object to ascertain its meaning.

ontological critic A critic who uses the assumptions of New Criticism and believes that a text is a concrete entity—like a painting, vase, or door lock—that can be analyzed to ascertain its meaning.

oral phase The first stage of child development as postulated by Sigmund Freud. In this stage, children suck at their mothers' breasts to be fed, but simultaneously the child's sexuality or libido is activated. Our mouths become erotogenic zones that will later cause us to enjoy sucking our tongues and, still later, kissing.

organic unity A term describing the concept that a text's structure is similar to a living plant, with all its parts supporting each other and living in a complex interrelationship. First advanced by the nineteenth-century poet–critic Samuel Taylor Coleridge, the concept of the organic unity of a work of art declares that each part of a text reflects and helps support the text's central idea, or as the New Critics would call it, the work's chief paradox. No part of a text is superfluous, but similar to a living organism, each part serves to enhance the whole. The whole is therefore greater than the sum of its parts. See **paradox**.

Orientalism A term introduced to postcolonist theory by Edward Said and refers to the creation of non-European stereotypes that suggest "Orientals" or Asians are indolent, thoughtless, sexually immoral, unreliable, and demented.

ostranenie A term used by Russian Formalists that translates as "making strange." Through syntax, rhyme, and a host of other literary devices, poetic diction or language has the capacity to "make strange" familiar words, thereby causing readers to reexamine and experience anew—a word, image, or symbol, for example—or their world. See **defamiliarization**.

Other A term used in feminist criticism (the "not-male" and thus unimportant) and postcolonialism (the colonized) to mean "different from" and unimportant, that which is dominated.

paradox A term used by the New Critics (especially Cleanth Brooks) to help explain the nature and essence of poetry. According to Brooks, scientific language must be precise and exact. On the other hand, poetry's chief characteristic is its many rich connotations, not the scientific denotations of words. The meaning of a poem is therefore built on paradox, a juxtaposition of connotations and meanings that all support the poem's central idea. Language, assert the New Critics, is complex and can sustain multiple meanings. According to Brooks, "the language of poetry is the language of paradox."

parapraxes A term coined by Sigmund Freud for slips of tongue, failures of memory, acts of misplacing an object, and a host of other so-called mistakes we make, all of which can be directly traced to our unconscious desires, wishes, or intentions.

parole A linguistic term used by Ferdinand de Saussure and other linguists to refer to an individual's actual speech utterances, as opposed to langue, the rules that comprise a language. An individual can generate countless examples of parole, but all are governed by the language's structure, its langue. For Saussure and other linguists, the proper study of linguistics is the system—the langue—not parole. See **langue**.

patriarchal A term used by feminist critics and others to describe a society or culture dominated by men; the adjective form of **patriarchy**.

patriarchy A societal or social organization in which men hold a disproportionate amount of power. In such a society, men define what it means to be human, including what it means to be female.

penis envy According to Sigmund Freud, the unfulfilled desire all women have for a penis; this desire causes them to possess a sense of lack throughout their lives. See **Electra complex**.

personal conscious A term used in psychoanalytic criticism to refer to the part of the human psyche that directly perceives and interacts with the external world. It is sometimes referred to as the *waking state* because the personal conscious is the image or thought of which we are aware at any given moment.

personal unconscious A term brought into literary criticism via the psychology of Carl Jung. According to Jung, the personal unconscious exists directly below the surface of the conscious and contains elements of private affairs that occur daily in each of our lives. Therefore, the personal unconscious is peculiar to one individual and not shared with any other.

personification A figure of speech that attributes human qualities to animals, ideas, or inanimate objects.

phallic stage The last stage of child development as theorized by Sigmund Freud. In this stage, the child's sexual desires or libido is directed toward the genitals.

phallic symbol A term used in psychoanalytic criticism to describe the male's symbol of power as represented by any penis-like image whose length exceeds its diameter, such as a tower, a sword, a knife, or a pen.

phallocentric A term used to describe any form of criticism, philosophy, or theory dominated by men and thus governed by a male way of thinking.

phallocentrism The belief that **phallus** is the source of power in culture and literature; usually accompanied by male-centered, male-dominant patriarchal assumptions.

phallus A symbol or representation of the penis. In much psychoanalytic theory (e.g., Jacques Lacan's ideas), the phallus becomes a **transcendental signified** and the ultimate symbol of power. Although neither males nor females can ever possess the phallus and therefore can never be complete or whole, males do have a penis and so have a slight claim to such power. See **transcendental signified**.

phenomenology Founded by Edmund Husserl, a modern philosophical tendency that emphasizes the perceiver. Objects exist and achieve meaning if and only if we register them on our consciousness. **Phenomenological critics** are therefore concerned with the ways that our consciousness perceives works of art.

philologist The name given to a linguist before the mid-twentieth century. A philologist is one who describes, compares, and analyzes the languages of the world to discover their similarities and relationships.

philology The science of linguistics before the mid-twentieth century; used now especially to refer to historical and comparative linguistics. Typically, whereas philology approached the study of language diachronically, present-day linguistics uses both the diachronic and synchronic approaches. See **diachronic, linguistics**, and **synchronic**.

phoneme A linguistic term for the smallest distinct and significant sounds that comprise a language. Phonemes are the primary building blocks of language. American English, for example, contains approximately 45 phonemes, such as /p/, /b/, and /k/.

phonetically The adverbial form of **phonetics**.

phonetics The study of how sounds are classified, described, and transcribed within a particular language.

phonocentrism A term coined by the French deconstructionist Jacques Derrida that asserts that Western culture privileges or prefers speech over writing. See **privileged**.

phonologically The adverbial form of **phonology**.

phonology The study of the various sound changes in a word or a particular language, often including the study of phonetics.

pleasure principle Introduced by Sigmund Freud in his economic model of the human psyche, defined as the part of the human psyche that craves only pleasures and desires instantaneous satisfaction of instinctual drives; it ignores moral and sexual boundaries established by society.

poem A term used by Louise M. Rosenblatt that refers to the creation of a new interpretation each time a reader transacts with a text, whether it is a first reading or any of countless rereadings of the same text. The interpretation becomes the poem, the new creation. New Critics also use this term to generically refer to any literary work.

Poetics Written by Aristotle, the earliest known work containing a definition of **literature**, particularly the genre of **tragedy**.

poetics A term used by the Russian Formalists to mean an analysis of a literary work's constituent parts, including all its linguistic and structural features. See **form**.

poetikes The Greek word meaning "things that are made or crafted." In critical theory, this word refers to Aristotle's text *Poetics*, which contains the component or "crafted parts" of a tragedy.

political unconscious A term coined by the Marxist critic Fredric Jameson. Borrowing Freud's idea of a repressed unconscious, Jameson posits the existence of a political unconscious, or repressed conditions of exploitation and oppression. The function of literary analysis, Jameson declares, is to uncover the political unconscious present in a text.

postcolonial criticism   Criticism that investigates ways that texts bear traces of colonialism's ideology and interpret such texts as challenging or promoting the colonizer's purposes and hegemony. Those who engage in this type of criticism analyze canonical texts from colonizing countries.

postcolonialism or **post-colonialism** One of the most recent approaches to literary analysis to appear on the literary scene. Postcolonialism concerns itself with literature written in English in formerly colonized countries and therefore excludes literature that represents either British or American viewpoints, concentrating on writings from colonized cultures such as Australia, New Zealand, Africa, and South America—to name a few—that were once dominated by but remained outside of the white male, European cultural, political, and philosophical tradition.

Often referred to as "third-world literature" by Marxist critics—a term many other critics think pejorative—postcolonial literature and theory investigate what happens when two cultures clash and when one of them, with its accompanying ideology, empowers and deems itself superior to the other. Postcolonial theorists include Fredric Jameson, Georg Gugelberger, Edward W. Said, Bill Ashcroft, Gareth Griffiths, Helen Tiffin, Frantz Fanon, Ian Adam, Gayatri Chakravorty Spivak, Homi K. Bhabha, and a host of others.

postcolonial theory   A strain of postcolonial criticism that moves beyond the bounds of literary studies and investigates social, political, and economic concerns of the colonized and the colonizer.

postist critics   Critics who "come after" structuralism, such as *post*modernists, *post*structuralists, and *post*colonialists

post-modern feminisms   One of four categories of contemporary feminist theory dating from 1990 to the present; includes theorists and critics such as Jane Gallop, Judith Butler, Uma Narayan, and Mary Daly.

postmodernism   A term used synonymously with deconstruction and poststructuralism. First used in literary circles in the 1930s, the term gained in popularity during the late 1960s and 1970s. Presently, it connotes a group of philosophers, literary critics, and contemporary scholars that denies the existence of objective reality. For these thinkers, reality is a human construct shaped by each individual's dominant social group.

poststructuralism   A term applied to a variety of literary theories and practical criticisms developed after structuralism. Dating from the late 1960s, poststructuralism is often used synonymously with **deconstruction**, although **poststructuralism** is much broader and includes such critical schools of thought as feminism, psychoanalysis (especially the ideas of Jacques Lacan), Marxism or any of its revisionist forms, New Historicism, and others.

Theoretically speaking, structuralism posits the objective reality of the text—that is, structuralists believe that one can examine a text using a standard and objective methodology and arrive at a conclusion. **Poststructuralists**, however, often assert the "undecidability" of a text's meaning and declare that a text may not in and of itself have any objective reality. Poststructuralists also question the long-held assumptions of the processes involved in both reading and writing and of the metaphysics of language.

poststructuralist feminisms One of four used to categorize contemporary feminist critics who use psychoanalytic, deconstruction, and postcolonial methodologies, such as Luce Irigaray, Gayatri Chakravorty Spivak, and Monique Wittig.

practical critic Critic who applies the theories and tenets of theoretical criticism to a particular work of art. Practical critics often define the standards of taste and explain, evaluate, or justify a particular text.

practical criticism See **applied criticism**.

preconscious A term used by Sigmund Freud in his typographic model of the human psyche to refer to that the part of the psyche that is the storehouse of memories and which the conscious part of the mind allows to be brought to consciousness without disguise in some other form. These memories are manageable in the consciousness without "masking."

prescriptive grammar Prescriptive rules dictated by grammarians who believe educated people should speak and write in the correct way, with the correct way specifically defined by these same grammarians.

private symbol See **symbol**.

privileged A term introduced into literary criticism by the French deconstructionist Jacques Derrida. According to Derrida, Western society bases its values and metaphysical assumptions on opposites, such as good/bad, light/dark, and true/false. In each of these pairs, Derrida asserts, Western culture values or privileges the first element and devalues or unprivileges the second.

production theory A term developed by the Marxist critic Louis Althusser that rejects the assumption of reflection theory that the superstructure must directly reflect the base. Althusser asserts that literature, for example, should not be strictly relegated to the superstructure; furthermore, he believes that the superstructure can and does influence the base. See **reflection theory** and **superstructure**.

proletariat A term used by Karl Marx and Friedrich Engels to refer to the working class of society. According to Marxist theory, the bourgeoisie (or upper class) oppresses and enslaves the proletariat by controlling the economic policies and the production of goods. The bourgeoisie, not the proletariat, defines and articulates a society's ideology.

prosody The mechanical or structural elements that comprise poetry, such as rhythm, meter, rhyme, stanza, diction, alliteration, and so forth. Used synonymously with *versification*.

psychoanalysis A method first used by Sigmund Freud in treating emotional and psychological disorders. During this type of therapy, the psychoanalyst has the patient talk freely about his or her childhood experiences and dreams.

psychoanalytic criticism The application of the methods of Sigmund Freud's psychoanalysis to interpreting works of literature. Because this approach to literary analysis attempts to explain the how and why of human actions without developing an aesthetic theory, a variety of critical approaches such as Marxism, feminism, and New Historicism use psychoanalytic methods in their interpretations without violating their own theoretical assumptions.

Central to psychoanalytic criticism is Freud's assumption that all artists are neurotic. Unlike other neurotics, the artist escapes many of the outward manifestations and end results of neurosis by finding in the act of creating art a pathway back to saneness and wholeness.

Freud believes that a literary text is really an artist's dream or fantasy. A text, then, can be analyzed like a dream. Freud assumes that the dream is a disguised wish. Just as if he were counseling a patient and trying to uncover the meaning of the disguised wish as it evidences itself in a dream, Freud believes we must apply the principles and methodology of psychoanalysis to a text to uncover its real meaning.

Although psychoanalytic criticism was founded by Freud, other critics, such as Carl Jung, Northrop Frye, and Jacques Lacan, have revised and expanded Freud's theories and developed their own methodologies for literary analysis. See **neurosis**.

psychoanalytic model   One of four approaches to feminist criticism devised by Elaine Showalter under the umbrella name **gynocriticism** to construct a female framework for the analysis of women's literature. This model analyzes the female psyche and demonstrates how such an analysis affects the writing process, emphasizing the flux and fluidity of female writing as opposed to male writing's rigidity and structure.

psychobiography   A method of interpreting texts that uses biographical data of an author gained through biographies, personal letters, lectures, and other sources to construct the author's personality, with all its idiosyncrasies, internal and external conflicts, and neuroses.

public symbol   See **symbol**.

queer theory   The most recent school of literary criticism (1991 to the present) that questions the terms we use to describe ourselves such as *heterosexual* or *homosexual*. Such words, claims queer theory, are socially constructed and do not define who we are. Disavowing **essentialism** and embracing **social constructivism**, queer theory assumes that our personal identities are unstable and in constant flux. As Eve Sedgwick, one of queer theory's leading theorists declares, "All people are different." What it means to be male or female is always in flux. Queer theory therefore challenges the assumptions of sexual identity, gender, and sexual difference, maintaining that our identities are not connected to our supposed essence but to what we do and who we are. Our identities are the effect, not the cause, of our performances. Who we are is performative, what we ourselves declare ourselves to be.

race   Used in postcolonial theory to refer to a class of people based on physical and cultural distinctions.

reader-oriented criticism   Rising to prominence in literary analysis in the early 1970s asserts that the reader is active, not passive, during the reading process. Both the reader and the text interact or share a transactional experience: The text acts as a stimulus for eliciting various past experiences, thoughts, and ideas of the reader, those found in both real life and in past reading experiences. Simultaneously, the text shapes the reader's experiences, selecting, limiting, and ordering the ideas that best conform to the text. The resulting interpretation is a new creation called a **poem**. For reader-oriented critics, the reader + the text = meaning or the poem.

Reader-oriented critics   ask a variety of theoretical questions, such as, What is a text? Who is the reader? Does the reader or the text or some combination of both determine a text's interpretation? What part does the author play in a work's interpretation? and perhaps most important, What is the reading process?

Composed of a diverse group of critics that emphasizes different elements of the reading process, reader-oriented critics include Roland Barthes, Gerard Genette,

Claude Lévi-Strauss, Wolfgang Iser, Louise Rosenblatt, Norman Holland, David Bleich and others. See also **poem**.

real order   According to Jacques Lacan, the third stage of psychic development, which consists of the physical world, including the material universe and everything in it. It also symbolizes everything a person is not. Objects within the real order continually function as symbols of primordial lack, leading to psychic fragmentation.

real reader   A term devised by the narratologist Gerard Prince to differentiate among the three kinds of readers—real, virtual, and ideal—to whom the narrator is speaking, the narratee. According to Prince, the real reader is the person actually reading the book. See **virtual reader, ideal reader**, and **narratee**.

reality principle   Introduced by Sigmund Freud in his economic model of the human psyche. Freud defines the reality principle as that part of the human psyche that holds the pleasure principle in check. The reality principle recognizes the need for societal standards and regulations on a person's desire for pleasure. See **pleasure principle**.

reception aesthetics   Another term for **affective stylistics**.

reception theory   A term used by reader-oriented critics to discuss how their theoretical assumptions are applied to textual analysis. A text's meaning, they argue, must be derived both from the present reader's personal response and from a critical examination of the history of the reception of the text through time, including contemporary critics of the author of the text in addition to critics living at the present moment.

referent   In linguistics, the entity—object, state of affairs, and so on—in the external world that is represented or symbolized by a word or term. For example, the referent for the word *desk* is the object *desk*.

reflection theory   One of the earliest theories developed by Marxist critics to explain the relationship between a society's base and its superstructure. A position held by Karl Marx early in his career, this theory asserts that the base or economic structure of society directly affects and determines a society's values; social, political, educational, and legal institutions; art; and beliefs—or, taken collectively, what Marx calls a society's superstructure. Simply put, the superstructure reflects or mirrors the base. Although a few Marxist critics still hold to this position, most now assert that the relationship between the base and the superstructure is much more complex than originally believed. The term **vulgar Marxism** is used to describe the form of Marxism that still holds to the reflection theory. See **base, Marxism**, and **superstructure**.

reflectionism   See **reflection theory**.

relativistic critic   Critic who uses various and even contradictory theories in critiquing a work of art.

rhetoric   Often defined as the art of speaking and writing effectively. Founded in Greece by Corax of Syracuse in the fifth century B.C.E., rhetoric set forth the principles and rules of composition for speech. Today, the term is used by such critics as Kenneth Burke, Northrop Frye, Roland Barthes, and Jacques Derrida and refers to patterns of structure found within texts. It has become the basis for much modern criticism.

rhetorical criticism A form of criticism that emphasizes the techniques and devices writers use to manipulate readers to interpret the writers' works in preconceived ways, emphasizing the art and techniques of persuasion.

romance phase One of four phases used by Northrop Frye, a mythic critic, to explain the one complete or whole story of literature, the **monomyth**. In the monomyth, the romance phase is the "summer" story when all our wishes are fulfilled and we achieve total happiness.

Romanticism A literary movement that dates to the publication of William Wordsworth and Samuel Taylor Coleridge's *Lyrical Ballads* in 1798. As a reaction against the eighteenth-century Age of Reason, Romanticism asserts that the world is similar to a living plant, ever growing, becoming, and aspiring. Denying reason as the sole path to truth, Romanticists declare that intuition can lead them to an understanding of themselves and their world. Individual concerns, the emotions, and the imagination are to be valued. As an approach to a text, Romanticism concerns itself with the artist's feelings and attitudes exhibited within the work of art.

Russian Formalism A school of criticism that flourished in the former Soviet Union from 1914 until its banishment by the Soviet government in 1930. Composed of two separate groups of scholars, writers, and theorists—the Moscow Linguistic Circle and the Society for the Study of Poetic Language—the Russian Formalists declared the autonomy of literature and poetic language. The proper study of literature, they asserted, was literature, not psychology, biography, sociology, politic or history. To study literature is to study **poetics**, the actual form and constituent parts of a work of literature, a text's internal devices.

Using the principles of science, the Russian formalists believed that to study a literary work is to study its **literariness**, or the language used in the text. Unlike everyday speech, literary language **foregrounds** itself, shouting, "Look at me; I am special." Through structure, imagery, syntax and a host of other literary devices, literary language has the capacity to make strange ordinary words, putting them in a new light, a process called **defamiliarization**. Such **estrangement** causes readers to slow down their perception of the word or image and experience afresh that word or image.

Because the Russian Formalists were not willing to view literature through the Stalinist regime's political and ideological perspectives, the former Soviet government disbanded their literary groups. Their influence flourished in the former Czechoslovakia in the writings of the Prague Linguistic Circle and indirectly influenced the Anglo-American New Criticism.

sadistic-anal phase Another term for Freud's **anal stage** in a child's development.

schools of criticism A group of fellow believers that shares common concerns about reading, writing, and interpretation. Examples of such schools are New Criticism, reader-oriented criticism, structuralism, deconstruction, and New Historicism.

semanalysis A new science developed by the psychoanalytic critic Julia Kristeva, who believes that during the Lacanian pre-mirror stage of development, a child experiences a lack or separation from the mother, who shapes meaning and gives significance, moving from this lack to desire. An emotional force develops which is tied to our instincts called **semiotique**. Using these ideas, Kristeva explores how signification or meaning continues to develop throughout our entire lives.

semantic features Used in linguistics to refer to those properties of words that help identify the different shades of meaning and relationships a word may have to surrounding phrases, clauses, and sentences.

semantics Used in linguistics to denote the study of how words combine to make meaning within a language.

semiology Proposed by the structuralist Ferdinand de Saussure, this new science would study how we create meaning through signs or codes in all our social behavioral systems. Because language was the chief and most characteristic of these systems, Saussure declared that it was to be the main branch of this new science. Although semiology never became the important new science Saussure envisioned, a similar science, semiotics, did develop and is still practiced today. See **semiotics** and **sign**.

semiotic interpretation A reading of signs to determine a text's interpretation. Developed by structuralist anthropologists, psychoanalysts, and literary critics, **semiotics** maintains that we all master codes or signs in our culture that allow us to interpret the culture and texts. Signs can be a direct means of communication such as a stop sign or indirect such as winking, hugging, or waving.

semiotique A term coined by the psychoanalytic feminist critic Julia Kristeva to refer to an emotional force that is tied to our instincts and exists in the prosody of language rather than symbols.

semiotics Founded by Charles Sanders Peirce and developing at the same time as Ferdinand de Saussure's proposed science of semiology, semiotics borrows linguistic methods used by Saussure and applies them to all meaningful cultural phenomena. Semiotics declares that meaning in society can be systematically studied, both in terms of how this meaning occurs and in terms of the structures that allow it to operate. Because it uses methods used by structuralism, **semiotics** and **structuralism** are often used interchangeably today. However, whereas semiotics denotes a particular field of study, structuralism is more an approach to literary analysis.

sentence A group of words that expresses a complete thought and conforms to the established syntactic structures of a language.

separatist feminism A contemporary feminist criticism that advocates separation from men, either total or partial, and assumes that women must first see themselves in a different context—separating themselves from men, at least for a while—before they can discover who they are as individuals. Such a separation is the necessary first step to achieving personal growth and individuality.

sexual instinct Another name for **eros**, one of two basic instincts that Freud asserts are part of everyone's unconscious. Later in his career, Freud referred to this term as **libido**.

sexual politics A term introduced by Kate Millett with her publication *Sexual Politics* (1969). The term has become synonymous with the second wave of feminism, which asserts that economic inequality and ideological indoctrination have been the chief causes of women's oppression and places patriarchy at the center of the feminist movement. Thanks to Millet, the term also denotes distinctions between sex and gender, the first being biological and the latter being psychological. Conforming or not conforming to prescribed cultural sex roles dictated by society becomes part of what Millet dubs sexual politics.

The term has also been used by Annette Kolodny to assert that feminist critics must accept a pluralistic approach to literary criticism. Kolodny assumes that any given text has the possibility of many different readings; such an approach, she argues, is both useful and illuminating.

sign   A term used in linguistics and first used by the French structuralist Ferdinand de Saussure to denote the definition for a word. According to Saussure, a word is not a symbol that equals something else; rather, a word is a sign (something that has meaning) composed of both a signifier and a signified. For Saussure, a word does not represent a referent in the objective world, but an abstract concept. See **referent, signifier**, and **signified**.

signification   A term used in literary criticism, theories of reading, and linguistics to denote the process by which we arrive at meaning through linguistic signs or other symbolic means.

signified   A term used by the French structuralist Ferdinand de Saussure that denotes one part of a word. Saussure proposed that all words are actually signs composed of two parts: the signifier and the signified. The signified is the concept to which the signifier—a written or spoken word or sound,—refers. Similar to the two sides of a sheet of paper, the linguistic sign is the union of the signifier and the signified. See **sign** and **signifier**.

signifier   A term used by the French structuralist Ferdinand de Saussure that denotes one part of a word. The signifier is the spoken or written constituent, such as the sound /t/ and the orthographic (written) symbol *t*. See **signified** and **sign**.

simile   A figure of speech that compares two unlike objects using the word *like* or *as*, such as: "His nose is like a cherry." The objects being compared cannot be from the same class. For example, the statement "London is like Paris" contains no simile because the objects being compared are from the same class (i.e., both are cities).

social constructivism   A theory concerning the nature of humanity that rejects the classical humanist's concept of **essentialism**. There exists no inner core of human essence that can be defined with finite terms. All terms used to describe people are socially constructed and steeped in ideological assumptions; these terms must be deconstructed before they can be reconstructed. Words such as *homosexual*, *heterosexual*, *male*, and *female* are laced with societal prejudices and must be reexamined. For social constructivists, the meaning of these words is always in flux.

spring phase   According to the mythic critic Northrop Frye, all literature tells one story, the **monomyth**, which consists of four phases. The spring phase relates the story of humanity's release from frustration and anxiety to freedom and happiness.

structural model   Another name for the **tripartite model** of Freud's model of the human psyche consisting of the **conscious, preconscious**, and **unconscious**.

structuralism   An approach to literary analysis that flourished in the 1960s. By using the techniques, methodologies, and vocabulary of linguistics as articulated by Ferdinand de Saussure, structuralism offers a scientific view of how we achieve meaning not only in literary works but also in all forms of communication and social behavior.

Structuralists believe that codes, signs, and rules govern all social and cultural practices, including communication, the "language" of sports, friendships, education, and literature. Structuralists want to discover the codes that they believe give meaning to all our social and cultural customs. The proper study of meaning and therefore reality is an examination of the system behind these practices, not the individual practices themselves.

For structuralist critics, the proper study of literature becomes a study of the conditions surrounding the act of interpretation itself, not an in-depth investigation of an individual work. Structuralists believe that a study of the grammar, or the system of rules that govern literary interpretation, becomes the critic's primary task.

Practiced by such critics as Jonathan Culler, Tzvetan Todorov, Roland Barthes, and Gerard Genette, structuralism challenges New Criticism's methodology for finding meaning within a text.

structuralist narratology A form of structuralism defined as the science of narrative and used by such critics as Vladimir Propp, Tzvetan Todorov, Roland Barthes, and Gerard Genette. **Narratologists** illustrate how a story's meaning develops from its overall structure, including elements such as theme, persona, voice, style, grammatical structure, and tone.

structural linguistics A term used synonymously with linguistics, the science of language.

stylistics A form of **structuralism** that interprets a text on the basis of its style—that is, diction, figurative language, syntax, vocabulary, sentence structure, and others.

subaltern writers A term coined by the Marxist critic Antonio Gramsci to refer to writers among those classes of people who are not in control of a culture's ideology or its **hegemony**. These writers, such as African Americans, provide new ways to see and understand cultural forces at work in literature and in ourselves.

superego A term used by Sigmund Freud to designate that part of the psyche that acts like an internal censor, causing us to make moral judgments in light of social pressures.

superstructure A term used by Karl Marx to designate that part of a culture that contains the social, legal, political, and educational systems along with the religious beliefs, values, and art of a society and which embodies a society's ideology that is controlled by the dominant social class or the bourgeoisie. By controlling the base, the bourgeoisie determines a society's superstructure and thus controls and oppresses the working class or proletariat. See **base** and **Marxism**.

supplement A term coined by the French deconstructionist Jacques Derrida to explain the relationship between two parts of any hierarchy upon which Western culture bases its metaphysics. For example, Derrida says Western society values light over darkness. The exact relationship between light and darkness, Derrida asserts, is not totally clear. Derrida uses the term *supplement* to refer to the unstable relationship between the two elements contained in this hierarchy. Rather than being two totally separate entities, light and dark supplement each other. Who, for example, can declare it to be light or dark when it is dusk? Each term thus helps define the other and is necessary for the other to exist.

supplementation The act of supplementing. See **supplement**.

symbol An image that represents something else and that can have multiple interpretations. There are two types: a **public symbol** embodies universal meaning, such as a rose representing love or water symbolizing life, and a **private symbol** obtains its meaning from the way in which it is used in a text, such as the scarlet *A* in Nathaniel Hawthorne's romance *The Scarlet Letter*.

symbolic order According to Jacques Lacan, the symbolic order is the second phase of our psychic development, during which we learn language. In this stage, we also learn to differentiate between genders, master gender differences, and learn cultural norms and laws. Furthermore, we learn that our fathers represent these cultural norms, and thus we master a male view of the world.

synchronic A linguistic term introduced by the French structuralist Ferdinand de Saussure and used to designate a process of language analysis that studies one language at one particular time in its evolution, emphasizing how that language functions, not its historical development through a long expanse of time. See **diachronic**.

syntax The study of the grammatical structure of a sentence, particularly the arrangement of words or word order. Used in linguistics to describe the rules governing the arrangement of words in phrases, clauses, and sentences.

synthesis A term used by the German philosopher Georg Hegel to explain how new ideas occur. According to Hegel, a **thesis** is presented followed by a counterstatement, the **antithesis**. What develops from the ensuing debate or discussion is a new idea call the synthesis.

syuzhet A termed coined by the Russian Formalist Victor Shklovsky. According to Shklovsky, all prose narrative has two aspects: fabula or syuzhet. Syuzhet (or plot) consists of all the literary devices a write uses to transform the story (see **fabula**) into plot. By using such literary devices as digressions, surprises, disruption, and so forth (syuzhet), the writer alters the fabula, making the text that has the potential "to make strange" the language of the text and render a new or fresh view of language or the reader's word. See **defamiliarization**.

teleological The adjective of the philosophical term *teleology*, the study of the evidence of design in the natural world. It denotes a worldview or philosophy of life that asserts a purposeful going forward toward some known end, especially one relating to nature.

tension A term used in literary criticism that is synonymous with conflict. It designates the oppositions or conflicts operating with a text.

text A term used by the Russian formalists and meaning a unified collection of various literary devices and conventions that can be objectively analyzed.

theoretical criticism Type of criticism that formulates the theories, principles, and tenets of the nature and value of art. By citing general aesthetic and moral principles of art, theoretical criticism provides the necessary framework for **practical criticism**.

thesis A term developed by the German philosopher Georg Hegel to explain how new ideas occur. Hegel asserts that a thesis (a statement) is presented, followed by a counterstatement, the **antithesis**. The new idea that will emerge from the debate or logical argument is the **synthesis**.

thick description Coined by the cultural anthropologist Clifford Geertz and brought into literary criticism via cultural poetics, this term is used by **cultural poetics** critics to describe the seemingly insignificant but abundant details present in any cultural practice. By focusing on these details, cultural poetics critics believe they can reveal the inherent contradictory forces at work within a culture. See **cultural poetics**.

third-world studies A term coined by the French demographer Alfred Sauvy at the beginning of the twentieth century. The term is no longer in use and has been replaced by **postcolonialism**.

touchstone theory   According to Matthew Arnold, a nineteenth-century critic, essayist, poet, and teacher, scholars and critics must "have always in [their] minds lines and expressions of the great masters, and apply them as a touchstone to other poetry." By comparing the newly written lines by contemporary poets to the classical poems that contain elements of the "sublime," the critic will instantly know whether a new poem is good or bad. Having mastered the "masters," good critics will themselves be touchstones, instantly knowing whether a contemporary work is good. In Arnold's theory, the critic functions as an authority on values, culture, and tastes, becoming a watchdog for high culture and its literature.

traditional historical approach   Methodology of interpretation that asserts that a critic place a work in its historical setting, paying attention to the author's life, the time period in which the work was written, and the cultural milieu of both the text and the author.

tragedy   Although the term is used in many different ways, in literary criticism, the term chiefly refers to Aristotle's definition found in the *Poetics*. Tragedy is "an imitation of a noble and complete action, having the proper magnitude; it employs language of linguistic adornment, applied separately in the various parts of the play; it is presented in dramatic, not narrative form, and achieves, through the representation of pitiable and fearful incidents, the catharsis of such pitiable and fearful incidents." See **catharsis, hamartia**, and **Poetics**.

transactional   A term introduced by Louise M. Rosenblatt to describe the process or event that takes place at a particular time and place when a reader transacts with a text. According to Rosenblatt, the text and the reader condition each other because the text acts as a stimulus or a blueprint for eliciting various past experiences, thoughts, and ideas of the reader—those found in both real life and in past reading experiences. The end result of this experience or "aesthetic transaction" is the creation of a poem, or what has been traditionally called the interpretation. See **aesthetic reading, poem**, and **transactional experience**.

transactional experience   According to the reader-oriented critic Louise M. Rosenblatt, a reader of a text and the text itself transact during the reading process. The text acts as a stimulus for eliciting various past experiences, thoughts, and ideas from the reader, those found in both our everyday existence and in past reading experiences. Simultaneously, the text shapes the reader's experiences, selecting, limiting, and ordering the ideas that best conform to the text. This overall event or act is what Rosenblatt dubs the transactional experience. See **transactional**.

transcendental signified   A term introduced into literary criticism by the French deconstructionist Jacques Derrida. In trying "to turn Western metaphysics on its head," Derrida asserts that from the time of Plato to the present, Western culture has been founded upon a classic, fundamental error: the searching for a transcendental signified, an external point of reference upon which one may build a concept or philosophy. Once found, this transcendental signified would provide ultimate meaning. It would guarantee a "center" of meaning, allowing those who believe in it to structure their ideas of reality around it. According to Derrida, Western metaphysics has invented a variety of such centers, including God, reason, origin, being, truth, humanity, and the self.

tripartite model   Sigmund Freud's most famous model of the human psyche. In this model, Freud divides the psyche into three parts: the **id**, the **ego**, and the **superego**.

trope A term synonymous with a figure of speech or a word or phrase not meant to be taken literally. The term has now been used by several schools of criticism in a variety of specialized meanings.

typographical model A model of the human psyche devised by Sigmund Freud. In this model, Freud divides the psyche into three parts: the **conscious**, **preconscious**, and **unconscious**.

unconscious A term used in Freudian psychoanalysis to refer to the part of the human psyche that receives and stores our hidden desires, ambitions, fears, passions, and irrational thoughts.

undecidability A term used by deconstructionists and other postmodern critics to decree that a text's meaning is always in flux, never final. Accordingly, foreclosure of meaning for any text is impossible. See **aporia, arche-writing, deconstruction, misspeaks**, and **poststructuralism**.

unfinalizability A term devised by the Russian formalists to assert that people can never be fully known, either to themselves or anyone else.

ungrammatical A term used to refer to phrases, clauses, and sentences that do not conform to the grammatical rules of a language.

unhomeliness A term coined by the postcolonial theorist Homi K. Bhabha; it refers to the way a colonial subject perceives the world as divided between two antagonistic cultures: that of the colonizer and of the indigenous community. This "double consciousness" often leaves the colonial subject feeling caught between two cultures, with neither of them providing a sense of belonging; the subject lacks the experience of having a "home" culture.

unprivileged A term introduced into literary criticism by the French deconstructionist Jacques Derrida. According to Derrida, Western society bases its values and its metaphysical assumptions on opposites, such as good/bad, light/dark, and true/false. In each of these pairs, Derrida asserts that Western culture values or privileges the first element, while devaluing or unprivileging the second. See **privileged** and **binary opposition**.

unvoiced In linguistics, any sound made without vibrating the vocal folds, such as /t/, /p/, and /k/.

Verhältnisse According to Marxist critics, implying nothing just "is" or exists in isolation.

Vermittlung A term used in Marxist criticism to assert the interrelatedness of all things; everything exists in a dynamic relationship with social forces.

virtual reader A term devised by the narratologist Gerard Prince to differentiate among the **real**, virtual, and **ideal reader**. According to Prince, the virtual reader is the reader to whom the author believes he or she is writing.

voiced In linguistics, any sound made during which the vocal folds are brought close together and made to vibrate, causing air to pass between them, such as /b/, /d/, and /g/.

vulgar Marxism A form of Marxism that holds to the reflection theory on the relationship of the base to the superstructure. Vulgar Marxism asserts that the superstructure directly reflects or mirrors the base. See **reflection theory**.

wage slaves Another term for the **proletariat** in Marxist criticism.

Weltanschauung The German word for worldview. See **worldview**.

the worker's paradise According to Karl Marx, the ultimate goal of society is to reach it highest stage, the worker's paradise in which benevolent self-rule will be established.

worldview According to James Sire in his text *The Universe Next Door* (1997), the set of assumptions or presuppositions that we all hold, either consciously or unconsciously, about the basic makeup of our world.

Wortkunst The German word for *literature* that automatically implies that the imaginative and creative aspects of literature are its essential components.

yonic symbol A term used in psychoanalytic criticism for any female symbol, such as a flower, a cup, a cave, or a vase.

INDEX